COREL WordPerfect 8
Complete Concepts
and Techniques

COREL WordPerfect 8
Complete Concepts and Techniques

Gary B. Shelly
Thomas J. Cashman
Steven G. Forsythe

SHELLY
CASHMAN
SERIES®

COURSE TECHNOLOGY
ONE MAIN STREET
CAMBRIDGE MA 02142

an International Thomson Publishing company

CAMBRIDGE • ALBANY • BONN • CINCINNATI • LONDON • MADRID • MELBOURNE

MEXICO CITY • NEW YORK • PARIS • SAN FRANCISCO • TOKYO • TORONTO • WASHINGTON

COURSE
TECHNOLOGY

© 1998 by Course Technology — ITP

For more information, contact:

Course Technology
One Main Street
Cambridge, Massachusetts 02142, USA

ITP Europe
Berkshire House
168-173 High Holborn
London, WC1V 7AA, United Kingdom

ITP Australia
102 Dodds Street
South Melbourne
Victoria 3205 Australia

ITP Nelson Canada
1120 Birchmount Road
Scarborough, Ontario
Canada M1K 5G4

International Thomson Editores
Saneca, 53
Colonia Polanco
11560 Mexico D.F. Mexico

ITP GmbH
Konigswinterer Strasse 418
53227 Bonn, Germany

ITP Asia
60 Albert Street, #15-01
Albert Complex
Singapore 189969

ITP Japan
Hirakawa-cho Kyowa Building, 3F
2-2-1 Hirakawa-cho, Chiyoda-ku
Tokyo 102, Japan

TRADEMARKS

Course Technology and the Open Book logo are registered trademarks and CourseKits is a trademark of Course Technology.

ITP The ITP logo is a registered trademark of International Thomson Publishing.

SHELLY CASHMAN SERIES® and **Custom Edition**® are trademarks of International Thomson Publishing. Some of the product names and company names used in this book have been used for identification purposes only and may be trademarks or registered trademarks of their respective manufacturers and sellers. International Thomson Publishing and Course Technology disclaim any affiliation, association, or connection with, or sponsorship or endorsement by, such owners.

DISCLAIMER

Course Technology reserves the right to revise this publication and make changes from time to time in its content without notice.

PHOTO CREDITS

Project 1, pages WP 1.4-5, Graduation cap and paper provided by PhotoDisc Inc. © 1996; Plato, degree background, pillar, and birth certificate edge, Courtesy of Corel Professional Photos CD-ROM Image usage; Huli Tribesmen photo, Courtesy of Christiane Emonin, Trans Niugini Tours. *Project 2, pages WP 2.2-3,* Astronaut, Courtesy of Corel Professional Photos CD-ROM Image usage; Flexing arm provided by PhotoDisc Inc. © 1996. *Project 4, page WP 4.3,* Werewolf, provided by Universal Studios/Motion Picture & Television Archives. *Project 5, page WP 5.3,* Map provided by PhotoDisc Inc. © 1996; Captain Gamma, fifteenth century ship, and Pony Express provided by North Wind Picture Archives; Newsletter, Courtesy of Joan Osborn.

ISBN 0-7895-4303-6

5 6 7 8 9 10   BC   02 01 00 99

COREL WordPerfect 8
Complete Concepts and Techniques

CONTENTS

Corel WordPerfect 8

▶ PROJECT THREE
CREATING A TERM PAPER

▶ PROJECT FOUR
GENERATING FORM LETTERS, MAILING LABELS, AND ENVELOPES

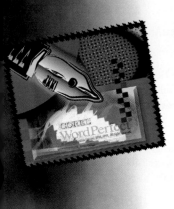

Preface

The Shelly Cashman Series® offers the finest textbooks in computer education. The Corel WordPerfect 8 book continues with the innovation, quality, and reliability that you have come to expect from this series. We are proud that earlier versions of WordPerfect were best sellers, and we are confident that Corel WordPerfect 8 will join their predecessors.

With WordPerfect 8, Corel has raised the stakes by adding a number of new features. The Power Bar contains buttons that change depending on the task you perform and the Application Bar lets you easily switch between documents, drag and drop information between documents, and easily work with multiple documents. Grammar-As-You-Go lets you recognize and fix common grammar problems as you type. QuickLinks automatically converts text that begins with the prefix, www, ftp, http, or mailto to an Internet hyperlink.

The Shelly Cashman Series team has responded with a WordPerfect 8 book that presents the fundamentals of word processing required in any introductory word processing course, as well new features such as PerfectExpert. PerfectExpert contains hundreds of projects that can guide you through a detailed project, such as creating a resume or a simpler project, such as inserting a graphics image.

In our WordPerfect 8 book, you will find an educationally sound and easy-to-follow pedagogy that combines a step-by-step approach with corresponding screens. The Other Ways and More About features have been increased and updated to offer in-depth knowledge of WordPerfect 8. The new project openers provide a fascinating perspective on the subject covered in the project. The Shelly Cashman Series WordPerfect 8 book will make your word processing class exciting and dynamic and one that your students will remember as one of their better educational experiences.

Objectives of This Textbook

Corel WordPerfect 8: Complete Concepts and Techniques is intended for a two-unit course that presents Corel WordPerfect 8. The objectives of this book are:

- To teach the fundamentals of Corel WordPerfect 8
- To foster an appreciation of word processing as a useful tool in the workplace
- To give students an in-depth understanding of creating announcements, business letters, resumes, term papers, form letters, and newsletters
- To provide a knowledge base of Corel WordPerfect 8 on which students can build
- To encourage independent study, and help those who are working alone in a distance education environment

When students complete the course using this textbook, they will have a firm knowledge and understanding of WordPerfect 8.

The Shelly Cashman Approach

Features of the Shelly Cashman Series WordPerfect 8 book include:

▶ **Project Orientation:** Each project in the book uses the unique Shelly Cashman Series screen-by-screen, step-by-step approach.

▶ **Screen-by-Screen, Step-by-Step Instructions:** Each of the tasks required to complete a project is identified throughout the development of the project. Then, steps to accomplish the task are specified. The steps are accompanied by screens. Students are not told to perform a step without seeing the result of the step on a color screen. Hence, students learn from this book the same as if they were using a computer.

▶ **Thoroughly Tested Projects:** The computer screens in the Shelly Cashman Series WordPerfect 8 book are shot directly from the author's computer. The screen is shot immediately after the author performs the step specified in the text. Therefore, every screen in the book is correct because it is produced only after performing a specific step, resulting in unprecedented quality in a computer textbook.

▶ **Multiple Ways to Use the Book:** The book can be used in a variety of ways, including: (a) Lecture and textbook approach – The instructor lectures on the material in the book. Students read and study the material and then apply the knowledge to an application on the computer; (b) Tutorial approach – Students perform each specified step on a computer. At the end of the project, students have solved the problem and are ready to solve comparable student assignments; (c) Other approaches – Many instructors lecture on the material and then require their students to perform each step in the project, reinforcing the material lectured. Students then complete one or more of the In the Lab exercises; and (d) Reference – Each task in a project is clearly identified. Therefore, the material serves as a complete reference.

▶ **Other Ways Boxes for Reference:** Windows 95 provides a wide variety of ways to carry out a given task. The Other Ways boxes displayed at the end of most of the step-by-step sequences specify the other ways to do the task completed in the steps. Thus, the steps and the Other Ways box make a comprehensive reference unit. You no longer have to reference tables at the end of a chapter or the end of a book.

▶ **More About Feature:** These marginal annotations provide background information that complements the topics covered, adding interest and depth to the learning process.

▶ **Other Ways**

1. Position insertion point on a blank line, click Format on menu bar, point to Paragraph, click Drop Cap, type paragraph

2. Press CTRL+SHIFT+C

◆ **More** *About* **PerfectExpert**

If you wish to create a cover letter without using PerfectExpert, we suggest you obtain a copy of *WordPerfect 6.1 for Windows* by Shelly/Cashman/ Forsythe. In Project 2, you create a letterhead, and then create a cover letter by entering and formatting text, changing tab settings, moving tab markers, and creating hanging indent paragraphs.

Organization of This Textbook

Corel WordPerfect 8: Complete Concepts and Techniques provides detailed instruction on how to use WordPerfect 8. The material is divided into five projects as follows.

Project 1 – Creating and Editing a WordPerfect Document   In Project 1, students are introduced to WordPerfect terminology, the WordPerfect screen, and the basic characteristics of a word processor. Topics include starting WordPerfect; knowing and changing default settings; understanding fonts; entering, selecting, and formatting text; correcting misspelled words; knowing the view modes; saving and printing a document; viewing and expanding codes; creating a bulleted list; downloading, inserting, sizing, and moving a graphics image; closing a document; quitting WordPerfect; opening a document; inserting and deleting text; recovering deleted text and codes; and using Help.

Project 2 – Creating a Resume and Cover Letter Using PerfectExpert   In Project 2, students add a name to the Address Book, learn the format of a resume, create a resume, learn the parts of a business letter, and create a cover letter. Topics include creating a resume using PerfectExpert; adding a section heading to a resume; selecting and replacing prompts within a resume with personalized information; understanding headers and tables; creating a cover letter using a PerfectExpert; personalizing the cover letter; creating and using AutoCorrect abbreviations; viewing the codes in a resume and cover letter; and working with two open documents.

Project 3 – Creating a Term Paper   In Project 3, students create a term paper using the recommended style of the Modern Language Association (MLA). Topics include creating a header with page numbers; double-spacing a report; using footnotes to include explanatory notes in the paper; typing parenthetical citations; changing the position of the Toolbar; creating a list of works cited at the end of the report; using WordPerfect Spell Checker and Thesaurus; and displaying document information. The Go To, Find, Replace, Drag and Drop Text, Cut, and Paste features also are covered.

Project 4 – Generating Form Letters, Mailing Labels, and Envelopes   In Project 4, students learn to generate form letters, mailing labels, and envelopes by creating a data file, creating a form file, and associating and merging the data and form files. Topics include entering records into a data file; editing a data file; creating the form file; associating the data file and form file; creating a letterhead with a horizontal graphics line; inserting date and field merge codes in the form file; creating a table; entering text and formulas into a table; formatting a table by applying a table style; formatting the cells of the table; and printing the form letters, mailing labels, and envelopes.

Project 5 – Creating a Professional Newsletter   In Project 5, students learn to check a document for writing problems using Grammatik and create a newsletter. Topics include understanding the parts of a newsletter; creating a nameplate; formatting the newsletter title by creating a TextArt design; formatting the newsletter subtitle, volume, and date using a table; searching for and retrieving files on disk; changing view modes; defining newspaper columns; formatting the text in newspaper columns; downloading and inserting a clip art image in the newsletter, wrapping text around a clip art image; creating a text box; and changing the border style and fill style of a text box.

End-of-Project Student Activities

A notable strength of the Shelly Cashman Series WordPerfect 8 book is the extensive student activities at the end of each project. Well-structured student activities can make the difference between students merely participating in a class and students retaining the information they learn. The activities in this Shelly Cashman Series WordPerfect 8 book include the following.

▶ **What You Should Know** A listing of the tasks completed within a project together with the pages where the step-by-step, screen-by-screen explanations appear. This section provides a perfect study review for students.

▶ **Test Your Knowledge** Four pencil-and-paper activities designed to determine students' understanding of the material in the project. Included are true/false questions, multiple-choice questions, and two short-answer activities.

▶ **Use Help** Any user of WordPerfect 8 must know how to use Help. Therefore, this book contains two Help exercises per project. These exercises alone distinguish the Shelly Cashman Series from any other set of WordPerfect 8 instructional materials.

▶ **Apply Your Knowledge** This exercise requires the student to open and manipulate a file on the Data Disk that accompanies the WordPerfect 8 book.

▶ **In the Lab** Three in-depth assignments per project require students to apply the knowledge gained in the project to solve problems on a computer.

▶ **Cases and Places** Seven unique case studies allow students to apply their knowledge to real-world situations.

Instructor's Resource Kit

A comprehensive Instructor's Resource Kit (IRK) accompanies this textbook in the form of a CD-ROM. The CD-ROM includes an *Electronic Instructor's Manual* (called *ElecMan*) and teaching and testing aids. The CD-ROM (ISBN 0-7895-4310-9) is available through your Course Technology representative or by calling one of the following telephone numbers: Colleges and Universities, 1-800-648-7450; High Schools, 1-800-824-5179; and Career Colleges, 1-800-477-3692. The contents of the CD-ROM are listed below.

▶ **ElecMan (*Electronic Instructor's Manual*)** ElecMan is made up of Corel WordPerfect 8 files. The files include lecture notes, solutions to laboratory assignments, and a large test bank. The files allow you to modify the lecture notes or generate quizzes and exams from the test bank using your own word processor. Where appropriate, solutions to laboratory assignments are embedded as icons in the files. When an icon appears, double-click it and the application will start and the solution will display on the screen. ElecMan includes the following for each project: project objectives; project overview; detailed lesson plans with page number references; teacher notes and activities; answers to the end-of-project exercises; test bank of 110 questions for every project (50 true/false, 25 multiple-choice, and 35 fill-in-the-blank) with page number references; and transparency references. The transparencies are available through the Figures on CD-ROM. The test bank questions are numbered the same as in Course Test Manager. Thus, you can print out a copy of the project and use the printed test bank to select your questions in Course Test Manager.

▶ **Figures on CD-ROM**   Illustrations for every screen in the textbook are available. Use this ancillary to create a slide show from the illustrations for lecture or to print transparencies for use in lecture with an overhead projector.

▶ **Course Test Manager**   A powerful testing and assessment package that lets you create and print tests from the available test bank. With access to a LAN, you can administer, grade, and track tests online. Online practice tests provide customized study for your students.

▶ **Lecture Success System**   Lecture Success System files are for use with the application software, a personal computer, and projection device to explain and illustrate the step-by-step, screen-by-screen development of a project in the textbook without entering large amounts of data.

▶ **Instructor's Lab Solutions**   Solutions and required files for all the In the Lab assignments at the end of each project are available.

▶ **Student Files**   All the files that are required by students to complete the Apply Your Knowledge exercises are included.

▶ **Interactive Labs**   Eighteen hands-on interactive labs that take students from ten to fifteen minutes to step through help solidify and reinforce mouse and keyboard usage and computer concepts. Student assessment is available in each interactive lab by means of a Print button. The assessment requires the student to answer questions about the contents of the interactive lab.

Shelly Cashman Online

Shelly Cashman Online is a World Wide Web service available to instructors and students of computer education. Visit Shelly Cashman Online at www.scseries.com. Shelly Cashman Online is divided into four areas.

▶ **Series Information**   Information on the Shelly Cashman Series products.

▶ **The Community**   Opportunities to discuss your course and your ideas with instructors in your field and with the Shelly Cashman Series team.

▶ **Teaching Resources**   This area includes password-protected data that can be downloaded, course outlines, teaching tips, and ancillaries such as ElecMan.

▶ **Student Center**   Dedicated to students learning about computers with Shelly Cashman Series textbooks and software. This area includes cool links, data from Data Disks that can be downloaded, and much more.

Several exercises in this book require the student to open and manipulate a file from the Shelly Cashman Series Corel WordPerfect 8 Project Files Web site (www.scsite.com/wp8). If your students do not have access to the World Wide Web, then copy the files from the Instructor's Resource Kit (IRK) to a folder to which they have access.

Acknowledgments

The Shelly Cashman Series would not be the leading computer education series without the contributions of outstanding publishing professionals. First, and foremost, among them is Becky Herrington, director of production and designer. She is the heart and soul of the Shelly Cashman Series, and it is only through her leadership, dedication, and tireless efforts that superior products are made possible. Becky created and produced the award-winning Windows 95 series of books.

Under Becky's direction, the following individuals made significant contributions to these books: Peter Schiller, production manager; Ginny Harvey, series specialist and developmental editor; Ken Russo, Mike Bodnar, Stephanie Nance, Greg Herrington, Dave Bonnewitz, and Mark Norton, graphic artists; Jeanne Black, Quark expert; Nancy Lamm, Marilyn Martin, Lyn Markowicz, Cherilyn King, and Steve Marconi, proofreaders; Cristina Haley, indexer; Sarah Evertson of Image Quest, photo researcher; and Susan Sebok and Nancy Lamm, contributing writers.

Special thanks go to Jim Quasney, our dedicated series editor; Lisa Strite, senior product manager; Lora Wade, associate product manager; Tonia Grafakos, editorial assistant; and Sarah McLean, product marketing manager. Special mention must go to Suzanne Biron, Becky Herrington, and Michael Gregson for the outstanding book design; Becky Herrington for the cover design; and Ken Russo for the cover illustrations.

Gary B. Shelly
Thomas J. Cashman
Steven G. Forsythe

**Visit Shelly Cashman Online at
www.scseries.com**

Shelly Cashman Series – Traditionally Bound Textbooks

The Shelly Cashman Series presents the following computer subjects in a variety of traditionally bound textbooks. For more information, see your Course Technology representative or call one of the following telephone numbers: Colleges and Universities, 1-800-648-7450; High Schools, 1-800-824-5179; and Career Colleges, 1-800-477-3692.

COMPUTERS	
Computers	Discovering Computers: A Link to the Future, World Wide Web Enhanced
	Discovering Computers: A Link to the Future, World Wide Web Enhanced Brief Edition
	Using Computers: A Gateway to Information, World Wide Web Edition
	Using Computers: A Gateway to Information, World Wide Web Brief Edition
	Exploring Computers: A Record of Discovery 2e with CD-ROM
	A Record of Discovery for Exploring Computers 2e
	Study Guide for Discovering Computers: A Link to the Future, World Wide Web Enhanced
	Study Guide for Using Computers: A Gateway to Information, World Wide Web Edition
	Brief Introduction to Computers 2e (32-page)

WINDOWS APPLICATIONS	
Integrated Packages	Microsoft Office 97: Introductory Concepts and Techniques, Brief Edition (6 projects)
	Microsoft Office 97: Introductory Concepts and Techniques, Essentials Edition (10 projects)
	Microsoft Office 97: Introductory Concepts and Techniques (15 projects)
	Microsoft Office 97: Introductory Concepts and Techniques Workbook
	Microsoft Office 97: Advanced Concepts and Techniques
	Microsoft Office 95: Introductory Concepts and Techniques (15 projects)
	Microsoft Office 95: Advanced Concepts and Techniques
	Microsoft Office 4.3 running under Windows 95: Introductory Concepts and Techniques
	Microsoft Office for Windows 3.1 Introductory Concepts and Techniques Enhanced Edition
	Microsoft Office: Advanced Concepts and Techniques
	Microsoft Works 4* • Microsoft Works 3.0*
Windows	Introduction to Microsoft Windows NT Workstation 4
	Microsoft Windows 95: Introductory Concepts and Techniques (96-page)
	Introduction to Microsoft Windows 95 (224-page)
	Microsoft Windows 95: Complete Concepts and Techniques
	Microsoft Windows 3.1 Introductory Concepts and Techniques
	Microsoft Windows 3.1 Complete Concepts and Techniques
Word Processing	Microsoft Word 97* • Microsoft Word 7* • Microsoft Word 6* • Microsoft Word 2.0
	Corel WordPerfect 8 • Corel WordPerfect 7 • WordPerfect 6.1* • WordPerfect 6* • WordPerfect 5.2
Spreadsheets	Microsoft Excel 97* • Microsoft Excel 7* • Microsoft Excel 5* • Microsoft Excel 4
	Lotus 1-2-3 97* • Lotus 1-2-3 Release 5* • Lotus 1-2-3 Release 4* • Quattro Pro 6
Database Management	Microsoft Access 97* • Microsoft Access 7* • Microsoft Access 2
	Paradox 5 • Paradox 4.5 • Paradox 1.0 • Visual dBASE 5/5.5
Presentation Graphics	Microsoft PowerPoint 97* • Microsoft PowerPoint 7* • Microsoft PowerPoint 4*

DOS APPLICATIONS	
Operating Systems	DOS 6 Introductory Concepts and Techniques
	DOS 6 and Microsoft Windows 3.1 Introductory Concepts and Techniques
Word Processing	WordPerfect 6.1 • WordPerfect 6.0 • WordPerfect 5.1
Spreadsheets	Lotus 1-2-3 Release 4 • Lotus 1-2-3 Release 2.4 • Lotus 1-2-3 Release 2.3
Database Management	dBASE 5 • dBASE IV Version 1.1 • dBASE III PLUS • Paradox 4.5

PROGRAMMING AND NETWORKING	
Programming	Microsoft Visual Basic 5*
	Microsoft Visual Basic 4 for Windows 95* (available with Student version software)
	Microsoft Visual Basic 3.0 for Windows*
	QBasic • QBasic: An Introduction to Programming • Microsoft BASIC
	Structured COBOL Programming (Micro Focus COBOL also available)
Networking	Novell NetWare for Users
	Business Data Communications: Introductory Concepts and Techniques, Second Edition
Internet	The Internet: Introductory Concepts and Techniques (UNIX)
	Netscape Navigator 4: An Introduction
	Netscape Navigator 3: An Introduction • Netscape Navigator 2 running under Windows 3.1
	Netscape Navigator: An Introduction (Version 1.1)
	Netscape Composer
	Microsoft Internet Explorer 4: An Introduction
	Microsoft Internet Explorer 3: An Introduction

SYSTEMS ANALYSIS	
Systems Analysis	Systems Analysis and Design, Third Edition

*Also available as a Double Diamond Edition, which is a shortened version of the complete book

Shelly Cashman Series – **Custom Edition**® Program

If you do not find a Shelly Cashman Series traditionally bound textbook to fit your needs, the Shelly Cashman Series unique **Custom Edition** program allows you to choose from a number of options and create a textbook perfectly suited to your course. Features of the **Custom Edition** program are:

- Textbooks that match the content of your course

- Windows- and DOS-based materials for the latest versions of personal computer applications software

- Shelly Cashman Series quality, with the same full-color materials and Shelly Cashman Series pedagogy found in the traditionally bound books

- Affordable pricing so your students receive the **Custom Edition** at a cost similar to that of traditionally bound books

The table on the right summarizes the available materials.

For more information, see your Course Technology representative or call one of the following telephone numbers: Colleges and Universities, 1-800-648-7450; High Schools, 1-800-824-5179; and Career Colleges, 1-800-477-3692.

For Shelly Cashman Series information, visit Shelly Cashman Online at **www.scseries.com**

COMPUTERS	
Computers	Discovering Computers: A Link to the Future, World Wide Web Enhanced
	Discovering Computers: A Link to the Future, World Wide Web Enhanced Brief Edition
	Using Computers: A Gateway to Information, World Wide Web Edition
	Using Computers: A Gateway to Information, World Wide Web Brief Edition
	A Record of Discovery for Exploring Computers 2e (available with CD-ROM)
	Study Guide for Discovering Computers: A Link to the Future, World Wide Web Enhanced
	Study Guide for Using Computers: A Gateway to Information, World Wide Web Edition
	Introduction to Computers (32-page)
OPERATING SYSTEMS	
Windows	Microsoft Windows 95: Introductory Concepts and Techniques (96-page)
	Introduction to Microsoft Windows NT Workstation 4
	Introduction to Microsoft Windows 95 (224-page)
	Microsoft Windows 95: Complete Concepts and Techniques
	Microsoft Windows 3.1 Introductory Concepts and Techniques
	Microsoft Windows 3.1 Complete Concepts and Techniques
DOS	Introduction to DOS 6 (using DOS prompt)
	Introduction to DOS 5.0 or earlier (using DOS prompt)
WINDOWS APPLICATIONS	
Integrated Packages	Microsoft Works 4*
	Microsoft Works 3.0*
Microsoft Office	Using Microsoft Office 97 (16-page)
	Using Microsoft Office 95 (16-page)
	Microsoft Office 97:Introductory Concepts and Techniques, Brief Edition (396-page)
	Microsoft Office 97: Introductory Concepts and Techniques, Essentials Edition (672-page)
	Object Linking and Embedding (OLE) (32-page)
	Microsoft Outlook 97 • Microsoft Schedule+ 7
	Introduction to Integrating Office 97 Applications (48-page)
	Introduction to Integrating Office 95 Applications (80-page)
Word Processing	Microsoft Word 97* • Microsoft Word 7* • Microsoft Word 6* • Microsoft Word 2.0
	Corel WordPerfect 8 • Corel WordPerfect 7 • WordPerfect 6.1* WordPerfect 6* • WordPerfect 5.2
Spreadsheets	Microsoft Excel 97* • Microsoft Excel 7* • Microsoft Excel 5* • Microsoft Excel 4
	Lotus 1-2-3 97* • Lotus 1-2-3 Release 5* • Lotus 1-2-3 Release 4* Quattro Pro 6
Database Management	Microsoft Access 97* • Microsoft Access 7* • Microsoft Access 2* Paradox 5 • Paradox 4.5 • Paradox 1.0 • Visual dBASE 5/5.5
Presentation Graphics	Microsoft PowerPoint 97* • Microsoft PowerPoint 7* • Microsoft PowerPoint 4*
DOS APPLICATIONS	
Word Processing	WordPerfect 6.1 • WordPerfect 6.0 • WordPerfect 5.1
Spreadsheets	Lotus 1-2-3 Release 4 • Lotus 1-2-3 Release 2.4 • Lotus 1-2-3 Release 2.3 Quattro Pro 3.0 • Quattro with 1-2-3 Menus
Database Management	dBASE 5 • dBASE IV Version 1.1 • dBASE III PLUS Paradox 4.5 • Paradox 3.5
PROGRAMMING AND NETWORKING	
Programming	Microsoft Visual Basic 4 for Windows 95* (available with Student version software) • Microsoft Visual Basic 3.0 for Windows*
	Microsoft BASIC • QBasic
Networking	Novell NetWare for Users
Internet	The Internet: Introductory Concepts and Techniques (UNIX)
	Netscape Navigator 4: An Introduction
	Netscape Navigator 3: An Introduction
	Netscape Navigator 2 running under Windows 3.1
	Netscape Navigator: An Introduction (Version 1.1)
	Netscape Composer
	Microsoft Internet Explorer 4: An Introduction
	Microsoft Internet Explorer 3: An Introduction

*Also available as a mini-module

Corel WordPerfect 8

Corel WordPerfect 8

Creating and Editing a WordPerfect Document

Objectives:

You will have mastered the material in this project when you can:

- ▶ Start WordPerfect
- ▶ Identify the elements of the WordPerfect screen
- ▶ List the WordPerfect default settings
- ▶ Change the default font size
- ▶ Describe and change font faces, font styles, and font sizes
- ▶ Enter, select, and format text
- ▶ Correct misspelled words
- ▶ Recognize the differences among Page view, Two Pages view, and Draft view modes
- ▶ Save and print a document
- ▶ View, expand, and delete WordPerfect codes
- ▶ Center a paragraph
- ▶ Create a bulleted list
- ▶ Save a modified document
- ▶ Download, insert, move, and size a graphics image
- ▶ Quit WordPerfect
- ▶ Open and close a document
- ▶ Insert, delete, and overtype text
- ▶ Recover deleted text and codes
- ▶ Use WordPerfect Help

Project 1

The Paper Trail of Life

How to process the documents on your journey from here to there, SUCCESSFULLY!

When John Jay Osborn wrote *The Paper Chase* in 1971, he portrayed the frenetic, often funny quest for a specific kind of document known as a law degree. Just as this piece of paper is a milestone in the life of a would-be attorney, our lives are defined by a *paper trail* of documents. Upon entering the world, a newborn receives a birth certificate to declare that he or she is, indeed, a real person. From that point forward, a succession of documents tracks our progress through life and even beyond. Medical records, school records, diplomas, military orders, death certificates, and wills are a smattering of the many kinds of specialized records that society keeps.

Our minds and our personalities are shaped by other documents such as the Bible, the Koran, or the Talmud, as well as the works of Plato, Aristotle, Shakespeare, Goethe, Paine, and countless other great thinkers. Yet, the most meaningful and gratifying kinds of documents usually are those we create

Inspiration!

ourselves, such as books, plays, poems, letters, term papers, and business and scientific reports. Later, when it is time to write the story of one's life, such papers form the basis upon which the biographer will build.

For many people, however, the act of creating a document ranks right up there in difficulty with the opening passage of Genesis —"In the beginning, God created the heaven and the earth." Causing the earth and the firmament to materialize from the void often seems easier than bringing about a document from the imagined lack of one's creativity.

Fortunately, you have a powerful tool with Corel WordPerfect. Rich in features designed to help you meet the most demanding requirements of a boss or an instructor, WordPerfect allows you to create documents in many fonts and styles and enhance them by importing attractive graphics, tables, and charts produced in other applications. Easy editing is another plus. At times when you need some friendly assistance, WordPerfect Help provides several ways of approaching a problem and solving it quickly.

Unlike those students in *The Paper Chase*, you have productivity tools that were not available when that book was written, including the capability of downloading text and images directly from the Internet. Using readily available research data, you can put your own unique spin on any subject. All you have to do is sit down and start.

As Goethe said, "Whatever you can do, or dream you can do, begin it. Boldness has a genius, magic, and power in it." Your genius plus the *magic* in WordPerfect can make an unbeatable team.

Aristotle
Shakespeare
Goethe
Paine

HARVARD LAW DEGREE

The trustees of Harvard, by virtue of the authority vested in them and on the recommendation of the faculty have conferred the degree of

JURIS DOCTOR

with all rights, privileges, and honors hereunto

Russell Neth

successful completion

SUCCESS.

"Whatever you can do, or dream you can do, begin it. Boldness has a genius, magic, and power in it."

PLATO

Project

1

Corel
WordPerfect 8

Case Perspective

New World Tours, known for its adventure tours to remote areas of the world, specializes in fully escorted group tours. An adventure tour can be a mentally, physically, and emotionally challenging experience. Excursions often include strenuous hikes through rain forests, scuba diving in dangerous ocean waters, and navigating rivers by canoe. New World Tours sends scouts to explore remote areas of the world. Upon their return, they design an adventure tour to the remote area. Scouts recently returned from Papua New Guinea, an island off the coast of Australia. Their explorations of Papua New Guinea revealed over 750 tribes, living in the stone age, that are separated by dense rain forests and high mountain ranges. Many of the tribesmen had never seen or heard English-speaking people. Others spoke limited English that they had learned from missionaries.

Your job is to prepare an announcement for a tour to Papua New Guinea. It should include information about the tour and how to contact New World Tours to obtain a copy of the New Guinea Vacation Planner.

Creating and Editing a WordPerfect Document

What Is Corel WordPerfect?

Corel WordPerfect 8 is a 32-bit word processing application that takes full advantage of Windows 95 and provides easy access to the Internet. WordPerfect allows you to create professional-looking personal and business documents, such as announcements, letters, memos, resumes, and reports, and revise them easily. WordPerfect's desktop publishing features allow you to add images to documents to create these professional-looking brochures, advertisements, and newsletters.

WordPerfect's many other features simplify the process of creating a document. **Spell-As-You-Go** underlines words that you may have misspelled while typing and allows you to correct the words as you type or after typing is complete. **QuickCorrect** automatically works with Spell-As-You-Go to correct common typing mistakes and capitalization errors as you type. In addition, **Grammar-As-You-Go** also recognizes and fixes grammar problems as you type and **Thesaurus** suggests alternative word choices in a document.

Other features facilitate the process of creating a document. **Property Bars** allow you to access frequently used features with the mouse. **QuickFonts** let you access up to twenty of the most recently used fonts. **Guidelines** indicate the margin positions with dotted lines in a document to permit you to change the margins easily.

Additional features allow you to work with the Internet and World Wide Web. **Send** lets you send **electronic mail**, or **e-mail**, over the Internet. **Internet Publisher** permits you to create Web pages, publish the pages on the World Wide Web, and browse other Web pages.

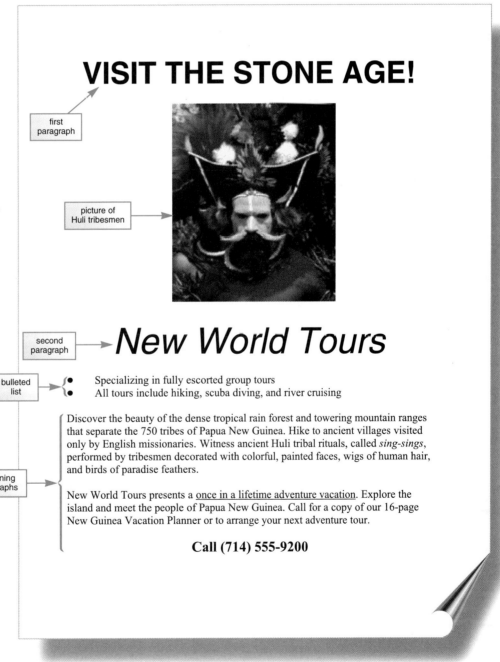

Project One—New Guinea Tour Announcement

This book presents a series of projects that allow you to use WordPerfect to create documents similar to those you will encounter in the academic and business environments. Project 1 produces the announcement illustrated in Figure 1-1.

The announcement, which informs the public of a new adventure tour to Papua New Guinea, consists of several paragraphs and a picture. A **paragraph** is a word or group of words ending with a hard return. The first paragraph, or heading, consists of the words, VISIT THE STONE AGE!. A picture of two Huli tribesmen displays below the first paragraph to catch the reader's attention.

The travel agency name, New World Tours, displays as the second paragraph, or sub-heading, and a bulleted list identifying the important aspects of their tours displays below the second paragraph. Three paragraphs follow the bulleted list. The first paragraph describes the tour and the second paragraph informs the reader of a New Guinea Vacation Planner.

FIGURE 1-1

The last paragraph contains a phone number to call to receive a copy of the vacation planner or arrange for a tour. The steps to create this document are explained on the following pages.

Document Preparation Steps

The document preparation steps give you an overview of how the document shown in Figure 1-1 will be developed. The following tasks will be completed in this project.

1. Start WordPerfect.
2. Change the default font size.
3. Enter the document text.
4. Correct incorrectly spelled words.
5. Save the document on a floppy disk.
6. Format the document text (center, enlarge, bold, underline, and italicize).
7. Add bullets to the list.
8. Save the document again.
9. Download the picture from the Internet.
10. Insert the picture.
11. Move and size the picture.
12. Save the document again.
13. Print the document.
14. Quit WordPerfect.

The following pages contain a detailed explanation of these tasks.

Mouse Usage

In this book, the mouse is used as the primary way to communicate with WordPerfect. You can perform six operations with a mouse: point, click, right-click, double-click, drag, and right-drag.

Point means you move the mouse across a flat surface until the mouse pointer rests on the item of choice on the screen. As you move the mouse, the mouse pointer moves across the screen in the same direction. **Click** means you press and release the left mouse button. The terminology used in this book to direct you to point to a particular item and then click is, Click the particular item. For example, Click the Bold button means point to the Bold button and then click.

Right-click means you press and release the right mouse button. As with the left mouse button, you usually will point to an item on the screen before right-clicking.

Double-click means you quickly press and release the left mouse button twice without moving the mouse. In most cases, you must point to an item before double-clicking. **Drag** means you point to an item, hold down the left mouse button, move the item to the desired location on the screen, and then release the left mouse button. **Right-drag** means you point to an item, hold down the right mouse button, move the item to the desired location, and then release the right mouse button.

The use of the mouse is an important skill when working with WordPerfect.

Starting WordPerfect

Follow these steps to start WordPerfect, or ask your instructor how to start WordPerfect on your system.

More *About* **the Mouse**

The mouse, although invented in the 1960's, was not widely used until the Apple Macintosh computer became available in 1984. Even then, some highbrows called mouse users wimps. Today, the mouse is an indispensable tool for every computer user.

More *About* **the Mouse**

Some mouse users experience wrist injuries because they bend their wrists frequently while moving the mouse. To help prevent wrist injuries, position the mouse at least six inches from the edge of a workstation. Repositioning the mouse forces the wrist to be flat and the elbow to bend when you move the mouse.

More *About* **Double-Clicking**

Double-clicking is the most difficult mouse skill to learn. Many people have a tendency to move the mouse before they click a second time, even when they do not want to move the mouse. You should find that with a little practice, double-clicking becomes quite natural.

Steps To Start WordPerfect

1 **Click the Start button on the taskbar, point to Corel WordPerfect Suite 8, and point to Corel WordPerfect 8.**

Windows 95 displays the Start *menu, highlights the* Corel WordPerfect Suite 8 *command, and then highlights the* Corel WordPerfect 8 *command (Figure 1-2).*

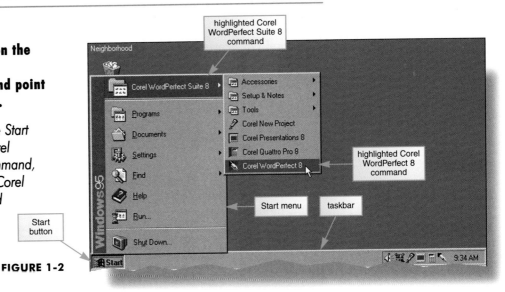

FIGURE 1-2

2 **Click Corel WordPerfect 8. If necessary, click the Maximize button in the Corel WordPerfect window and when the Document1 window displays, if necessary, click the Maximize button.**

A box containing the version number, Corel WordPerfect name, and copyright notice displays briefly on the screen while WordPerfect starts. The maximized Corel WordPerfect application window displays, and then a blank document titled Document1 and the status, (unmodified) displays in a maximized document window (Figure 1-3).

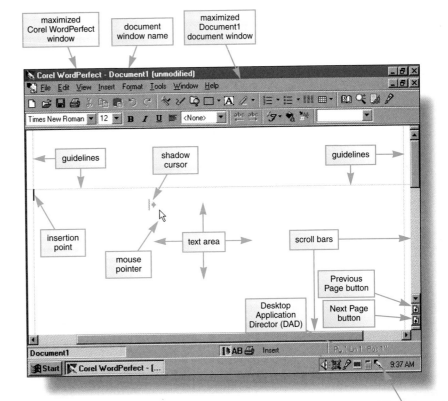

FIGURE 1-3

When Corel WordPerfect 8 is installed as part of the Corel WordPerfect Suite 8 software package, the **Desktop Application Director (DAD)** displays in the status tray area of the taskbar (see Figure 1-3). The DAD contains several icons, including the Corel WordPerfect 8 icon to start Corel WordPerfect 8. Clicking the icon starts WordPerfect and displays the application and document windows shown in Figure 1-3.

OtherWays

1. Click Corel WordPerfect 8 button on Desktop Application Director (DAD).

2. Right-click Start button, click Open, double-click Corel WordPerfect Suite 8 icon, double-click Corel WordPerfect 8 icon

The Corel WordPerfect Screen

The **Corel WordPerfect screen** consists of the maximized Corel WordPerfect application window and maximized Document1 document window (see Figure 1-3 on the previous page). Both windows contain elements that make working with WordPerfect 8 faster and easier than working with previous versions.

WordPerfect Document Window

The WordPerfect document window contains several elements common to all document windows, as well as some elements that are unique to WordPerfect. The main elements in the WordPerfect document window are the text area, insertion point, mouse pointer, and scroll bars (see Figure 1-3).

TEXT AREA   As you type text or insert graphics, the text and graphics display in the **text area**.

INSERTION POINT   The **insertion point** is a flashing vertical line that indicates the point at which text typed on the keyboard will display on the screen. As you type, the insertion point moves to the right, and when you reach the end of a line, it moves downward to the beginning of the next line. When you insert a graphics image into a document, the image displays close to the location of the insertion point. You can move the insertion point by clicking a new position in the text area or using the arrow keys to move the insertion point through the text one character or line at a time.

MOUSE POINTER AND SHADOW CURSOR   The **mouse pointer** allows you to point to items on the desktop or different areas in a window and indicates which item or area will be affected when you click the left or right mouse button. The mouse pointer changes shape when it points to different items or areas in a window. The mouse pointer in Figure 1-3 on the previous page is in the shape of a **left-pointing block arrow**. A shadow cursor displays next to the mouse pointer. The **shadow cursor** displays when you point to white space in the text area. The shadow cursor indicates where the insertion point will display when you click the mouse and changes its appearance to indicate the justification (left, right, or center) of any text you type.

SCROLL BARS   A **scroll bar** is a bar that displays at the right edge and bottom of a window when an area of the window is not completely visible. A scroll bar contains a **scroll box** and two **scroll arrows** that enable you to view areas of the window not currently visible. In Figure 1-3, a vertical scroll bar displays at the right edge of the document window and a horizontal scroll bar displays at the bottom. Two buttons at the bottom of the vertical scroll bar allow you to display the previous page or the next page in a multiple page document. Clicking the **Previous Page button** causes the top of the previous page to display in the document window. Clicking the **Next Page button** causes the top of the next page to display. The insertion point, however, does not move when either button is clicked.

GUIDELINES   The **guidelines** show the margins or measurements of elements in a document, such as page margins, tables, columns, headers, and footers. Guidelines appear as dotted lines in the document window but do not print. You can change the format of the document by dragging a guideline to a new position. In Figure 1-3, two vertical guidelines show the left and right margins and a horizontal guideline shows the top margin. Although not visible, a horizontal guideline also shows the bottom margin.

More About Scroll Bars

Clicking the vertical scroll bar moves the document window a full screen up or down and allows you to step through a document screen by screen. Clicking the horizontal scroll bar moves the contents of the window to the left and right and allows you to view hidden text or margins.

More About Scrolling

Follow these general scrolling guidelines to improve scrolling efficiency: (1) To scroll short distances (line-by-line), click the scroll arrows; (2) To scroll one screen at a time, click the scroll bar; (3) To scroll long distances, drag the scroll box.

More About Guidelines

Guidelines were available for the first time in Corel WordPerfect 7. Using the guidelines, WordPerfect users can change margins and columns directly in the document window. Previously, they were restricted to using buttons and menu commands.

The Corel WordPerfect Application Window

The main elements in the Corel WordPerfect application window are the title bar, menu bar, Toolbar, Property Bar, and Application Bar (see Figure 1-4). The title bar, menu bar, Toolbar, and Property Bar display at the top of the window and the Application Bar displays at the bottom. In addition, the Ruler displays below the Property Bar. Unlike the Toolbar and Property Bar, the Ruler does not display when you start WordPerfect. To display it, you must click View on the menu bar and then click Ruler on the View menu.

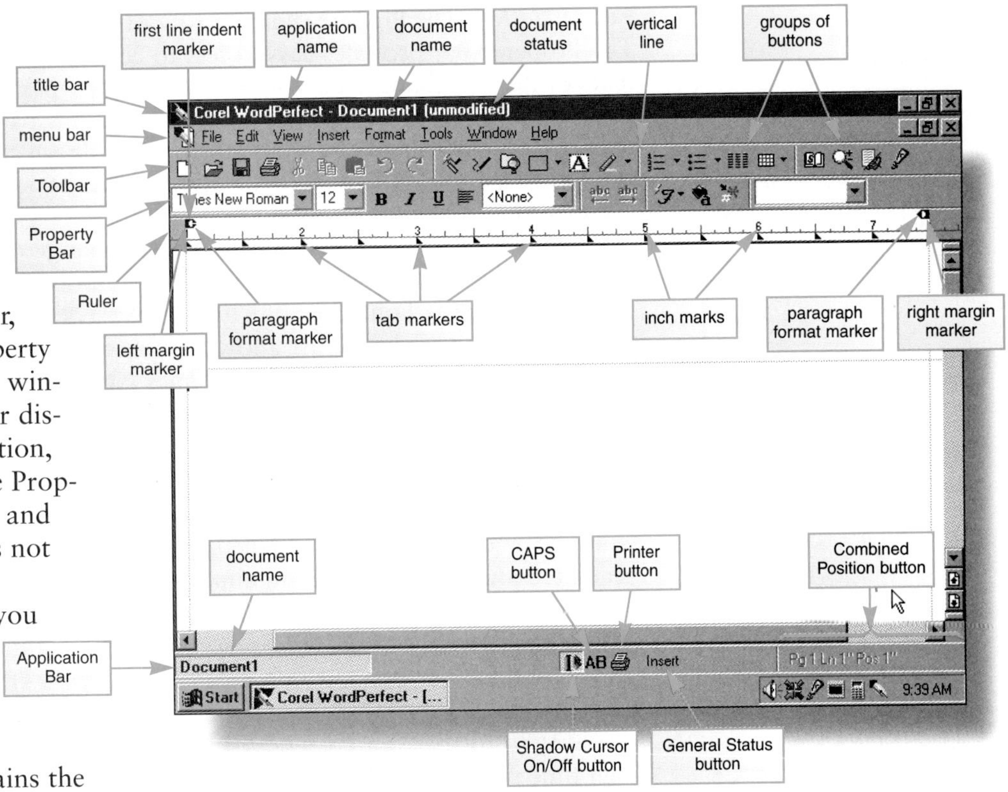

FIGURE 1-4

TITLE BAR The **title bar** contains the application name (Corel WordPerfect), a hyphen (-), document name (Document1), and document status enclosed in brackets (unmodified). Document1 is the name assigned by WordPerfect to the first document you create. WordPerfect uses this name until you name the document and save it on disk.

MENU BAR The **menu bar** contains eight menu names. Each menu name represents a **menu** containing commands, such as Open, Close, Save, Print, or Exit, that you can use to access WordPerfect features. Click the menu name on the menu bar to display a menu. Click the command name on the menu to access a command on a menu.

TOOLBAR The **Toolbar** is the row of buttons below the menu bar that allow you to accomplish basic tasks, such as opening, saving, and printing a document. The **WordPerfect 8 Toolbar** shown in Figure 1-4 is one of fourteen Toolbars available in WordPerfect and displays when you start WordPerfect. Clicking a button on the Toolbar is often faster than using the commands on a menu. The twenty-three buttons on the Toolbar are organized into four groups, and each button has a pictorial representation to help you remember the button function. A thin vertical line separates each group of buttons from the other buttons.

If a small vertical scroll bar displays at the right side of the Toolbar on your computer, the Toolbar contains more buttons than can display on the Toolbar. Clicking the down scroll arrow replaces the buttons currently on the Toolbar with another row of buttons. Clicking the up scroll arrow displays the original buttons on the Toolbar. To remove the Toolbar, click View on the menu bar, click Toolbars, click WordPerfect 8 in the Toolbars dialog box, and then click the OK button.

You must use the mouse to click a button on the Toolbar. To click a button, position the mouse pointer on the button and click. Several dimmed buttons display on the Toolbar illustrated in Figure 1-4 to indicate you must click other buttons or features before you can click the button.

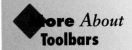
ore About Toolbars

If the WordPerfect 8 Toolbar does not display in the Corel WordPerfect application window, it has been hidden. To display the Toolbar, click View on the menu bar, click Toolbars on the View menu, click the WordPerfect 8 check box, and click the OK button.

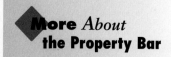

PROPERTY BAR   The **Property Bar** is a row of boxes and buttons below the Toolbar. The Property Bar provides easy access to commonly used features and the contents of the bar changes depending upon what work is being performed. The Property Bar shown in Figure 1-4 on the previous page contains four boxes and nine buttons that display when you start WordPerfect. These list boxes and buttons allow you to quickly access features designed specifically for the work being performed.

The first box (Font Face) allows you to change the font. **Font** is a term used to describe a group of letters, numbers, and symbols with a common design (typeface). Clicking the Font Face box arrow displays a list of fonts. Selecting text and then clicking a font in the list allows you to format the selected text using that font. The name of the default font (Times New Roman) identifies the box. The default font size (12) identifies the second box (Font Size). The font size is measured in points. Clicking the Font Size box arrow allows you to change the font size. Text entered from the keyboard will display on the screen in Times New Roman 12-point font. The Times New Roman font is one of many fonts contained in a collection of fonts called **TrueType fonts**. TrueType fonts are graphically generated and can be printed in almost any size.

The next four buttons (Bold, Italic, Underline, and Justification) allow you to change the font style (bold, italic, and underline) and justification (left, right, and center) of text. The entry, <None>, identifies the next box (Select Style). When you click the Select Style box arrow, you can select a style. A **style** provides an easy way to format similar types of text, such as headings or lists in the same way each time they are used.

The next two groups of buttons allow you to search for text within a document (QuickFind Previous and QuickFind Next), select a font in a list of recently used fonts (QuickFonts), change the font color (Font Color), and insert special characters (Insert Symbol).

The last box (Prompt-As-You-Go) displays suggestions while you type. Depending upon where the insertion point is located, the **Prompt-As-You-Go** feature can display spell-checker, grammar checker, or thesaurus information in the box.

You must use the mouse to click a button or box arrow on the Property Bar. To click a button or box arrow, position the mouse pointer on the button or box arrow and click. To remove the Property Bar, click View on the menu bar, click Toolbars, click Property Bar in the Toolbars dialog box, and click the OK button.

APPLICATION BAR   The **Application Bar** is located at the bottom of the Corel WordPerfect window (see Figure 1-4 on the previous page). The Application Bar displays information and allows you to access information about documents in the WordPerfect application window. When you open a document, a button identified by the document's name displays at the left end of the Application Bar. When multiple documents are open, clicking a button displays the chosen document in the window. The buttons also allow you to drag information from one document to another.

In addition, the Application Bar contains buttons that allow you to turn the shadow cursor on or off (Shadow Cursor On/Off), enter capitalized text (CAPS), print a document, and display messages that assist you when using WordPerfect (General Status). The word, Insert, displays on the General Status button in Figure 1-4 to indicate that when you enter text, the text will be inserted between the existing text and will not delete any of the existing text. If the word, Typeover, displays on this button, you will delete the text to the right of the insertion point as you enter text.

At the right end of the Application Bar, the Combined Position button contains the page number (Pg 1), line number (Ln 1"), and position number (Pos 1"). The Page entry (Pg 1) indicates the page of the document on which the insertion point is located. The value, 1, indicates the insertion point displays on page one. The Line entry (Ln 1") measures how far down the insertion point is from the top of the page. The value, 1, indicates the insertion point displays one inch from the top of the page. The Position entry (Pos 1") registers how far the insertion point is from the left edge of the page. The value, 1, shows the insertion point is one inch from the left edge of the page.

To remove the Application Bar, click View on the menu bar, click Toolbars, click Application Bar in the Toolbars dialog box, and click the OK button.

RULER Although the Ruler appears to display in the Corel WordPerfect window in Figure 1-4 on page WP 1.11, the Ruler actually displays at the top of the maximized Document1 document window. Unlike the Toolbar and Property Bar, the Ruler does not display when you start WordPerfect. As a result, before you can use the Ruler you must click View on the menu bar and then click Ruler.

In the upper left corner and upper right corner of the Ruler are two margin markers. **Margin markers** indicate the positions of the left and right margins. Below the margin markers are the inch marks numbered from one to seven. The **left margin marker** displays above the 1-inch mark to indicate the left margin is set at 1 inch. The **right margin marker** displays halfway between the 7- inch and 8-inch marks, at 7.5 inches. Assuming you have a paper width of 8½ inches, the right margin marker indicates the right margin is set at 1 inch (1 = 8.5 − 7.5). You change the left or right margin by dragging the corresponding margin marker on the Ruler to the left or right or by dragging the left margin guideline or right margin guideline to a new position in the text area.

To the right of the left margin marker are two triangles. The top triangle is the **first line indent marker**. This marker specifies the point to which the first line of each paragraph will be indented. The bottom triangle to the right of the left margin marker and the triangle to the left of the right margin marker are **paragraph format markers**. The paragraph format markers are used to adjust the margins of individual paragraphs.

Below the inch and half-inch marks are the tab markers. **Tab markers** display every half inch and are denoted by small triangles. You can change a tab setting by dragging the tab marker to the left or right.

WordPerfect Default Settings

Before you enter the text to create the New Guinea Tour announcement, you should know about the **default settings** that affect the way a document looks on the screen and the way a document prints. The following settings are among those default settings that are important when creating the announcement.

1. Margins – WordPerfect places a one-inch top, bottom, left, and right margin on each printed page, based on a paper size of 8.5 inches by 11 inches.
2. Font Face and Font Size – Text displays using the Times New Roman Regular 12-point font.
3. Line Spacing – Text is single-spaced.
4. Tab Set – Tabs are set at one-half inch intervals, beginning at the left margin.
5. Justification – Text is left-justified.

6. View Mode – The document on the screen displays in Page view mode.
7. Toolbar – The WordPerfect 8 Toolbar displays.
8. Spelling Mode – QuickCorrect and Spell-As-You-Go are turned on.
9. Zoom Percentage – The zoom percentage is 100%.
10. Default Drive – Drive C, the hard disk, is the default drive for saving and retrieving documents.
11. Default Folder – The MyFiles folder on the hard drive is the default folder for saving and retrieving documents.

You can change many of these default settings by clicking File on the menu bar, pointing to Document, and then clicking Current Document Style.

Understanding Fonts

To create the document shown in Figure 1-1 on page WP 1.7, you must format the page. **Formatting** is the process of controlling the appearance of text on the screen and the printed document.

With WordPerfect, you can specify the font face (such as Arial or Times New Roman), font style (such as bold or italic), and font size (such as 12 point) of one or more characters, words, sentences, or paragraphs in a document.

Font Faces

Recall that a font is a group of letters, numbers, and symbols with a common design, or typeface. A font consists of three elements: font face, font style, and font size. Each **font face** is a style of type identified by a name. Some of the commonly used font faces are Arial, Courier New, and Times New Roman (Figure 1-5). Each of the font faces shown in Figure 1-5 has a unique design. There are a variety of fonts available for use with WordPerfect.

Most font faces fall into one of two major categories: (1) serif or (2) sans serif. A serif font face has small, curved finishing strokes in the characters. The Times New Roman and Courier New font faces are examples of a serif font face. Serif font faces are considered easy to read when large blocks of text are involved and are normally used in books and magazines for the main text.

A **sans serif font face** is relatively plain with straight letter forms. The Arial font face in Figure 1-5 is a sans serif font face. Sans serif font faces are commonly used in headlines and short titles.

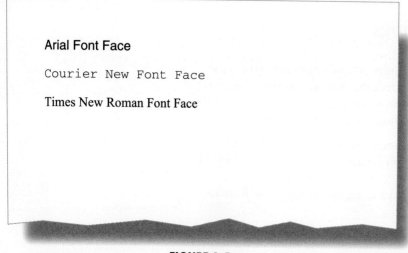

Arial Font Face

Courier New Font Face

Times New Roman Font Face

FIGURE 1-5

Font Styles

In WordPerfect, **font style** is the term used to describe the special appearance of text and numbers. Widely used font styles include bold, italic, and underline (Figure 1-6). The bold, italic, and underline styles can be applied to the same set of characters, if you so desire. In WordPerfect terminology, text formatted without the bold, italic, or underline font style is referred to as the **regular style**.

Font Sizes

You change the size of text by selecting a font size. Font sizes are measured in points. There are seventy-two points to one inch. Thus, a font size of thirty-six points is approximately one-half inch in height. The measurement is made from the top of the tallest character in a font face (such as a lowercase l) to the bottom of a character that extends below a line (such as a lowercase p). Figure 1-7 illustrates various font sizes of the Arial font face.

Changing the Default Font Size

The **default font size** is 12 point. If the majority of text in a document you wish to create requires a different font size, you can easily change the font size before you enter the document text. In the announcement, a majority of the text (bulleted list and last three paragraphs) displays in 14-point font size instead of the default font size (12 point). Perform the following steps to change the font size before you begin entering text.

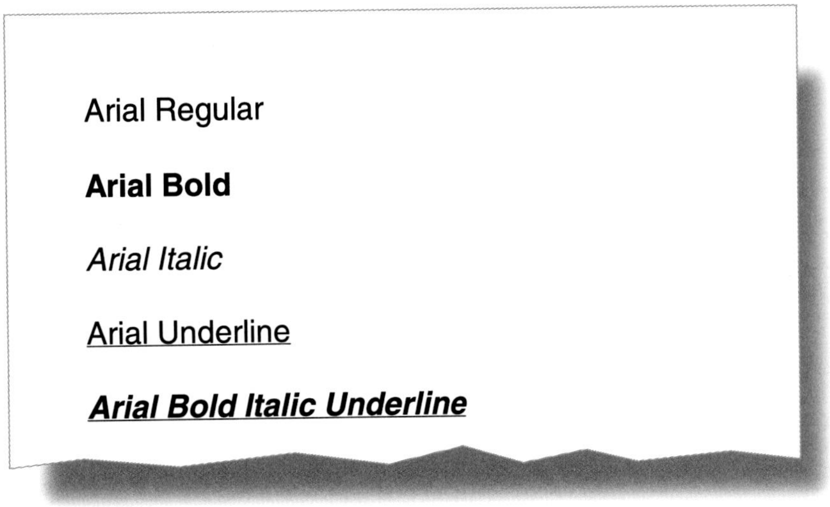

Arial Regular

Arial Bold

Arial Italic

Arial Underline

Arial Bold Italic Underline

FIGURE 1-6

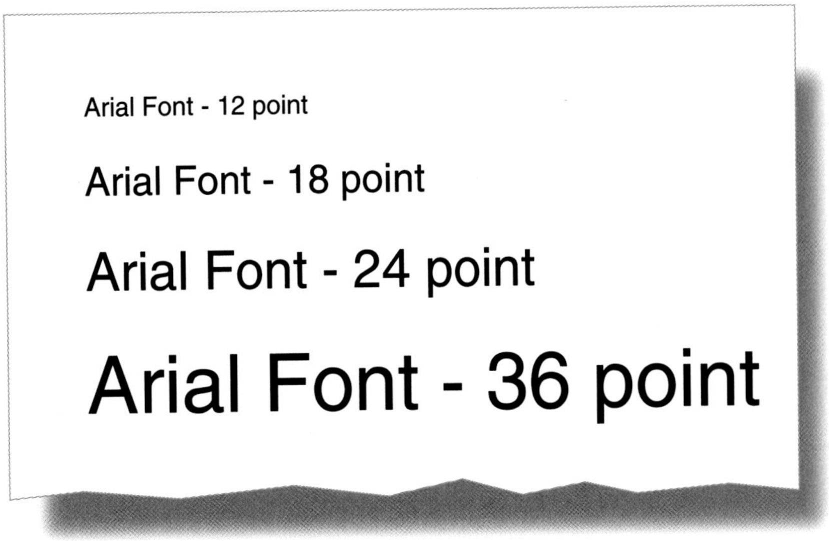

Arial Font - 12 point

Arial Font - 18 point

Arial Font - 24 point

Arial Font - 36 point

FIGURE 1-7

 Steps To Change the Default Font Size

1 Point to the Font Size box arrow on the Property Bar.

The mouse pointer points to the Font Size box arrow, and a QuickTip (Font Size - Change the font size) displays below the mouse pointer (Figure 1-8). The default font size (12) displays in the Font Size box.

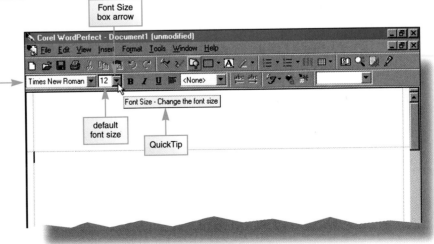

FIGURE 1-8

2 **Click the Font Size box arrow. When the Font Size drop-down list displays, point to 14.**

WordPerfect displays the Font Size list, highlights the 14-point font size in the Font Size list, and highlights the 12-point font size in the Font Size box (Figure 1-9). The mouse pointer points to font size 14.

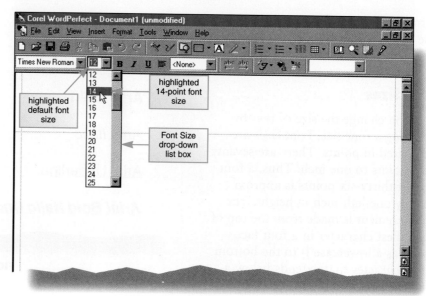

FIGURE 1-9

3 **Click 14.**

The font size changes to 14 point and 14 displays in the Font Size box (Figure 1-10).

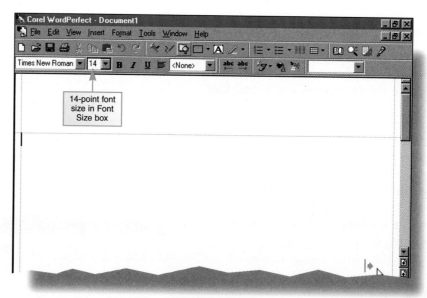

FIGURE 1-10

Entering Text

To prepare a document in WordPerfect, you enter text by pressing the keys on the keyboard. In the announcement, the first paragraph (VISIT THE STONE AGE!) is capitalized. Perform the following steps to enter the first paragraph in all capital letters.

Steps **To Enter Text in All Capital Letters**

1 **If the CAPS button on the Application Bar is not recessed, click the CAPS button on the Application Bar. Type** VISIT THE STONE AGE! **as the text of the first paragraph. If you make an error while typing or if red diagonal lines display below a word to indicate the word is not found in the dictionary, press the BACKSPACE key until you have deleted the text if it is in error and then type the text correctly.**

WordPerfect recesses the CAPS button on the Application Bar, turns on the CAPS LOCK indicator light on the keyboard, changes the Pos 1" entry on the Application Bar to Pos 3.08" when you have completed entering the text, and displays the last word typed (AGE) in the Prompt-As-You-Go box (Figure 1-11). As you type, the characters display in capital letters and the insertion point moves to the right, one character at a time.

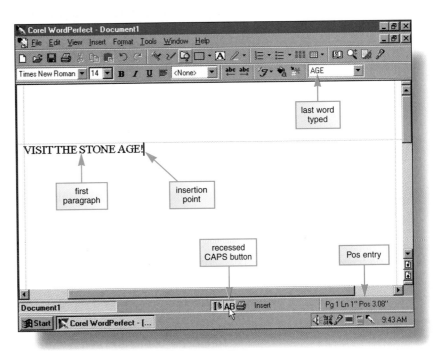

FIGURE 1-11

2 **Click the CAPS button and then press the ENTER key to complete the first paragraph.**

The CAPS button is no longer recessed, the CAPS LOCK indicator light on the keyboard is turned off, and the insertion point moves to the beginning of the next line (Figure 1-12). Pressing the ENTER key ends the entry of text and creates a paragraph in the document. On the Application Bar, the Ln 1" entry changes to Ln 1.23" and the Pos 3.08" entry changes to Pos 1" to indicate the new position of the insertion point.

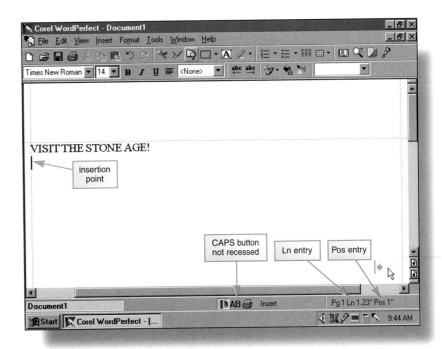

FIGURE 1-12

*Other***Ways**

1. Press CAPS LOCK key, type paragraph, press CAPS LOCK key

2. Hold down SHIFT key, type paragraph, release SHIFT key

Spell-As-You-Go and QuickCorrect

As you enter text, you may notice the spelling of some incorrectly spelled words is corrected automatically as you type. In addition, you may notice red diagonal lines below some words to indicate they may be incorrectly spelled. These actions are caused by Spell-As-You-Go and QuickCorrect. The default setting for spelling is that Spell-As-You-Go and QuickCorrect are turned on.

Spell-As-You-Go displays red diagonal lines below words that may be misspelled, so that you can decide whether to correct them. You can correct the word as you type or after you finish typing the document. To correct an incorrectly spelled word, right-click the word to display a **QuickMenu** and click the correct replacement word. Later in this project, you will learn how to correct all misspelled words in a document.

QuickCorrect checks the text you type for commonly misspelled words and capitalization errors. For example, if you incorrectly type the word, teh, instead of the word, the, QuickCorrect automatically corrects the problem. When the SPACEBAR is pressed to begin another word, QuickCorrect replaces the incorrectly spelled word, teh, with the correctly spelled word, the. QuickCorrect also fixes capitalization errors, such as automatically capitalizing the first character of a sentence and replacing the word, july, with the word, July.

Entering a Blank Line in a Document

To enter a blank line in a document, press the ENTER key twice after you have completed entering the text of a paragraph. The following step illustrates how to enter a blank line below the first paragraph.

ore *About*
QuickCorrect

QuickCorrect is one of twenty-one WordPerfect Quick features. Other Quick features mentioned in this book include Quick-Finder, QuickFormat, Quick-Menu, QuickLines, QuickTasks, and QuickTip.

Steps To Enter a Blank Line in a Document

1 **Press the ENTER key to insert a blank line.**

When the line containing the insertion point does not contain text and you press the ENTER key, WordPerfect inserts a blank line in the document (Figure 1-13).

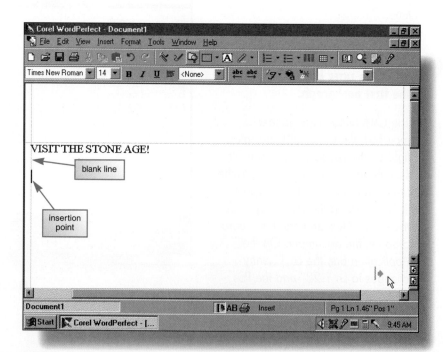

FIGURE 1-13

*Other*Ways

1. Move shadow cursor to beginning of second blank line following paragraph and click

Entering Regular Text

The next step is to enter the second paragraph, New World Tours, and the two paragraphs for the bulleted list. Perform the step below to enter the three paragraphs.

 Steps To Enter the Next Three Paragraphs

1 **Type** New World Tours **and then press the ENTER key twice to end the line and insert a blank line following the paragraph. Type** Specializing in fully escorted group tours **and then press the ENTER key. Type** All tours include hiking, scuba diving, and river cruising **and then press the ENTER key twice.**

The three paragraphs display (Figure 1-14). A blank line displays below the second and fourth paragraphs.

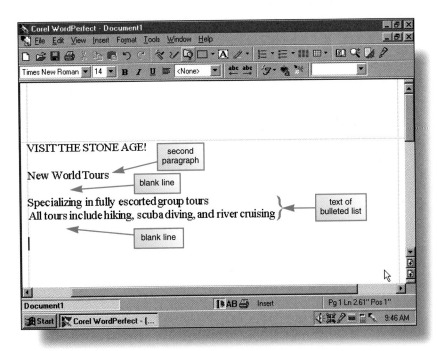

FIGURE 1-14

Wordwrap

Before typing the next two paragraphs in the document, it is important to understand what occurs when you type multiple lines. When you type text that requires more than one line, the insertion point continues to move toward the right margin. **Wordwrap** automatically drops the word down to the beginning of the next line when the word extends beyond the right margin. Wordwrap is an important feature of WordPerfect because it facilitates rapid entry of data and allows WordPerfect to rearrange characters, words, and sentences within a paragraph easily when you make changes. Perform the steps on the next page to enter the next two paragraphs in the document.

 **More** *About* **Entering Text**

In the days of typewriters, the lowercase letter l was used for both the lowercase letter l and the number one. Keyboards, however, have both a lowercase letter l and a number one. Also, keyboards have both the number zero and the letter O. Be careful to press the correct keyboard character when creating a word processing document.

Steps **To Use WordWrap**

1 **Begin typing the first paragraph with multiple sentences as shown in Figure 1-15. Do not press the ENTER key at the end of each line. Press the ENTER key only to end the paragraph. Press the ENTER key again to insert a blank line following the paragraph.**

The paragraph and a blank line display (Figure 1-15). Wordwrap occurs at the end of the first four lines of the paragraph. Red diagonal lines display below the word, Huli. Although Spell-As-You-Go detected this as an incorrectly spelled word, the word is the name of a New Guinea tribe and is correctly spelled.

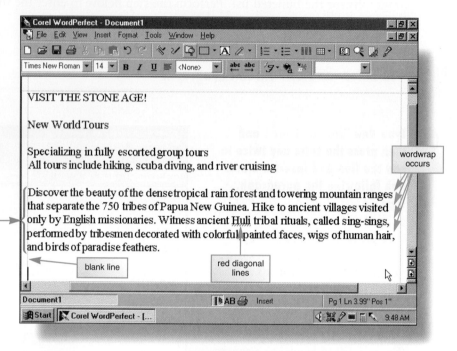

FIGURE 1-15

2 **Type the next paragraph as shown in Figure 1-16. Press the ENTER key twice. Type** Call (714) 555-9200 **as the last paragraph. Press the ENTER key.**

The last five paragraphs in the document display (Figure 1-16). Wordwrap occurs while typing the second to last paragraph and a blank line separates the last two paragraphs.

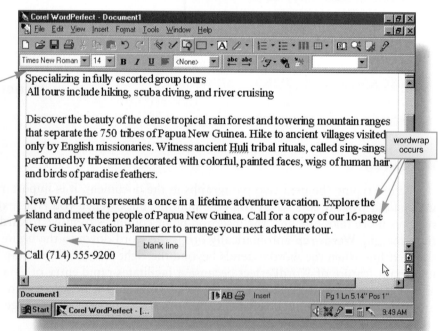

FIGURE 1-16

In Figure 1-16, the top portion of the document no longer displays in the document window. As you type more lines of text than can display in the text area, WordPerfect scrolls the top portion of the document upward off the screen. Although you cannot see the text once it scrolls off the screen, it remains in the document.

Correcting Incorrectly Spelled Words

Spell-As-You-Go checks each word in the document against a list of correctly spelled words, called a **dictionary**. When a word is found in the document that does not match any of the words in the dictionary, Spell-As-You-Go displays red diagonal lines below the word. Although it is a matter of personal choice whether you correct misspelled words as you type or after you have finished typing, it is important to spell check every document and correct any incorrectly spelled words.

While entering the text of the announcement, red diagonal lines display below the word, Huli, to indicate it may be incorrectly spelled (see Figure 1-16). The word Huli is a proper name, or proper noun, and is spelled correctly. Assume that while entering the text of the announcement, you enter the incorrectly spelled word, paradice, instead of the correctly spelled word, paradise, in the same paragraph. The word, paradice, is incorrectly spelled and should be corrected. Perform the following steps to check the document for red diagonal lines that display below words.

 Steps To Correct Incorrectly Spelled Words

 1 **Locate the first incorrectly spelled word (Huli). Point to the space before the word, Huli, and then right-click. Point to Skip in Document on the QuickMenu.**

A QuickMenu displays and a replacement word displays in the Prompt-As-You-Go box (Figure 1-17). The top area of the Quick-Menu contains three replacement words. Because the word, Huli, is a proper name and is spelled correctly, you should click Skip in Document to skip all occurrences of the word, Huli, in the document. Clicking Skip in Document removes the red diagonal lines from other occurrences of the word, Huli, in the document. The incorrectly spelled word, paradice, also displays while you are checking the same paragraph.

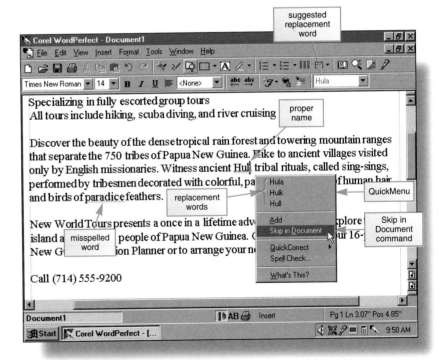

FIGURE 1-17

2 **Click Skip in Document. Locate the next incorrectly spelled word (paradice) in the document. Point to the word, paradice.**

WordPerfect removes the red diagonal lines below the word, Huli (Figure 1-18). If the document had contained other occurrences of the word, Huli, the red diagonal lines below those words also would have been removed. The I-beam pointer is located in the word, paradice.

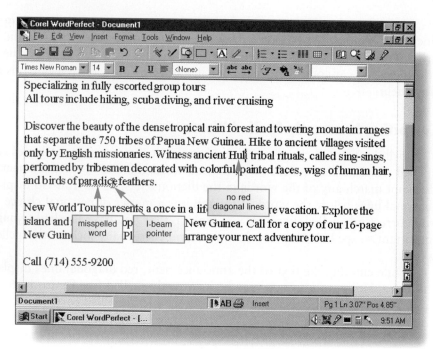

FIGURE 1-18

3 **Right-click paradice. Point to the word, paradise, on the Quickmenu.**

A QuickMenu displays (Figure 1-19). The first area contains six replacement words and the More entry. The first replacement word (paradise) is highlighted on the QuickMenu and displays in red text in the Prompt-As-You-Go box. The word, paradice, is misspelled and should be replaced with the word, paradise.

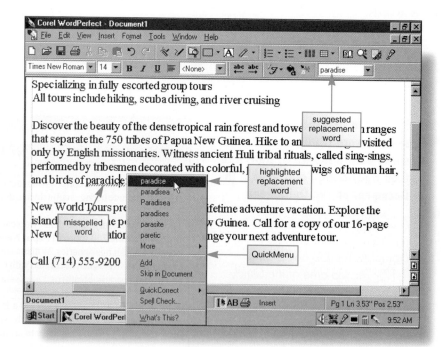

FIGURE 1-19

4 **Click paradise.**

WordPerfect replaces the misspelled word (paradice) with the replacement word (paradise) and removes the red diagonal lines below the word (Figure 1-20).

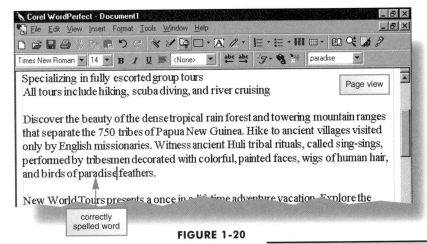

FIGURE 1-20

Other Ways

1. Click Prompt-As-You-Go box arrow, click correctly spelled word
2. On WordPerfect 8 Toolbar click Spell Check button, correct misspelled words
3. Right-click text area, click Spell Check, correct misspelled words
4. Press CTRL+F1

Spell-As-You-Go also checks for duplicate words and irregular capitalization. If duplicate words exist together in a document, you can delete the second occurrence of the word by clicking Delete Duplicate in the QuickMenu. If an irregularly capitalized word, such as sPeaking, is found, you can replace the uppercase letter (P) with a lowercase letter (p) by right-clicking the word, Speaking, and then clicking speaking in the QuickMenu.

View Modes

You can work with a WordPerfect document in one of three **view modes**: Draft, Page, and Two Pages. **Draft view** displays the document in approximately the same way it will look when it is printed. Special features (headers, footers, footnotes, and watermarks) do not display in the document window. As a result, you can move through the document more quickly in Draft view.

Page view displays a document on the screen exactly as it will appear when it is printed. Page view displays the special features in the document. Each time you begin a new page in Page view, WordPerfect creates the entire page. As a result, you can scroll to the bottom of the page even though it is blank. When you start WordPerfect, the **default view mode setting** is Page view. **Two Pages view** is similar to Page view, except that two consecutive pages display side-by-side in the document window. The announcement shown in the document window in Figure 1-20 displays in Page view.

A fourth view mode also is provided by WordPerfect. When you create a Web document, you can view it through the Web Editor before publishing it to the Web. **Web view** (accessed through the Web Editor) displays a document in the format required to publish the document to the World Wide Web.

Saving a Document

When you create a document, the document is stored only in your computer's main memory until you save the document on the hard disk or on a floppy disk. If you turn off the computer or there is a power loss before you save a document, your work will be lost. You should, therefore, save all documents on either the hard disk or a floppy disk when you have completed a large amount of the work.

More About Filenames

Because of restrictions with Microsoft DOS, older versions of WordPerfect allowed filenames of only eight or fewer characters. JOHNLETR, and similar difficult to understand names, were common. Longer filenames are a significant breakthrough and should be used to create readable and meaningful filenames.

When saving a document for the first time, you must create a filename. The filename is the name used to reference the file (document) on the hard disk or floppy disk. The filename can contain up to 255 characters, including spaces. Any uppercase or lowercase characters are valid when creating a filename, except the backslash (\), slash (/), colon (:), asterisk (*), question mark (?), quotation mark ('), less than symbol (<), greater than symbol (>), or vertical bar (|). Filenames cannot be CON, AUX, COM1, COM2, COM3, COM4, LPT1, LPT2, LPT3, PRN, or NUL. These are reserved filenames for system functions.

In addition to the filename, WordPerfect automatically assigns an extension consisting of a period and three characters (.wpd) to each document name. A good, descriptive name for the document is New Guinea Tour. When you save the document, WordPerfect will add the .wpd extension and save the file on disk using the New Guinea Tour.wpd filename.

The next step in creating the announcement is to save the document on a floppy disk in drive A using the filename, New Guinea Tour. Because this is the first project in the book, you will need a blank, formatted floppy disk to save all the documents you create in this book. You will label the floppy disk by writing the words, Corel WordPerfect 8 Files, on the paper label attached to the floppy disk.

Because the **default drive setting** for storing files is drive C and the **default folder setting** is the MyFiles folder, you must change the default drive and folder when saving the document on drive A. Perform the following steps to save the document on a floppy disk in drive A using the filename, New Guinea Tour.wpd.

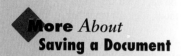

More *About*
Saving a Document

Most word processor users can tell at least one horror story of working on their computer for a long period of time and then losing the work because of a malfunction with the computer or application software. Be Warned! Save and save often to protect your documents.

Steps To Save a Document

1. **Label a blank formatted floppy disk by writing the words, Corel WordPerfect 8 Files, on the paper label attached to the floppy disk. Insert the Corel WordPerfect 8 Files disk into drive A.**

2. **Point to the Save button on the Toolbar.**

   The mouse pointer points to the Save button on the Toolbar and a QuickTip (Save - Save the current document) displays (Figure 1-21).

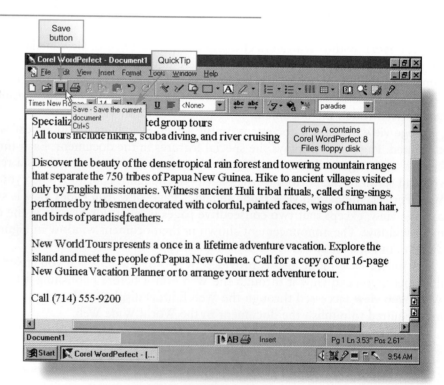

FIGURE 1-21

3 **Click the Save button. When the Save File dialog box displays, type** New Guinea Tour **in the File name box. Point to the Save in box arrow.**

WordPerfect opens the Save File dialog box (Figure 1-22). The New Guinea Tour filename displays in the File name box. The default MyFiles folder icon and name display in the Save in box, and one folder in the MyFiles folder on drive C (Backup) displays in the list box.

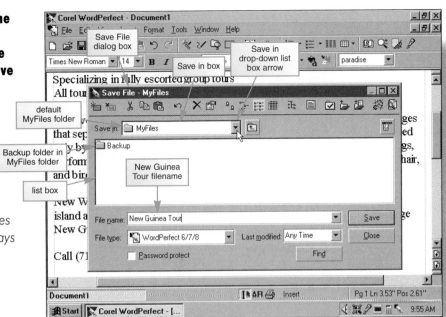

FIGURE 1-22

4 **Click the Save in box arrow, scroll the Save in list until 3½ Floppy (A:) displays, and then point to 3½ Floppy (A:).**

The Save in drop-down list box displays (Figure 1-23). The Save in list contains various elements of your computer, including Desktop, My Computer, and 3½ Floppy (A:). Depending upon how your computer is configured, the contents of the list may differ.

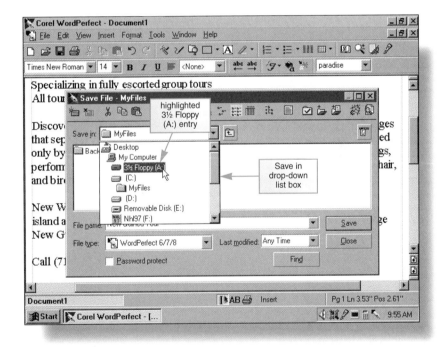

FIGURE 1-23

5 **Click 3½ Floppy (A:). Point to the Save button.**

When you click 3½ Floppy (A:) in the Save in list, 3½ Floppy (A:) displays on the title bar and in the Save in box and the contents of the floppy disk in drive A display in the list box (Figure 1-24). This indicates the file will be saved on the floppy disk in drive A using the filename specified in the File name box. Currently, no files display in the list box.

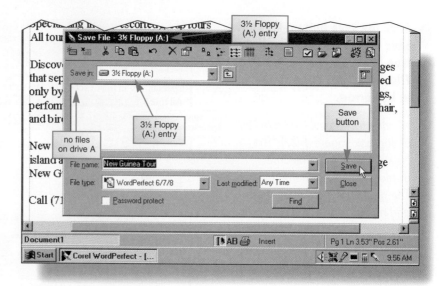

FIGURE 1-24

6 **Click the Save button.**

Windows 95 displays an hourglass icon while saving the New Guinea Tour.wpd document on the floppy disk in drive A, closes the Save File dialog box, and replaces the Document1 entry in the Corel WordPerfect window title with the A:\New Guinea Tour.wpd (unmodified) entry (Figure 1-25).

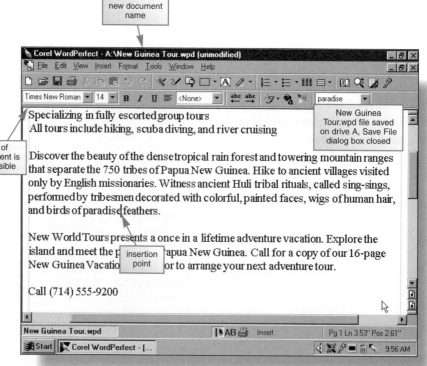

FIGURE 1-25

OtherWays

1. On File menu click Save, type filename, select location, click Save button
2. On File menu click Save As, type filename, select location, click Save button
3. Press CTRL+S

After saving a document for the first time, continue to save the document often to avoid losing the information in case there is a power loss. When saving the document again using the same filename, click the Save button on the Toolbar. If you use the Save button on the Toolbar, WordPerfect saves the document without changing the filename. If you want to save the document using a different filename, use the **Save As command** on the **File menu**.

Codes in a Document

When you create a document, WordPerfect places **codes** in the document. Codes determine how a document will display on the screen and print on the printer. Codes are placed in a document when you change the font face, font size, or font style; when you press the ENTER key; and when wordwrap occurs. The codes do not print and currently do not display in the document window.

You view the codes by opening the Reveal Codes window. To view codes, you may have to move the insertion point to a different area in the document before opening the Reveal Codes window. The following sections illustrate how to view codes in different areas of the document.

Scrolling

In Figure 1-25, the insertion point displays toward the bottom of the document, and the top portion of the document is not visible in the document window. To view the codes in the top of the document, it is necessary to scroll the document window and move the insertion point.

You can use the scroll bar or the keyboard keys to scroll the document window. **Scrolling** can be accomplished in three ways using the scroll bar: 1) clicking the scroll arrows; 2) clicking the scroll bar; and 3) dragging the scroll box. Perform the following steps to scroll the document window until the top of the document is visible in the document window.

 Steps **To Scroll to the Top of a Document**

1 **Point to the vertical scroll bar above the scroll box (Figure 1-26).**

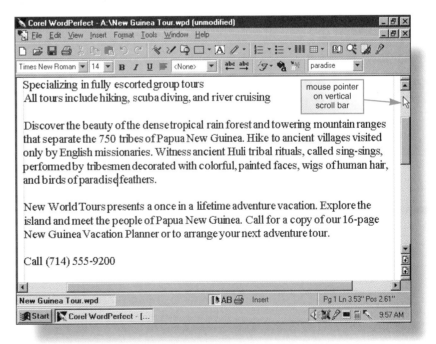

FIGURE 1-26

2 Click the scroll bar.

The top of the document displays in the document window (Figure 1-27).

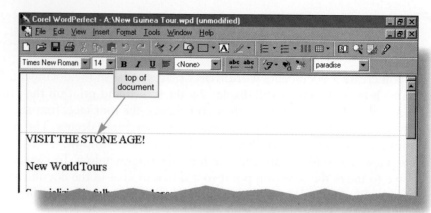

FIGURE 1-27

OtherWays

1. Drag scroll box up or down vertical scroll bar
2. Click up or down scroll arrows
3. Press PAGE UP key or PAGE DOWN key

Moving the Insertion Point

After scrolling, you must move the insertion point to the beginning of the document. You can move the insertion point using the mouse or the keyboard keys. To move the insertion point using the keyboard, use the arrow keys.

To move the insertion point using the mouse, point to where you want the insertion point to display and click. When you point to a position within text, the I-beam pointer displays. The **I-beam pointer** indicates where in the document the insertion point will display when you click. After the I-beam pointer displays, clicking will move the insertion point to the position the I-beam pointer occupies. Perform the following steps to move the insertion point from its current position to the beginning of the first paragraph.

Steps **To Move the Insertion Point**

1 With the top of the document visible, point to the text area to the left of the first character in the first paragraph (the letter V).

The I-beam pointer displays to the left of the letter V (Figure 1-28). Although not visible, the insertion point continues to display toward the end of the document.

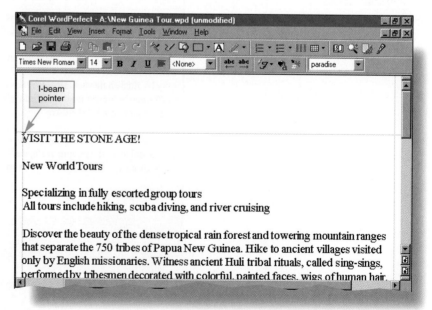

FIGURE 1-28

Click the text area.

The insertion point moves to the beginning of the first paragraph (Figure 1-29).

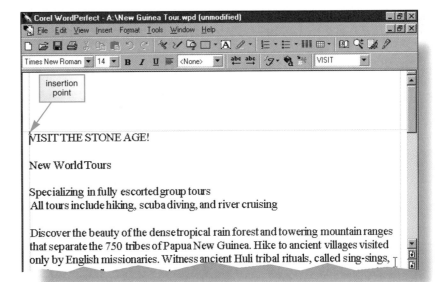

FIGURE 1-29

Opening the Reveal Codes Window

After moving the insertion point, open the Reveal Codes window to make the codes at the beginning of the document visible. Perform the following steps to open the Reveal Codes window and view the codes.

Steps **To Open the Reveal Codes Window**

1 **Right-click the text area. Point to Reveal Codes on the QuickMenu.**

WordPerfect displays a QuickMenu, highlights the Reveal Codes command, and moves the insertion point to a new location in the document (Figure 1-30).

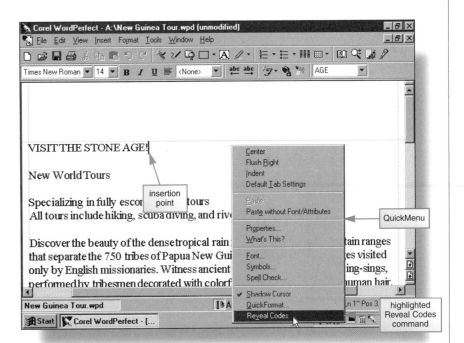

FIGURE 1-30

2 Click Reveal Codes.

*A thick double line, called the **divider line**, displays across the document window. The divider line separates the document window into two areas (Figure 1-31). The mouse pointer displays as an I-beam pointer in the Reveal Codes window.*

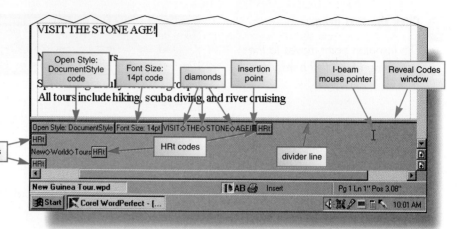

FIGURE 1-31

The area above the divider line is the text area and contains only text. The area below the divider line, called the **Reveal Codes window**, contains text and codes. You can make the Reveal Codes window larger or smaller by dragging the divider line up or down.

The first code in the Reveal Codes window, the **Open Style: DocumentStyle code**, controls the default settings for the document. This code is inserted in a document when you start WordPerfect or create a new document.

The **Font Size: 14pt code** displays in the document because you changed the default font size to 14 point. This code causes all text to the right and below the code to display in 14-point font size. To the right of the Font Size code is the text of the first paragraph (VISIT THE STONE AGE!). Diamonds between the words in this paragraph correspond to the blank spaces between words in the text area. The colored rectangle, or **insertion point**, to the right of the first paragraph indicates the position of the insertion point in the text area.

Several **HRt codes**, or **Hard Return codes**, display in the Reveal Codes window. An HRt code represents the end of a paragraph or a blank line. In Figure 1-31, the HRt codes to the right of the first and second paragraphs indicate the end of the paragraph. The two HRt codes on lines by themselves indicate you pressed the ENTER key to create a blank line in the document.

To view the codes in the bottom section of the document, perform the following steps to move the insertion point to the beginning of the second to last paragraph in the document.

TO MOVE THE INSERTION POINT

1 Point to the vertical scroll bar below the scroll box.
2 Click the scroll bar.
3 Point to the text area to the left of the first character (the letter N) in the second to last paragraph.
4 Click the text area.

*The insertion point displays at the beginning of the paragraph (Figure 1-32). A **SRt code**, or **Soft Return code**, displays at the end of each of the first two lines of the paragraph to indicate wordwrap has occurred. An HRt code displays at the end of the paragraph to indicate the end of the paragraph.*

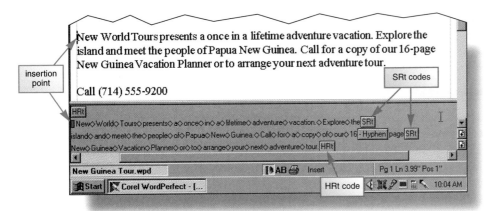

FIGURE 1-32

Formatting the Document

The entry of the text of the announcement is complete. The next step in preparing the announcement is to format the document. **Formatting** is the process of conforming a document to a specific visual appearance. You will format the document in this project by selecting text and specifying the font face, font style and font size for the text; centering selected lines, and adding bullets. The formatting requirements of the New Guinea Tour document are illustrated in Figure 1-33.

The first paragraph (VISIT THE STONE AGE!) displays in all capital letters in Arial Bold 38-point font. A picture downloaded from the Internet displays below the first paragraph. The second paragraph (New World Tours) displays in Arial Italic 45-point font. The first and second paragraphs are centered. A bulleted list, consisting of two bulleted items, displays below the second paragraph.

The two paragraphs below the bulleted list describe the New Guinea adventure tour. A single word in the first paragraph, sing-sings, displays in italics. A group of words in the second paragraph, once in a lifetime adventure vacation, is underlined. The last paragraph contains a phone number, displays in Times New Roman Bold 18-point font, and is centered. The

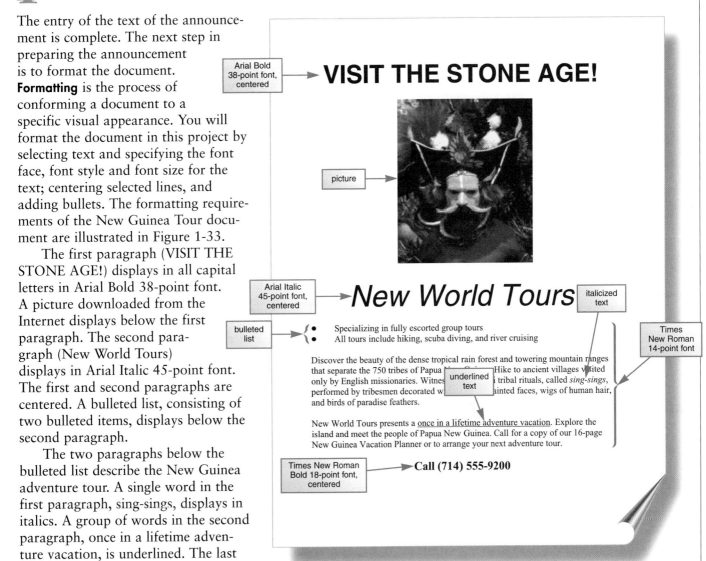

FIGURE 1-33

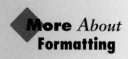

bulleted list and the three paragraphs below the list display in the Times New Roman 14-point font. The following sections illustrate how to format the announcement.

Selecting Text

Before you can change the format of a document, you must **select** the text you want to change. Selected text displays in reverse video in the text area. The Select code, or **Beginning of Selection code**, displays before the text in the Reveal Codes window, and the insertion point indicates the end of the selected text.

WordPerfect provides a variety of ways to select text. One common method is to move the I-beam pointer to the first character of the text and drag across the text until all the text you wish to format is selected. Table 1-1 explains other techniques you can use to select text.

If you select text and then wish to remove the highlighting for any reason, click anywhere in the text area or Reveal Codes window. The highlighting will be removed.

Selecting Text Using a QuickMenu

WordPerfect displays a QuickMenu when you right-click an area of the document window or an object in the document window. The QuickMenu illustrated in Figure 1-34 opens when you right-click the left margin. To open this QuickMenu, move the mouse pointer into the left margin until the mouse pointer changes to a **right-pointing block arrow**. If you have difficulty pointing to the left margin area because only a small portion is visible in the document window, click the left scroll arrow on the horizontal scroll bar to make more of the left margin visible.

The QuickMenu contains three areas separated by horizontal lines. Use the commands in the first area (Select Sentence, Select Paragraph, Select Page, and Select All) to select text in the document window. Table 1-2 on the opposite page explains how to use the QuickMenu to select text.

Table 1–1	
TO SELECT	*ACTION TO BE PERFORMED*
A word	Double-click when the I-beam is located anywhere in the word.
A sentence	Click the left margin beside the sentence, or triple-click when the I-beam pointer is located anywhere in the sentence.
A paragraph	Double-click the left margin beside the paragraph, or quadruple-click when the I-beam pointer is located anywhere in the paragraph.
Several words	Point to the first word to be selected and drag the I-beam pointer to the left or right.
Several lines or paragraphs	Position the mouse pointer in the left margin and drag the mouse pointer up or down.

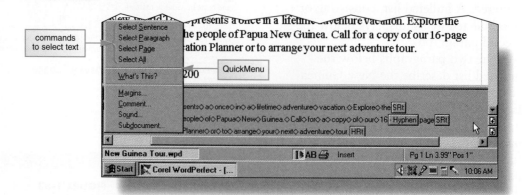

FIGURE 1-34

Formatting the First Paragraph

The default font face is Times New Roman Regular 12-point font size. Before you entered the text of the announcement, you changed the default font size to 14 point. The text in the announcement now displays in Times New Roman 14-point font and the current font face and font size (Times New Roman and 14) display in the first and second boxes on the Property Bar. The first paragraph (VISIT THE STONE AGE!) should display in Arial Bold 38-point font (see Figure 1-33). Thus, the font face must be changed to Arial, the font style changed to bold, and the size changed to 38 point.

Justification is the process of aligning a line of text between the left and right margins. You can align text at the left margin (left-justification), at the right margin (right-justification), or center text between the margins (center-justification). In addition, you can instruct the computer to add space between words to spread text to both margins (full-justification) or add spaces between words and letters (all-justification). Currently, the first paragraph is aligned at the left margin (left-justified) and needs to be centered between the margins (see Figure 1-31).

As mentioned earlier, selected text displays highlighted in a document. For example, if your screen normally displays dark letters on a light background, then selected text displays as light letters on a dark background. Once selected, you can format text by right-clicking the text and clicking Font on the QuickMenu to display the Font dialog box. Perform the following step to select the first paragraph.

Table 1–2	
TO SELECT	ACTION TO BE PERFORMED
A sentence	Position the insertion point in the sentence, right-click the left margin, and click Select Sentence.
A paragraph	Position the insertion point in the paragraph, right-click the left margin, and click Select Paragraph.
A page	Position the insertion point on the page, right-click the left margin, and click Select Page.
All text	Right-click the left margin, and click Select All.

More *About*
Selecting
Paragraphs

Pressing the ENTER key terminates the entry of a paragraph and inserts HRT code. In the case of a single sentence paragraph followed by a blank line, quadruple-clicking will select the sentence and blank line. When this is undesirable, triple-click to select only the paragraph.

Steps To Select a Paragraph

1 **Click the vertical scroll bar above the scroll box to display the top of the document. Move the I-beam pointer into the first paragraph and triple-click.**

The I-beam pointer changes to a left-pointing block arrow and the first paragraph is selected (Figure 1-35).

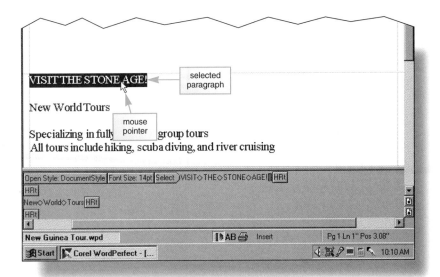

FIGURE 1-35

After selecting the first paragraph, perform the following steps to format it by using the Arial Bold 38-point font and centering the paragraph.

 Steps **To Format a Paragraph Using a QuickMenu**

1 **With the first paragraph selected, right-click the paragraph. Point to Font on the QuickMenu.**

WordPerfect displays a QuickMenu and highlights the Font command on the QuickMenu (Figure 1-36).

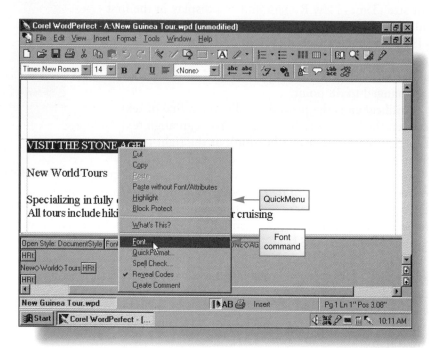

FIGURE 1-36

2 **Click Font.**

The Font dialog box displays (Figure 1-37). The highlighted Times New Roman entry displays in the Font face list box, the highlighted Regular entry displays in the Font style list box, and the number 14 displays in the Font size text box. The highlighted Regular entry indicates the paragraph is formatted without the bold, italic, or underline style. A sample of Times New Roman Regular 14 point text displays in the Preview window.

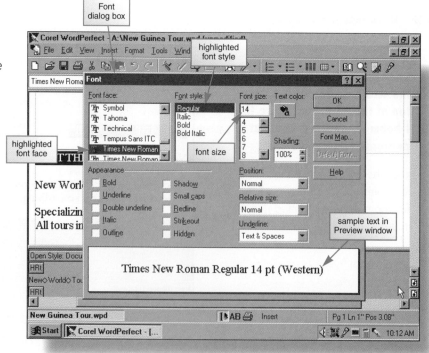

FIGURE 1-37

3 Scroll the Font face list box until Arial displays and then click Arial. Click Bold in the Font style list box. Scroll the Font size list box to display 38 and then click 38. Point to the OK button.

WordPerfect highlights the Arial entry in the Font face list box, Bold entry in the Font style list box, font size 38 in the Font size list box and Font size text box, and displays a sample of the Arial Bold 38-point font in the Preview window (Figure 1-38).

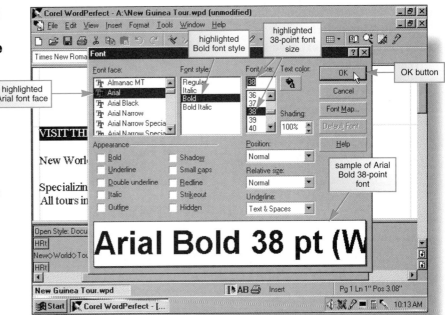

FIGURE 1-38

4 Click the OK button. Click the Justification button on the Property Bar to display the Justification menu. Point to the Center button.

*WordPerfect closes the Font dialog box, formats the first paragraph (Arial Bold 38-point font), inserts two **Font codes** and two **Font size codes** in the document, recesses the Justification button, and opens the Justification menu (Figure 1-39). Five buttons display on the Justification menu. The Left button is recessed to indicate the default justification is Left justification. When you point to the Center button, the button changes to a three-dimensional button. The Font and Font size codes are visible in the Reveal Codes window.*

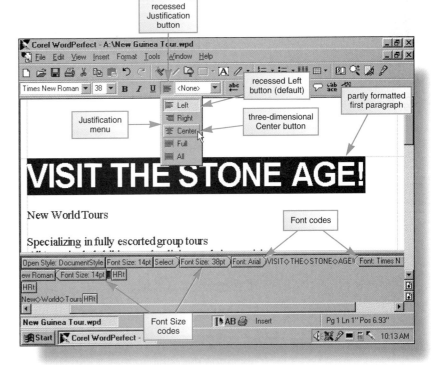

FIGURE 1-39

5 **Click the Center button in the Justification palette. Click anywhere in the text area to remove the highlight.**

*WordPerfect closes the Justification palette, centers the paragraph, removes the highlighting, and inserts two **Justification codes** in the document (Figure 1-40). The Justification codes are visible in the Reveal Codes window.*

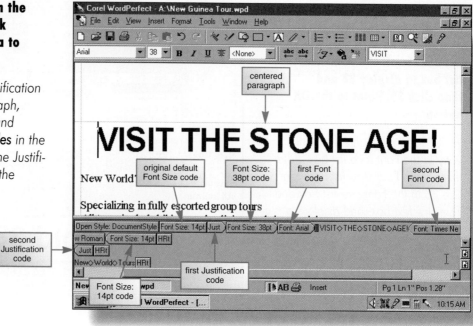

FIGURE 1-40

As a result of changing the font face of the first paragraph and centering the paragraph, WordPerfect inserts sets of two Font codes, two Font Size codes, and two Justification codes in the document. The first code in the set displays at the beginning of the affected text in the Reveal Codes window, and the second code displays following the text. Together, a set of two codes, called **revertible codes**, causes the text between the codes to be formatted.

As an example, the first Font code (Font: Arial) points to the right to indicate the text following the code displays in the Arial font. The second Font code (Font: Times New Roman) points to the left to indicate the end of the Arial text and the continuation of the original font (Times New Roman). Together, the two Font codes cause the text between the codes to display in Arial font while not altering the font of the other text in the document. The Font Size and Justification codes operate in a similar manner.

Expanding a Code

Some codes, like the Font and Justification codes, display in the Reveal Codes window in an abbreviated form to conserve space. Clicking the code or using the arrow keys to move the insertion point immediately to the left of the code expands the code so that additional text displays on the code. In Figure 1-40, the description, Font: Arial, displays on the first Font code and the description, Font: Times New Roman, displays on the second Font code. Neither code is expanded. Clicking the first Font code moves the insertion point to the left of the code, expands the code, and displays the description, Font: Arial Bold. Perform the following step to expand the Font: Arial code.

To Expand a Code

① Click the Font: Arial code in the Reveal Codes window.

WordPerfect moves the insertion point to the left of the code and expands the Font code (Figure 1-41). The description changes to Font: Arial Bold.

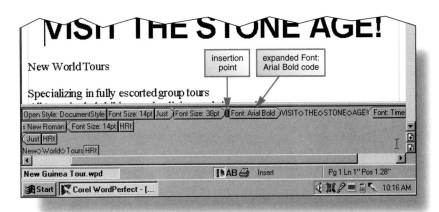

FIGURE 1-41

▶**Other Ways**

1. Position insertion point to left of code in Reveal Codes window

When the other Font code (Font: Times New Roman) is expanded, the description changes to Font: Times New Roman Regular. The word Regular indicates the text following the code is not formatted with the bold, italic, or underline font style. The first code (Font: Arial Bold) precedes the paragraph in the document and the second code (Font: Times New Roman Regular) displays following the paragraph. The two revertible Font codes cause the text between the codes to display in Arial Bold font and the text following the paragraph to display in Times New Roman font.

Formatting the Second Paragraph

The second paragraph (New World Tours) is formatted using Arial Italic 45-point font and is centered (see Figure 1-33 on page WP 1.31). Perform the following steps to format the second paragraph.

TO FORMAT A PARAGRAPH USING A QUICKMENU

① Move the I-beam pointer into the second paragraph and triple-click.
② Right-click the paragraph to display a QuickMenu.
③ Click Font on the QuickMenu.
④ Scroll the Font face list box until the Arial font name displays and then click Arial.
⑤ Click Italic in the Font style list box.
⑥ Scroll the Font size list box until the font size 45 displays and then click 45.
⑦ Click the OK button.
⑧ Click the Justification button on the Property Bar to display the Justification palette.
⑨ Click the Center button.
⑩ Click anywhere in the text area to remove the highlight.

WordPerfect formats and centers the second paragraph, and then inserts two Font codes, two Font size codes, and two Justification codes in the document (Figure 1-42 on the next page). The codes are visible in the Reveal Codes window.

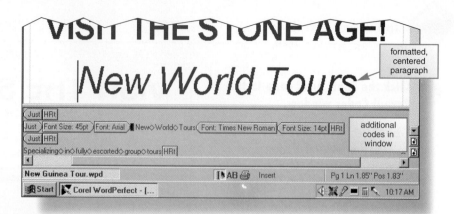

FIGURE 1-42

Continuing the Formatting of the Document

The next step is to create a **bulleted list**. The bulleted list consists of the third paragraph (Specializing in fully escorted group tours) and fourth paragraph (All tours include hiking, scuba diving, and river cruising) in the document (see Figure 1-33 on WP 1.31). To create a bulleted list using the two paragraphs, you must first select the paragraphs.

Selecting Multiple Paragraphs

The method used to select the third and fourth paragraphs in the following steps is to point to the left margin of the first paragraph and drag downward until both paragraphs are highlighted. Before selecting the paragraphs, you must scroll the document window to make the paragraphs visible and then enlarge the left margin by clicking the left scroll arrow on the horizontal scroll bar. Perform the following steps to enlarge the left margin and select the two paragraphs.

Steps **To Enlarge the Left Margin and Select Multiple Paragraphs**

1 **Scroll the document window until the third and fourth paragraphs display. Click the left scroll arrow on the horizontal scroll bar to increase the size of the left margin. Point to the left margin next to the third paragraph until the mouse pointer changes to a right-pointing block arrow.**

The left margin increases in size, the two paragraphs are visible, and the mouse pointer changes to a right-pointing block arrow when positioned in the left margin (Figure 1-43).

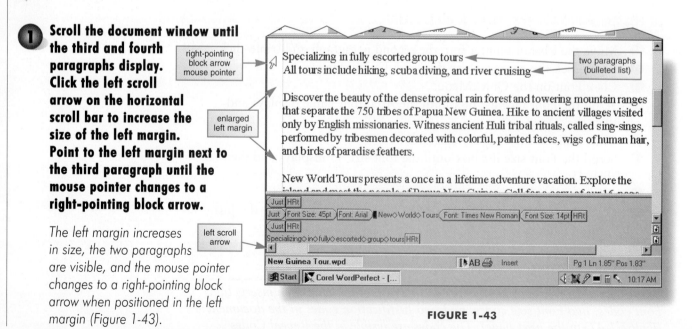

FIGURE 1-43

② **Drag downward until the two paragraphs are selected.**

The pointer changes to an I-beam pointer as you drag, and the two paragraphs are highlighted (Figure 1-44).

selected paragraphs

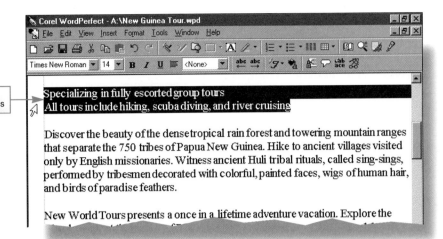

FIGURE 1-44

Other Ways

1. Position I-beam pointer to left of first character in first paragraph, drag down

Creating a Bulleted List

Next, create the bulleted list using the Bullets button on the Toolbar. When you select text and click the Bullets button, a bulleted list is created using the selected text and the default bullet list style. When you click the down arrow on the Bullets button, a palette of bullet list styles displays. Clicking a bullet list style creates a bulleted list using the style you selected. Perform the following steps to create a bulleted list using the down arrow on the Bullets button.

More About Bulleted Lists

To use the default bullet list style, click the Bullets button on the WordPerfect 8 Toolbar. WordPerfect inserts the default bullet in the document.

 Steps To Create a Bulleted List

① **Point to the down arrow on the Bullets button on the Toolbar.**

The mouse pointer points to the down arrow on the Bullets button and a QuickTip displays (Figure 1-45).

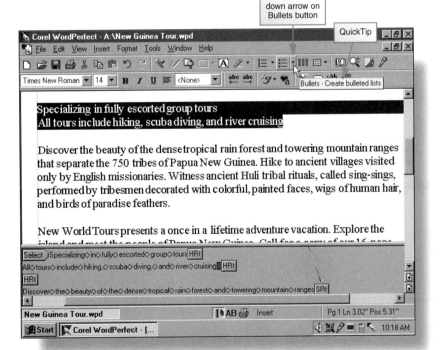

FIGURE 1-45

2 **Click the down arrow. When the Bullets palette displays, point to the second bullet in first row (Large Circle bullet).**

WordPerfect displays the Bullets palette (Figure 1-46). When you point to the Large Circle bullet, the bullet becomes three-dimensional. Although the first two bullets in the first row of the palette look similar, the second bullet displays a larger bullet than the first bullet.

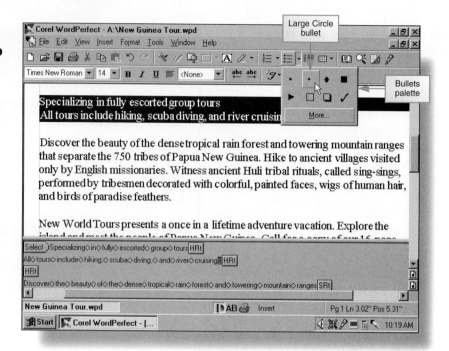

FIGURE 1-46

3 **Click the bullet. Press the DELETE key to remove one of the blank lines following the bulleted list. Click the right scroll arrow on the horizontal scroll bar.**

*Clicking the bullet creates a bulleted list, removes the highlight from the bulleted list, and inserts a blank line following the list (Figure 1-47). Pressing the DELETE key removes the blank line. Clicking the right scroll arrow returns the left margin to its original size. WordPerfect inserts an **Outline code** before the first bulleted item, a **Para Style code** and **Style code** preceding each bulleted item, a Para Style code following each item, and an Outline code and **Para Num Set code** following the bulleted list. The codes preceding and following the second bulleted item are visible in Figure 1-47.*

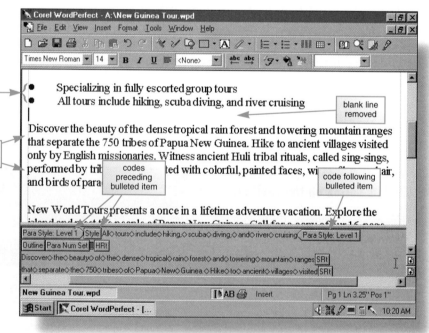

FIGURE 1-47

Changing the Font Style of a Single Word

A single word in the fifth paragraph, sing-sings, should display in italics. Previously, to create a bulleted list you first had to select two paragraphs and then format the paragraphs. When you format a single word, you do not need to select the text before formatting. Perform the following steps to italicize the word, sing-sings, in the document.

Steps To Italicize a Single Word

1 **Scroll the document window until the last three paragraphs display. Click sing-sings in the last sentence of the first paragraph on the screen. Point to the Italic button on the Property Bar.**

When you point to the word, sing-sings, the I-beam pointer displays. When you click the word, the insertion point replaces the I-beam pointer (Figure 1-48).

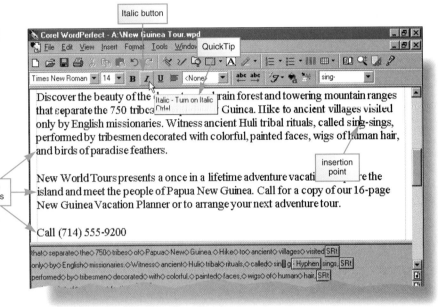

FIGURE 1-48

2 **Click the Italic button.**

WordPerfect recesses the Italic button and italicizes the word, singsings (Figure 1-49). Although not visible in Figure 1-49, two Italic codes are inserted in the document.

Other Ways

1. Right-click word, click Font on QuickMenu, click Italic, click OK button
2. With insertion point in word, on Format menu click Font, click Italic, click OK button
3. With insertion point in word, press CTRL+I
4. Press CTRL+I, type text, press CTRL+I

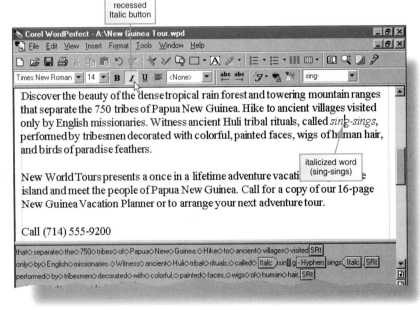

FIGURE 1-49

Selecting a Group of Words

The words, once in a lifetime adventure vacation, in the first sentence of the next paragraph should be underlined (see Figure 1-33 on page WP 1.31). To underline the text, select the group of words and then click the Underline button on the Property Bar. Before formatting, select the group of words by performing the following steps.

Steps: To Select a Group of Words

1 **Position the I-beam pointer immediately to the left of the first character (o) in the first word (once) to be selected.**

The I-beam pointer displays at the beginning of the word, once (Figure 1-50).

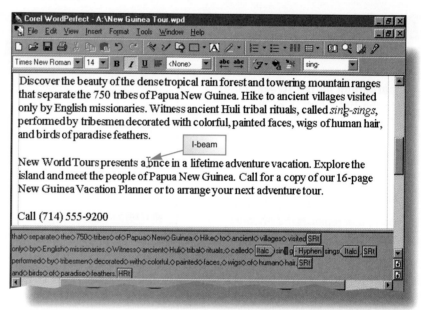

FIGURE 1-50

2 **Drag across the six words (once in a lifetime adventure vacation) to select the words.**

WordPerfect selects the phrase, once in a lifetime adventure vacation (Figure 1-51).

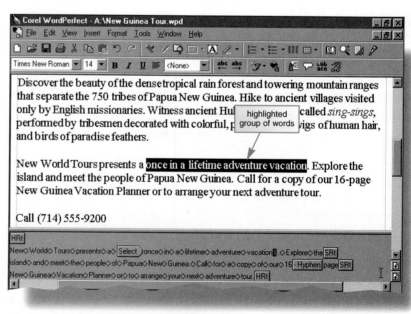

FIGURE 1-51

OtherWays

1. Position insertion point left of words, hold down SHIFT key, press right arrow key
2. Position insertion point left of words, press SHIFT+CTRL, press arrow keys
3. Position insertion point left of words, press F8, press arrow keys until all words are highlighted

Changing the Font Style of a Group of Words

After selecting the group of words, underline them by clicking the Underline button on the Property Bar. Perform the following step to underline the group of words.

 Steps **To Underline a Group of Words**

1 **Click the Underline button on the Property Bar. Click anywhere in the underlined text to remove the highlight.**

*WordPerfect recesses the Underline button, underlines the group of words, and inserts two **Und codes**, or **Underline codes**, in the document (Figure 1-52).*

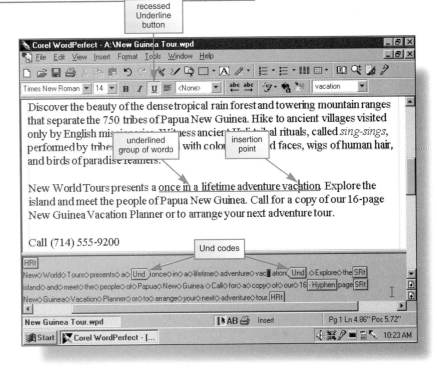

FIGURE 1-52

Formatting the Last Paragraph

The last paragraph, Call (714) 555-9200, is formatted using the Bold font style, 18-point font size, and center justification (see Figure 1-33 on page WP 1.31). Perform the steps below and on the next page to format the paragraph.

TO FORMAT A PARAGRAPH USING A QUICKMENU

1 Move the I-beam pointer into the last paragraph and then triple-click.

2 Right-click the paragraph to display a QuickMenu.

3 Click to Font on the QuickMenu.

4 Click Bold in the Font style list box.

5 Scroll the Font size list box until font size 18 displays and then click 18.

6 Click the OK button.

▶*Other*Ways

1. Select text, right-click words, click Font button on Quick-Menu, click Underline, click OK button

2. Select text, on Format menu click Font, click Underline, click OK button

3. Select text, press CTRL+U

4. Press CTRL+U, type text, press CTRL+U

⑦ Click the Justification button on the Property Bar.
⑧ Click the Center button.
⑨ Click anywhere in the text area to remove the highlight.

WordPerfect formats and centers the last paragraph, and inserts two Font Size codes and two Justification codes in the document (Figure 1-53). The codes are visible in the Reveal Codes window.

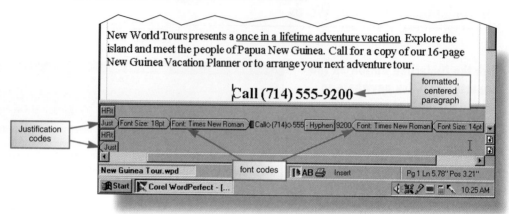

FIGURE 1-53

Saving a Modified Document Using the Same Filename

Earlier in this project, you entered the announcement and saved it on the Corel WordPerfect 8 Files floppy disk in drive A using the filename, New Guinea Tour. After modifying the document by formatting the text, you should save the modified document on the same floppy disk using the same filename. To save a modified document on the floppy disk, click the Save button on the Toolbar. Perform the following steps to save the modified document using the same filename.

 To Save a Modified Document Using the Same Filename

① Click the Save button on the Toolbar.

WordPerfect saves the modified document on the floppy disk in drive A using the New Guinea Tour.wpd filename. The document remains on the screen (Figure 1-54).

FIGURE 1-54

Closing the Reveal Codes Window

After formatting the document and to make more room available in the document window for inserting the Huli tribesmen picture, close the Reveal Codes window by performing the following steps.

TO CLOSE THE REVEAL CODES WINDOWS

1 Right-click the text area.
2 Click Reveal Codes on the QuickMenu.

WordPerfect closes the Reveal Codes window.

Graphics Images and WordPerfect Documents

The next formatting step is to insert the graphics image (two tribesmen picture) shown in Figure 1-33 on page WP 1.31 in the document. Before inserting the picture, change the zoom percentage to make it easier to insert, size, and move a graphics image.

Changing the Zoom Percentage

The default setting for the view mode is Page view. **Page view** causes the text in the document window to display at a zoom percentage of 100%. A 100% zoom percentage causes the text on the screen to look similar to the printed text. The zoom percentage is often changed to make working with graphic images easier. The Zoom button on the Toolbar is used to change the zoom percentage (see Figure 1-54).

In Draft and Page view, you can use **Zoom** to change the size of text or graphics in a document. You can specify a zoom percentage from 50% to 200%, or you can specify one of three zoom options (Margin Width, Page Width, or Full Page) and have WordPerfect automatically calculate the zoom percentage. Perform the following steps to change the zoom percentage to 50%.

 Steps To Change the Zoom Percentage

---

1 **Click the Zoom button on the Toolbar. When the Zoom menu displays, point to 50%.**

WordPerfect recesses the Zoom button and displays the Zoom menu (Figure 1-55). The default zoom percentage button (100%) is recessed, and the mouse pointer points to the three-dimensional 50% button.

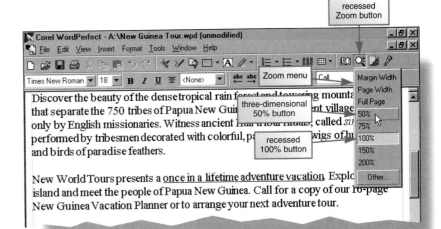

FIGURE 1-55

2 **Click 50%. Scroll the document window to make the top of the document visible.**

WordPerfect displays the document in the document window at a zoom percentage of 50% (Figure 1-56). The left, top, and right guidelines are visible on the screen. Although not visible, the 50% zoom percentage button on the Zoom menu is recessed.

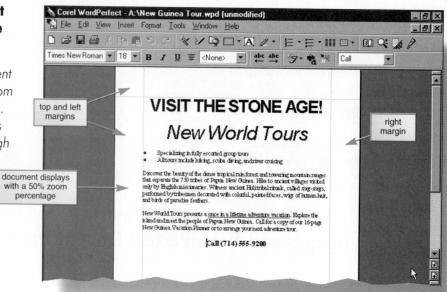

FIGURE 1-56

Downloading a Graphics File

The graphics images that are required to complete the projects and assignments in this book are available on the Internet. The **Internet** is a collection of computer networks, each of which is composed of a collection of smaller computer networks. The **World Wide Web** is an easy-to-use graphical interface for locating and viewing documents on the Internet. The documents on the Internet and the links among the documents comprise a *web* of information.

The World Wide Web consists of many individual Web sites. A **Web site** can consist of a single **Web page** or multiple Web pages linked together. The first Web page in the web site is called the **home page**. A unique address, called a **uniform resource locator (URL)**, identifies each Web page. A software tool, called a **browser**, allows you to locate Web pages by entering the URL for the Web page. The more widely used browser, **Netscape Navigator**, is available on the Corel WordPerfect Suite 8 CD-ROM disk and is used in this book to download graphic files.

The files that are required to complete the projects and assignments in this book are located on the Corel WordPerfect 8 Web site established by the publisher of this book. The URL for the home page of this Web site is:

http://www.scsite.com/wp8

Knowing the URL and using a browser, you can **download**, or copy, the files from the Web site to a floppy disk. Once the files are stored on disk, you can use WordPerfect to insert them into a document.

Another source for these files may be your network server. If your computer is connected to a network, ask your instructor if the files are available on the network server and how you can access the files. The files are also available to your instructor on a CD-ROM disk from the publishing company.

If you do not have access to the Internet or your computer network, ask your instructor how to obtain these files.

In this project, you will store the graphic files required to complete the projects and assignments in this book on the Corel WordPerfect 8 Files floppy disk. The following steps illustrate how to download the file containing the two tribesmen picture to the Corel WordPerfect 8 Files floppy disk.

Steps To Download a Graphics Image From the Internet

1 Verify the Corel WordPerfect 8 Files floppy disk is inserted in drive A.

2 Click File on the menu bar and point to Internet Publisher.

WordPerfect opens the File menu and highlights the Internet Publisher command (Figure 1-57).

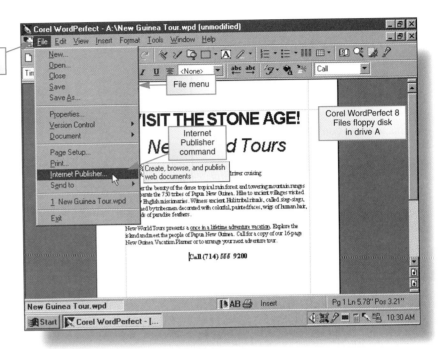

FIGURE 1-57

3 Click Internet Publisher. Point to the Browse the Web button.

WordPerfect closes the File menu and displays the Internet Publisher dialog box (Figure 1-58). The mouse pointer points to the Browse the Web button.

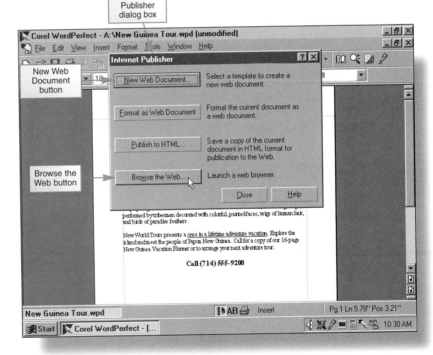

FIGURE 1-58

4 **Click the Browse the Web button. If the Netscape window is not maximized, maximize the window.**

WordPerfect starts the Netscape program and then WordPerfect displays the maximized Welcome to Netscape window (Figure 1-59). This window contains the Navigator Toolbar, Location Toolbar, Personal Toolbar, and Netscape home page. The location box contains the URL of the Netscape home page (http://home.netscape.com/).

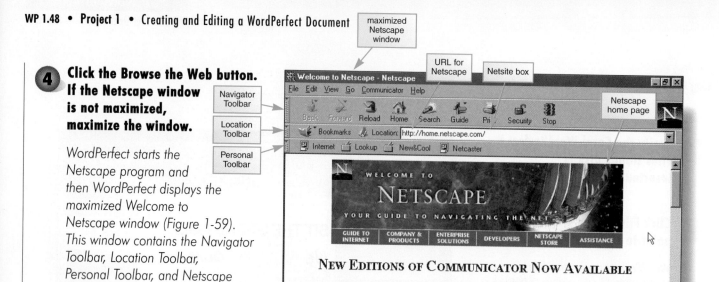

FIGURE 1-59

5 **Click the location box to highlight the URL. Type** http://www.scsite.com/wp8 **in the box.**

The URL for the home page of the Corel WordPerfect 8 Web site displays in the Go To box (Figure 1-60).

FIGURE 1-60

6 **Press the ENTER key. Point to Project 1.**

WordPerfect displays the home page in the **Corel WordPerfect 8 Web site** (Figure 1-61). The home page is divided into three areas, or **frames**. The frame on the left side of the page contains the Web site name (Corel WordPerfect 8), author's names (Shelly Cashman Forsythe), textbook cover and ISBN number, and links to Project 1, Project 3, Project 4, and Project 5. The top frame on the right side of the page contains the instructions to download a graphics file or a Corel WordPerfect file. The bottom frame contains general information about the Web site.

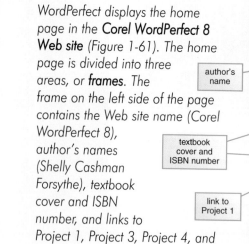

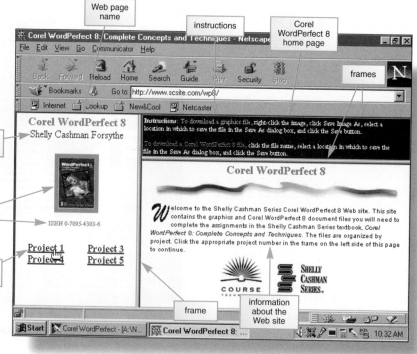

FIGURE 1-61

7 Click Project 1. Right-click the Huli_Tribesmen image and then point to Save Image As.

When you click Project 1, the Project 1 title (Creating and Editing a WordPerfect Document) and the files required to complete Project 1 display in the bottom frame on the right side of the page and the underline below the Project 1 link is removed (Figure 1-62). When you right-click the Huli_Tribesmen image and point to the Save Image As command, WordPerfect displays a QuickMenu and highlights the command.

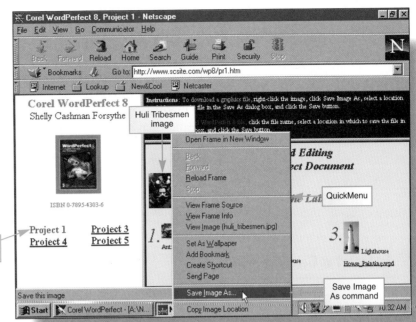

FIGURE 1-62

8 Click Save Image As. Verify the 3½ Floppy (A:) entry displays in the Save in box. Point to the Save button.

The Save As dialog box displays (Figure 1-63). The huli_tribesmen filename displays in the File name box, 3½ Floppy (A:) displays in the Save in box, and the type of file (JPEG) displays in the Save as type box. No folders and files display in the list box below the Save in box.

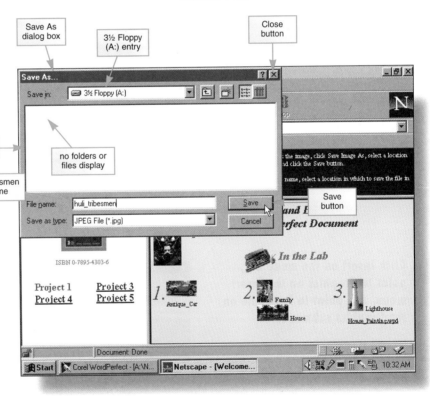

FIGURE 1-63

9 Click the Save button. Click the Close button in the WordPerfect 8, Project 1 window. Click the Close button in the Shelly Cashman WordPerfect 8 window

A Saving Location dialog box displays as WordPerfect copies the file on the floppy disk in drive A. When the download is complete, WordPerfect removes the Saving Location dialog box and closes the Netscape windows.

▶**Other Ways**

1. On WordPerfect 8 Toolbar, click Browse the Web, type URL, right-click filename, click Save As Image, select location to save file, click Save button, click OK button

Inserting a Graphics Image in a Document

The size and position of the picture of the two tribesmen is shown in Figure 1-33 on page WP 1.31. The picture is centered between the left and right margins and positioned between the first and second paragraphs.

You insert a picture in a document by positioning the insertion point close to where the picture should display, inserting the graphics image in a **graphics box**, or **frame**, and then moving the picture to its final position in the document and sizing it.

If you followed the steps to download the huli_tribesmen file, the file containing the Huli tribesmen picture is located on the Corel WordPerfect 8 Files floppy disk in drive A. Perform the following steps to insert the graphics image in the document.

Steps To Insert a Graphics Image

1 Move the insertion point to the blank line between the first and second paragraphs (Figure 1-64).

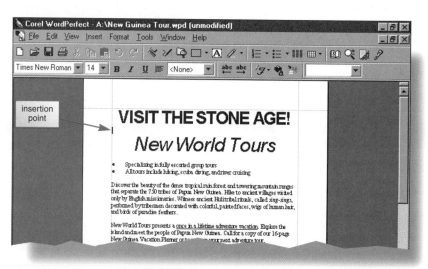

FIGURE 1-64

2 Click Insert on the menu bar, point to Graphics on the Insert menu, and point to From File on the Graphics submenu.

*WordPerfect displays the **Insert** menu, highlights the **Graphics command** and **From File command**, and displays a QuickTip (Figure 1-65).*

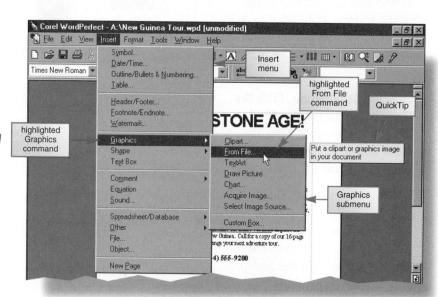

FIGURE 1-65

3 **Click From File. Click the Look in box arrow in the Insert Image dialog box, scroll the Look in list box until 3½ Floppy (A:) displays, and click 3½ Floppy (A:). Click huli_tribesmen. Point to the Insert button.**

WordPerfect opens the Insert Image dialog box (Figure 1-66). As indicated by the 3½ Floppy (A:) entry in the Look in box, the graphics image file is located on the disk in drive A. The huli_tribesmen filename is highlighted in the list box below the Look in box and displays in the File name box.

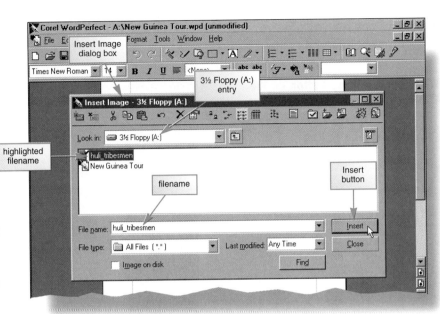

FIGURE 1-66

4 **Click the Insert button.**

When you click the Insert button, a Conversion dialog box displays momentarily while WordPerfect retrieves the picture from the floppy disk in drive A. WordPerfect displays the huli_ tribesmen picture in a graphics box, wraps the text around the right side of the graphics box, and changes the buttons on the Property Bar (Figure 1-67). The buttons on the Property Bar are designed to make working with graphic images easier.

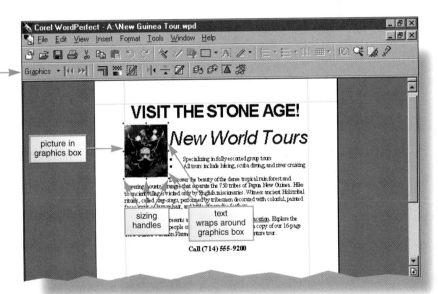

FIGURE 1-67

Darkened boxes, called **sizing handles**, display at each corner and in the middle of each side of the graphics box illustrated in Figure 1-67. Although not visible, WordPerfect inserts a **Box code** in the document.

Preventing Text from Wrapping Around a Graphics Box

The default text wrap setting controls how the text in Figure 1-67 wraps around the graphics box. The **default text wrap setting** (Square/Both Sides) wraps text around the square edge of both the left and right sides of a graphics box. To prevent the text from wrapping around both sides of the graphics box and to cause the text to display below the graphics box, you must change the default text wrap setting. Perform the steps on the next page to change how the text wraps around the graphics box.

Other Ways

1. On WordPerfect 7 Toolbar click Image From File button, select location and filename of image, click Insert button

Steps To Prevent Text Wrap

1 **Click the Wrap button on the Property Bar. When the Wrap menu displays, point to the Neither Side button.**

WordPerfect recesses the Wrap button and displays the Wrap menu (Figure 1-68). The default text wrap button (Square/Both Sides) is recessed and the mouse pointer points to the three-dimensional Neither Side button.

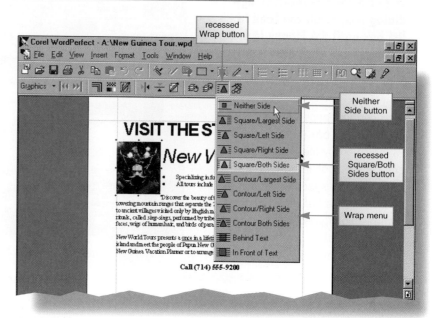

FIGURE 1-68

2 **Click the Neither Side button.**

WordPerfect closes the Wrap menu, prevents the text from wrapping around the right side of the graphics box, and moves the text below the graphics box (Figure 1-69).

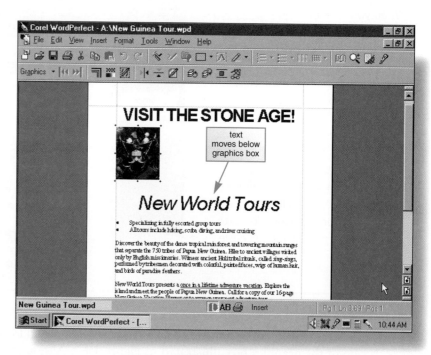

FIGURE 1-69

OtherWays

1. Right-click image, click Wrap, click Neither Side, click OK button

Moving a Graphics Box

After inserting the graphics box and preventing text wrap, you must center the graphics box between the left and right margins by moving the graphics box. The following steps illustrate how to move the graphics box.

Steps To Move a Graphics Box

1 **Point to the graphics box.**

When you point to the graphics box, the I-beam pointer changes to a four-directional pointer (Figure 1-70).

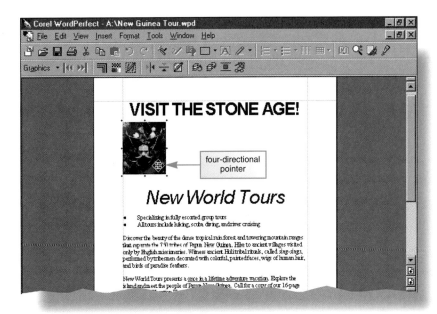

FIGURE 1-70

2 **Drag the graphics box to the position shown in Figure 1-71.**

A dotted outline displays as you drag the graphics box. After dragging, WordPerfect removes the dotted outline and displays the graphics box in its new location between the left and right margins (Figure 1-71).

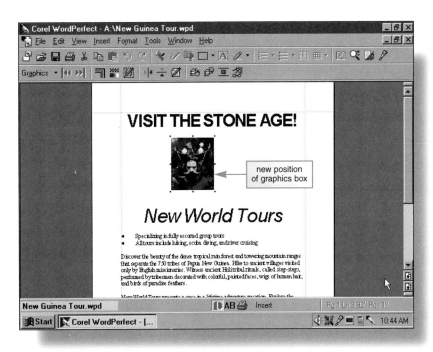

FIGURE 1-71

Sizing a Graphics Box

After moving the graphics image, you should center the graphics box between the left and right margins. The steps that follow size the graphics image.

Steps To Size a Graphics Box

1 Point to the lower right corner sizing handle.

The I-beam pointer changes to a two-headed arrow and points to the lower right corner sizing handle (Figure 1-72).

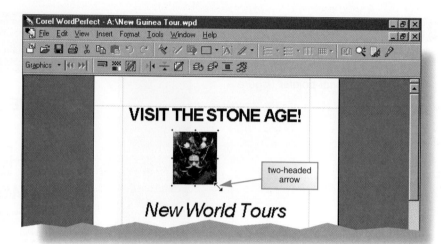

FIGURE 1-72

2 Drag the sizing handle until the graphics box is positioned as shown in Figure 1-73.

As you drag the corner sizing handle, a dotted outline displays. After dragging, WordPerfect removes the outline and displays the graphics box in its new location centered horizontally between the left and right margins (Figure 1-73).

3 If necessary, continue to move and size the graphics box until the box is positioned as shown in Figure 1-73.

After moving and sizing a graphics box, you often will need to make minor adjustments in the position of the box by moving and sizing the box until it occupies the position you want.

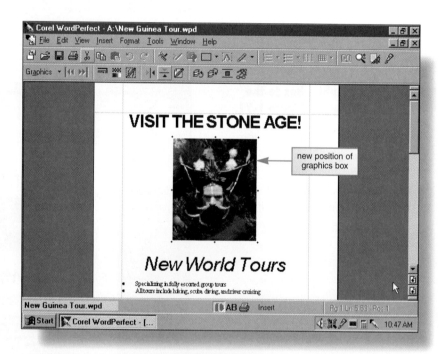

FIGURE 1-73

Saving a Modified Document with the Same Filename

After inserting and positioning the graphics image in the New Guinea Tour document, the document is complete and you should again save the document. Perform the following steps to save the finished New Guinea Tour document.

TO SAVE A MODIFIED DOCUMENT

① Verify the Corel WordPerfect 8 Files floppy disk is in drive A.

② Click the Save button on the Toolbar.

WordPerfect saves the modified document on the Corel WordPerfect 8 Files floppy disk in drive A using the New Guinea Tour filename. The document remains on the screen.

Printing a Document

The next step is to print the document on the printer. A printed version of the document is called a **hard copy**, or **printout**. Perform the following steps to print the document.

More *About* **Printing**

To print multiple copies of a document, click the Print button on the Toolbar, enter the number of copies in the Number of copies text box, and then click the Print button. To print a section of a document, select the section, click the Print button on the Toolbar, and click the Print button.

 Steps To Print a Document

① **Click the Print button on the Toolbar. Click the Print tab in the Print to dialog box. Point to the Print button.**

WordPerfect displays the Print to dialog box (Figure 1-74). The printer name in the dialog box will vary depending upon the printer installed on your computer. Review the Print sheet. Check to ensure the Full document option button is selected and the number 1 displays in the Number of copies text box. These settings indicate all pages will print one time.

② **Click the Print button. When the printing is complete, retrieve the document.**

The Corel WordPerfect window, containing the current status of the print operation (Preparing Document), displays momentarily and then the document is printed as shown in Figure 1-1 on page WP 1.7.

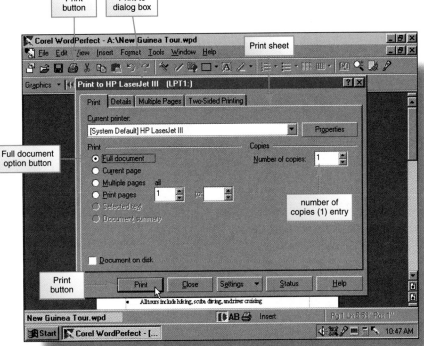

FIGURE 1-74

OtherWays

1. Click Print button on Application Bar, click Print button
2. On menu bar click File, click Print, click Print button
3. Press CTRL+P; or press F5

If you have a color printer, the document will print as illustrated in Figure 1-1 on page WP 1.7. If you do not have a color printer, the text will print in black, and the picture will print in shades of gray.

Quitting WordPerfect

When you have finished using WordPerfect, you should quit WordPerfect. It is important to quit WordPerfect using the Close button and not just turn off the computer after completing a document. The following steps explain how to quit WordPerfect.

Steps | To Quit WordPerfect

1 Click the Close button in the Corel WordPerfect window.

If you made changes to the document since the last time you saved the document, WordPerfect displays the Corel WordPerfect dialog box containing a message asking if you want to save the changes (Figure 1-75). Click the Yes button to save changes; click the No button to ignore the changes; or click the Cancel button to return to the document. If you made no changes since saving the document, this dialog box does not display.

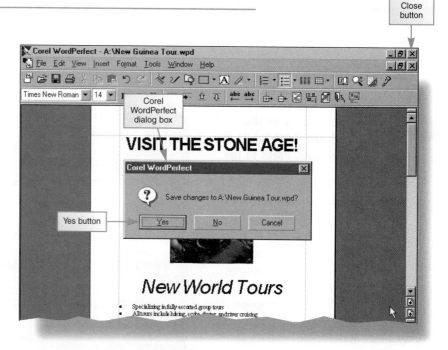

FIGURE 1-75

OtherWays

1. Double-click WordPerfect icon on title bar
2. Right-click title bar, click Close
3. Click File on menu bar, click Exit
4. Press ALT+F4

Project 1 is now complete. You created and formatted a document, checked for and corrected misspelled words, inserted a graphics image, and saved and printed the document. You may, however, decide to change the announcement at a later date. To do this, you must start WordPerfect and retrieve the announcement from the Corel WordPerfect 8 Files floppy disk.

Opening a Document

Earlier, you saved the document created in Project 1 on the Corel WordPerfect 8 Files floppy disk using the filename, New Guinea Tour.wpd. If you wish to revise or print the document after creating and saving it, you must open the file. The following steps illustrate how to open the New Guinea Tour.wpd file.

Steps **To Open a Document**

① Start WordPerfect as explained on page WP 1.9. Click the Open button on the Toolbar.

WordPerfect opens the Open File dialog box (Figure 1-76). The MyFiles folder icon displays in the Look in box. The contents of the MyFiles folder (the Backup folder) display in the list box.

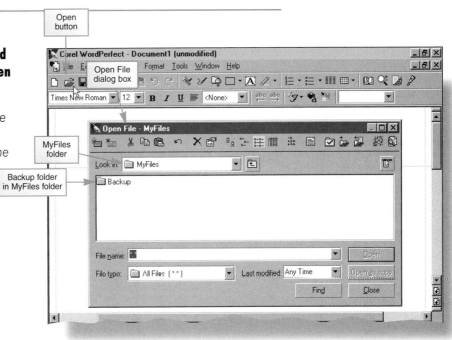

FIGURE 1-76

② Click the Look in box arrow. Scroll the Look in list box until 3½ Floppy (A:) displays and then click 3½ Floppy (A:). Click New Guinea Tour in the Look in list box. Point to the Open button.

WordPerfect displays the file or folder names on drive A in the list box. Clicking the New Guinea Tour filename highlights the filename in the list box and displays the filename in the File name box (Figure 1-77).

③ Click the Open button.

WordPerfect displays the top of the New Guinea Tour document in the document window. Now you can revise or print the document as required.

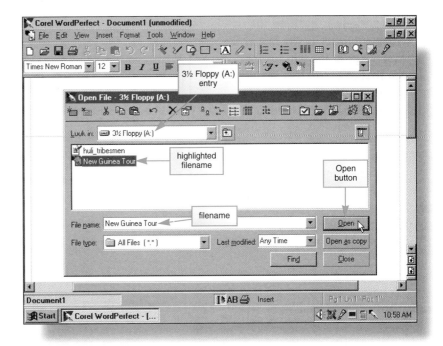

FIGURE 1-77

▶*Other***Ways**

1. On menu bar click File, click Open, select filename, select location, click Open button
2. On menu bar click File, on File menu click filename
3. Press CTRL+O; or press F4, select filename, select location, click Open button

More *About*
Opening a Document

You can open a recently closed document by clicking File on the menu bar and clicking the document name on the File menu. To prevent the names from displaying, click Tools on the menu bar, click Settings, double-click Environment, click Interface tab, click Display last open documents on the File menu check box if a check mark displays, click the OK button, and click Close button.

Correcting Errors

After creating a document, often you will find you must make changes to the document. Changes are made because the document contains an error or because of new circumstances. The types of changes made to documents normally fall into one of three categories: additions, deletions, or modifications. The following sections explain how to insert and delete text in a document.

Inserting Text into an Existing Document

The **default typing mode** is the insert mode. **Insert mode** allows you to insert new text without deleting any of the existing text. As you type, the text to the right of the text you type moves to the right and downward to accommodate the new text. Perform the following steps to add the word, primitive, before the word, tribes, in the first sentence of the first paragraph below the bulleted list.

Steps **To Insert Text into an Existing Document**

1 **Scroll the document window until the last three paragraphs display in the window. Position the I-beam pointer to the left of the first letter in the word, tribes, in the first paragraph in the window. Click the position to display the insertion point.**

The insertion point displays to the left of the letter t in the word, tribes (Figure 1-78). The Insert message displays on the General Status button to indicate you are in the Insert mode.

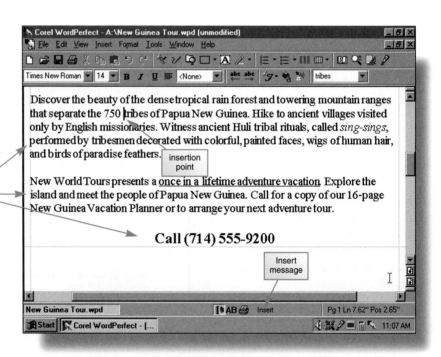

FIGURE 1-78

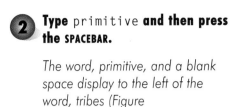

2 **Type** primitive **and then press the** SPACEBAR.

The word, primitive, and a blank space display to the left of the word, tribes (Figure 1-79).

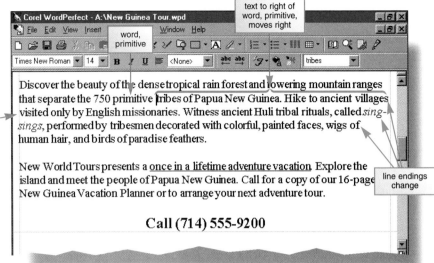

word, visited, wraps to next line

FIGURE 1-79

The text to the right of the word, primitive, in Figure 1-79 moved to the right and downward to accommodate the insertion of the word, primitive. The word, visited, moves down to the beginning of the next line, the word, sing-sings, is hyphenated at the hyphen, and sings drops down to the next line. The words, human hair, drop down to the next line.

Overtyping Existing Text

Sometimes you may prefer to type over existing text. To accomplish this, you can switch to overtype mode by clicking the General Status button on the Application Bar. In **overtype** mode, the word, Typeover, displays on the General Status button and any existing text will be typed over. For example, if a document contains July 1, 1999, and it should contain June 1, 1999, position the insertion point immediately to the left of the J in July, click the General Status button, and type June. The word, June, will replace the word, July. To return to insert mode, click the General Status button again.

Deleting Text

It is not unusual to type characters or words you later wish to change in a document. In such a case, you may want to delete these letters or words to correct the error. A variety of methods exist to delete text. Table 1-3 summarizes these methods.

Table 1–3	
METHOD	*RESULT*
Press DELETE **key**	Deletes the character to the right of the insertion point.
Press BACKSPACE **key**	Deletes the character to the left of the insertion point.
Hold down CTRL **key and press** BACKSPACE **key**	Deletes the word containing the insertion point.
Hold down CTRL **key and** SHIFT **keys and press** DELETE **key**	Deletes from the insertion point to the end of the page.
Select text and press DELETE **or** BACKSPACE **key**	Deletes the selected text.
Select text, right-click selected text, and then click Cut on QuickMenu; or select text, click Cut on Toolbar	Deletes the selected text.
Select text by dragging and type new text	Deletes the selected text and inserts new text.

Deleting a Code in a Document

Sometimes unwanted codes or codes placed in the wrong position cause a document to display or print incorrectly. To correct these problems, you may have to move the insertion point in the Reveal Codes window and delete a code. The travel agency name, New World Tours, displays in 45-point font size. Assume that the font size should be 55 point. One method to make this change is to delete the Font Size: 45pt code and format the line again.

To delete the code, move the insertion point in the Reveal Codes window to make the Font Size: 45pt code visible and then drag the code out of the Reveal Codes window. The insertion point is currently located to the left of the word, tribes, in the paragraph below the bulleted list. Perform the following steps to move the insertion point and delete the Font Size: 45pt code.

Steps To Delete a Code

① **Right-click the text area. Click Reveal Codes on the QuickMenu. Use the arrow keys to move the insertion point to the left of the letter N in the word, New, in the second paragraph and to the right of the Font: 45pt code in the Reveal Codes window.**

WordPerfect opens the Reveal Codes window and moves the insertion point (Figure 1-80). The insertion point displays to the left of the letter N in the word, New, in the document window and to the right of the Font Size: 45 pt code in the Reveal Codes window.

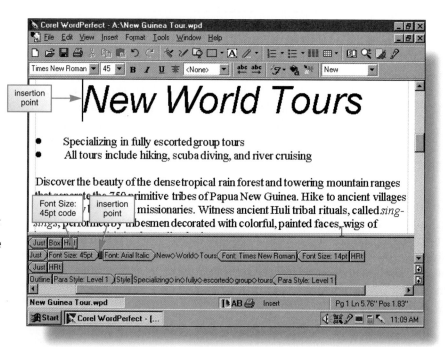

FIGURE 1-80

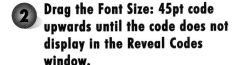

2 **Drag the Font Size: 45pt code upwards until the code does not display in the Reveal Codes window.**

As you drag the code, the mouse pointer and Font Size code move, and the location where the code used to be is visible in the window. After dragging, the Font Size: 45pt code no longer displays in the Reveal Codes window, and the paragraph displays in 14-point font size (Figure 1-81).

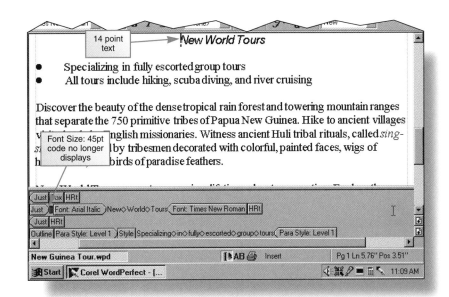

FIGURE 1-81

◗ *Other***Ways**

1. Move insertion point left of code, press DELETE key
2. Move insertion point right of code, press BACKSPACE key

To complete the change in format after deleting the Font Size: 45pt code, select the paragraph and change the font size to 55.

Undoing Previous Actions

If you edit a document and want to undo the last insertion or deletion, use the **Undo button** on the Toolbar. **Undo** reverses an editing action, such as changes made to text or graphics images. Clicking the Undo button the first time will reverse the last change made. Additional clicks of the button will reverse the next nine changes. Some actions, such as scrolling or saving a document, cannot be reversed. Perform the following step to reverse the deletion of the Font Size: 45pt code.

TO UNDO YOUR MOST RECENT ACTION

① Click the Undo button on the Toolbar.

The Font Size: 45pt code displays in the Reveal Codes window in its original location and the travel agency name displays in 45-point font size.

To reverse the most recent Undo action, use the **Redo button** on the Toolbar. Perform the following step to reverse the last undo action and delete the Font Size: 45pt code.

TO REVERSE THE LAST UNDO ACTION

① Click the Redo button on the Toolbar.

WordPerfect removes the Font Size: 45pt code from the Reveal Codes window and displays the travel agency name in 14-point font size.

To reverse any of the last 10 actions in your document, use the **Undo/Redo History command** on the Edit menu as explained in the following steps.

TO UNDO MULTIPLE ACTIONS

1. Delete the word, escort, in the first bulleted item using the DEL key.
2. Delete the word, fully, in the first bulleted item using the DEL key.
3. Click Edit on the menu bar.
4. Click Undo/Redo History on the Edit menu. Two actions (SelectDelete and SelectDelete) display at the top of the Undo list box.
5. Click the second Cut entry in the Undo list box to select the Cut action and all prior actions in the list box (Cut).
6. Click the Undo button in the dialog box to display the words, fully and escorted, in the document.
7. Click the Close button in the Undo/Redo History dialog box.

You can also redo an action by clicking the action you wish to redo in the Redo list box and then clicking the Redo button.

Closing the Document

After learning how to undo, redo, and undelete text, close the document. Closing the document removes the document you are working on from the window. If no other documents are open, WordPerfect displays a blank document window.

If you make changes to a document and then close it before saving the modified document, WordPerfect displays a dialog box asking if you want to save the changes before closing. Because changes were made to the New Guinea Tour document while learning to undo prior actions, the changes to the document should not be saved. Perform the following steps to close the document.

TO CLOSE A DOCUMENT

1. Click File on the menu bar and then click Close.
2. Click the No button in the Corel WordPerfect dialog box.

WordPerfect closes the document and displays a blank document in the document window.

WordPerfect Help

At any time while using WordPerfect, you have access to **WordPerfect Help** to obtain answers to questions you may have about WordPerfect. Used properly, Help can minimize the time you spend learning to use WordPerfect and increase your productivity.

Accessing Help

To access Help, click Help on the menu bar to display the **Help menu**. The commands on the Help menu give you access to a wide range of help features. **Help Topics** allow you to search for a help topic. **Ask the PerfectExpert** allows you to obtain help by entering your own words, phrases, or sentences. **PerfectExpert** displays a list of word processing tasks you can perform in WordPerfect and assists you in the completion of those tasks. **Corel Web Site** connects you to the Corel Corporation Web site on the World Wide Web. Perform the steps below to access Help.

 **To Access Help**

1 **Click Help on the menu bar. Point to Help Topics on the Help menu.**

*WordPerfect opens the Help menu and highlights the **Help Topics command** (Figure 1-82). The Help menu contains the Help Topics, Ask the PerfectExpert, PerfectExpert, and Corel Web Site commands.*

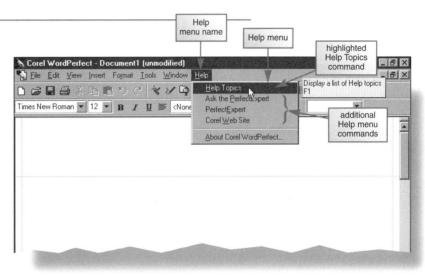

FIGURE 1-82

2 **Click Help Topics. If necessary, click the Contents tab.**

The Help Topics: WordPerfect Help dialog box displays (Figure 1-83). This dialog box contains four tabbed sheets: Contents, Index, Find, and Ask the PerfectExpert. The Contents sheet displays in the Help Topics: WordPerfect Help dialog box.

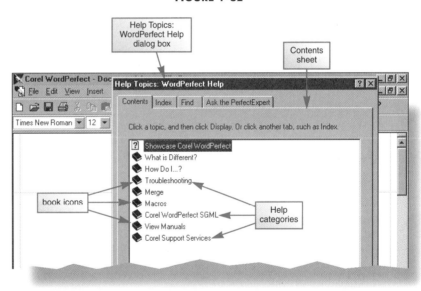

FIGURE 1-83

1. Press F1

Searching for Help Using the Contents Sheet

WordPerfect provides a variety of methods to obtain information. One method to find a help topic uses the Contents sheet. The **Contents sheet** allows you to browse through help topics by category. In the Contents sheet shown in Figure 1-83, each help category is preceded by a book icon. A **book icon** indicates help topics or additional help categories are associated with the help category and can be viewed by double-clicking the book icon. The steps on the next page show how to use the Contents sheet to obtain information about inserting graphics images.

Steps To Search for Help Using the Contents Sheet

1 **Double-click the How Do I book. Double-click the Add Images (Graphics) book. Double-click the Add Images book. Point to Insert Images (Graphics/ClipArt).**

WordPerfect opens the How Do I book, Add Images (Graphics) book, and the Add Images book (Figure 1-84). Several help topics display below the opened Add Images book.

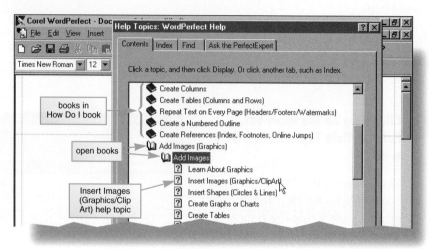

FIGURE 1-84

2 **Double-click Insert Images (Graphics/ClipArt).**

WordPerfect closes the Help Topics: WordPerfect Help dialog box and opens the Corel WordPerfect Help window (Figure 1-85). The window contains three buttons (Help Topics, Back, and Options), steps to insert clipart, and several tips. Although not visible, links to About Scrapbooks, Related Topics, and About Types of Graphics You Can Insert also display in the window.

3 **After reading the information in the WordPerfect Help window, click the Help Topics button.**

WordPerfect displays the Help Topics: WordPerfect Help window on top of the Corel WordPerfect Help window.

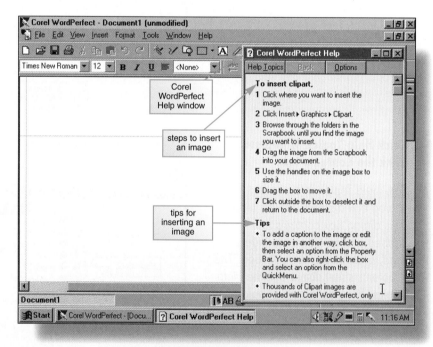

FIGURE 1-85

Clicking the Help Topics button in the Corel WordPerfect Help window displays the Help Topics: WordPerfect Help window. In Figure 1-85, if you click the Back button (when the button is not dimmed), WordPerfect displays the previously displayed Help topic. Clicking the Options button allows you to annotate a Help topic, copy or print the help topic, change the font and color scheme of Help windows, and control how Help windows display in relation to other windows on the desktop. You can also display information about the version of Help that the program uses.

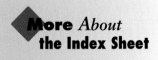
Searching for Help Using the Index Sheet

A second method to find information uses the Index Sheet. The **Index sheet** lists a large number of index entries, each of which references one or more help screens. For example, if you want help on bulleted lists, display the Index sheet and then enter bulleted list. Perform the following step to obtain information about bulleted lists.

1 **Click the Index tab. Type** bulleted list **in the text box.**

The Index sheet displays containing a list of entries that can be referenced. When you type an entry, the list automatically scrolls and the entry you type, such as bulleted list, is highlighted. Six Help topics are indented and display below the highlighted bulleted list entry (Figure 1-86). Double-clicking any of these topics opens the Help Topics: WordPerfect Help dialog box and displays information about the topic in the window.

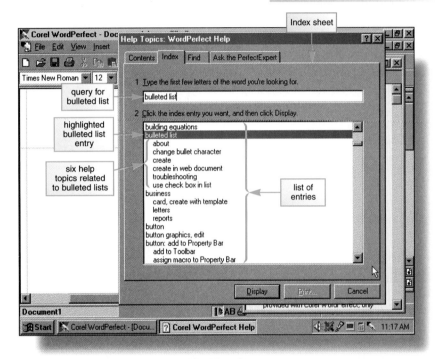

FIGURE 1-86

Searching for Help Using the Find Sheet

A third method to find information uses the Find Sheet. The **Find sheet** allows you to locate a help topic based upon a particular word or phrase. For example, if you want to locate information about Spell-As-You-Go, click the Find tab, and then type spell-as-you-go in the text box. WordPerfect displays a list of topics related to Spell-As-You-Go. Double-clicking one of those topics displays the Corel WordPerfect Help window containing information about the topic.

Obtaining Help Using Ask the PerfectExpert

Another method to obtain information uses the Ask the PerfectExpert sheet. The **PerfectExpert sheet** allows you to obtain help by entering a word, phrase, or sentence and searching for associated help topics. Perform the steps on the next page to obtain help about selecting text.

Steps **To Search for Help Using the Ask the PerfectExpert Sheet**

① Click the Ask the PerfectExpert tab. Type select text **in the What do you want to know? box. Click the Search button. Click the About Selecting Text topic. Point to the Display button.**

WordPerfect displays the Ask the PerfectExpert sheet, and the words, select text, display in the What do you want to know? box. When the Search button is clicked, the help topics associated with selecting text display in the Search Results list box (Figure 1-87). The About Selecting Text topic is highlighted. The mouse pointer points to the Display button.

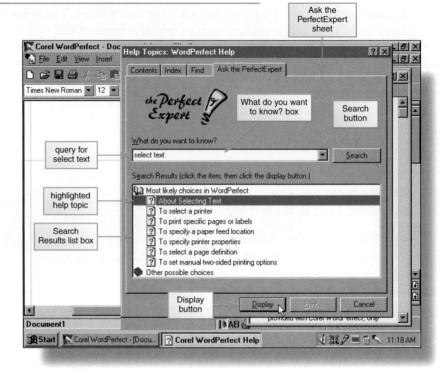

FIGURE 1-87

② Click the Display button.

WordPerfect closes the Help Topics: WordPerfect Help dialog box and opens the Corel WordPerfect Help window (Figure 1-88). The window contains eight buttons. Although not visible, a link to Related Topics also displays in the window. Clicking a button displays a new help screen containing information about the associated topic.

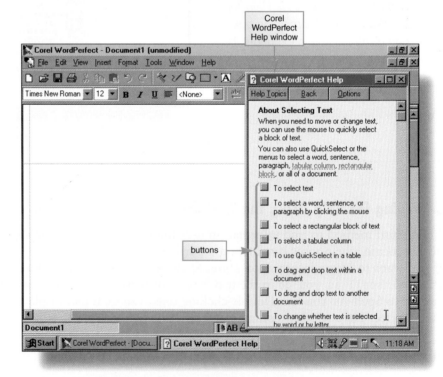

FIGURE 1-88

Exiting Help and Quitting WordPerfect

When you are ready to exit Help, exit the Help system and Quit WordPerfect by performing the following steps.

TO QUIT HELP, QUIT WORDPERFECT, AND REMOVE THE FLOPPY DISK

1 Click the Close button in the Corel WordPerfect Help window.

2 Click the Close button in the Corel WordPerfect window.

3 Remove the Corel WordPerfect 8 Files floppy disk from drive A.

WordPerfect closes the Corel WordPerfect window and quits WordPerfect, and the Corel WordPerfect 8 Files floppy disk is removed from drive A.

Project Summary

The purpose of this project was to teach you many of the capabilities of WordPerfect. Important topics covered included starting WordPerfect, entering text, changing font faces and font styles, changing font size, centering text, inserting graphics images, moving and sizing graphics images, saving and printing a document, quitting WordPerfect, opening a document, inserting and deleting text, restoring deleted text, and using Help. With a knowledge of these WordPerfect features you can create a variety of documents.

What You Should Know

Having completed this project, you now should be able to perform the following tasks:

▶ Access Help *(WP 1.63)*

▶ Change the default font size *(WP 1.15)*

▶ Change the zoom percentage *(WP 1.45)*

▶ Close a document *(WP 1.62)*

▶ Close the Reveal Codes window *(WP 1.45)*

▶ Correct incorrectly spelled words *(WP 1.21)*

▶ Create a bulleted list *(WP 1.39)*

▶ Delete a code *(WP 1.60)*

▶ Download a graphics image from the Internet *(WP 1.47)*

▶ Enlarge the left margin and select multiple paragraphs *(WP 1.38)*

▶ Enter a blank line in a document *(WP 1.18)*

▶ Enter text in all capital letters *(WP 1.17)*

▶ Enter the next three paragraphs *(WP 1.19)*

▶ Expand a code *(WP 1.37)*

▶ Format a paragraph using a QuickMenu *(WP 1.34, WP 1.37, WP 1.43)*

▶ Insert a graphics image *(WP 1.50)*

▶ Insert text into an existing document *(WP 1.58)*

▶ Italicize a single word *(WP 1.41)*

▶ Move a graphics box *(WP 1.53)*

▶ Move the insertion point *(WP 1.28, WP 1.30)*

▶ Open a document *(WP 1.57)*

▶ Open the Reveal Codes window *(WP 1.29)*

▶ Prevent text wrap *(WP 1.52)*

▶ Print a document *(WP 1.55)*

▶ Quit Help *(WP 1.67)*

▶ Quit WordPerfect *(WP 1.56, WP 1.67)*

▶ Reverse the last Undo action *(WP 1.61)*

▶ Save a document *(WP 1.24)*

▶ Save a modified document *(WP 1.55)*

▶ Save a modified document with the same filename *(WP 1.44)*

▶ Scroll to the top of a document *(WP 1.27)*

▶ Search for help using the Ask the PerfectExpert sheet *(WP 1.66)*

▶ Search for help using the Contents sheet *(WP 1.64)*

▶ Search for help using the Index sheet *(WP 1.65)*

▶ Select a group of words *(WP 1.42)*

▶ Select a paragraph *(WP 1.33)*

▶ Size a graphics box *(WP 1.54)*

▶ Start WordPerfect *(WP 1.9)*

▶ Underline a group of words *(WP 1.43)*

▶ Undo multiple actions *(WP 1.62)*

▶ Undo your most recent action *(WP 1.61)*

▶ Use wordwrap *(WP 1.20)*

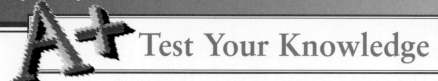

Test Your Knowledge

1 True/False

Instructions: Circle T if the statement is true or F if the statement is false.

T F   1. Corel WordPerfect is a 32-bit, full-featured word processing application that allows you to take full advantage of the Windows 95 environment.

T F   2. The Toolbar contains buttons that allow you to accomplish basic tasks, such as opening, saving, and printing a document.

T F   3. Bold, italic, and underline are examples of fonts.

T F   4. The default WordPerfect font face and font size are Times New Roman and 14 point.

T F   5. To open the Reveal Codes window, right-click the text area and then click Reveal Codes on the QuickMenu.

T F   6. The mouse pointer and shadow cursor are identical when they point to text in a document.

T F   7. To select multiple paragraphs, move the insertion point into one of the paragraphs and then triple-click.

T F   8. The red diagonal lines below a word indicate the word may be incorrectly spelled.

T F   9. When you insert a picture in a document, a graphics box displays centered between the left and right margins.

T F   10. You can delete a code by double-clicking the code in the Reveal Codes window.

2 Multiple Choice

Instructions: Circle the correct response.

1. The _____ contains buttons that allow easy access to commonly used editing and text formatting features, such as changing the font style and font size.
   a. Property Bar
   b. menu bar
   c. Toolbar
   d. Application Bar

2. Serif and sans serif are examples of _____.
   a. font styles
   b. font faces
   c. point sizes
   d. font sizes

3. Bold, italic, and underline are examples of _____.
   a. font sizes
   b. fonts
   c. font styles
   d. font faces

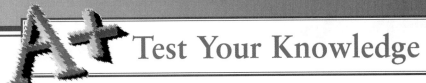

4. The default view mode in WordPerfect is _____.
   a. Draft view
   b. Page view
   c. Two Page view
   d. Full Page view

5. To save a new document on disk, use the _____ button on the Toolbar.
   a. Save
   b. Open
   c. New
   d. Close

6. The _____ code represents the end of a paragraph or a blank line.
   a. Select
   b. Soft Return
   c. Hard Return
   d. Open Styles

7. To highlight a paragraph, you should _____ the left margin beside the paragraph.
   a. click
   b. double-click
   c. triple-click
   d. quadruple-click

8. You display a QuickMenu near the left margin by _____ the left margin.
   a. clicking
   b. double-clicking
   c. right-clicking
   d. triple-clicking

9. When you insert a graphics image in a document, the graphics box containing the image always displays _____.
   a. at the left margin
   b. at the right margin
   c. centered between the margins
   d. at the position of the insertion point

10. The easiest way to reverse your last action in a document is to use the _____.
    a. Redo button
    b. Undo/Redo History command
    c. Undelete command
    d. Undo button

Test Your Knowledge

3 Understanding the Corel WordPerfect Screen

Instructions: In Figure 1-89, arrows point to major elements of the Corel WordPerfect screen. Identify the various elements of the screen in the spaces provided.

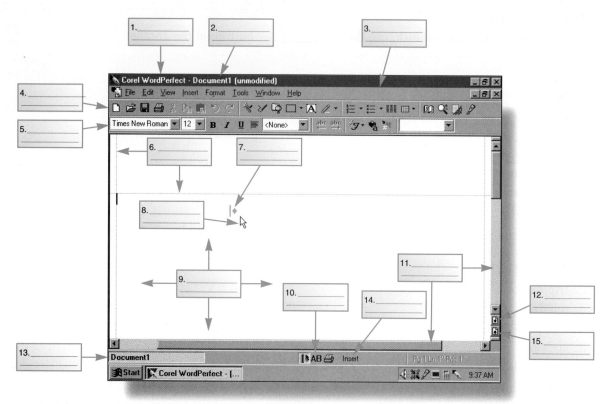

FIGURE 1-89

4 Understanding the Toolbar and Property Bar

Instructions: In Figure 1-90, arrows point to several of the objects on the Toolbar and Property Bar. In the space provided, name the object and briefly explain the function of each object.

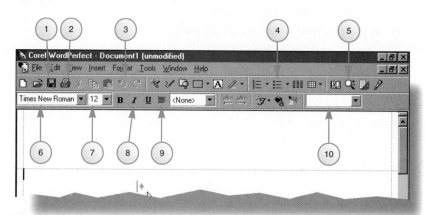

FIGURE 1-90

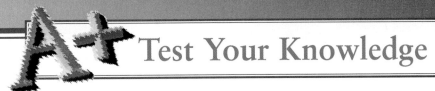

OBJECT NAME	OBJECT FUNCTION
1. _____	_____
2. _____	_____
3. _____	_____
4. _____	_____
5. _____	_____
6. _____	_____
7. _____	_____
8. _____	_____
9. _____	_____
10. _____	_____

1 Obtaining Additional Help

Instructions: Another help feature, called the **Reference Center,** is located on the Corel WordPerfect 8 CD-ROM disk and contains a copy of all the manuals available for the Corel WordPerfect Suite. Perform the following tasks on a computer and answer any questions on a separate piece of paper.

Part 1: Starting the Reference Center

1. If you do not have access to the Corel WordPerfect 8 CD-ROM disk, go to Part 4.
2. Insert the Corel WordPerfect 8 CD-ROM disk into your CD-ROM drive. If the Corel WordPerfect Suite 8 Applications Disc window displays when you insert the CD-ROM disk, click Reference Center in the window and go to Step 4.
3. Click the Start button, point to Corel WordPerfect 8 Suite, point to Setup & Notes, and click Reference Center. If the Problem with Shortcut dialog box displays, the CD-DOM disk is not in the CD-ROM drive and the Reference Center cannot be accessed.
4. Click the WordPerfect icon in the Corel Reference Center window.

Part 2: Finding Information Using the Reference Center

1. Click the Getting Around button. Familiarize yourself with the buttons on the Toolbar by pointing to each button and reading its QuickTip.
2. Click the First Page button on the Toolbar.

(continued)

Use Help

Obtaining Additional Help *(continued)*

3. Click the Contents button on the first page.
4. Click the Zoom in button on the Toolbar. Click the text area once to enlarge the text area. Click the Select button on the Toolbar.
5. Scroll the Envoy Viewer window to make the Table of Contents visible.
6. Scroll the Table of Contents to display the topics in Chapter 4.
7. On what page is the Changing the Look of Text Using Fonts topic located?
8. Click Edit on the menu bar, click Go To Page on the Edit menu, type the page number from Step 7 above, and click the OK button.
9. Scroll the document to find the Tips box associated with this topic.
10. What is the name of the Toolbar that lets you quickly access font attributes such as small caps and superscript?
11. How do you display this Toolbar?

Part 3: Searching for Information

1. Click the First Page button on the Toolbar. Click the Find button on the Toolbar.
2. Type scrapbook in the text box in the Find dialog box. Click the Find Next button.
3. What does the Scrapbook contain?
4. How do you access the objects in the Scrapbook?
5. How do you insert an object from the Scrapbook in a document?
6. Click the Close button in the Envoy Viewer window. Click the Close button in the Corel Reference Center window. If necessary, click the Close button in the Corel WordPerfect Suite 8 Applications Disc window.

Part 4: Inserting a Clipart Image in a Document

1. Start WordPerfect. Type your name and press the enter key. Select your name, format it using the Arial Bold 24-point font, and center justification. Click the blank line below your name to remove the highlight.
2. Click Insert on the menu bar, point to Graphics on the Insert menu, and click Clipart.
3. Drag one of the clipart images from the scrapbook into your document.
4. Close the Scrapbook window.
5. Center the graphics box below your name that contains the clipart by moving and sizing the box.
6. Save the document on the Corel WordPerfect 8 Files floppy disk using Clipart as the filename. Print the document. Exit WordPerfect.
7. If necessary, remove the Corel WordPerfect 8 CD-ROM disk from the CD-ROM drive.

2 Expanding on the Basics

Instructions: Perform the following tasks using a computer, and then answer the questions on a separate piece of paper.

WordPerfect allows you to format text in many different ways. Using the Contents sheet and the How Do I book in the Help Topics: WordPerfect dialog box, answer the following questions.

1. What is a drop cap and how do you add a drop cap to a paragraph?
2. What is QuickFormat and how would you use it to format a heading?
3. What is TextArt and what does it allow you to do?

Using the Index tab in the Help Topics: WordPerfect dialog box, answer these questions about shortcut keys.

1. Which key(s) move(s) the insertion point before the codes at the beginning of a document?
2. Which key(s) move(s) the insertion point to a specific page in a document?
3. Which key(s) insert(s) a Hard Return code in a document?
4. Which key(s) change(s) selected text from uppercase to lowercase (convert case)?
5. Which key(s) select(s) one word to the right in a document?

WordPerfect allows you to password-protect a file. Use the Find tab in the Help Topics: WordPerfect Help dialog box to answer the following questions.

1. What dialog box allows you to assign a password to a file?
2. How do you assign a password to a file?
3. How do you open a password-protected file?
4. What dialog box allows you to enter your password to obtain access to a password-protected file?

WordPerfect allows you to spell check a document as you type (Spell-As-You-Go) or spell check an entire document at one time (Spell Checker). Using WordPerfect Help, answer the following questions about the Spell Checker.

1. What buttons and/or commands do you use to start Spell Checker?
2. How do you spell check an entire document?
3. When Spell Checker finds a word not in the dictionary, what four operations can you perform on the word?
4. What is a word list? What are the two types of word lists? Describe the two word lists?

Apply Your Knowledge

1 Correcting Misspelled Words

Instructions: Start WordPerfect. The House_Painting.wpd file is located on the Corel WordPerfect 8 Web site. Perform the following steps to download the file and check for incorrectly spelled words. Perform the following tasks:

1. Start WordPerfect.
2. Insert the Corel WordPerfect 8 Files floppy disk in drive A.
3. If you do not have access to the Internet, obtain a copy of the House_Painting.wpd file from your instructor, place the file on the Corel WordPerfect 8 Files floppy disk, and go to Step 10.
4. Click File on the menu bar, click Internet Publisher, and click Browse the Web to display the Netscape home page.
5. Type http://www.scseries.com/wp8 in the Netsite box and press the ENTER key to display the Corel WordPerfect 8 home page.
6. Click Project 1. Click the house_painting.wpd filename to open the Save As dialog box.
7. Click the Save in box arrow in the Save As dialog box, scroll the Save in list box until 3½ Floppy (A:) displays, and click 3½ Floppy (A:).
8. Click the Save button.
9. Click the Close button in all Netscape windows.
10. Click the Open button on the Toolbar and then open the house_painting.wpd document located on the Corel WordPerfect 8 Files floppy disk (see Figure 1-91). When displayed in the document window, red diagonal lines will display beneath many words in the house_painting document to indicate possible spelling problems.
11. Right-click each underlined word and then fix the problem.
12. Save the corrected document on the same floppy disk using a different filename (Corrected House Painting).
13. Print the corrected document.
14. Quit WordPerfect.
15. Remove the Corel WordPerfect 8 Files floppy disk.

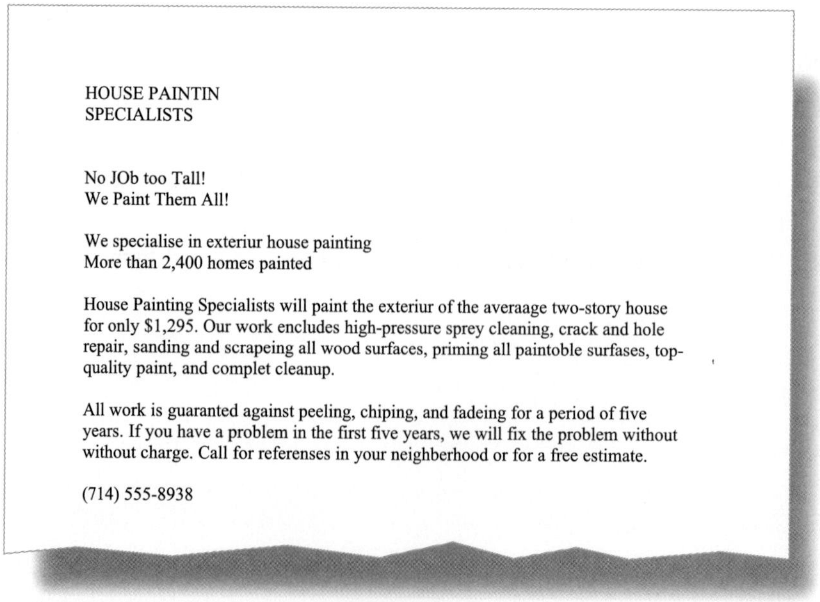

HOUSE PAINTIN
SPECIALISTS

No JOb too Tall!
We Paint Them All!

We specialise in exteriur house painting
More than 2,400 homes painted

House Painting Specialists will paint the exteriur of the averaage two-story house for only $1,295. Our work encludes high-pressure sprey cleaning, crack and hole repair, sanding and scrapeing all wood surfaces, priming all paintoble surfases, top-quality paint, and complet cleanup.

All work is guaranted against peeling, chiping, and fadeing for a period of five years. If you have a problem in the first five years, we will fix the problem without without charge. Call for referenses in your neighborhood or for a free estimate.

(714) 555-8938

FIGURE 1-91

In the Lab

1 Creating an Announcement Containing a Picture

Problem: As the president of the Car Club of Anaheim, you are responsible for announcing an upcoming car rally. You have obtained a photo of an antique car you would like to use in the announcement. The unformatted document is shown in Figure 1-92, and the formatted document is shown in Figure 1-93.

Antique Car Owners!

17th Annual Goofball Rally

$30.00 entry fee includes road rally and steak barbecue
1st Place, 2nd Place, and 3rd Place trophies will be awarded
Bring a map, compass, and knowledge of American history

Join us on April 23 for the running of the 17th Annual Goofball Rally. This year's event is sponsored by the MGB Car Club of Anaheim. The Rally will begin precisely at 11:00 a.m. in the Anaheim Mall parking lot.

An information envelope, available only at the starting line, explains the rules and regulations of the Goofball Rally and contains your first clue. Solving the first clue will take you to the first checkpoint. At each of the seven checkpoints, your time and distance will be recorded and you will be given your next clue. The car with the best time and distance wins. For information, contact Frank Anderson.

Call (714) 555-6738

FIGURE 1-92

Instructions:

1. Change the default font size to 14 point.
2. Enter the text of the announcement as shown in Figure 1-92.
3. Check the document for incorrectly spelled words and then correct any spelling problems.
4. Save the document on the Corel WordPerfect 8 Files floppy disk using the Goofball Road Rally.wpd filename.
5. Format the first paragraph (Antique Car Owners!) using the Arial font face, Bold and Italic font styles, and 40-point font size. Center the paragraph.

Antique Car Owners!

17th **Annual Goofball Rally**

$30.00 entry fee includes road rally and steak barbecue
1st Place, 2nd Place, and 3rd Place trophies will be awarded
Bring a map, compass, and knowledge of American history

Join us on April 23 for the running of the 17th Annual Goofball Rally. This year's event is sponsored by the MGB Car Club of Anaheim. The Rally will begin *precisely* at 11:00 a.m. in the Anaheim Mall parking lot.

An information envelope, available only at the starting line, explains the rules and regulations of the Goofball Rally and contains your first clue. Solving the first clue will take you to the first checkpoint. At each of the seven checkpoints, your time and distance will be recorded and you will be given your next clue. The car with the <u>best time and distance wins</u>. For information, contact Frank Anderson.

Call (714) 555-6738

FIGURE 1-93

(continued)

In the Lab

Creating an Announcement Containing a Picture *(continued)*

6. Format the second paragraph (17th Annual Goofball Rally) using the Arial font face, Bold font style, and 30-point font size. Center the paragraph.

7. Select the next three paragraphs. Create a bulleted list using the three paragraphs and the Large Circle bullet style.

8. Italicize the word, precisely, in the paragraph following the bulleted list.

9. Select the words, best time and distance wins, in the next paragraph. Underline the words.

10. Format the last paragraph (Call (714) 555-6738) using the Bold font style and 18-point font size. Center the paragraph.

11. Save the announcement again using the same filename.

12. If you have access to the Internet, download the Antique_Car file containing the picture of an antique car from the Corel WordPerfect 8 Web site to the Corel WordPerfect 8 Files floppy disk you created in this project. Use the URL, http://www.scsite.com/wp8. Otherwise, obtain the Antique_Car file from your instructor.

13. Insert the antique_car file between the first and second paragraph. Prevent text from wrapping around the graphics box. Size and move the graphics box containing the picture to resemble the picture shown in Figure 1-93 on the previous page.

14. Save the announcement again.

15. Print the announcement.

2 Creating an Announcement Containing Multiple Pictures

Problem: You are the manager of The Real Estate Professionals, a real estate company. You wish to design an announcement to be placed on the doorsteps of possible home buyers using two pictures you have already obtained. While there is still a buyer's market, you decide to prepare the announcement shown in Figure 1-94.

Instructions:

1. Change the default font size to 14 point.

2. Enter the text of the announcement as shown in Figure 1-94.

3. Check the document for incorrectly spelled words and correct any spelling problems.

4. Save the document on a floppy disk using the Real Estate Professionals.wpd filename.

5. Format the first two paragraphs (Matching People and Houses Is Our Job!) using the Arial Bold 30-point font. Center the paragraphs.

6. Format the third paragraph (The Real Estate Professionals) using the Arial Bold, Italic, 30-point font. Center the paragraph.

7. Underline the word, The, in the group of words.

8. Select the next two paragraphs. Create a bulleted list using the two paragraphs and the Triangle bullet style.

9. In the bulleted list, select the words, 24-hour a day, and then italicize the words.

In the Lab

10. In the bulleted list, select the words, experienced professionals, and then italicize the words.
11. Select the words, The Real Estate Professionals, in the paragraph following the bulleted list. Bold the words. Underline the word, The, in the same paragraph.
12. Select the words, latest computer technology, in the next paragraph. Underline the words.
13. Select the words, full-color interior and exterior photographs, in the same paragraph. Underline the words.
14. Format the last paragraph, Now is the Time to Buy!, using the Italic font style, 18-point font size. Center the paragraph.
15. Save the announcement again using the same filename.
16. If you have access to the Internet, download the Family and House files to the Corel WordPerfect 8 Files disk you created in this project. These files contain the pictures of a family and a house from the Corel WordPerfect 8 Web site. Use the URL (http://www.scsite.com/wp8). Otherwise, obtain the files from your instructor.
17. Insert the family file between the second and third paragraphs.
18. Insert the house file between the second and third paragraphs.
19. Prevent the text from wrapping around both graphics boxes.
20. Move and size the two graphics boxes containing the pictures to resemble the images shown in Figure 1-94.
21. Save the announcement again using the same filename.
22. Print the announcement.

Matching People and Houses Is Our Job!

The Real Estate Professionals

- Local offices open *24-hours a day*, seven-days a week
- Personal service from *experienced professionals*

Whether relocating to another state or looking to buy in the same town, **_The Real Estate Professionals_** will match your needs to the home of your dreams. Our agents are receptive to your requirements, familiar with the market, and dedicated to making your home-acquiring experience pleasurable.

In the comfort of our offices, and using the <u>latest computer technology</u>, your agent can show you hundreds of <u>full-color interior and exterior photographs</u> of homes for sale in any area. This new, time-saving service allows you to narrow the search for your new home and eliminate driving from house to house. View each home on a computer monitor, select the ones that match your needs and pocketbook, and we will arrange a personal tour at your convenience.

Call or come in to one of our conveniently located offices today and talk to a friendly, experienced real estate professional. To arrange an appointment or for additional information, call (714) 555-8473.

Now is the Time to Buy!

FIGURE 1-94

In the Lab

3 Composing an Announcement from a Draft

Problem: You own and operate House Painting Specialists, a house painting business. You wish to design an announcement that you can distribute door-to-door to prospective customers. You obtained a picture of a lighthouse and wish to include the picture in the announcement.

Instructions: You are to create the unformatted announcement shown in Figure 1-95. If you performed the Apply Your Knowledge assignment in this project, use the text in the Corrected House Painting.wpd file for this announcement. If you have access to the Internet, using the URL, http://www.scsite.com/wp8, download the Lighthouse file from the Corel WordPerfect 8 Web site to the Corel WordPerfect 8 Files

floppy disk you created in this project. Otherwise, obtain the file from your instructor. Then, format the announcement using the techniques presented in this project, save the document, and then print the document. Below are some general guidelines for formatting the announcement.

1. Center the first four paragraphs and the last paragraph.

2. Increase the font size of the first four paragraphs to emphasize the paragraphs.

3. Create bulleted lists as needed to emphasize important aspects of the house painting service.

4. Use the bold, italic, and underline font styles to emphasize important words or phrases.

5. Change the font face and font size to emphasize text.

HOUSE PAINTING
SPECIALISTS

No Job Too Tall!
We Paint Them All!

We specialize in exterior house painting
More than 2,400 homes painted

House Painting Specialists will paint the exterior of the average two-story house for only $1,295. Our work includes high-pressure spray cleaning, crack and hole repair, sanding and scraping all wood surfaces, priming all paintable surfaces, top-quality paint, and complete cleanup.

All work is guaranteed against peeling, chipping, and fading for a period of five years. If you have a problem in the first five years, we will fix the problem without charge. Call for references in your neighborhood or for a free estimate.

(714) 555-8938

FIGURE 1-95

Cases and Places

The difficulty of these case studies varies: ❱ are the least difficult; ❱❱ are more difficult; and ❱❱❱ are the most difficult.

1 ❱ Seven families who live on Conners Street in your neighborhood are having a garage sale. Ms. Martinez, the organizer of the sale, asked you to design an announcement she could distribute to houses in the area. The garage sale is scheduled for Saturday, August 15 from 8:00 a.m. to 3:00 p.m. She asked you to emphasize there would be many baby clothes, two ten-speed bicycles, living room and dining room furniture, and a collection of old electric trains. Use a bulleted list and insert an appropriate graphics image. Use the concepts and techniques presented in this project to create the announcement.

2 ❱ Mr. Santos is the owner of Extreme Exteriors, a garage door business. He would like to distribute an announcement advertising an end-of-summer garage door sale. The top-of-the-line Weatherguard 1500 doors are on sale. The doors in the 1500 series are insulated steel sectional garage doors available in two sizes: eight feet by seven feet and sixteen feet by seven feet. The smaller door sells for $525.00 and the larger door sells for $730.00. Both prices include installation, weather stripping, sales tax, and removal of old garage doors. Mr. Santos is a licensed contractor (license number 650542) and his phone number is (414) 555-3782. Use the concepts and techniques presented in this project to create the announcement. Use a bulleted list and insert an appropriate graphics image.

3 ❱❱ The graduating class of Pennington High School will be celebrating their tenth high school reunion this year. Betty Arnold, the reunion coordinator, asked you to prepare an announcement that she can send to all students in her graduating class. The reunion consists of dinner at the Cosmic Celery restaurant, music by The Granite Horses, and a special guest appearance by Bobby Dunlap, a local celebrity. It will be held on Saturday, August 22, at 8:00 p.m. Guests are encouraged to bring old photographs and yearbooks and to wear clothing that was popular in high school. More information can be obtained by calling Betty Arnold at (313) 555-1938. Use a bulleted list and insert an appropriate graphics image. Use the concepts and techniques presented in this project to create the announcement.

4 ❱❱ The graphics image used to create the New Guinea Tour document in Project 1 contains a picture of two New Guinea tribesmen. Graphics images such as this one can be obtained from many different sources. Sources include the Corel WordPerfect Suite 8 CD-ROM, CD-ROMs that you can purchase at a computer retail store, stores that are in the business of selling their pictures, and various Web sites on the Internet (Corel, Kodak, Polaroid, Adobe, and so on). Using the sources mentioned previously, obtain copies of at least two other pictures of people from New Guinea. Identify who the people are, where they live in New Guinea, their habits and customs, and the source of the picture.

Cases and Places

5 ▶▶ Many announcements you receive in the mail or on your doorstep are poorly designed and not formatted to catch the reader's attention. Obtain a copy of one of these announcements. Create a WordPerfect document and enter the text of the announcement in the document. Using this text and the concepts and techniques presented in this project, create an announcement that would be more likely to catch a reader's eye. Format the announcement and include a bulleted list and suitable graphics images.

6 ▶▶▶ The classified section of the newspaper contains advertisements for employment. Most of the advertisements are small and unnoticeable. Larger advertisements (quarter and half page size) draw the attention of the reader and are, therefore, more effective. Look through the classified section of your newspaper to find a small classified advertisement that you think could be enlarged and formatted. Using the smaller advertisement and the concepts and techniques presented in this project, redo the advertisement to fill one-quarter of a newspaper page. Format the announcement and include a bulleted list and suitable graphics images.

7 ▶▶▶ The Foreign Language Club is sponsoring an ethnic dinner. The club is composed of students taking Spanish, French, German, Russian, and Italian classes. Mr. Perez, the Spanish teacher in room 201, asked you to design an announcement that could be distributed to other classes. The dinner, which costs $7.00, is scheduled for Wednesday, September 16 from 6:00 p.m. to 8:00 p.m. in the cafeteria. Ethnic dishes will be served by all five classes. Using the Internet, a language textbook, a foreign language student or teacher, and the concepts and techniques presented in this project, create the announcement in one of the five languages mentioned above. Use a bulleted list and insert an appropriate graphics image.

Corel *WordPerfect 8*

Creating a Resume and Cover Letter Using PerfectExpert

Objectives:

You will have mastered the material in this project when you can:

- ▶ Add a name to the Address Book
- ▶ Create a resume using PerfectExpert
- ▶ Personalize a resume by selecting and replacing prompts
- ▶ Create a section heading in a resume
- ▶ View the codes in the resume
- ▶ Explain the components of a business letter
- ▶ Explain the spacing between the components of the letter
- ▶ Understand the concept of headers with tables
- ▶ Create a cover letter using PerfectExpert
- ▶ Personalize a cover letter
- ▶ Define and use AutoCorrect abbreviations
- ▶ View the codes in the cover letter
- ▶ Open two document windows
- ▶ Switch between open documents

NEXT STOP: MARS

Suppose a meteorite from Antarctica, bearing traces of primitive life that may have existed on Mars billions of years ago, has spurred a feverish push to land a team on the Red Planet. You are one of a select group of private citizens who has been asked to submit résumés for a place on the long-awaited mission. It is an assignment you want more than wealth, fame, or stardom. As a noted paleoecologist, you specialize in analyzing the remains of dead organisms and reconstructing the environment and events that led to their demise. Even in this relatively esoteric field, others want your dream job, too.

Sound far-out? In August 1996, after studying a Martian meteorite for two years, scientists announced the discovery of the remains of microscopic organisms, rekindling the world's fascination with the idea of exploring Earth's neighbor. Though a *job* on such a mission may be years in the future, the problem is no different from today's reality: competition for jobs is tough and sophisticated.

ONLY THOSE WITH A STRONG DESIRE FOR SUCCESS NEED APPLY!!!

Making your education pay off may rest on two documents that seem deceptively simple: namely, a cover letter and résumé. Yet, these are vitally important and require your *best* writing. Daily, human resources specialists in business and government must consider thousands of such documents. First — just to be read — your cover letter and résumé must stand out; otherwise, they land in the circular file. Only then does the real evaluation begin.

Besides neatness and accuracy, you must compose these two pieces to present your unique qualifications in the most advantageous light. Remember . . . they are a sales tool, designed to convince a potential employer to invite you for a face-to-face interview.

Although preparing a cover letter and résumé may seem to be a daunting task, Corel WordPerfect has several built-in tools to help the job seeker clear this first mighty hurdle. Using PerfectExpert and the Resume project, even a novice can create a professional looking self-promotion package in minutes. By taking care of the mechanical tasks of formatting and style, WordPerfect lets the author concentrate on content. Within the Resume project, the Resume template creates a document and prompts the author to provide essential information. Spell-As-You-Go and QuickCorrect detect misspelled words and typographical errors as you compose.

The trip to Mars likely will require the teamwork of many nations: Australia, Russia, Japan, the United States, and others. Certainly, the competition will be fierce to see who takes the ride. You may be one of the lucky few who get to don space suits and go bounding over red rocks beneath a pink Martian sky. Think of how *that* will look on a résumé!

Creating a Resume and Cover Letter Using PerfectExpert

Case Perspective

Kate Summers will graduate next month from California College with a Bachelor of Science degree in Computer Education. Kate decides to prepare a resume to send to prospective employers before graduating. She wants the resume to look professional and highlight her employment and educational experience, so Kate decides to create her resume using PerfectExpert.

While reading last Sunday's edition of the *Southern California News*, she located a classified advertisement for a computer columnist at the Southern California News Agency, owner of the newspaper. Because of her love of writing (her minor in college was English), Kate decides to apply for the position. In addition to a resume, Kate needs to create a personalized cover letter to send to Mr. Edward Andrews at the agency. In her cover letter, she wants to emphasize her computer and writing skills, so Kate decides to create it using PerfectExpert. After creating the resume and cover letter, Kate plans to send a copy of both documents to Mr. Andrews and wait for his response.

Introduction

Whether searching for your first job or a new job, you will want to prepare a resume and a personalized cover letter to send to prospective employers. A **resume** summarizes an applicant's job experience, educational background, and qualifications. Because employers receive large numbers of resumes for a single job opening, you should carefully design a resume to make yourself look like the best candidate for the job.

Along with each resume, you should attach a personalized cover letter. A **cover letter** allows you to emphasize the strong points in your resume and gives the reader an opportunity to see your written communication skills. Thus, it is important to prepare a well-written cover letter using the established rules for writing business letters. Cover letters also contain a personalized letterhead. A **letterhead** is the information at the top of the letter that contains the writer's name, address, and phone number. You can use graphics, such as horizontal lines, and different font faces, styles, and sizes to enhance the appearance of a letterhead.

Templates and PerfectExpert

A difficult process for many people is creating a resume and cover letter. In response, WordPerfect provides an easier method to create documents such as a resume and cover letter. This method uses a template to assist you in creating these documents. A **template** is a predefined document that contains a customized format, content, and certain features. Every WordPerfect document you create is based on a template. Even the blank document that displays when you start WordPerfect is based on a template. A template can be as simple as a memo you fill in or as complex as a multiple-page newsletter.

In Project One, you used Ask the PerfectExpert to search for information from Help by entering words, phrases, or sentences. **PerfectExpert** also can assist you in creating documents based on templates. To create a document based upon a template, you select one of the hundreds of projects available in WordPerfect. Typical **projects** include creating a balance sheet, expense report, fax cover sheet, resume, business letter, brochure, newsletter, and so on. Each project uses a template that controls the formatting and content of the project. You can display a list of projects by using the New command on the File menu.

To help locate a project quickly, projects are organized in categories and given names, such as business correspondence, legal, and time management. When you open a project within a category, PerfectExpert displays a panel on the left side of the Corel WordPerfect application window. The PerfectExpert panel allows you to customize the document on which you are working.

To create a resume, you select the **Resume project** within the **Job Search category**. The Resume project uses the Resume template to create the resume. The **Resume template** creates a document based upon a resume style (contemporary, cosmopolitan, and so on). After creating the resume, you replace the prewritten text in the document, called **prompts**, with personal information, such as employment and educational information. When you have completed the document, check it for incorrectly spelled words and then save and print the document.

To create a business letter, you select the **Business Letter project** within the **Business Correspondence category**. The **Letter template** steps you through the process of creating a letter by prompting you to select a letterhead style (contemporary, cosmopolitan, and so on) and a business letter style (full block, modified block, or semiblock). Then, the template creates the letter, displays the letter on the screen, and allows you to enter personalized information. When you have finished, check for incorrectly spelled words, and then save the document, and print it.

Project Two—Resume and Cover Letter

In Project 2, you will use WordPerfect to produce the cover letter shown in Figure 2-1 on the next page and the resume shown in Figure 2-2 also on the next page. As you will recall from the Case Perspective, Kate Summers graduates next month and is seeking a full-time position as a newspaper columnist with a major news agency in southern California. In addition to her resume, she would like to send a personalized cover letter to Mr. Edward Andrews at the Southern California News Agency.

cover
letter

Kate Summers

2098 Vista Drive
Mission Viejo, CA 92692
(714) 555-1211

May 5, 1999

Edward Andrews
Southern California News Agency
3637 Front Street
Yorba Linda, CA 92882

Dear Mr. Andrews:

I read your advertisement for a full-time computer columnist in the May 3 edition of *Southern California News*. I will be graduating from California College with a major in Computer Education and a minor in English, and feel I have the necessary qualifications for the position.

With my college education, I have gained up-to-date computer and software skills, a fresh writing style, and a strong desire to be a columnist. I have experience with personal computers and many software packages, and my research skills include using the Internet and World Wide Web.

As a part-time employee at the college, it is my responsibility to train Business department faculty and staff to use presentation graphics and word processing software. I also write a weekly article on personal computer or application software topics for the faculty newsletter, *Faculty Update*.

I am very interested in the columnist position and would appreciate the opportunity to discuss employment with the Southern California News Agency in a personal interview. Please contact me at (714) 555-1211 to arrange an appointment. I have enclosed a copy of my resume so you can review my qualifications before the interview. Thank you for your consideration.

Sincerely,

Kate Summers

Enclosure

FIGURE 2-1

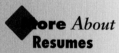

ore *About*
Resumes

A resume is a chance to advertise yourself to a potential employer. A good resume promotes your qualifications and is accurate, truthful, and up-to-date. For best results, review the advertisement that made you aware of the job, review the contents of your resume, and customize your resume to fit that job.

resume

KATE SUMMERS

2098 Vista Drive • Mission Viejo, CA 92692 • (714) 555-1211

Objective

To obtain a computer columnist position with a major news agency in southern California.

Employment

FACULTY ASSISTANT   YEARS EMPLOYED (1996 - 99)
California College   *Los Angeles, California*

Several times a year, I train small groups of Business department faculty and staff to use presentation graphics and word processing software. Weekly, I write an article about an interesting aspect of personal computers or application software for the faculty newsletter.

MANAGER   YEARS EMPLOYED (1995 - 96)
Bob's Burgers   *El Toro, California*

When required, I trained new employees to use cash registers. On an ongoing basis, I monitored customer service by overseeing cashiers, cooks, and drive-through operators. Weekly, I designed work schedules for all employees using word processing and spreadsheet software.

Education

B.S. IN COMPUTER EDUCATION   YEARS ATTENDED (1995 - 99)
California College   *Los Angeles, California*

In 1998 and 1999, I was named Computer Education Student of the Year. I was awarded this honor for my high academic achievement and for starting the Student Tutorial Program. My estimated grade point average upon graduation from college is 3.9/4.0.

HIGH SCHOOL DIPLOMA   YEARS ATTENDED (1991 - 95)
Mission Viejo High School   *Mission Viejo, California*

In 1994, I was voted the high school student most likely to succeed by the Mission Viejo Civic Club and awarded the prestigious Civic Pride college scholarship. I attained the Principal's Honor Roll in all four years of high school and my grade point average was 3.7/4.0.

Skills

- In-depth knowledge of personal computers and application software
- Extensive writing experience
- Internet and World Wide Web research skills

References

Carol Packard, Instructor, California College, Los Angeles, California
Bob Robertson, Owner, Bob's Burgers, El Toro, California

FIGURE 2-2

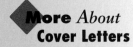

Document Preparation Steps

Document preparation steps give you an overview of how the documents in Figure 2-1 and Figure 2-2 will be developed. The following tasks will be completed in this project.

1. Start WordPerfect.
2. Add the resume and cover letter writer's name to the Address Book.
3. Use PerfectExpert to create a resume.
4. Personalize the resume.
5. Correct misspelled words.
6. Save the resume on a floppy disk.
7. Print the resume.
8. Add the cover letter recipient's name to the Address Book.
9. Use PerfectExpert to create a cover letter.
10. Personalize the cover letter.
11. Correct misspelled words.
12. Save the cover letter on a floppy disk.
13. Print the cover letter.

The following pages contain a detailed explanation of these tasks.

Starting WordPerfect

Before you can create the resume and cover letter, you need to start WordPerfect by following the procedures explained in Project 1 on page WP 1.8. These procedures are summarized below.

TO START WORDPERFECT

1 Click the Start button on the taskbar.
2 Point to Corel WordPerfect Suite 8.
3 Click Corel WordPerfect 8 on the Corel WordPerfect Suite 8 submenu.
4 If necessary, click the Maximize button in the Corel WordPerfect window.
5 If necessary, click the Maximize button in the Document1 window.

WordPerfect displays the maximized Corel WordPerfect application window and a blank document titled Document1 in a maximized document window

The Address Book

The **Address Book** is an application included with WordPerfect that enables you to keep the address information for many individuals in one place. The Address Book can store names, addresses, e-mail addresses, telephone numbers, and fax numbers. This information can be useful when creating letters, addressing envelopes, creating mailing labels, producing mass mailings, and using PerfectExpert. You can also dial telephone and fax numbers using the Address Book.

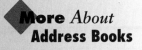

More *About*
Cover Letters

Always send a personalized cover letter with every resume. A cover letter should highlight your accomplishments that are relevant to the position. To remember those accomplishments, create a WordPerfect document and update the document when appropriate. Save the document in the same location as your cover letter and resume.

More *About*
Address Books

An address book, which holds up to 1,000 address entries, can be your phone book and complete information center. You can use the addresses when creating letters, addressing envelopes, and printing mailing labels. If a single address book is not enough, you can create and name additional address books.

Adding a Name to the Address Book

Prior to creating the resume and cover letter in this project, you should add the name of the individual for whom the resume and cover letter are being created to the Address Book and enter the required information to create the resume and cover letter. The required information includes first name, last name, street address, city, state, zip code, and home telephone number. Perform the following steps to add the name, Kate Summers, to the Address Book.

Steps To Add a Name to the Address Book

1 Click Tools on the menu bar and point to Address Book (Figure 2-3).

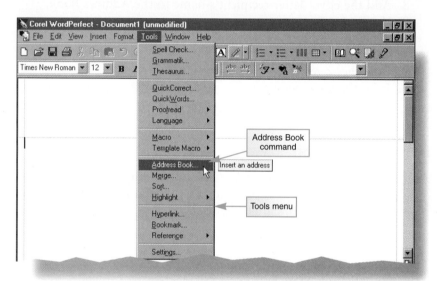

FIGURE 2-3

2 Click Address Book. If necessary, click the My Addresses tab. Point to the Add button in the Corel Address Book dialog box.

The My Addresses sheet in the Corel Address Book dialog box contains several Search List text boxes, a list box containing several column markers, three address entries that are sorted by first name, and a row of several buttons (Figure 2-4). A column name identifies each Search List box and column marker. The entries are in order by Name (first column) and the Art Stanley entry is highlighted. You can use the Search List boxes to search for an entry in the Address Book. The column names in the My Addresses sheet on your computer may be different or in a different order.

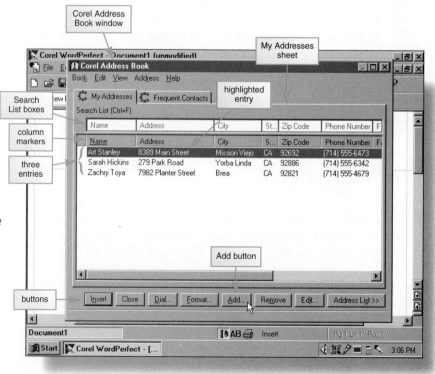

FIGURE 2-4

3 **Click the Add button. Point to the OK button in the New Entry dialog box.**

WordPerfect displays the New Entry dialog box (Figure 2-5). Two entries, Person and Organization, display in the list box and the Person entry is highlighted.

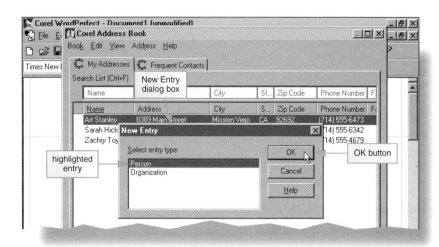

FIGURE 2-5

4 **Click the OK button. If necessary, click the Personal tab.**

*The Personal sheet in the New Person Properties dialog box contains a text box, or **property field**, for each piece of information you can enter in the new entry (Figure 2-6). Three other tabs also display in the dialog box. The insertion point is located in the First name text box.*

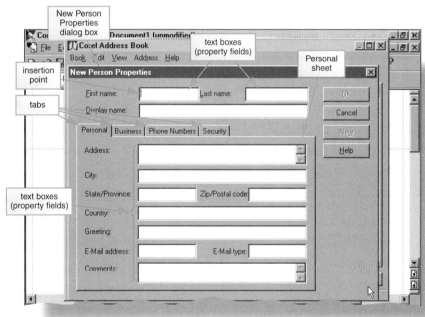

FIGURE 2-6

5 **Type** Kate **in the First name text box. Press the TAB key. Type** Summers **in the Last name text box.**

Each character of the first name displays in the First name text box and Display name text box as you type it. As you type the last name, each character displays in the Last name text box and Display name text box. The first name displays in the First name text box, the last name displays in the Last name text box, and the first and last names separated by a space display in the Display name text box (Figure 2-7).

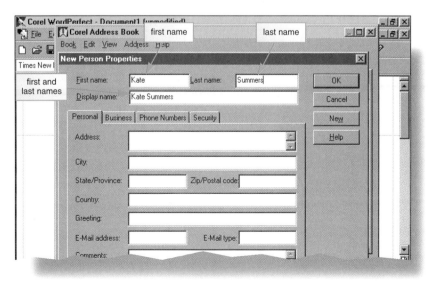

FIGURE 2-7

6 Click the Address text box and then type 2098 Vista Drive in the text box. Click the City text box and then type Mission Viejo in the text box. Click the State/Province text box and then type CA in the text box. Click the Zip/Postal code text box and then type 92692 in the text box. Point to the Phone Numbers tab.

The address, city, state, and zip code display in the appropriate text boxes (Figure 2-8).

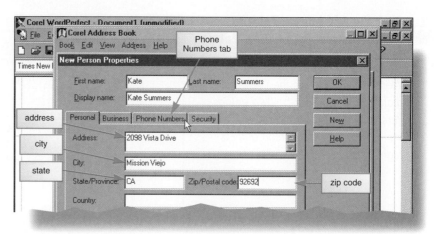

FIGURE 2-8

7 Click the Phone Numbers tab. Click the Home phone text box and then type (714) 555-1211 in the text box. Point to the OK button.

WordPerfect displays the Phone Numbers sheet, selects the Home phone option button, and displays Kate Summers's home telephone number in the Home phone text box (Figure 2-9).

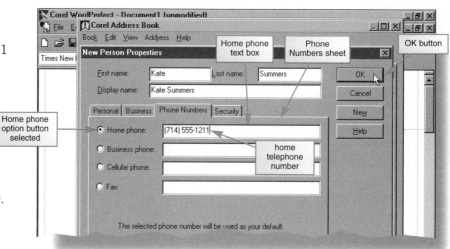

FIGURE 2-9

8 Click the OK button. Point to the Close button in the Corel Address Book window.

The New Person Properties dialog box closes, and the Kate Summers entry is added to the list of entries in the list box in the Corel Address Book window (Figure 2-10).

9 Click the Close button.

WordPerfect closes the Corel Address Book window.

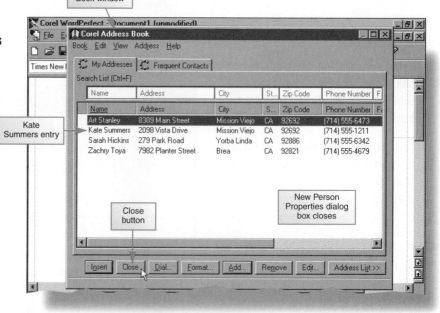

FIGURE 2-10

OtherWays

1. Click Start button, point to Corel WordPerfect Suite 8, point to Accessories, click Corel Address Book 8

After adding a name to the Corel Address Book, you can delete the name by selecting the entry in the list box, clicking the Remove button in the window, and clicking the Yes button in the Address Book - Question dialog box. In addition, you can search for an entry or sort the entries in the list box. To search for an entry, click the Search List box you wish to use in the search and then type the text you are searching for in the list box. To sort the entries, drag the column marker of the column you wish to sort on to the leftmost column marker in the list box.

The Resume

To create a resume, you may use one of two methods. This first method begins with a blank document window and requires you to create a resume design, enter text, and format the resume. With the second method, you select the Job Search category, select the Resume project, and then let PerfectExpert and the Resume template design and format the resume. When PerfectExpert has finished designing and formatting the resume, you can customize the resume by selecting prompts in the document and replacing the prompts with text you enter from the keyboard. The **prompt** will tell you what information to type and where to type it.

Styles

When you use PerfectExpert and a template to create a document, WordPerfect formats the document using styles. A **style** is a customized format applied to text in a document. Using a style to format similar types of text saves time and ensures that the document has a consistent format. The **Select Style box** on the Property Bar indicates whether or not a style has been applied to the text surrounding the insertion point. The <None> entry in the Select Style box indicates no style has been applied. Otherwise, the name of the style applied to the text displays in the box. Perform the following steps to create a resume using PerfectExpert and the Resume project.

More *About* Styles

WordPerfect has four kinds of styles. A character style formats text in a paragraph. A paragraph style formats entire paragraphs. An automatic paragraph style formats a group of paragraphs. Changing the format of one paragraph changes all paragraphs. A document style formats text from the insertion point to the end of the document.

 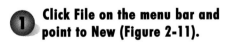
To Create a Resume Using PerfectExpert

1 **Click File on the menu bar and point to New (Figure 2-11).**

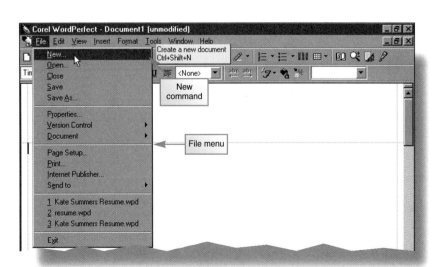

FIGURE 2-11

2 **Click New. If necessary, click the Create New tab. Click the Options button in the New dialog box. Point to Personal Information.**

The Create New sheet and Options menu display in the New dialog box (Figure 2-12). The sheet contains a graphics image, a Category box containing the highlighted default category ([Corel WordPerfect 8]), a list box containing the highlighted default project ([WordPerfect Document]), a list of projects in the Corel WordPerfect 8 category, a description of the WordPerfect Document project, and several buttons.

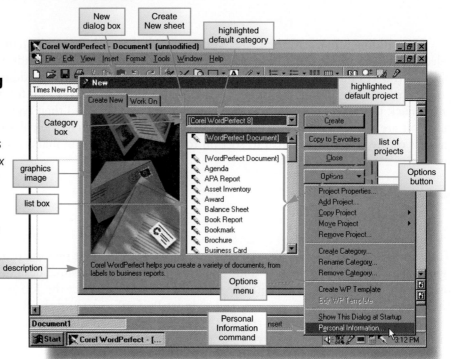

FIGURE 2-12

3 **Click Personal Information. Point to the OK button in the Corel PerfectExpert dialog box.**

The Corel PerfectExpert dialog box displays (Figure 2-13). The messages in the dialog box indicate you should add a new entry to the address book or select an existing entry to become the personal information used by the project to create the resume. Currently, no Address Book entry has been selected.

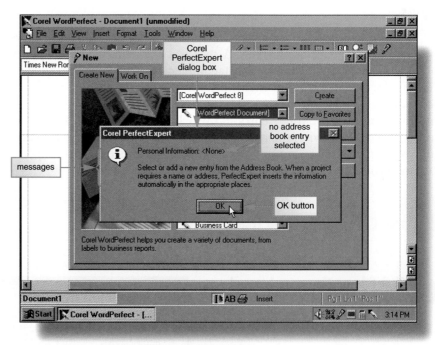

FIGURE 2-13

4 **Click the OK button. Verify the Kate Summers entry is highlighted. Point to the Select button in the Corel Address Book dialog box.**

The My Addresses sheet displays in the Corel Address Book dialog box (Figure 2-14). Four address entries, including the Kate Summers entry, display in the list box. The last entry added, Kate Summers, is highlighted. The entries in the list box may be different on your computer. Clicking the Select button causes WordPerfect to use selected information from the high-lighted entry to create the resume.

FIGURE 2-14

5 **Click the Select button. Click the Category box arrow in the New dialog box. Point to Job Search.**

The Corel Address Book dialog box closes, the New dialog box displays, the Create New sheet displays in the dialog box, and the Category drop-down list box displays (Figure 2-15). The Job Search category is highlighted in the Category list.

FIGURE 2-15

6 Click Job Search. Click Resume in the list box. Point to the Create button.

The Category drop-down list box closes, Job Search displays in the Category box, and the project name, Resume, is highlighted in the list box (Figure 2-16). A message about the Resume project displays at the bottom of the New dialog box.

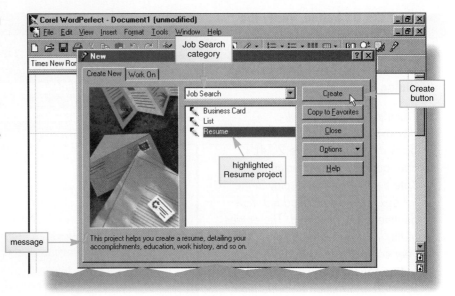

FIGURE 2-16

7 Click the Create button.

WordPerfect closes the New dialog box, displays the PerfectExpert panel, recesses the PerfectExpert button on the Toolbar, and displays the resume in the window (Figure 2-17). The resume contains Kate Summers's personal information from the Address Book, two section headings, and several horizontal graphics lines. Several prompts display in the resume, and the left margin guidelines indicate the left margin is 1" at the top of the document and changes to 2" below the address and phone number line. The PerfectExpert panel contains the Resume project name, several buttons, a tip, and the More Help on button.

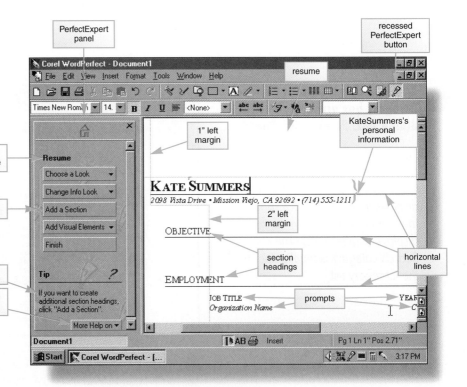

FIGURE 2-17

Other Ways

1. Click Corel PerfectExpert button on Desktop Application Director (DAD), select Job Search, select project, click Create button
2. On Help menu click Ask the PerfectExpert, type resume, click Search button, click Resume, click Display button

The Resume Template

Each project is based upon a template. The Resume project that you chose to create the resume document shown in Figure 2-17 was designed according to the instructions in the Resume template. The **Resume template** retrieved Kate Summers's personal information from the Address book and displayed it at the top of the resume.

In addition, the template created the section headers (Objective, Employment, and so on) and the prompts below each header (Job Title, Organization Name, and so on). Additional section headers and prompts are visible by scrolling the document window.

The Resume template also changed the left and right margins of the document to cause the prompts to be indented within each section. As illustrated by the left margin guideline in Figure 2-17, the left margin is one inch from the top of the document to the bottom of the address and phone number line in the heading and then changes to two inches below the address and phone line. The 2" left margin causes the prompts in the Employment section to be indented. Although not visible, a similar situation exists with the right margin guideline. The right margin guideline is one inch from the top of the document to the bottom of the address and phone number line and then changes to 1.25" below the address and phone number line.

Applying a Style to the Resume

After creating a resume, you may wish to apply a style to the resume. The Resume template allows you to choose one of three styles (Contemporary, Cosmopolitan, and Traditional). To apply a style, use the Choose a Look button on the PerfectExpert panel. Perform the following steps to apply the Contemporary style to the resume.

  Steps To Apply a Style to a Resume

 Click the **Choose a Look** button. Point to **Contemporary**.

WordPerfect recesses the Choose a Look button, displays the Choose a Look menu, and highlights the Contemporary command (Figure 2-18).

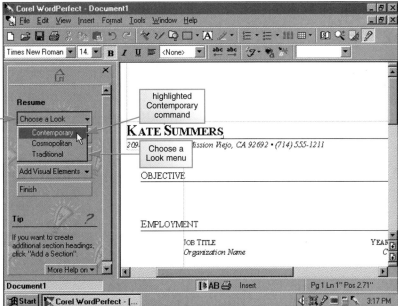

FIGURE 2-18

2 Click Contemporary.

The Choose a Look menu closes, the Choose a Look button is no longer recessed, and the resume is formatted using the contemporary style (Figure 2-19). WordPerfect removes the horizontal lines and changes the appearance of the section headings.

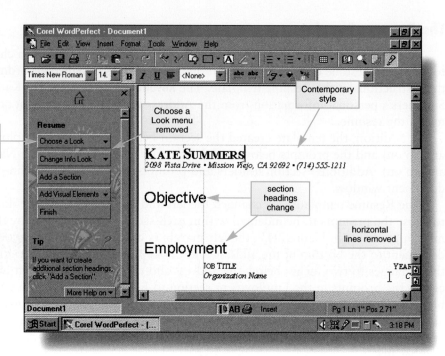

FIGURE 2-19

Applying a Style to the Personal Information

The Resume template allows you to choose one of three styles (Left Justified, With Bullets; Centered, With Bullets; and Centered, Without Bullets) to apply to the personal information in the resume. To apply a personal information style, use the Change Info Look button on the PerfectExpert panel. Perform the following steps to apply the Centered, With Bullets style to the resume.

To Apply a Style to the Personal Information

1 Click the Change Info Look button. Point to Centered, With Bullets.

WordPerfect recesses the Change Info Look button, displays the Choose Info Look menu, and highlights the Centered, With Bullets command (Figure 2-20).

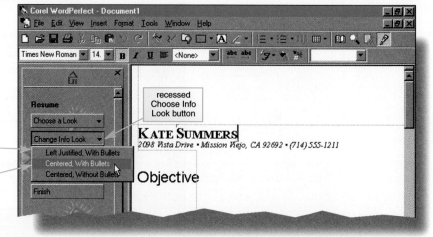

FIGURE 2-20

② Click Centered, With Bullets.

*The personal information is format-
ted using the Centered, With Bullets
style and displays centered with
bullets following the address and
zip code (Figure 2-21).*

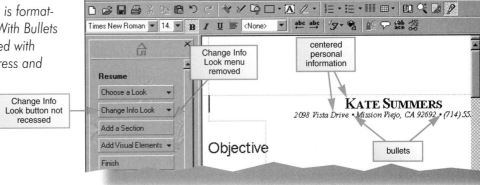

FIGURE 2-21

Removing the PerfectExpert Panel

After applying styles to the resume and personal information, remove the
PerfectExpert panel to make more of the resume visible in the document
window. The panel will be returned to the document window after formatting
and customizing the resume. Perform the following steps to remove the panel.

Steps **To Remove the PerfectExpert Panel**

① Point to the recessed PerfectExpert button on the Toolbar (Figure 2-22).

FIGURE 2-22

② Click the PerfectExpert button.

*WordPerfect removes the Perfect-
Expert panel, the PerfectExpert
button is no longer recessed, and
the top portion of the resume is
visible in the document window
(Figure 2-23).*

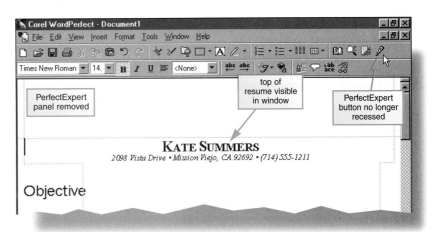

FIGURE 2-23

*Other***Ways**

1. Click the Close button on
   the PerfectExpert panel

Codes in the Resume

As mentioned in Project 1, WordPerfect places **codes** in the document when you create and format a document. Codes are also inserted in a document when creating a document using PerfectExpert. To view the codes, open the Reveal Codes window and, if necessary, scroll the document and move the insertion point to the different areas of the resume. The following section illustrates how to view the codes at the beginning of the resume and at the beginning of a section heading.

 Steps To View the Codes in the Resume

1 **Right-click the text area and then click Reveal Codes on the QuickMenu. Click the text area to the left of the first character (the letter K) in the first paragraph.**

*The Reveal Codes window displays and the insertion point is located at the beginning of the document (Figure 2-24). The **Open Style: DocumentStyle code** changes the default font size to 10 point. The **Tab Set code** displays a tab marker at the 1" setting on the Ruler, and every .33" inch thereafter. The **Sm Cap code** causes the lowercase letters of the first and last name to display in small capital letters. The **Named Region codes** identify where the personal information begins and ends and where each piece of information from the Address Book begins and ends. The **Bookmark codes** mark a location you can find again quickly. Other codes control the format of the first and last name, address, and telephone number.*

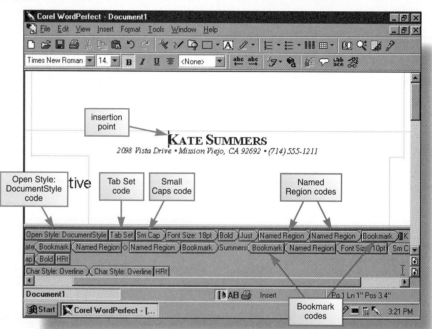

FIGURE 2-24

2 **Position the insertion point in the text area on the blank line above the Objective section heading.**

Several codes display in the Reveal Codes window (Figure 2-25). The **Lft Mar** *and* **Rgt Mar** *codes control the indentation of the text in the sections. The* **Just** *code to the right of the Rgt Mar code causes the text to be fully justified. The* **Para Style: _Section** *and* **Style** *codes control the format of the Objective heading (Arial 18-point font).*

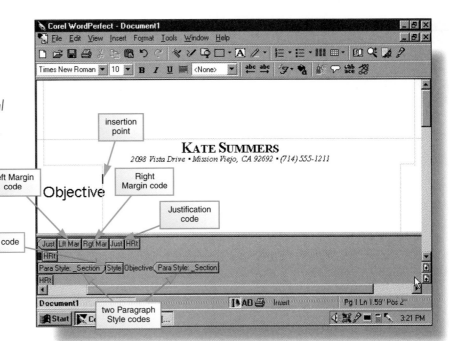

FIGURE 2-25

3 **Right-click the text area and then click Reveal Codes on the QuickMenu.**

The Reveal Codes window closes.

Personalizing the Resume

The next step is to personalize the resume. First, change the top and bottom margins to one-half inch to allow more room for the text in the resume. Next, format the name, Kate Summers, and type the objective. Using the prompts that display in the resume, type the employment, education, and skills information in the appropriate positions. Finally, add the References heading following the Skills section (see Figure 2-2 on page WP 2.6) and type the two references. The following pages show how to personalize the resume.

Changing the Top Margin

The default setting for the top and bottom margins is one inch. To make more room on the page for the text of the resume, the top and bottom margins should be changed from their default settings to .5 inch. Perform the steps on the next page to accomplish this task.

Steps To Change the Top Margin

1 **Point to the top margin guideline. Hold down the left mouse button.**

When you point to the guideline, the mouse pointer changes to a horizontal bar with a vertical double-headed arrow to indicate you can move the guideline by dragging. When you hold the mouse button down, WordPerfect displays a dotted guideline on top of the top margin and a QuickTip indicating the top margin is 1" inch (Figure 2-26).

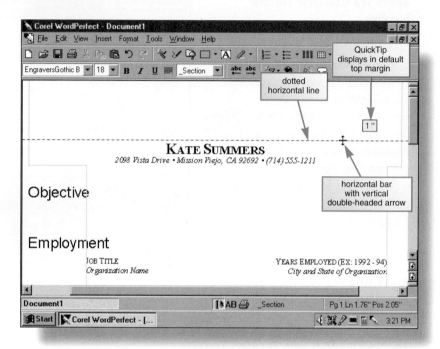

FIGURE 2-26

2 **Without releasing the left mouse button, drag the dotted guideline up until the QuickTip indicates the margin is 0.5".**

When you drag the dotted guide-line, the value in the QuickTip changes to reflect the location of the dotted guideline, and the top margin guideline remains in its original location (Figure 2-27).

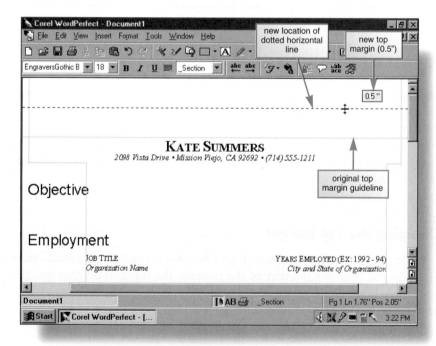

FIGURE 2-27

3 **Release the left mouse button.**

WordPerfect removes the dotted guideline, displays the top margin guideline where the dotted guideline used to be, and removes the horizontal bar with a vertical double-headed arrow and the QuickTip (Figure 2-28).

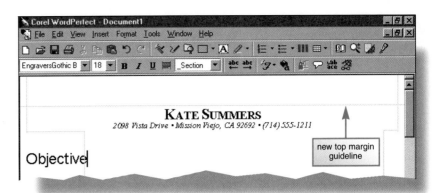

FIGURE 2-28

Changing the Bottom Margin

Next, change the bottom margin from its default setting to .5 inch. Perform the following steps to change the bottom margin.

TO CHANGE THE BOTTOM MARGIN

1 Scroll the document window to display the bottom margin guideline.

2 Point to the bottom margin guideline.

3 Hold the left mouse button down.

4 Without releasing the left mouse button, drag the dotted guideline down until the QuickTip indicates the margin is 0.5".

5 Release the left mouse button.

The bottom margin changes to .5 inch (Figure 2-29).

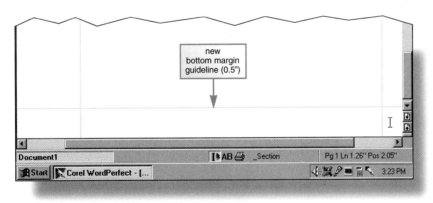

FIGURE 2-29

Formatting the Personal Information

Formatting the personal information consists of formatting the name, Kate Summers, using the Arial font and 32-point font size. Perform the steps on the next page to format the name.

OtherWays

1. Click Page Margins button on Format Toolbar, change top margin, click OK button

2. Double-click margin marker or area between margin markers on Ruler, change top margin, click OK button

3. On Format menu click Margins, change top margin, click OK button

4. Press CTRL+F8, change top margin, click OK button

FIGURE 2-30

TO FORMAT THE NAME

1 Scroll the document window to make the top of the document visible.

2 Select the paragraph containing the name, Kate Summers.

3 Right-click the name to display a QuickMenu.

4 Click Font on the QuickMenu.

5 Scroll the Font face list box to display Arial and then click Arial.

6 Scroll the Font size list box until 32 displays and then click 32.

7 Click the OK button.

8 Click anywhere within the text to remove the highlight.

WordPerfect formats the first paragraph by changing the font face to Arial and the font size to 32 point (Figure 2-30).

Typing the Objective

The next step in personalizing the resume is to enter the objective. You enter the objective by positioning the insertion point in the text area on the first blank line following the Objective heading and typing the objective. Perform the following steps to enter the objective.

TO TYPE THE OBJECTIVE

1 Position the insertion point in the text area on the first blank line following the Objective heading.

2 Type To obtain a computer columnist position with a major news agency in southern California. as the objective.

The objective displays in the Objective section (Figure 2-31).

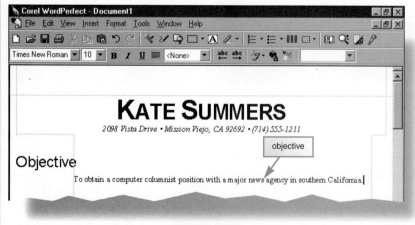

FIGURE 2-31

Selecting and Replacing Prompts in the Employment Section

The next step in personalizing the resume is to select each prompt in the resume and replace it with personal information. The first section containing prompts is the Employment section. The Employment section contains five prompts (Job Title, Organization Name, Years Employed, City and State of Organization, and Job Description). You replace a prompt by selecting the prompt and entering the associated information from the keyboard. When you type the first character, WordPerfect removes the highlight from the prompt and displays the character in place of the prompt. Additional characters entered from the keyboard will display following the first character. Perform the following steps to type the information for the first job.

 Steps To Select and Replace the Prompts for the First Job

① **Scroll the document window until the Employment heading and section display at the top of the window. Select the JOB TITLE prompt and type** FACULTY ASSISTANT **as the job title. Select the EX: 1992 - 94 entry in the YEARS EMPLOYED prompt and type** 1996 - 99 **as the years employed.**

The job title, FACULTY ASSISTANT, replaces the JOB TITLE prompt and the years employed, 1996 - 99, replace the years in the YEARS EMPLOYED prompt in the resume (Figure 2-32).

② **Select the Organization Name prompt and then type** California College **as the organization name. Select the City and State of Organization prompt and then type** Los Angeles, California **as the city and state.**

The organization name, California College, and city and state of the organization, Los Angeles, California, replace the prompts in the resume (Figure 2-33).

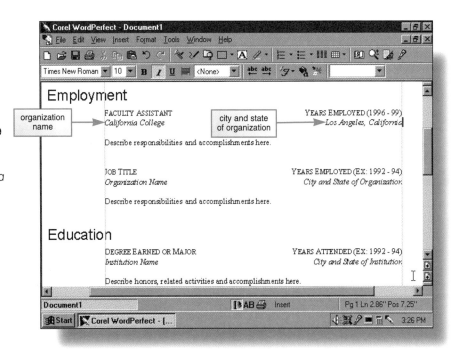

FIGURE 2-32

FIGURE 2-33

3 **Select the Describe responsibilities and accomplishments here. prompt and then type** Several times a year, I train small groups of Business department faculty and staff to use presentation graphics and word processing software. Weekly, I write an article about an interesting aspect of personal computers or application software for the faculty newsletter. **as the job description.**

The job description replaces the Describe responsibilities and accomplishments here. prompt in the resume project (Figure 2-34).

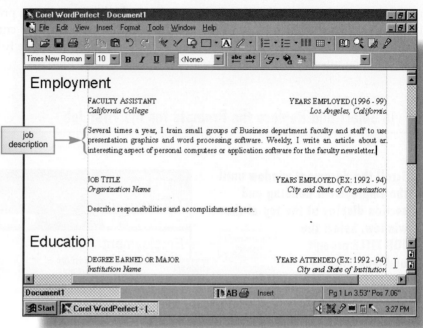

FIGURE 2-34

Next, select the first prompt in the Employment section that describes the second job and type the appropriate entry. Repeat this process until all prompts in this section have been replaced with the correct information. Perform the following steps to type the information for the second job.

TO SELECT AND REPLACE THE PROMPTS FOR THE SECOND JOB

1 Select the JOB TITLE prompt and type Manager as the job title.

2 Select the EX: 1992 - 94 entry in the YEARS EMPLOYED prompt and then type 1995 - 96 as the years employed.

3 Select the Organization Name prompt and then type Bob's Burgers as the organization name.

4 Select the City and State of Organization prompt and then type El Toro, California as the city and state.

5 Select the Describe responsibilities and accomplishments here. prompt and then type When required, I trained new employees to use cash registers. On an ongoing basis, I monitored customer service by overseeing cashiers, cooks, and drive-through operators. Weekly, I designed work schedules for all employees using word processing and spreadsheet software. as the job description.

The job title, years employed, organization name, city and state of the organization, and job description replace the prompts for the second job entry in the resume (Figure 2-35).

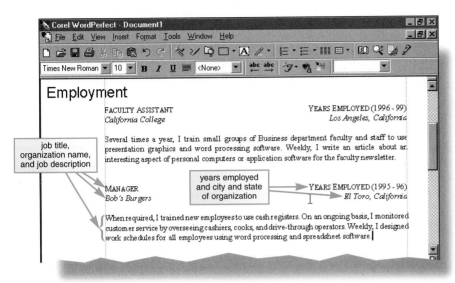

FIGURE 2-35

Selecting and Replacing the Prompts in the Education Section

Next, select the prompts in the Education section that describe the schools you attended and type the appropriate entry for each prompt. Perform the following steps to type the information for the first school.

To Select and Replace the Prompts for the First School

1 Scroll the document window until the Education heading and section display at the top of the window. Select the DEGREE EARNED OR MAJOR prompt and then type B.S. in Computer Education as the degree earned. Select the EX: 1992 - 94 entry in the YEARS ATTENDED prompt and then type 1995 - 99 as the years attended.

The degree earned, B.S. in Computer Education, replaces the DEGREE EARNED OR MAJOR prompt and the years attended, 1995 - 99, replace the YEARS ATTENDED prompt in the resume (Figure 2-36).

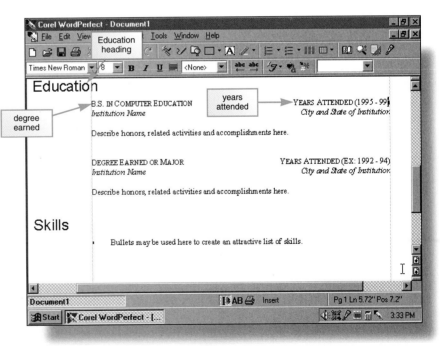

FIGURE 2-36

Select the Institution Name prompt and then type California College **as the institution name. Select the City and State of Institution prompt and then type** Los Angeles, California **as the city and state.**

The institution name, California College, and city and state of the institution, Los Angeles, California, replace the prompts in the resume (Figure 2-37).

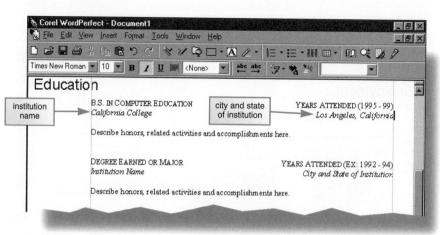

FIGURE 2-37

 Select the Describe honors, related activities and accomplishments here. prompt and then type In 1998 and 1999, I was named Computer Education Student of the Year. I was awarded this honor for my high academic achievement and for starting the Student Tutorial Program. My estimated grade point average upon graduation from college is 3.9/4.0. **as the honors.**

The honors and accomplishments replace the prompt (Figure 2-38).

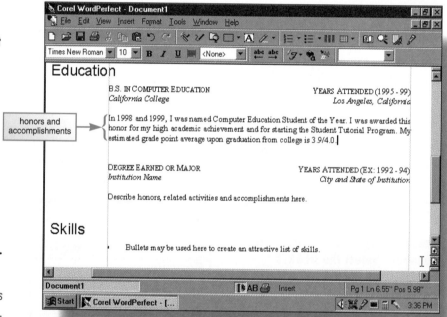

FIGURE 2-38

Next, select each prompt in the Education section that describes the second school and type the appropriate entry for each prompt. Perform the following steps to type the information for the second school.

TO SELECT AND REPLACE THE PROMPTS FOR THE SECOND SCHOOL

1. Select the DEGREE EARNED OR MAJOR prompt and then type High School Diploma to replace the prompt.
2. Select the EX: 1992 - 94 entry in the YEARS ATTENDED prompt and then type 1991 - 95 as the years attended.
3. Select the Institution Name prompt and then type Mission Viejo High School as the institution name.

④ Select the City and State of Institution prompt and then type Mission Viejo, California as the city and state.

⑤ Select the Describe honors, related activities and accomplishments here. prompt and then type In 1994, I was voted the high school student most likely to succeed by the Mission Viejo Civic Club and awarded the prestigious Civic Pride college scholarship. I attained the Principal's Honor Roll in all four years of high school and my grade point average was 3.7/4.0. as the honors.

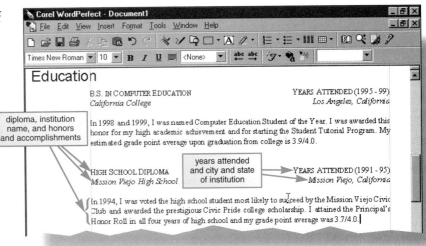

FIGURE 2-39

The diploma earned, years attended, institution name, city and state of the institution, and honors and accomplishments replace the prompts for the second school entry (Figure 2-39).

Selecting and Replacing the Prompt in the Skills Section

The Skills section contains a single prompt. Select the prompt and then type the first bulleted item in the resume. Perform the following step to select and replace the bulleted item.

 Steps **To Select and Replace the Prompt for the Bulleted Item**

① **Scroll the document window until the Skills heading and section are visible in the window. Select the bulleted item and then type** In-depth knowledge of personal computers and application software **and press the ENTER key.**

The first skill replaces the prompt, a second bullet displays, and the style name (_ . displays in the Select Style box on the Property Bar (Figure 2-40). Although not visible, the _ . style name displays on the General Status button on the Application Bar.

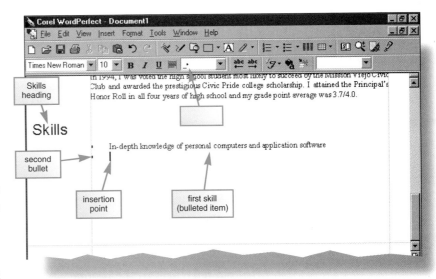

FIGURE 2-40

Typing Additional Skills

Next, add the additional skills section to the resume by typing two additional items in the bulleted list. Perform the following step to add two additional skills to the bulleted list.

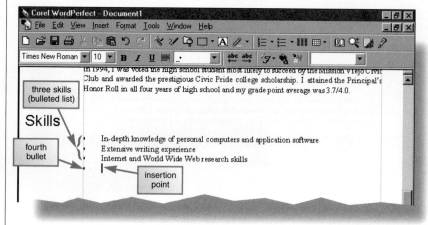

FIGURE 2-41

TO ADD ADDITIONAL SKILLS TO THE BULLETED LIST

1. Type Extensive writing experience and then press the ENTER key. Type Internet and World Wide Web research skills and then press the ENTER key.

Three skills, or bulleted items, display in the resume (Figure 2-41). A fourth bullet and the insertion point display on the line following the three bulleted items.

Creating a Section Heading

Next, create the heading for the References section of the resume and type the two references (see Figure 2-1 on page WP 2.6). To create the new section heading, display the PerfectExpert panel and use the Add a Section button. Perform the following steps to display the panel.

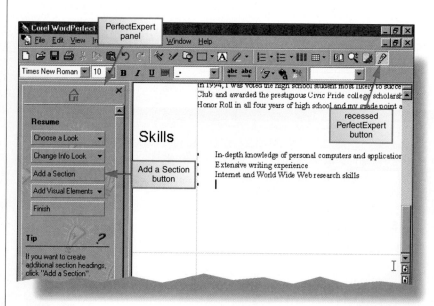

FIGURE 2-42

TO DISPLAY THE PERFECTEXPERT PANEL

1. Point to the PerfectExpert button on the Toolbar.
2. Click the PerfectExpert button.

WordPerfect displays the PerfectExpert panel in the document window and recesses the PerfectExpert button (Figure 2-42).

Next, perform the following steps to create the References heading and add the two references to the resume.

Steps To Create a Section Heading

1 **Verify the insertion point is located following the fourth bullet in the bulleted list. Click the Add a Section button on the PerfectExpert panel. Type** References **and then press the ENTER key.**

The section heading, References, displays in the resume, the insertion point displays in the text area below the section heading, and the fourth bullet is removed (Figure 2-43).

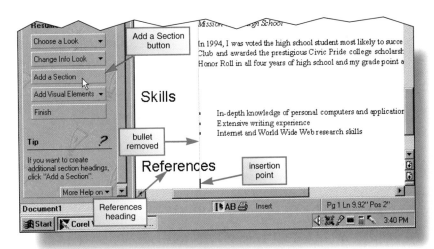

FIGURE 2-43

2 **Type** Carol Packard, Instructor, California College, Los Angeles, California **and then press the ENTER key. Type** Bob Robertson, Owner, Bob's Burgers, El Toro, California **and then press the ENTER key.**

Two references display in the completed resume (Figure 2-44).

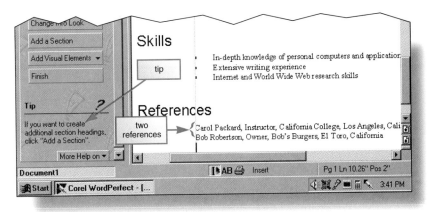

FIGURE 2-44

Finishing the Resume

When the resume is complete, correct any misspelled words, save the resume on the Corel WordPerfect 8 Files floppy disk using the Kate Summers Resume filename, and print it on the printer. To perform these operations, either follow the steps explained in Project 1 to spell check, save, and print a document or use the **Finish template** included with PerfectExpert. In this project, misspelled words will be corrected using the techniques illustrated in Project 1, and the resume will be saved and printed using the Finish template.

Using the Finish Template

Click the Finish button on the PerfectExpert panel to start the Finish template. Perform the steps on the next page to use the Finish template.

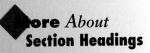

ore *About* **Section Headings**

To give a potential employer an unbiased look at your qualifications, section headings containing personal information (age, height, weight, gender, physical appearance, health, and marital status) should not be included in your resume. Many modern-day resume guides recommend the statement, References will be provided upon request, in place of the References section.

Steps To Use the Finish Template

1 Point to the Finish button on the PerfectExpert panel.

A QuickTip displays with the message, Save, check for types, create an HTML version, and print (Figure 2-45).

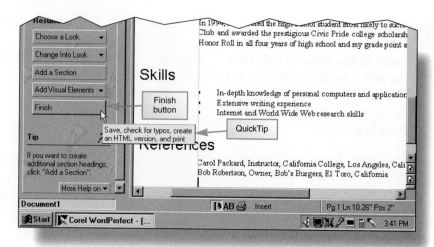

FIGURE 2-45

2 Click the Finish button.

WordPerfect replaces the five buttons (Choose a Look, Change Info Look, Add a Section, Add Visual Elements, and Finish) on the PerfectExpert panel with the Check the Spelling, Make It Fit, Save, Print, and Save in Other Format buttons and displays a new Tip. (Figure 2-46).

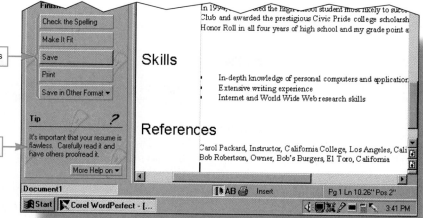

FIGURE 2-46

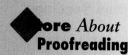

More *About* Proofreading

It is important that a resume be error free. Use Spell Checker and Grammatik to check for misspelled words and problems in grammar. Create and proofread your resume, set the resume aside for several days, and then proofread the resume again. Ask a parent, friend, or teacher to proofread your resume also.

Correcting Misspelled Words in the Resume

In Project 1, you spell checked a document by right-clicking each word that had red diagonal lines below it and either skipping the word in the remainder of the document or selecting a replacement word. Another method of checking the spelling of a document is to click the **Check the Spelling button** on the PerfectExpert panel. Clicking the button starts the **WordPerfect Spell Checker**. The Spell Checker checks from the beginning of the document to the end of the document for words not found in the WordPerfect Dictionary. The WordPerfect Spell Checker will not be used to spell check the resume in this project but will be explained in detail in Project 3.

Check the resume in this project for incorrectly spelled words by right-clicking each word in the resume that has red diagonal lines below it. Then either skip the word in the remainder of the resume or select a replacement word.

Saving the Resume

After spell checking the resume, save the document on the Corel WordPerfect 8 Files floppy disk created in Project 1 by using the **Save button** on the PerfectExpert panel. Perform the following steps to save the resume.

 Steps To Save the Resume

1 Insert the Corel WordPerfect 8 Files floppy disk into drive A, and point to the Save button on the PerfectExpert panel (Figure 2-47).

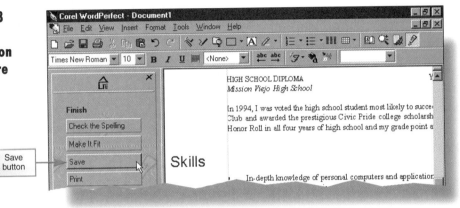

FIGURE 2-47

2 Click the Save button. When the Save As dialog box displays, type Kate Summers Resume in the File name box. Click the Save in box arrow, scroll the Save in list until 3½ Floppy (A:) displays, and click 3½ Floppy (A:). Point to the Save button.

The Kate Summers Resume filename displays in the File name box, the 3½ Floppy (A:) entry displays in the Save in box, and the mouse pointer points to the Save button (Figure 2-48). Additional files may display in the list box on your computer.

3 Click the Save button.

WordPerfect displays an hourglass icon while saving the Kate Summers Resume.wpd document on the floppy disk in drive A, closes the Save As dialog box, and replaces the Document1 entry in the Corel WordPerfect window title with the A:\Kate Summers Resume.wpd (unmodified) entry.

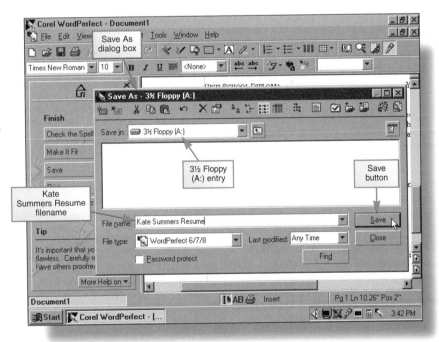

FIGURE 2-48

Printing the Resume

After saving the resume, print the document on the printer. Perform the following steps to print the document using the Print button on the PerfectExpert panel.

Steps To Print the Resume

1 **Point to the Print button on the PerfectExpert panel (Figure 2-49).**

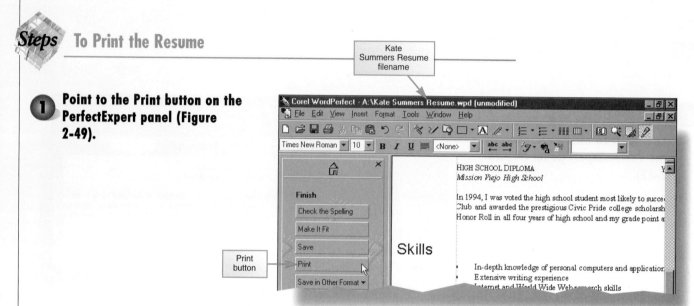

FIGURE 2-49

2 **Click the Print button. Click the Print tab in the Print to dialog box. Point to the Print button.**

WordPerfect displays the Print to dialog box (Figure 2-50). Check to ensure the Full document option button is selected and the number 1 displays in the Number of copies text box.

3 **Click the Print button. When printing is complete, retrieve the document.**

The Corel WordPerfect window, containing the current status of the print operation (Preparing Document), displays momentarily and then the document is printed as shown in Figure 2-2 on page WP 2.6.

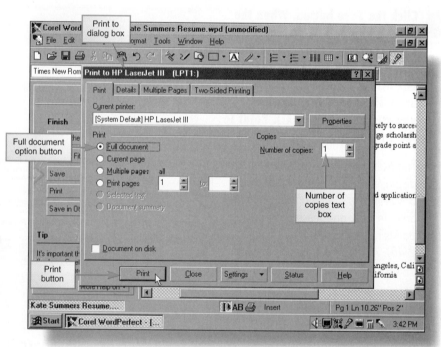

FIGURE 2-50

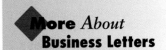
Removing the PerfectExpert Panel and Closing the Document

After saving and printing the resume, remove the PerfectExpert panel and close the document window.

TO REMOVE THE PERFECTEXPERT PANEL AND CLOSE THE DOCUMENT

1 Click the PerfectExpert button on the Toolbar.

2 Click File on the menu bar and then click Close on the File menu.

WordPerfect removes the PerfectExpert panel and closes the Kate Summers Resume document.

> **More** *About* **Business Letters**
>
> The appearance of any business letter is important. To capture the attention of the reader, the letterhead should be attractive and contain appealing graphic elements. The letter should contain all the basic business letter components in a visually pleasing arrangement, correct spelling, proper grammar, and concisely worded sentences.

he Cover Letter

Previously in this project, you created a personalized resume to send to prospective employers. The next step is to create a cover letter to attach to the resume. The **cover letter** allows you to emphasize the strong points in your resume and gives the reader an opportunity to see your written communication skills. Cover letters usually contain a personalized letterhead. The **letterhead** is the information at the top of the letter that contains the name, address, and phone number of the sender. Graphics, such as horizontal lines and bars, and different fonts enhance the appearance of a letterhead. The following pages illustrate how to use PerfectExpert to create and personalize a cover letter.

Components of a Business Letter

During your professional career, you will create many business letters. A cover letter is one type of business letter. Every business letter contains the same basic components—date line, inside address, salutation, message, complimentary close, and signature block (Figure 2-51).

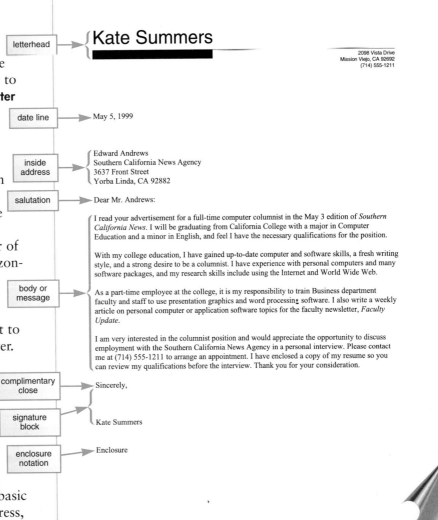

FIGURE 2-51

More *About*
the Inside Address

Check and recheck the spelling and punctuation in the inside address. Verify the name, company name, and address are correct and complete. If you are uncertain of the gender of the recipient, contact the company to find out. Check all abbreviations used in the inside address. If necessary, call the business to verify this information.

The **date line** consists of the month, day, and year the letter is written and is positioned two to six lines below the letterhead. Next, the **inside address** usually contains the addressee's full name and title; business affiliation and address and can be placed three to eight lines below the date. The **salutation** (Dear recipient's name:) begins two lines below the inside address.

The body of the letter, or message, begins two lines below the salutation. The lines within each paragraph are single-spaced and the paragraphs are double-spaced. Two lines below the body of the letter is the **complimentary close** (Sincerely, Yours truly, and so on). The **signature block** is typed at least four lines below the complimentary close. An **enclosure notation**, typed three lines below the signature block, indicates an additional document or documents are included with the letter.

The letter in this project will use mixed punctuation and the full block letter style. **Mixed punctuation** requires a colon after the salutation (Dear Mr. Andrews:) and a comma after the complimentary close (Sincerely,).

Creating a Cover Letter Using PerfectExpert

PerfectExpert steps you through the process of creating a letter. In the process, you will select a category and project, letterhead style (simple, traditional, contemporary, cosmopolitan, or elegant), select a business letter style (full block, modified block, semiblock, or simple), and enter personalized information (inside address, salutation, body, and closing).

More *About*
Salutations

Salutations such as, Dear Sir and To whom it may concern, should not be used. If you are unsure of the name and gender of an individual, use his or her title in the salutation. The salutation, Dear Personnel Director, is preferred over the impersonal salutations mentioned above. If you are writing to a company and do not have an individual's name for the salutation, Ladies and Gentlemen is acceptable.

To create the cover letter in this project, you will select the **Business Correspondence category, Business Letter project**, contemporary letterhead style, and full block letter style. Based upon your choices and the information you supply, PerfectExpert creates the letter, displays the letter on the screen, and allows you to enter personalized information. When you have finished, check for incorrectly spelled words, save the document, and print the document. The steps on the following pages use PerfectExpert to create the cover letter shown in Figure 2-51 on the previous page.

Adding the Recipient's Name to the Address Book

Before you create the cover letter, you should add the name and address of the individual to whom the cover letter is being sent to the Address Book. Perform the following steps to add the name, Edward Andrews, to the Address Book.

More *About*
Enclosures

If a document contains multiple enclosures, place the total number of enclosures in parenthesis (Enclosures 3). Multiple enclosures also can be numerically listed and described (Enclosures: Quarterly Report (next line contains the second entry; align the enclosure itemizations at the first letter following the colon). If an enclosure is mailed separately, the enclosure should indicate a separate mailing and a description (Separate mailing: Yearly Profits Report).

TO ADD A NAME TO THE ADDRESS BOOK

1. Click Tools on the menu bar.
2. Click Address Book.
3. If necessary, click the My Addresses tab. Click the Add button on the My Addresses sheet.
4. Click the OK button in the New Entry dialog box.
5. If necessary, click the Personal tab. Type Edward in the First name text box. Press the TAB key. Type Andrews in the Last name text box.
6. Select the Address text box and then type 3637 Front Street in the text box.
7. Select the City text box and then type Yorba Linda in the text box.
8. Select the State/Province text box and then type CA in the text box.
9. Select the Zip/Postal code text box and then type 92882 in the text box.

⑩ Select the Greetings text box and then type Dear Mr. Andrews in the text box.

⑪ Select the OK button in the New Person Properties dialog box.

⑫ Click the Close button in the Corel Address Book dialog box.

WordPerfect opens the Corel Address Book dialog box, adds the Edward Andrews entry to the Address book, and closes the Corel Address Book dialog box.

Selecting a Category and Project

Next, select the Business Correspondence category and Business Letter project to start the process of creating the cover letter. Perform the following steps to select the Business Correspondence category and Business Letter project.

TO SELECT A CATEGORY AND PROJECT

① Click File on the menu bar.

② Click New.

③ Click the Category box arrow in the New dialog box.

④ Click Correspondence, Business in the Category list.

⑤ Click Letter, Business in the list box.

⑥ Click the Create button in the New dialog box.

WordPerfect displays the New dialog box, displays the Category drop-down list, highlights the Correspondence, Business category in the list, displays the projects in the Business Correspondence category, highlights the Letter, Business project, displays the Letter panel, and displays the Letter PerfectExpert dialog box on top of a sample business letter (Figure 2-52).

The Letter PerfectExpert panel shown in Figure 2-52 contains the Letter project name, a list of pre-written letters, and several buttons. Although not visible, the sample business letter displays in the default letterhead style (Traditional) and business letter style (Full Block). The Letter PerfectExpert dialog box contains the Select element to modify box, the To area containing two text boxes, and the Address Book, Finished, Cancel, and Zoom buttons.

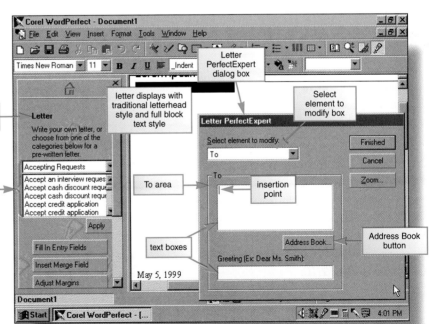

FIGURE 2-52

Creating the Cover Letter

Currently, the insertion point is located in the To text box. Continue the creation of the business letter by using the Edward Andrews entry in the Address Book to display the recipient's name and address (inside address) in the first text box and display the greeting in the second text box. Then, verify that the Kate Summers entry in the Address Book will be used for the personal information, select the Contemporary letterhead style, and select an enclosure notation. Perform the following steps to accomplish these tasks.

Steps **To Customize the Cover Letter**

① **Point to the Address Book button (Figure 2-53).**

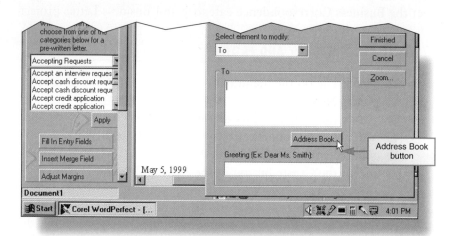

FIGURE 2-53

② **Click the Address Book button. Click the Edward Andrews entry in the Select Letter Recipient window. Point to the Select button.**

WordPerfect displays the Select Letter Recipient window and highlights the Edward Andrews entry in the list box (Figure 2-54). The Select Letter Recipient window in Figure 2-54 is similar to the Corel Address Book window illustrated in Figure 2-10 on page WP 2.10.

FIGURE 2-54

③ Click the Select button. Position the insertion point following the Edward Andrews name in the first text box, press the ENTER key to insert a blank line, and type Southern California News Agency **as the business name. Point to the Select element to modify box arrow.**

The inside address displays in the first text box in the To area and body of the letter, and the salutation displays in the second text box and the body of the letter (Figure 2-55).

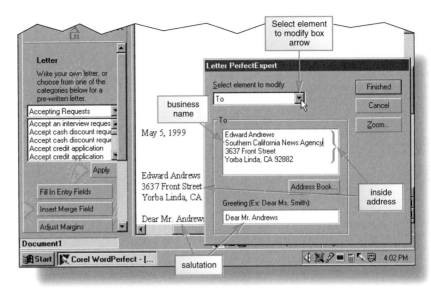

FIGURE 2-55

④ Click the Select element to modify box arrow and then point to From.

The Select element to modify drop-down list displays (Figure 2-56). The From element is highlighted in the list box.

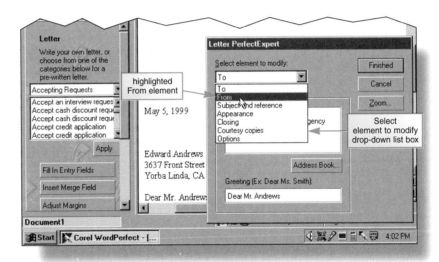

FIGURE 2-56

⑤ Click From. Point to the Select element to modify box arrow.

The highlighted From element displays in the Select element to modify box and the From area replaces the To area (Figure 2-57). The name, Kate Summers, displays in the From area to indicate Kate Summers's personal information will be used to create the cover letter. The business name (Southern California News Agency) is added to the inside address in the letter.

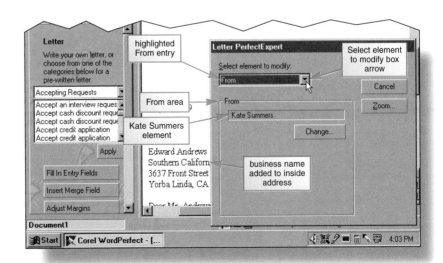

FIGURE 2-57

Click the Select element to modify box arrow and then point to Appearance.

The Select element to modify drop-down list box displays (Figure 2-58). The Appearance element is highlighted in the list box.

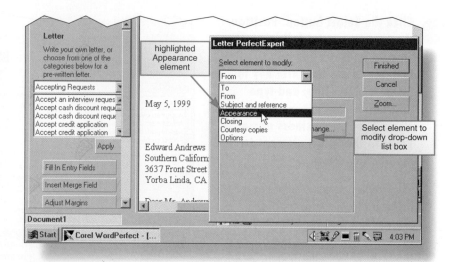

FIGURE 2-58

Click Appearance. Point to the Letterhead style box arrow.

When you click Appearance, the highlighted word, Appearance, displays in the Select element to modify box and the Appearance area displays (Figure 2-59). The default letterhead style (Traditional) displays in the Letterhead style box, the default text format (Full Block) displays in the Text format box, and a message displays describing the text format. The default letterhead style and text format may be different on your computer.

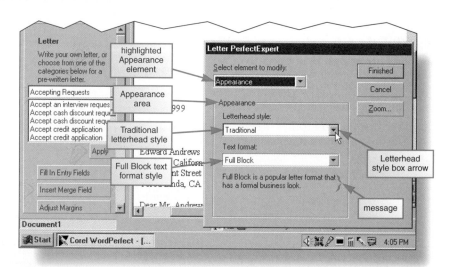

FIGURE 2-59

Click the Letterhead style box arrow and then point to Contemporary.

WordPerfect displays the Letterhead style drop-down list box and highlights the Contemporary element in the list (Figure 2-60).

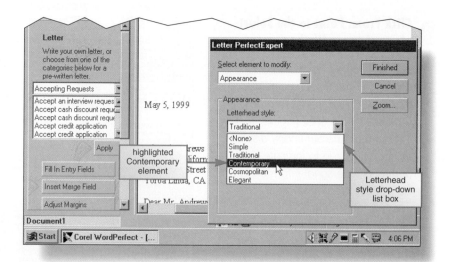

FIGURE 2-60

9 **Click Contemporary. Point to the Select element to modify box arrow.**

When you click Contemporary, the highlighted word, Contemporary, displays in the Letterhead style box and WordPerfect formats the sample business letter using the Contemporary style (Figure 2-61).

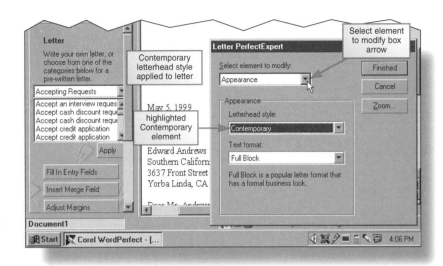

FIGURE 2-61

10 **Click the Select element to modify box arrow and then point to Closing.**

The Select element to modify drop-down list box displays (Figure 2-62). The Closing element is highlighted in the list.

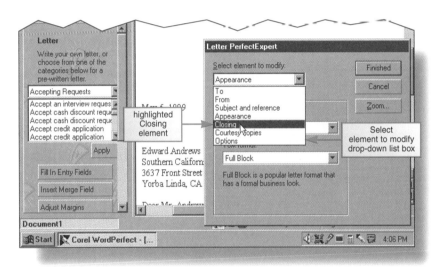

FIGURE 2-62

11 **Click Closing. Click the Enclosure(s) check box. Point to the Finished button.**

WordPerfect displays the word, Closing, in the Select element to modify box, displays a check mark in the Enclosure(s) check box, and adds an enclosure notation to the sample business letter (Figure 2-63).

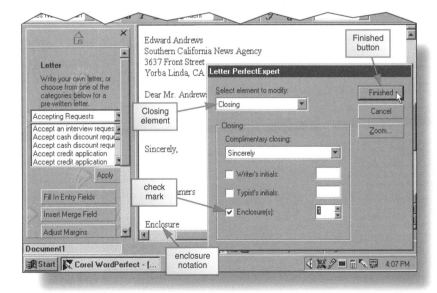

FIGURE 2-63

12 Click the Finished button.

WordPerfect displays the top portion of the business letter in the Corel WordPerfect - Document1 window (Figure 2-64). The insertion point displays between two markers to indicate where the body of the letter should be typed.

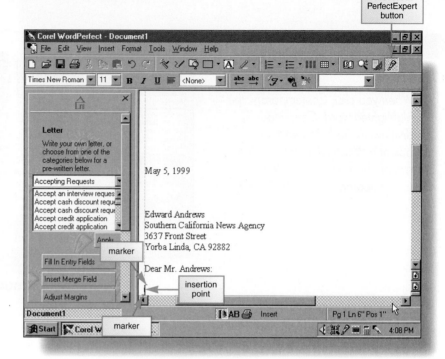

FIGURE 2-64

Removing the PerfectExpert Panel

After creating the business letter, remove the PerfectExpert panel to display more of the letter in the document window. The panel will be returned to the document window when you save and print the letter. Perform the following steps to remove the panel.

TO REMOVE THE PERFECTEXPERT PANEL

1. Point to the recessed PerfectExpert button on the Toolbar.
2. Click the PerfectExpert button.

WordPerfect removes the PerfectExpert panel, the PerfectExpert button is no longer recessed, the top portion of the letter is visible in the document window, and the marks indicating the area in which to type the body text are removed (Figure 2-65).

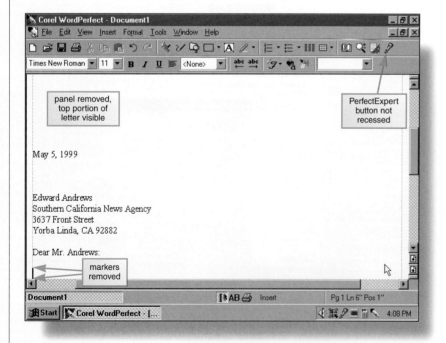

FIGURE 2-65

QuickCorrect Abbreviations

You can define a **QuickCorrect abbreviation** to speed up entering the body text. By defining an abbreviation as small as a single letter, you can replace single words, multiple words, or phrases. For example, you can define the abbreviation, wp, so that QuickCorrect inserts the word, WordPerfect, each time you type wp and press the SPACEBAR. QuickCorrect abbreviations are case-sensitive. If you define the abbreviation, so, for the word, software, and then type the letters, So, QuickCorrect inserts the word, Software. QuickCorrect also recognizes possessive forms of an abbreviated word. If you define the abbreviation, bob, for the word, Robert, and then type bob's, QuickCorrect displays the word, Robert's, in the document.

More *About*
QuickCorrect
Abbreviations

Be careful when creating abbreviations. In writing this book, the abbreviation, wp, was created to insert the word, WordPerfect. As a result, the abbreviation caused the page number to display incorrectly. When the page number, WP 2.1, was typed, the abbreviation caused the page number to incorrectly display as WordPerfect 2.1.

Typing the Body of the Cover Letter

The next step is to type the body of the cover letter. Perform the following steps to type the first two paragraphs in the body of the letter.

TO TYPE THE FIRST TWO PARAGRAPHS

1 Type I read your advertisement for a full-time computer columnist in the May 3 edition of Southern California News. I will be graduating from California College with a major in Computer Education and a minor in English, and feel I have the necessary qualifications for the position. and press the ENTER key.

2 Select the words, Southern California News, in the first paragraph, click the Italic button on the Property Bar, and click the second blank line following the paragraph.

3 Type With my college education, I have gained up-to-date computer and software skills, a fresh writing style, and a strong desire to be a columnist. I have experience with personal computers and many software packages, and my research skills include using the Internet and World Wide Web. and press the ENTER key.

The first and second paragraphs in the body of the letter display in the document window (Figure 2-66). The words, Southern California News Agency, in the first paragraph display in italics. Pressing the ENTER key after typing a paragraph inserts a blank line in the document and allows you to type on the line following the blank line.

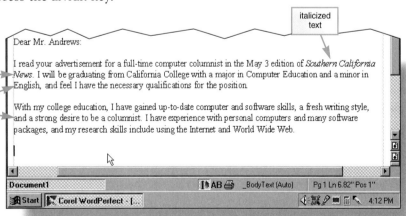

FIGURE 2-66

Creating a QuickCorrect Abbreviation

After typing the second paragraph, create a QuickCorrect abbreviation for the words, personal computers, in the second paragraph. A QuickCorrect abbreviation speeds up the entry of text by allowing you to create an abbreviation as small as a single letter. If you define the QuickCorrect abbreviation to be the two characters, pc, and then type pc and press the SPACEBAR, QuickCorrect replaces the characters you typed with the words, personal computer. Follow the steps below to create the QuickCorrect abbreviation.

 Steps To Create a QuickCorrect Abbreviation

1 **Select the words, personal computers, in the second paragraph. Click Tools on the menu bar. Point to QuickCorrect.**

WordPerfect highlights the words, personal computers, in the second paragraph, displays the Tools menu, and highlights the QuickCorrect command (Figure 2-67).

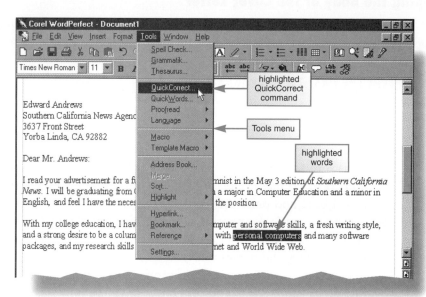

FIGURE 2-67

2 **Click QuickCorrect. Type pc in the Replace text box in the QuickCorrect dialog box.**

WordPerfect displays the Quick-Correct dialog box (Figure 2-68). The dialog box contains the Replace text box, With text box, and a list box containing the current abbreviations and associated word or words. The abbreviation, pc, displays in the Replace text box and the words, personal computers, display in the With text box.

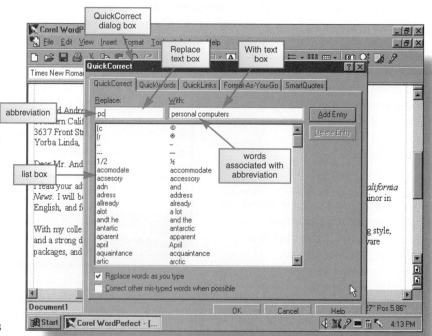

FIGURE 2-68

③ **Click to the right of the words, personal computers, in the With text box, press the BACKSPACE key to erase the s in the word, computers. Point to the Add Entry button.**

The letter s is removed from the word, computer, in the With text box (Figure 2-69).

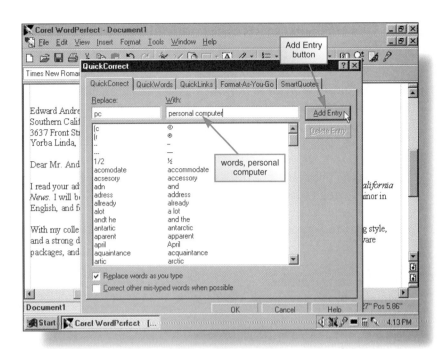

FIGURE 2-69

④ **Click the Add Entry button. Point to the OK button.**

WordPerfect adds the abbreviation, pc, and the associated words, personal computer, to the list box (Figure 2-70).

⑤ **Click the OK button.**

WordPerfect closes the QuickCorrect dialog box.

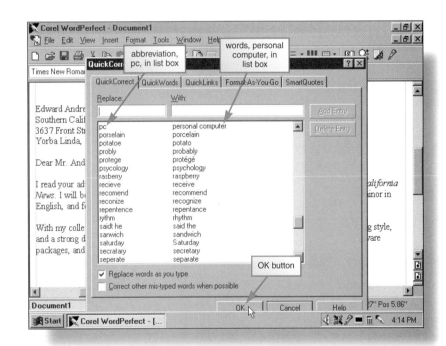

FIGURE 2-70

❯OtherWays

1. Press CTRL +SHIFT+F1, type appropriate entries in dialog box, click Add Entry button, click OK button

Inserting a QuickCorrect Entry

The next step is to enter the last two paragraphs in the body of the cover letter. In the process, you will use the QuickCorrect abbreviation (pc) in the next steps to simplify entering the words, personal computer, in the second sentence of the third paragraph.

Steps To Insert a QuickCorrect Entry

1 **Move the insertion point to the second blank line below the second paragraph. Type** As a part-time employee at the college, it is my responsibility to train Business department faculty and staff to use presentation graphics and word processing software. I also write a weekly article on pc **as the beginning of the paragraph.**

The beginning of the third paragraph and the QuickCorrect abbreviation, pc, display in the document window (Figure 2-71).

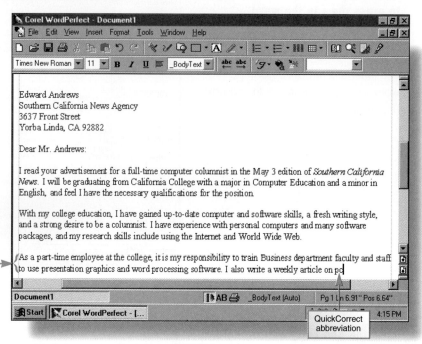

FIGURE 2-71

2 **Press the SPACEBAR.**

WordPerfect replaces the abbreviation, pc, with the words, personal computer (Figure 2-72).

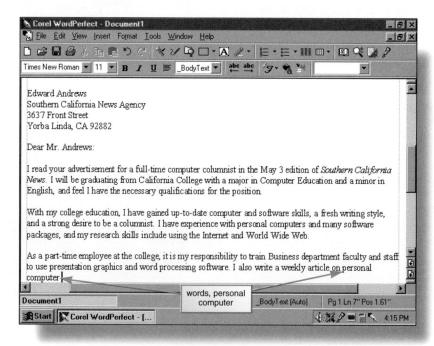

FIGURE 2-72

3 **Type** or application software topics for the faculty newsletter, Faculty Update. **and press the ENTER key. Select the words, Faculty Update, in the paragraph, click the Italic button on the Property Bar, and click the second blank line following the paragraph. Type** I am very interested in the columnist position and would appreciate the opportunity to discuss employment with the Southern California News Agency in a personal interview. Please contact me at (714) 555-1211 to arrange an appointment. I have enclosed a copy of my resume so you can review my qualifications before the interview. Thank you for your consideration. **as the last paragraph of the body of the letter.**

The last two paragraphs of the body of the cover letter display in the document window. (Figure 2-73)

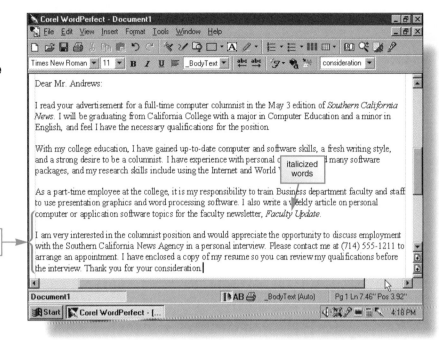

FIGURE 2-73

More *About* **Headers**

Detailed information about headers is available in Projects 3 and 5. In Project 3, you use a header to number the pages of a term paper. In Project 5, you use a header to number the pages of a newsletter. To find out more about headers, see the What You Should Know section at the end of each project.

Headers With Tables

The letterhead that displays at the top of the cover letter contains the name, address, and telephone number of Kate Summers (see Figure 2-74). The PerfectExpert displays the letterhead using the personal information from the Address Book and the contemporary letterhead style. To position the letterhead at the top of the document, PerfectExpert uses a header. A **header** is special text that displays at the top of printed pages in a document. Usually, a header contains the page number, titles, or other types of information, but in this project, you will enter other information. The dotted guidelines define the letterhead.

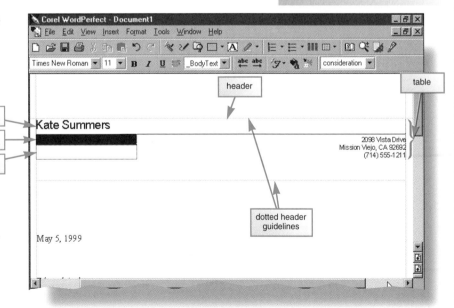

FIGURE 2-74

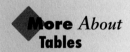

More About
Tables

Detailed information about tables is available in Project 4. In Project 4, you use a table to graphically present the costs of three vehicle maintenance services to new car buyers. To find out more about tables, see the What You Should Know section at the end of the project.

The PerfectExpert created a table within the header to organize the name, address, and telephone number. A **table** consists of **rows**, which run horizontally, and **columns**, which run vertically. Guidelines in the document window divide the table into rectangular areas called **cells**. A cell can contain text, a numeric value, or a mathematical formula. The columns, rows, and cells of the table in the letterhead have been manipulated to allow the placement of the name, address, and telephone number. The name, Kate Summers, displays left-justified in the first row. The second row contains a horizontal black bar at the beginning and the address and telephone number are right-justified at the end.

Additional information about creating and formatting the tables and header will be covered in later projects in this book.

Codes in the Cover Letter

When PerfectExpert creates the header containing the table, WordPerfect places codes in the document. To view these codes, open the Reveal Codes window and move the insertion point to different areas of the letter. The following section illustrates how to view the codes in the cover letter.

 To View the Codes in the Cover Letter

1 **Right-click the text area and then click Reveal Codes on the QuickMenu. Scroll the document window to display the top of the document and then click the text area to the left of the first character (the letter M) in the date.**

The Reveal Codes window opens and the insertion point displays to the left of the date (Figure 2-75). The Cntr Cur Pg code centers the text of the letter vertically on the page. The Top Mar code changes the top margin to .75 inch so the letterhead starts three-quarters of an inch from the top of the paper. The Header A code defines the header. The Font: Times New Roman and Font Size: 11pt codes set the default font and font size to Times New Roman 11-point font. If the letter requires more than one page, the Delay code causes the top margin to return to its default value (1") and the header not to print on the additional pages. The Date Fmt code controls the format of the date.

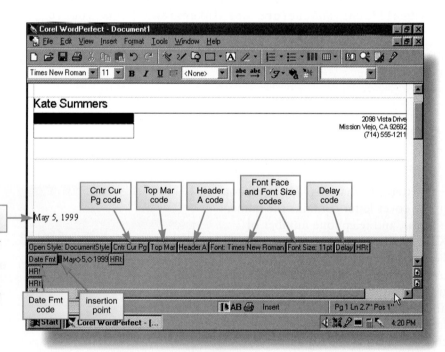

FIGURE 2-75

2 **Move the insertion point to the left of the Header A code in the Reveal Codes window.**

*The insertion point displays to the left of the expanded Header A code (Figure 2-76). Although not completely visible, the expanded Header A code contains the codes to set the default settings for the header (**Open Style code**), define the table (**Tbl Def code**) and control the format of text in the table using other Font and Font Size codes.*

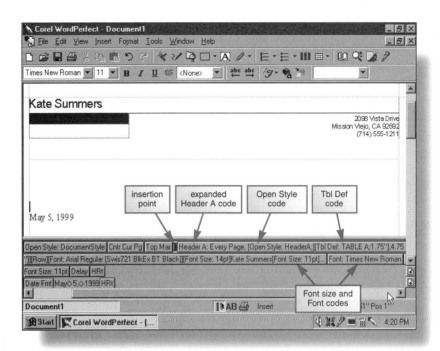

FIGURE 2-76

3 **Move the insertion point into the header by clicking the text area to the left of the first character (the letter K) in the letterhead.**

*The insertion point displays to the left of the name in the letterhead (Figure 2-77). All the codes in the Header A code display in the Reveal Codes window. These codes include the Open Style code, **Table Definition code**, Font codes, Row codes, and Cell codes. A **Row code** displays for each row in the table and a Cell code displays for each cell in the table. The TABLE A Cell A1 entry on the General Status button indicates the insertion point is located in cell A1 (first row, first column) in Table A (first table).*

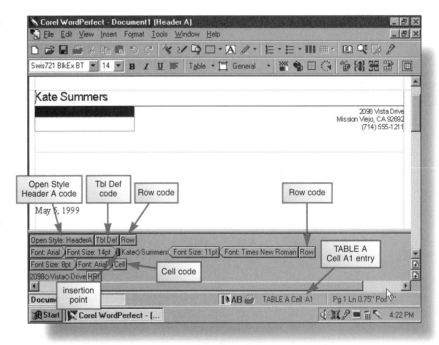

FIGURE 2-77

4 Scroll the document window to display the third paragraph in the body of the letter. Move the insertion point to the beginning of the second line in the third paragraph.

Two Para Style: Auto _BodyText *codes display in the paragraph, and the text between the codes is formatted using the* Auto _BodyText *style (Figure 2-78). The Style code changes the spacing between paragraphs to 2.0-inch, which allows you to press the ENTER key once instead of twice to insert a blank line between the paragraphs and begin the next paragraph. The _Body Text(Auto) entry on the General Status button and the _Body Text entry in the Select Style Box on the Property Bar indicates the style used to format the paragraph.*

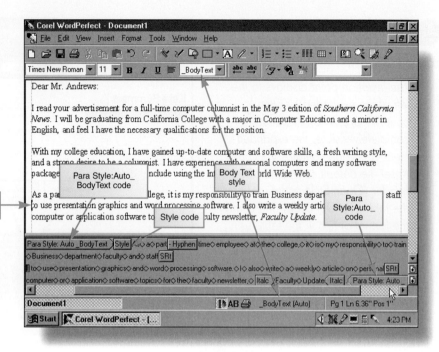

FIGURE 2-78

5 Right-click the text area and then click Reveal Codes on the QuickMenu.

WordPerfect closes the Reveal Codes window.

Personalizing the Cover Letter

First, format the name, Kate Summers, by changing the font size to 28 point. Next, change the width of the horizontal black bar below the name to match the width of the name. Last, change the font size of the body text to 12 point. The following steps show how to personalize the cover letter.

Steps To Personalize the Cover Letter

1 **Scroll the document window to display the name, Kate Summers, at the top of the window. Select the name, Kate Summers, in the letterhead. Click the Font size box arrow on the Property Bar. Click 28. Click inside the text to remove the highlight. Point to the dotted vertical line (column line) below the right side of the horizontal black bar to change the mouse pointer to a vertical bar with a horizontal two-headed arrow.**

The name, Kate Summers, changes to the 28-point font size, and a vertical bar with a horizontal two-headed arrow displays on the dotted vertical line, or column line, in the document window (Figure 2-79).

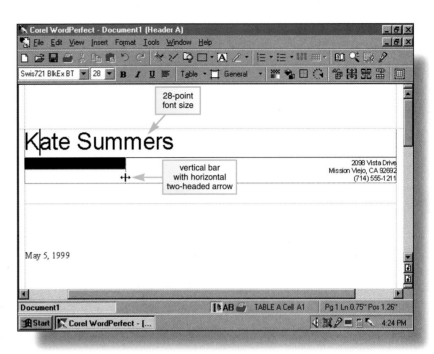

FIGURE 2-79

2 **Hold down the left mouse button.**

When you hold down the left mouse button, an extended column line and a QuickTip display (Figure 2-80). The two entries in the Quick-Tip (1.75" and 4.75") indicate the distance of the column line from the left margin (1.75") and the right margin (4.75").

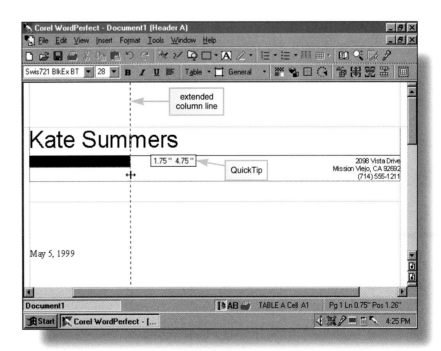

FIGURE 2-80

3 Drag the column line until the QuickTip contains 2.56" and 3.94". Release the mouse button.

WordPerfect removes the extended column line and QuickTip and extends the length of the horizontal bar (Figure 2-81).

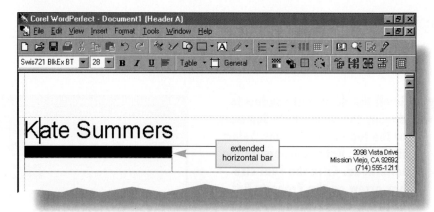

FIGURE 2-81

4 Click any area outside the letterhead to move the insertion point into the body of the letter. Click Edit on the menu bar, point to Select, and then point to All.

WordPerfect opens the Edit menu, highlights the **Select command,** opens the Select submenu, and highlights the **All command** on the Select submenu (Figure 2-82).

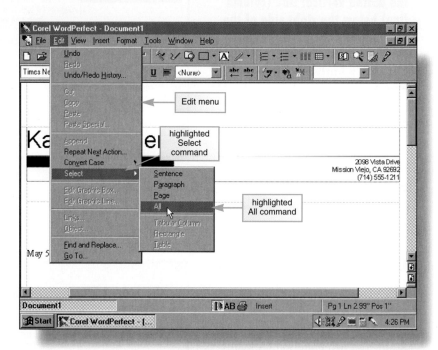

FIGURE 2-82

5 Click All. Click the Font size box arrow on the Property Bar. Click 12 in the Font size list box. Click inside the text to remove the highlight.

All text in the body of the letter displays in 12-point font size (Figure 2-83).

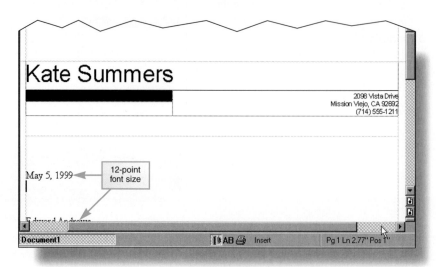

FIGURE 2-83

Finishing the Letter Project

When the letter is complete, correct any misspelled words in it, and then save the letter on the Corel WordPerfect 8 Files floppy disk in drive A using Mr. Andrews Letter as the filename. Print the letter on the printer. In this project, misspelled words will be corrected using the techniques illustrated in Project 1 and the letter will be saved and printed using the Finish template.

Check the letter for incorrectly spelled words by right-clicking each word in the letter that has red diagonal lines below it and either skip the word in the remainder of the letter or select a replacement word.

Perform the following steps to display the PerfectExpert panel, save the letter, and print it.

TO DISPLAY THE PERFECTEXPERT PANEL

① Click the PerfectExpert button on the Toolbar.

WordPerfect displays the PerfectExpert panel in the document window and recesses the PerfectExpert button.

Next, use the Finish template to save and print the letter by performing the following steps.

TO SAVE THE COVER LETTER

① Verify the Corel WordPerfect 8 Files floppy disk is in drive A.
② Scroll the PerfectExpert panel to display the Finish button.
③ Click the Finish button to display the Finish menu.
④ Click the Save button on the PerfectExpert panel. When the Save As dialog box displays, type Mr. Andrews Letter in the File name box. Click the Save in box arrow and scroll the Save in list until 3½ Floppy (A:) displays. Then click 3½ Floppy (A:) and click the Save button.

WordPerfect saves the Mr. Andrews Letter.wpd document on the floppy disk in drive A, closes the Save As dialog box, and replaces the Document1 entry in the Corel WordPerfect window title with A:\Mr. Andrews Letter.wpd (unmodified).

After saving the letter, print the document on the printer. Perform the following steps to print the document by using the Print button on the Finish menu.

TO PRINT THE COVER LETTER

① Click the Finish button on the PerfectExpert panel.
② Click the Print button on the Finish menu.
③ Click the Print tab in the Print to dialog box.
④ Click the Print button. When printing is complete, retrieve the document.

The Corel WordPerfect window, which contains the current status of the print operation (Preparing Document), displays momentarily and then the document is printed as illustrated in Figure 2-1 on page WP 2.6.

More *About* Printing

Print the cover letter and resume on standard letter-size white or ivory paper. Print a copy for yourself, send the cover letter and resume to potential employers, and then read both documents immediately before an interview. The interviewer will have a copy of both documents and generally will ask questions about their contents.

Removing the PerfectExpert Panel

After saving and printing the letter, remove the PerfectExpert panel.

TO REMOVE THE PERFECTEXPERT PANEL

① Click the PerfectExpert button on the Toolbar.

WordPerfect removes the PerfectExpert panel.

Multiple Document Windows

WordPerfect allows you to have multiple document windows open within the Corel WordPerfect window. Currently, the cover letter displays in the first document window in the Corel WordPerfect window. To open the Kate Summers Resume document and switch between the two documents, perform the steps described below and in the paragraphs on the following pages.

Working with Multiple Document Windows

If, after creating the cover letter, you want to view both the cover letter and the resume, you can open the file containing the resume (Kate Summers Resume.wpd) and display this document in a second document window. Perform the following steps to open the Kate Summers Resume.wpd file using the File menu.

More *About*
Multiple Document Windows

To view multiple windows at the same time, cascade or tile the windows using commands on the Window menu. Cascaded windows display on top of each other in an organized manner. Tiled windows display so that a portion of each window is visible. To switch between windows, click the part of the window that is visible.

Steps **To Open a Document**

① **Click File on the menu bar and point to Kate Summers Resume.wpd.**

WordPerfect displays the File menu (Figure 2-84). The Kate Summers Resume.wpd filename displays at the bottom of the File menu.

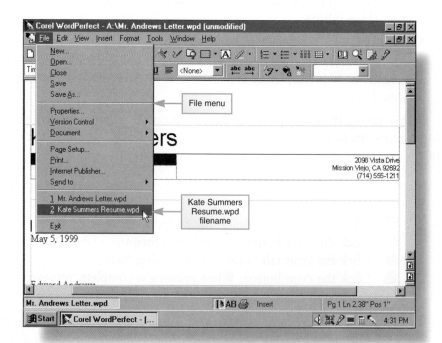

FIGURE 2-84

2 Click Kate Summers Resume.wpd.

*WordPerfect opens the
Kate Summers Resume.wpd file
and displays the resume
in a second document
window (Figure 2-85).*

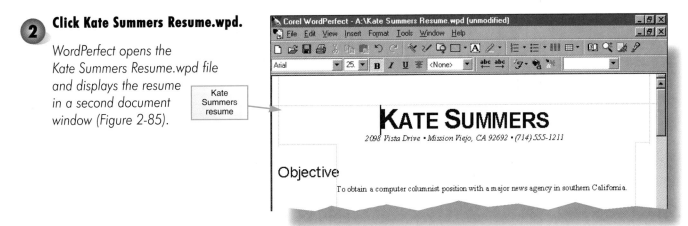

Kate
Summers
resume

FIGURE 2-85

Switching Between Document Windows

Currently, the resume displays in the document window in the Corel WordPerfect window. If you wish to view the cover letter in the other document window, you can easily display the cover letter by opening the first document window. Perform the following steps to open the first document window and display the cover letter.

Steps To Switch Between Document Windows

1 Point to the Mr. Andrews
Letter.wpd button on the
Application Bar (Figure 2-86).

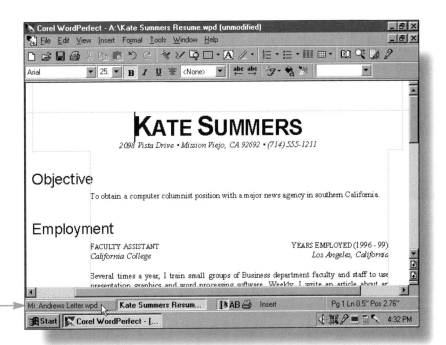

Mr. Andrews
Letter.wpd
button

FIGURE 2-86

2 **Click the Mr. Andrews Letter.wpd button.**

WordPerfect displays the cover letter, which is the Mr. Andrews Letter.wpd file (Figure 2-87). You may review or change the cover letter as necessary.

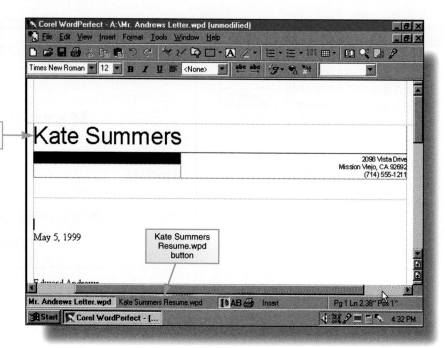

FIGURE 2-87

3 **To display the resume again, click the Kate Summers Resume.wpd button on the Application Bar.**

WordPerfect displays the resume again (Figure 2-88).

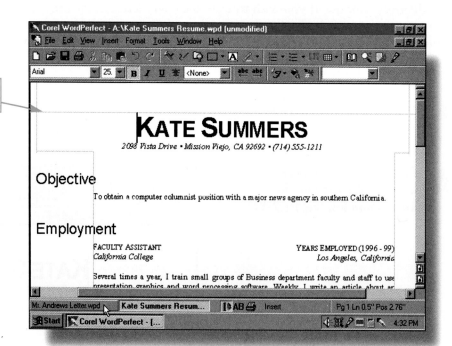

FIGURE 2-88

Other Ways

1. Click Window on the menu bar, click filename
2. Click anywhere on document window if visible

The ability to work with documents in multiple document windows is an important feature of WordPerfect. This feature can be useful when you are creating two or more documents that contain related information.

Removing a Name from the Address Book

In a school environment, you always want to return the computer system to its original state before you quit your session with Windows. Therefore, before quitting WordPerfect, you should remove the Kate Summers and Edward Andrews entries from the Address Book and remove the QuickCorrect abbreviation (pc) you created earlier. Then quit WordPerfect and remove the Corel WordPerfect 8 Files floppy disk from drive A. Perform the following steps to remove the names, Kate Summers and Edward Andrews, from the Address Book.

TO REMOVE NAMES FROM THE ADDRESS BOOK

1. Click Tools on the menu bar.
2. Click Address Book.
3. If necessary, click the My Addresses tab. Click the Kate Summers entry in the list box.
4. Click the Remove button.
5. Click the Yes button in the Address Book - Question dialog box.
6. Click the Edward Andrews entry in the list box.
7. Click the Remove button.
8. Click the Yes button in the Address Book - Question dialog box.
9. Click the Close button in the Corel Address Book dialog box.

WordPerfect removes the Edward Andrews and Kate Summers entries from the Address Book.

Removing a QuickCorrect Abbreviation

Next, perform the following steps to delete the QuickCorrect abbreviation (pc) created in this project.

TO REMOVE A QUICKCORRECT ABBREVIATION

1. Click Tools on the menu bar.
2. Click QuickCorrect.
3. Scroll the list box to display the pc entry.
4. Click pc.
5. Click the Delete Entry button.
6. Click the Yes button in the Corel WordPerfect dialog box.
7. Click the OK button in the QuickCorrect window.

WordPerfect deletes the pc abbreviation.

Quitting WordPerfect

When you have finished these tasks, quit WordPerfect by clicking the Close button in the Corel WordPerfect window. Clicking the Close button closes both document windows and quits WordPerfect. Then, remove the Corel WordPerfect 8 Files floppy disk from drive A.

TO QUIT WORDPERFECT AND REMOVE THE COREL WORDPERFECT 8 FILES FLOPPY DISK

1 Click the Close button in the Corel WordPerfect window.

2 Remove the Corel WordPerfect 8 Files floppy disk from drive A.

WordPerfect closes the Kate Summers Resume and Edward Andrews Letter documents, closes the Corel WordPerfect window, and the WordPerfect Document Files floppy disk is removed from drive A.

Project Summary

In this project, you added a name to the Address Book and created a resume and cover letter using Perfect-Expert. While creating the resume, you added a name to the Address Book, used the Contemporary resume style, added a section heading, selected and replaced prompts with personalized information, and learned about headers and tables. While creating the cover letter, you learned the parts of a business letter, added a name to the Address Book, created and used a QuickCorrect abbreviation, and used the contemporary letterhead style and full block text format. In addition, you viewed the codes in the resume and cover letter and learned to view two open documents using buttons on the Application Bar.

What You Should Know

Having completed this project, you now should be able to perform the following tasks:

- Add a name to the Address Book *(WP 2.8, WP 2.34)*
- Add additional skills to the bulleted list *(WP 2.28)*
- Apply a style to a resume *(WP 2.15)*
- Apply a style to the personal information *(WP 2.16)*
- Change the bottom margin*(WP 2.21)*
- Change the top margin *(WP 2.20)*
- Close the Document *(WP 2.52)*
- Create a QuickCorrect abbreviation *(WP 2.42)*
- Create a resume using PerfectExpert *(WP 2.11)*
- Create a section heading *(WP 2.29)*
- Customize the cover letter *(WP 2.36*
- Display the PerfectExpert panel *(WP 2.28, WP 2.51)*
- Format the name *(WP 2.22)*
- Insert a QuickCorrect entry *(WP 2.44)*
- Open a document *(WP 2.52)*
- Personalize the cover letter *(WP 2.49)*
- Print the cover letter *(WP 2.51)*
- Print the resume *(WP 2.32)*
- Quit WordPerfect and remove the Corel WordPerfect 8 Files floppy disk *(WP 2.56)*
- Remove a QuickCorrect abbreviation *(WP 2.55)*

- Remove names from the Address Book *(WP 2.55)*
- Remove the PerfectExpert panel *(WP 2.17, WP 2.33, WP 2.40, WP 2.52)*
- Save the cover letter *(WP 2.51)*
- Save the resume *(WP 2.31)*
- Select a category and project *(WP 2.35)*
- Select and replace the prompt for the bulleted item *(WP 2.27)*
- Select and replace the prompts for the first job *(WP 2.23)*
- Select and replace the prompts for the first school *(WP 2.25)*
- Select and replace the prompts for the second job *(WP 2.24)*
- Select and replace the prompts for the second school *(WP 2.26)*
- Start WordPerfect *(WP 2.7)*
- Switch between document windows *(WP 2.53)*
- Type the first two paragraphs *(WP 2.41)*
- Type the objective *(WP 2.22)*
- Use the Finish template *(WP 2.30)*
- View the codes in the cover letter *(WP 2.46)*
- View the codes in the resume *(WP 2.18)*

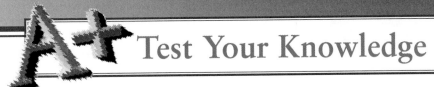 Test Your Knowledge

1 True/False

Instructions: Circle T if the statement is true or F if the statement is false.

T F   1. A resume summarizes an applicant's job experience, educational background, and qualifications.

T F   2. A cover letter is a predefined document that contains a customized format, customized content, and customized features.

T F   3. You can create either a letter or resume using PerfectExpert.

T F   4. A prompt tells you what information to type and where to type the information.

T F   5. The Resume template does not insert codes into the document.

T F   6. Personalizing a resume involves selecting a prompt and replacing the prompt with personalized information.

T F   7. A cover letter allows you to emphasize your strong points in the resume and gives the reader the opportunity to evaluate your written communication skills.

T F   8. When using mixed punctuation, you place a colon after the salutation.

T F   9. When you create a resume using PerfectExpert, the Finish template allows you to save and print the resume.

T F   10. WordPerfect does not allow two document windows to be open at the same time.

2 Multiple Choice

Instructions: Circle the correct response.

1. A _____ summarizes an applicant's job experience, educational background, and qualifications.
   a business letter   b. letterhead   c. resume   d. none of the above

2. To create a resume, _____.
   a. select a category and then select a project   c select only a project
   b. select a project and then select a category   d. select only a category

3. _____ is an application that lets you keep address information for many individuals in one place.
   a. Notepad   b. Corel WordPerfect   c. Address Book   d. Phone Book

4. A _____ tells you what information to type and where to type the information.
   a. template   b. property field   c. message   d. prompt

5. The format of a section heading is controlled by the _____.
   a. Para Style:_Style and Style codes   c. Bookmark code
   b. Tab Set code   d. Lft Mar and Rgt Mar codes

(continued)

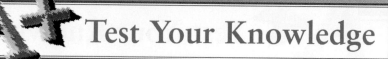

Test Your Knowledge

Multiple Choice *(continued)*

6. A _____ allows you to emphasize your strong points and gives the reader the opportunity to evaluate your written communication skills.
   a. letterhead
   b. cover letter
   c. resume
   d. business letter

7. The correct order of the complimentary close, date line, inside address, and salutation in a business letter is _____.
   a. date line, inside address, salutation, complimentary close
   b. date line, salutation, inside address, complimentary close
   c. inside address, dateline, salutation, complimentary close
   d. none of the above

8. To begin the process of creating a resume using PerfectExpert, click the _____.
   a. Create Letter QuickTask button
   c. File menu name on the menu bar
   b. Start button
   d. Tools menu name on the menu bar

9. To insert a QuickCorrect entry, type the abbreviation and then press the _____.
   a. INSERT key
   b. SPACEBAR
   c. F3 key
   d. ENTER key

10. To switch between two open document windows, you _____.
    a. click a button on the Application bar
    b. click Switch on the menu bar
    c. click File on the menu bar, and then click a filename on the File menu
    d. none of the above

3 Understanding the Components of a Business Letter

Instructions: In Figure 2-89, arrows point to various components of a business letter. Identify the components of the letter in the space provided.

 Test Your Knowledge

Kate Summers
2098 Vista Drive
Mission Viejo, CA 92692
(714) 555-1211

1. _____

2. _____ May 5, 1999

3. _____
Edward Andrews
Southern California News Agency
3637 Front Street
Yorba Linda, CA 92882

4. _____ Dear Mr. Andrews:

I read your advertisement for a full-time computer columnist in the May 3 edition of *Southern California News*. I will be graduating from California College with a major in Computer Education and a minor in English, and feel I have the necessary qualifications for the position.

With my college education, I have gained up-to-date computer and software skills, a fresh writing style, and a strong desire to be a columnist. I have experience with personal computers and many software packages, and my research skills include using the Internet and World Wide Web.

5. _____
As a part-time employee at the college, it is my responsibility to train Business department faculty and staff to use presentation graphics and word processing software. I also write a weekly article on personal computer or application software topics for the faculty newsletter, *Faculty Update*.

I am very interested in the columnist position and would appreciate the opportunity to discuss employment with the Southern California News Agency in a personal interview. Please contact me at (714) 555-1211 to arrange an appointment. I have enclosed a copy of my resume so you can review my qualifications before the interview. Thank you for your consideration.

6. _____ Sincerely,

7. _____ Kate Summers

8. _____

Enclosure

FIGURE 2-89

4 Understanding the New Dialog Box

Instructions: In Figure 2-90, arrows point to different elements of the New dialog box. Identify these various elements of the dialog box in the space provided.

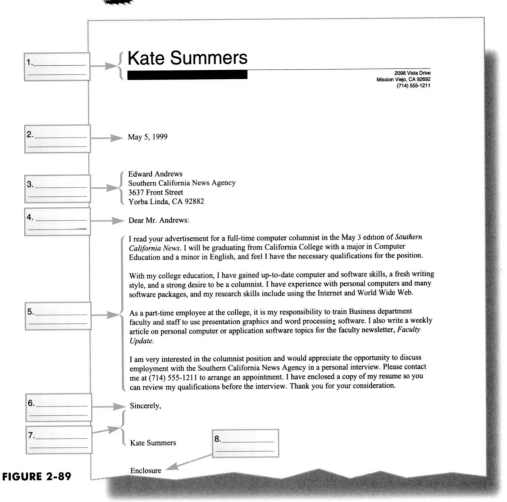
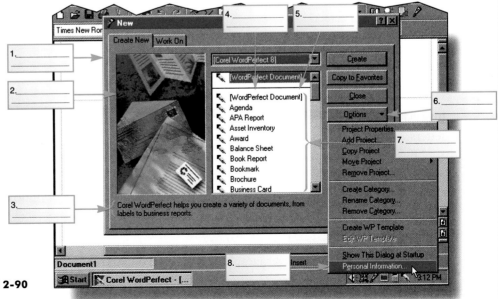

FIGURE 2-90

Use Help

1 Reviewing Project Activities

Instructions: Perform the following tasks on a computer.

1. Start WordPerfect.
2. Press the F1 key. Click the Contents tab. Double-click the How Do I book. Double-click the Create Documents book. Double-click the Correspondence book.
3. Double-click the Business Letters topic. Click the Create headers/footers for subsequent pages button. Read the information about headers and footers.
4. Scroll the topics list if necessary. Click the To edit a header or footer button. Read the information about editing a header or footer.
5. Click the Options button, click Print Topic, and click the OK button.
6. Click the Help Topics button. Scroll the list box to make the How Do I book visible. Double-click the How Do I book to close the book.
7. Double-click the What is Different book. Double-click the About Creating Documents book. Double-click The Address Book topic. Read the information about the Address Book.
8. Scroll the topics list if necessary. Click the To select addresses button. Click the Options button, click Print Topic, and click the OK button.
9. Click the Help Topics button. Click the Index tab. Type template and then double-click the about topic. Read the information about templates. Click the Options button, click Print Topic, and click the OK button.
10. Click the Help Topics button. Type table and then double-click the about tables topic. Read the information about tables.
11. Click the Help Topics button. Type quickcorrect and then double-click the abbreviation, about topic. Double-click the About QuickCorrect Abbreviations topic.
12. Click the Options button, click Print Topic, and click the OK button.
13. Close any open Help windows by clicking the Close buttons.
14. Quit WordPerfect.

2 Expanding on the Basics

Instructions: Perform the following tasks using a computer and answer the questions about business letters.

Business letters remain a common method of communication. To obtain additional information about them, start Help, double-click the Showcase Corel WordPerfect topic in the Contents sheet, and click the Ex Animo image in the upper left corner of the Examples window. Answer the following questions about business letters:

1. How do you create a business letter?
2. How do you format a paragraph by adjusting the margin of the paragraph?
3. How do you quickly create a horizontal line in a business letter?

The Application Bar displays information about open documents and allows you to switch between open documents. Using Help, answer the following questions about the Application Bar:

1. How do you add information to the Application Bar?
2. How do you drag information from one document to another?
3. How do you hide the Application Bar?

A resume is valuable when applying for your first job or a new job. Using Help, answer the following questions about creating your own resume without using PerfectExpert:

1. What feature do you use to check whether you are saying the right thing in a resume?
2. How do you quickly add a line across the page?
3. What feature do you use to make all headings look the same?

PerfectExpert is a tool that lets you select a project to perform common operations in WordPerfect. Answer the following questions about categories and projects.

1. What category contains the project to create a brochure?
2. What category contains the project to create a household inventory list?
3. What category contains the project to create a balance sheet?

1 Enhancing a Document

Instructions: Start WordPerfect and perform the following tasks:

Part 1: Create a Name and Address Entry

1. Click Tools on the menu bar and click Address Book. If necessary, click the My Addresses tab.
2. Click the Add button in the Corel Address Book window. Click the OK button in the New Entry dialog box.
3. Type Frank in the First name text box. Press the TAB key. Type Tanner in the Last name text box. Click the Address text box and type 3874 Fairview Drive in the text box.
4. Click the City text box and type Chicago in the text box. Click the State/Province text box and type IL in the text box. Click the Zip/Postal code text box and type 60601 in the text box.
5. Click the Phone Numbers tab. Click the Home phone text box and type (312) 555-1736 in the text box.
6. Click the OK button.
7. Click the Close button in the Corel Address Book window.

(continued)

Apply Your Knowledge

Enhancing a Document *(continued)*

Part 2: Insert an Address Entry in a Blank Document

1. Click Tools on the menu bar and click Address Book. If necessary, click the My Addresses tab.
2. Double-click the Frank Tanner entry in the Address Book.
3. Print a copy of the document containing Frank Tanner's name and address.

Part 3: Removing a Name from the Address Book

1. Click Tools on the menu bar and click Address Book. Click the My Addresses tab.
2. Click the Frank Tanner entry in the list box. Click the Remove button.
3. Click the Yes button in the Address Book - Question dialog box.
4. Click the Close button in the Corel Address Book window.
5. Quit WordPerfect. Do not save changes to the document.

In the Lab

1 Using PerfectExpert to Create a Resume

Problem: You are a senior at Orange College and expect to graduate with Bachelor of Science degree in information systems at the end of the semester. Close to the end of the semester, you begin to search for full-time employment. As the end of the semester approaches, you realize you need a resume. You prepare the resume shown in Figure 2-91 using PerfectExpert.

Instructions:

1. Create an entry in the Address Book using the name, address, and home telephone information for Peter Barnett shown in Figure 2-91.
2. Use PerfectExpert to create the resume. Use the traditional resume style. Use the Centered, With Bullets style for the personal information. Change the top and bottom margins to .5-inch.
3. Name the resume Peter Barnett Resume and save the resume on the Corel WordPerfect 8 Files floppy disk you created in Project 1.
4. Personalize the resume by increasing the font size of the name to 36 point and the address and telephone line to 12 point.
5. Personalize the resume by replacing each prompt with the information shown in Figure 2-91.
6. Add the three bulleted items in the Skills section.
7. Add the References section as shown in Figure 2-91.
8. Check the resume for misspelled words and correct the errors. Save the resume again using the same filename.

In the Lab

9. Print the resume on the printer.
10. If you do not plan to perform the In the Lab 2 assignment next, remove the Peter Barnett entry from the Address Book.

2 Using PerfectExpert to Create a Cover Letter

Problem: You have just prepared the resume shown in Figure 2-91 and now are ready to create a cover letter to send to a prospective employer. In last Sunday's edition of the *Northern California News*, you noticed an advertisement for a computer training position at Computer Trainers. You prepare the cover letter shown in Figure 2-92 on the next page to send with your resume.

Instructions:

1. If necessary, create an entry in the Address Book using the name, address, and telephone information for Peter Barnett shown in Figure 2-91.
2. Create an entry in the Address Book using the name, address, and telephone information for Sandra Peterson as shown in Figure 2-92 on the next page.
3. Use PerfectExpert to create the letter. Use the cosmopolitan letterhead style and full block letter style.
4. Personalize the letter by increasing the font size of the name to 32 point, the address and telephone to 12 point, and the body text to 12 point.
5. Check the letter for misspelled words and correct the errors.
6. Name the file Ms. Peterson Letter. Use the Finish template to save the letter on the Corel WordPerfect 8 Files floppy disk you created in Project 1 and print it on the printer.
7. Remove the Sandra Peterson and Peter Barnett entries from the Address Book.

PETER BARNETT

36784 Summerset Dr. • Irvine, CA 92583 • (714) 555-9839

OBJECTIVE

To obtain an application software training position, specializing in Corel WordPerfect Suite 8 software, with a major computer training company in northern California.

EMPLOYMENT

| SOFTWARE TRAINER | YEARS EMPLOYED (1996 - 99) |
| *New Beginnings* | *Los Angeles, California* |

Two days a week, I train small groups of business people to use Corel WordPerfect 8 and Corel Presentations 8 software.

| SALESMAN | YEARS EMPLOYED (1995 - 96) |
| *Software Unlimited* | *Mission Viejo, California* |

As a part-time employee, I demonstrated and sold various business software packages..

EDUCATION

| B.S. IN INFORMATION SYSTEMS | YEARS ATTENDED (1997 - 99) |
| *Orange College* | *El Toro, California* |

In 1997, I was awarded first place in the Information Systems examination. In 1999, I was named Information Systems student of the year. My estimated grade point average upon graduation from college is 3.9/4.0.

| A.A. IN BUSINESS | YEARS ATTENDED (1995 - 97) |
| *Placentia Community College* | *Placentia, California* |

In 1995, I was granted a two-year scholarship to Placentia Community College from the Henry R. Farnsworth Foundation. My graduating grade point average was 3.8/4.0.

SKILLS

- In-depth knowledge of personal computers and application software
- Extensive Internet and World Wide Web experience
- Fluency in two foreign languages (Russian and Japanese)

REFERENCES

Randy Truman, Instructor, Orange College, El Toro, California
Sally Maynard, Manager, New Beginnings, Los Angeles, California
Franklyn Peterson, Owner, Software Unlimited, Mission Viejo, California

FIGURE 2-91

In the Lab

Using PerfectExpert to Create a Cover Letter (*continued*)

3 Creating a Resume and Cover Letter

Problem: You recently registered with an employment agency to assist you in finding an employment opportunity in the computer field. You received a letter from the agency that included a copy of the advertisement shown in Figure 2-93.

The letter asked you to prepare a cover letter and resume to respond to the employment opportunity in the advertisement. You have the biographical information shown in Figure 2-94 to assist you in preparing the letter and resume.

Instructions:

1. Create an entry in the Address Book using the name, address, and telephone information for Angela Perez.

2. Use PerfectExpert to create the resume. Use the traditional resume style. Use the Centered, With Bullets style for the personal information. Change the top and bottom margins to .5-inch.

3. Personalize the resume as you wish.

4. Use bulleted items where appropriate.

Peter Barnett
36784 Summerset Dr.
Irvine, Ca 92583
(714) 555-9839

June 23, 1999

Sandra Peterson
Computer Trainers
3870 Business Park Drive
San Jose, CA 95100

Dear Ms. Peterson:

I am responding to your advertisement for a full-time computer trainer in the May 3 edition of *Northern California News*. I will be graduating from Orange College with a major in Information Systems and feel I have the necessary qualifications for the position.

While attending classes at Orange College, I gained up-to-date computer and application software skills and a strong desire to be a computer trainer. I have experience with personal computers and many software packages, and my research skills include using the Internet and World Wide Web.

My past employment experience includes demonstrating and selling business software packages at Software Unlimited. Currently, I work part-time at New Beginnings training small groups of business people to use Corel WordPerfect Suite 8.

I am interested in the computer trainer position and would appreciate the opportunity to discuss employment with Computer Trainers in a personal interview. Please contact me at (714) 555-9839 to arrange an appointment. I have enclosed a copy of my resume so you can review my qualifications before the interview. Thank you for your consideration.

Sincerely,

Peter Barnett

Enclosure

FIGURE 2-92

Personal Computer Software Installer
Individual needed to assist customers in the installation of word processing, spreadsheet, and database software. An understanding of how these applications work is essential. Please send resume to Mr. Sean Overton, Personnel Director, Computer System Services, 345 Fifth Avenue, Fullerton, California 91789.

FIGURE 2-93

In the Lab

5. Add a References section.

6. Check the resume for misspelled words and correct the errors.

7. Save and print the resume.

8. Use PerfectExpert to create the letter. Use the traditional letterhead and full block letter styles.

9. Personalize the letter as you wish.

10. Check the letter for misspelled words and correct the errors.

11. Save and print the letter.

12. Remove the Angela Perez entry from the Address Book.

Angela Perez

I was born in Sarnia Hills, Michigan on February 23, 1977. I graduated with honors from Sarnia Hills High School in 1995. I attended Southern Michigan University for four years and graduated in 1999 with a bachelor of arts degree. I majored in Computer Education. My grade point average for the four years I attended Southern Michigan University was 3.65/4.0.

During my first year at Southern Michigan University, I took first place in the Freshman Information Systems examination. This test is given at the end of the first semester. Any freshman student can take the exam. I was awarded first place and a complete set of Time-Life books on the subject of computers. During my last year at Southern Michigan University I was awarded the Robert Ford Software Application scholarship. This scholarship is awarded based on overall grade point average.

While attending the university, I took both introductory computer and software application classes. In the software application classes, I learned to use Windows 95-based word processing, database, and spreadsheet software. I completed each class successfully with a grade of A.

I worked as a computer laboratory assistant in the Information Systems Department the last two years I attended the university. Dr. Mack Stanton was my supervisor.

During the two summers before graduation, I worked in the business office at Southern Michigan University. My job responsibilities included composing business letters using Corel WordPerfect Suite 8 software and entering data into the Registration database. Mrs. Alice Ramirez was my supervisor. The two summers prior to that I worked for my father, who owns Perez Construction. I was the receptionist in his office. In addition to my receptionist duties, I entered and printed customer invoices.

My current address is 3694 Oak Avenue, Yorba Linda, California 92686. My telephone number is (714) 555-3022.

FIGURE 2-94

Cases and Places

The difficulty of these case studies varies: ❱ are the least difficult; ❱❱ are more difficult; and ❱❱❱ are the most difficult.

1 ❱ Ms. Allegro is the owner of Interior Designs, an interior design business. She would like all employees to use the same memo for interoffice communication. The memo should be very cosmopolitan and have entries that identify the sender, recipient, and subject of the memo. Send a memo with the new design to Ms. Allegro indicating you have designed a memo for the business and would like her opinion of the memo. Use PerfectExpert to create the memo.

Cases and Places

2 ▶ Your second year at the junior high school you volunteer as an office aid for the principal. The principal, Ms. Beard, would like certificates of excellence for the two eighth grade students graduating with 4.0 grade point averages. Both Michael Wong and Alicia Landers will receive certificates. Because you took computer classes last year, she asks you to design the certificates. She requests that each certificate contain the current date, description of achievement, Summa Cum Laude Graduate (4.0 GPA), and appropriate clipart, if available. When they are completed, she will sign each certificate. Use PerfectExpert to create the certificates.

3 ▶▶ Businesses use a variety of business letter styles to write business letters. In this project, a cover letter was created using the full block business letter style. Using the Internet, a library, or another resource, determine the three most widely used business letter styles. Write a brief report summarizing the characteristics of each business letter style. Then create one business letter and format it using each of the three business letter styles. Print the three business letters. On each printed letter, identify the features of each style.

4 ▶▶ The letterhead on a business letter draws the reader's attention to the letter. WordPerfect has five letterhead styles (simple, traditional, contemporary, cosmopolitan, and elegant). Using the Internet, a library, or another resource, determine what makes a good letterhead design. Write a brief report summarizing your findings. Then create one business letter using the full block style and format the letter using any three of the five WordPerfect letterhead styles. Print the three each business letters. Based upon your findings, indicate the good and bad points of letterhead style.

5 ▶▶▶ Microsoft Office Suite allows you to create a resume using Word's Resume Wizard. Visit a software store, friend's house, or local business to find a computer that has the Microsoft Office software installed. Use the Resume Wizard to create the resume illustrated in Figure 2-2 in this project. Write a brief report comparing the Resume Wizard and WordPerfect PerfectExpert.

6 ▶▶▶ Microsoft Word allows you to create a cover letter using a template. Visit a software store, friend's house, or local business to find a computer that has the Microsoft Word software installed. Use the Letter Template to create the cover letter illustrated in Figure 2-1 in this project. Write a brief report comparing the Letter Template and WordPerfect PerfectExpert.

7 ▶▶▶ You found the perfect used car (1966 Ford Mustang) for the perfect price ($6,500) and would like to finance the car through a bank. Contact three banks or other financial institutions to obtain the best interest rate for a 4-year (48-month) used car loan. Using the best interest rate, create a loan amortization using PerfectExpert and the Mortgage Amortization project. If necessary, use Help to understand the Quattro Pro 8 spreadsheet software used to create the amortization. Write a brief report explaining what information PerfectExpert requires to produce the amortization report, what the monthly payment (principal & interest payment) is, how much cumulative interest is paid, and the total amount of money that will be paid for the car

Corel WordPerfect 8

Creating a Term Paper

Objectives:

You will have mastered the material in this project when you can:

◗ Describe the MLA formatting standards for reports
◗ Display, hide, and move a Toolbar
◗ Set the top margin
◗ Use a header to number pages in a document
◗ Adjust the line spacing
◗ Insert the current date
◗ Center a line of text before typing
◗ Indent paragraphs
◗ Create footnotes and parenthetical citations
◗ Identify and insert soft and hard page breaks
◗ Create a Works Cited page
◗ Create a hanging indent
◗ Drag and drop text
◗ Find and replace text
◗ Use WordPerfect's Thesaurus and Spell Check
◗ Display document information
◗ Use shortcut keys to move the insertion point

The Two-Edged Sword of Time

"Time is the best teacher," a philosopher once wrote. "Unfortunately, it kills all its pupils." This tongue-in-cheek appraisal of a commodity that even Nobel laureates cannot properly define is a view shared by nearly everyone at some point.

The ancient Greeks acknowledged that time can be both friend and foe by creating two different words for it. *Chronos*, the root for English words such as chronometer and chronology, embodies the concept of "rush time," when hours seem like seconds. Paradoxically, you can perceive this phenomenon during a good experience or a bad one, such as the night of the senior prom or the hours before a young soldier goes into battle. *Kairos* reflects the perception that time can seem to slow down, for example, when you are absorbed totally in a creative endeavor such as composing music or writing a novel. Some refer to this latter state as "flow."

Doctor Wayne Dyer, noted modern philosopher and author of *Real Magic*, tells of an instance when he was playing tennis. An opponent's torrid serve appeared to

The Roman Empire
Term Paper

EMPERORS AND THE PAX ROMANUM

In 25 B.C. Julius Caesar's once obscure nephew Octavian and his lowlyborn General Agrippa, defeated Rome's golden boy, Marcus Antonius and his lover Cleopatra. Augustus then set about 'restoring' the Republic, though in fact he institutionalized the 'Imperium', a term that referred to his direct rule of a number of provinces (in particular the bread basket of the Mediterranean, Egypt). The term Imperium soon came to mean the absolute rule of Augustus over Rome and her provinces with a veneer of Republican democracy over it.

This Roman Empire world endured for fifteen hundred years (in various forms), bringing peace and prosperity to Europe until the fifth century. The reason this Pax Romanum ended so well... alone never found a proper method of... century, kept civil war more or less at bay... when decades of uninterrupted civil... Empire. Strong Emperors like Dio... brought brief periods of peace, but nothing could stem the tide of decay and the pending... rmanic Barbarians. By 400 A.D., the glory was gone, and by 476A.D., the last... of Emp... West went with it. The Eastern Empire went on for another thousand years, but for m... Europe, the... wing centuries were ones of chaosand violence known as the Dark Ages.

Rome, which had virtua... ME DU... THE REIGN

series of battles. Having defeat... up and defeated the mighty Carthaginian navy in a drained their own power fighti... rthaginians... the Hellenistic Kingdoms having long since War (219-202 B.C.), the brilli... ginian Genera... master of the Mediterranean. In the Second Punic and defeated the Romans in a... l marched into Italy at Cannae. But Hannibal, wh... win all the... massive bloodbath battles, could not win the... Romans fought a war... gic attrition and finally defeated the Cartha... at Zama (202 B.C.), ou... thage itself. Finally the in the Third... r (149 - 146 B.C.) the Rm... literated Carthage. By that time Rome had... spread its power beyond th... rn Mediterranean and gradually conqu... nce and the eastern Mediterran... werful began to

As Rome... however, the weapon that made... were kept on turn against her... holding farmers who made up the... l and bought campaign for... in their absence their holdings were fo... orm were... up by ari... ndowners and worked on by slaves. Attemp... by Sulla and his conservative allies. After victory, Sulla... he had opposed in war. The Legions became professional, their o...

CUT AND PASTE
DRAG AND DROP
FIND AND REPLACE

hang suspended in the air, giving Dr. Dyer time to reach the ball and return it. Police, firefighters, and others in high-stress situations have perceived this same quirk of suspended animation, or slow motion, which bears the tongue-twisting label **tachypsychia**.

College students understand perfectly the double edge of time. A school semester can seem like a life sentence when anticipating the fun of a summer break. Or it can flash by in a nanosecond when a term paper looms as a deadline. Imagine when students were using typewriters to assemble term papers. The mechanics of formatting, typing, and editing were major obstacles in the path of a superior grade. Correcting errors or rearranging text might have required numerous hours and reams of paper, as well as the major stress and worry as the deadline neared.

With Corel WordPerfect, you can construct a term paper that looks sharp and is easy to change, and you can do it quickly even when you need to rewrite, revise, and reorganize. WordPerfect gives you potent features for handling formatting details such as headers and footers, line spacing, and indentation. After supplying the paper's content based on your semester of hard work, you may decide that the document needs major revision. With WordPerfect, you can perform the operation with facility and precision using such powerful features as drag and drop, cut and paste, find and replace, Spell Check, and the WordPerfect Thesaurus.

While the next semester flashes — or drags — by, consider how you are influenced by the passing of time; whether you are on time or trying to beat the clock, you always will have the need for tools that will help you reach your objectives. In the words of John F. Kennedy, "We must use time as a tool, not as a couch."

Corel
WordPerfect 8

Creating a Term Paper

Case Perspective

Janice Flanders is a freshmen at Washtenaw Community College, majoring in Electrical Engineering. The instructor teaching Janice's introductory computer class, Introduction to Computers 101, has assigned a term paper. The term paper must discuss some aspect of using a personal computer and be 500 to 550 words in length. It also must be written according to the Modern Language Association (MLA) guidelines specified for report preparation. Carol Seeger, Janice's computer instructor, indicated the term paper must contain at least two footnotes, three parenthetical citations, and a bibliography. Each student in the class received a summary of the MLA guidelines.

Before she left for college, Janice's father bought her a laptop computer. Although the laptop has a modem, Janice has never used the modem to communicate with other computers or access the Internet. As a result, Janice decides to research the techniques available to access the Internet and write her term paper about the methods she finds. Janice looks for information about the Internet in the college library. She finds a book, magazine article, and Web site that contain information related to accessing the Internet and using the World Wide Web.

Introduction

In the academic and business environments, you will be required to write reports. In the business world, you may perform research and write reports for salespeople, managers, or customers. In the academic world, you will probably write a term paper to satisfy the requirements of an instructor. Whether preparing a report in the business world or meeting a requirement of an instructor in the academic world, you should follow a standard format when preparing the report.

Various professional associations have proposed specific standards and recommendations for writing term papers. The three styles recognized by WordPerfect for writing term papers are the ones from the Modern Language Association (MLA), Chicago Manual of Style (Tiburian) and American Psychological Association (APA). Although the term paper styles are similar from one source to another, the placement of information and the format of the documentation may be different. Many instructors and schools throughout the United States regard the MLA as their authority. The term paper illustrated in Project 3 is prepared using the MLA style.

Project Three—Term Paper

A short term paper titled "Online Services and Internet Service Providers" is illustrated in Figure 3-1. The term paper provides information about accessing the Internet using an online service and an Internet service provider. The term paper contains approximately 510 words and requires two pages of text. Explanatory notes, or **footnotes**, are placed at the bottom of a page when the text on the page requires a further explanation.

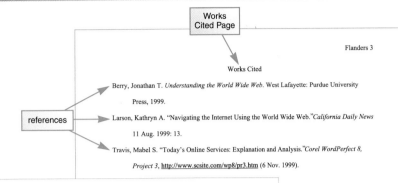

Works Cited Page

Flanders 3

Works Cited

Berry, Jonathan T. *Understanding the World Wide Web*. West Lafayette: Purdue University

Press, 1999.

references

Larson, Kathryn A. "Navigating the Internet Using the World Wide Web."*California Daily News*

11 Aug. 1999: 13.

Travis, Mabel S. "Today's Online Services: Explanation and Analysis."*Corel WordPerfect 8,*

Project 3, http://www.scsite.com/wp8/pr3.htm (6 Nov. 1999).

Flanders 2

often and do not expect to use the other services offered by an online service, an Internet service

provider may be best for you.[2]

Once connected to the Internet, you can navigate the World Wide Web in a graphical

environment to locate and view different Web sites (Larson 13). A Web site might consist of a

single Web page or multiple Web pages. When you first access a Web site, you are connected to

the site's home page, which is the starting point for exploring the Web site. A unique address,

called a Uniform Resource Locator (URL), identifies each Web page and is used to access the

Web page (Berry 12 14).

Whether you use an online service or an Internet service provider, accessing the Internet

and using the World Wide Web bring the exciting and constantly changing world of cyberspace

to your computer.

Flanders 1

Janice Flanders

Instructor Carol Seeger

Introduction to Computers 101

December 10, 1999

Online Services and Internet Service Providers

The Internet is a global network of computers. Using the Internet, you can send and

receive electronic mail, see the latest news and sports, research topics of interest, and engage in

live conversations with other individuals. Connecting to the Internet requires a computer and a

modem.[1] With a modem, you can access the Internet using either an online service or Internet

service provider.

Online services, such as America Online, give you access to the Internet (Travis, 6 Nov.

1999). An online service imposes a monthly fee to connect to the Internet for a specific number of

hours or a flat rate for unlimited use of the Internet. Hours in excess of those covered by the

monthly fee are billed a fixed amount for each additional hour. An online service provides other

services such as electronic mail (e-mail) exchange; posting to and reading bulletin boards; chat

with other members; and the latest news, sports, weather, and financial information.

You also can access the Internet using an Internet service provider. An Internet service

provider (ISP) maintains a computer, called a server, that is connected to the Internet. To access

the Internet, you must set up an account. When you set up an account, you are billed a flat

monthly fee for unlimited access to the Internet. The added services available from an online

service are not available from an Internet service provider. If you anticipate using the Internet

[1] Another method to access the Internet is to connect your computer to a network of

computers that has a direct connection to the Internet.

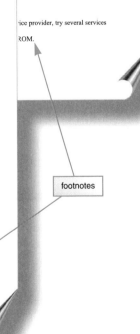

...ice provider, try several services

...ROM.

footnotes

FIGURE 3-1

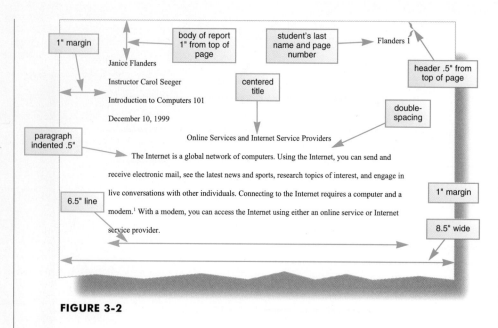

FIGURE 3-2

The **references**, names of books, magazine or newspaper articles, or other materials used in the preparation of the term paper, are listed alphabetically on the Works Cited page of the term paper.

Modern Language Association Guidelines

When writing a term paper, you should follow a number of important standards related to formatting the paper. The term paper in this project follows the guidelines authorized by the Modern Language Association. These guidelines are described in this section and are illustrated in Figure 3-2. Follow these standards when you create the term paper.

When using the MLA style, double-space all pages of the term paper and provide a one-inch bottom, left, and right margin. Indent the first line of a paragraph .5 inch. Number all pages consecutively in the upper right corner of the page one-half inch below the top of the page. This entry should consist of your last name followed by the page number. Leave one space between your name and the page number. This is called the **header**.

The MLA style does not require a title page. Instead, begin one inch down from the top of the first page at the left margin. On separate lines, type the author's name, instructor's name, course name and number, and date. Center the term paper title below the name and course information.

One space follows a period when using Times New Roman font or a similar font and the term paper is printed on standard-sized 8.5 inches wide by 11 inches long paper.

Document Preparation Steps

Document preparation steps give you an overview of how the document in Figure 3-1 on page WP 3.5 will be developed. The following tasks will be completed in this project.

1. Start WordPerfect.
2. Display the Format Toolbar.
3. Set the top margin to .5 inch.
4. Create a header to number pages.
5. Change line spacing to double-space.
6. Enter the author's name, instructor's name, course information, and date.
7. Center the term paper title.
8. Enter the body of term paper.
9. Enter the footnotes and parenthetical citations.
10. Save the document.
11. Create the Works Cited Page.

12. Save the document again.
13. Edit the term paper.
14. Spell check the term paper.
15. Print the term paper.
16. Display the document information.

The following pages contain a detailed explanation of these tasks.

Starting WordPerfect

Before you can create the term paper, you need to start WordPerfect by following the procedures explained in Project 1 and Project 2. These procedures are summarized below.

TO START WORDPERFECT

① Click the Start button on the taskbar.
② Point to Corel WordPerfect Suite 8 on the Start menu.
③ Click Corel WordPerfect 8 on the Corel WordPerfect Suite 8 submenu.
④ If necessary, click the Maximize button in the Corel WordPerfect window.
⑤ If necessary, click the Maximize button in the Document1 window.

WordPerfect displays the maximized Corel WordPerfect application window and a blank document titled Document1 in a maximized document window.

Displaying the Format Toolbar

Fourteen Toolbars are available in WordPerfect. Each Toolbar contains a collection of buttons designed to assist you in performing a related group of tasks. In the previous two projects, the default Toolbar (WordPerfect 8 Toolbar) was used to perform the tasks required to create the announcement, cover letter, and resume.

In preparation for creating the term paper, you will display the Format Toolbar. The **Format Toolbar** contains buttons to change page margins, justify text, and create hanging indent paragraphs. You will use these features while creating the term paper. Perform the following steps to display the Format Toolbar.

 Steps To Display a Toolbar

1 **Point to the Bullets button on the WordPerfect 8 Toolbar.**

*The mouse pointer points to the **Bullets button** on the WordPerfect 8 Toolbar (Figure 3-3). You can point to any button or blank area on the Toolbar and then follow Step 2 to obtain the same results.*

Bullets button

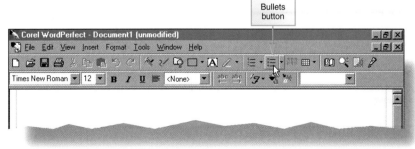

FIGURE 3-3

② **Right-click the Bullets button. Point to Format.**

WordPerfect displays a QuickMenu (Figure 3-4). The fourteen Toolbar names display at the top of the menu followed by a horizontal line. A check mark precedes the WordPerfect 8 Toolbar name and the Format Toolbar name is highlighted. Three commands display at the bottom of the menu.

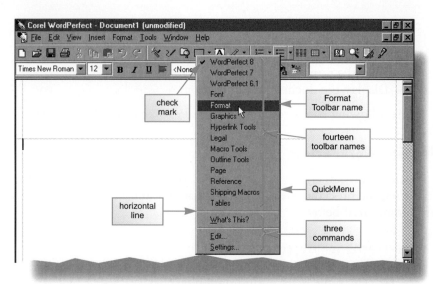

FIGURE 3-4

③ **Click Format.**

The Format Toolbar, containing two boxes and fifteen buttons, displays below the WordPerfect 8 Toolbar (Figure 3-5). The Font Face and Font Size boxes and the Bold, Italic, and Underline buttons are located on both the Format Toolbar and the Property Bar. You will use five buttons (Hanging Indent, Page Margins, Justify Left, Justify Center, and Justify Right) to create the term paper. The recessed Justify Left button indicates the text to be entered will be left justified.

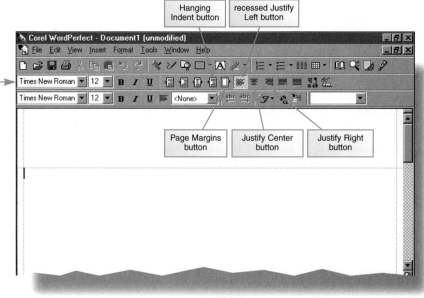

FIGURE 3-5

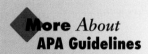

More *About* **APA Guidelines**

Until recently, the APA style required 1.5" top, bottom, left, and right margins. Now, the APA guidelines require 1" margins.

Changing the Top Margin

Currently, the default margin settings are one inch for the top, bottom, left, and right margins. Before typing the term paper, you should set the margins as specified by the MLA style. When you print a WordPerfect document, the header automatically prints just below the top margin. Because the MLA style for a term paper indicates the header should print .5 inch from the top of the page, you must change the default setting for the top margin to .5 inch. You do not need to change the default setting for the left, right, and bottom margins.

In Project 2, you changed the top and bottom margins of the resume by dragging the top and bottom guidelines. In this project, you will change the top margin using the Page Setup dialog box. Perform the following steps to change the top margin.

Steps To Change the Top Margin

1 **Point to the Page Margins button on the Format Toolbar (Figure 3-6).**

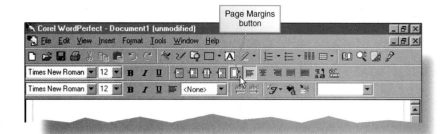

FIGURE 3-6

2 **Click the Page Margins button. Click the Page Margins tab in the Page Setup dialog box.**

WordPerfect displays the Page Margins sheet in the Page Setup dialog box (Figure 3-7). The Page Margins sheet contains a text box for each margin (Left, Right, Top, and Bottom), the Make all margins equal check box, and a sample document illustrating the current margin settings.

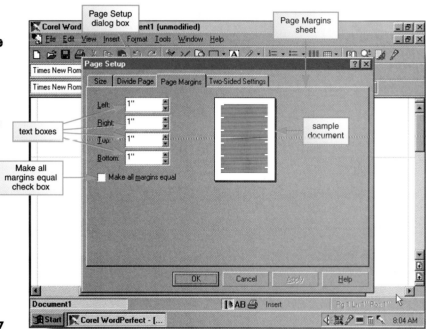

FIGURE 3-7

3 **Double-click the Top text box and then type .5 in the text box. Point to the OK button.**

The value .5 displays in the Top text box, and the top margin in the sample document changes to reflect the new top margin (Figure 3-8).

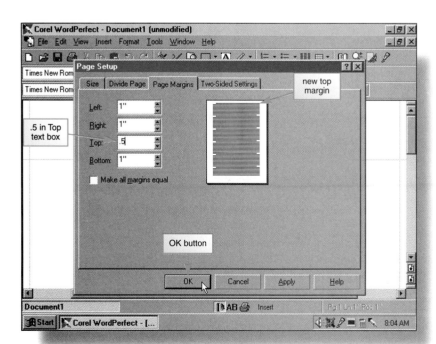

FIGURE 3-8

Click the OK button.

WordPerfect repositions the top margin guideline and changes the top margin to .5 inch (Figure 3-9).

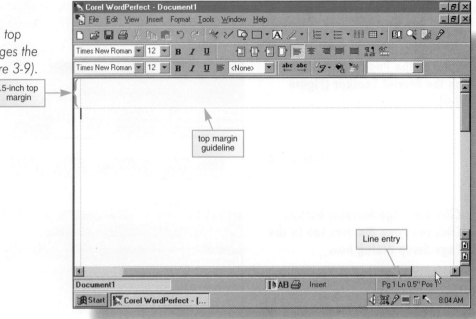

FIGURE 3-9

As indicated by the Line entry (Ln 0.5") in the Combined Position area on the Application Bar, the insertion point is located .5 inch from the top of the page. Thus, the top margin is .5 inch. Although not visible in Figure 3-9, a **Top Margin code** is inserted in the document. The left and right default margin settings of 1"(2 inches total) provide a 6.5-inch line on an 8.5-inch wide document.

Creating the Term Paper

The text of the term paper should display in Times New Roman Regular 12-point font. Because the WordPerfect default font is Times New Roman Regular 12 point, no change is necessary. The next step in preparing the term paper is to type the last name (Flanders) followed by a blank space and the page number.

Headers and Footers

A **header** is special text that appears at the top of printed pages in a document. A **footer** is special text that appears at the bottom of printed pages in a document. You use headers and footers to number pages and add a title or other types of information to the top or bottom of a document. In the term paper, you use a header to identify the student and number the pages in the document. The term paper does not use a footer.

Calculating the Distance Between the Header and First Line of Text

Currently, the top margin is set to .5 inch. Because WordPerfect always prints the header just below the top margin, the header will print one-half inch from the top of the paper. This satisfies the MLA requirement for the header to print one-half inch from the top of the paper. Another MLA requirement is for the first line of text in the term paper to print one inch from the top of the paper. To guarantee the position of the first line of text, you must calculate the distance between the header and the first line of text before you create the header. To make this calculation you must know the **line height** of each line in the document is .197. Figure 3-10 illustrates this calculation.

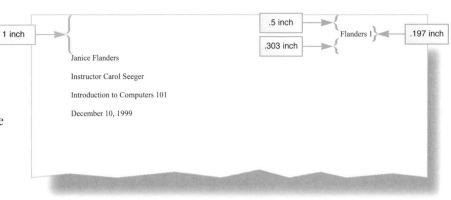

FIGURE 3-10

The distance from the top of the paper to the first line of print is 1 inch. The distance from the top of the paper to the header is .5 inch. The height of the line containing the header is .197. To find the distance from the header to the first line of text, subtract the sum of the distance from the top of the page to the header (.5 inch) and the line height (.197 inch) from the distance between the top of the page and the first line of text (1 inch). Thus, the distance between the header and first line of text is .303 inch (1 − .5 − .197). This value is required to create the header.

Perform the following steps to create and format the header.

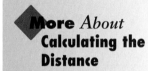

 Steps To Create and Format a Header

More *About* **Calculating the Distance**

In Step 9 through Step 11 on pages WP 3.13 and WP 3.14, the distance is calculated by entering a value in the Distance between text and header text box in the Distance dialog box. An alternative method of setting the distance is to drag the lower pink guideline until .303 displays in the QuickTip.

1 **Point to the area above the top margin guideline in the document window.**

The I-beam pointer displays in the area above the top margin guideline (Figure 3-11).

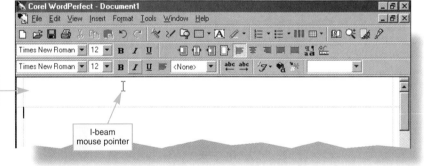

FIGURE 3-11

2 **Right-click the area. Point to Header/Footer.**

*WordPerfect displays a QuickMenu and highlights the **Header/Footer** command (Figure 3-12).*

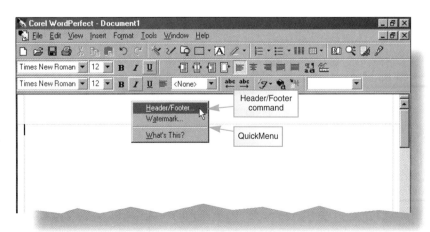

FIGURE 3-12

3 **Click Header/Footer. Point to the Create button.**

WordPerfect displays the Headers/Footers dialog box and selects the Header A option button (Figure 3-13). You can create a new header using the Create button, edit an existing header using the Edit button, or stop the display of the header on certain pages by using the Discontinue button.

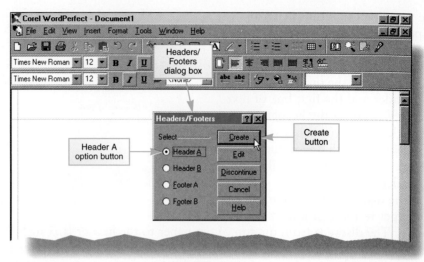

FIGURE 3-13

4 **Click the Create button.**

WordPerfect creates the header, changes several buttons on the Property Bar, and changes the title in the document window to contain the (Header A) entry (Figure 3-14). A dotted guideline (header guideline) defines the area in which the header will display. The new buttons on the Property Bar are designed to make working with headers and footers easier.

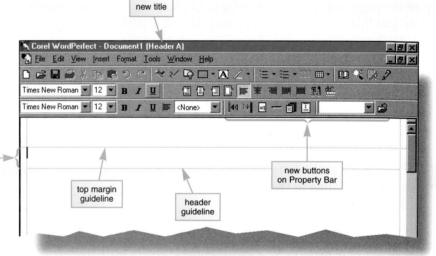

FIGURE 3-14

5 **Type** Flanders **for the last name. Press the SPACEBAR. Point to the Page Numbering button on the Property Bar.**

*The name, Flanders, and a blank space display at the left margin of the page (Figure 3-15). The Property Bar contains the **Page Numbering button**.*

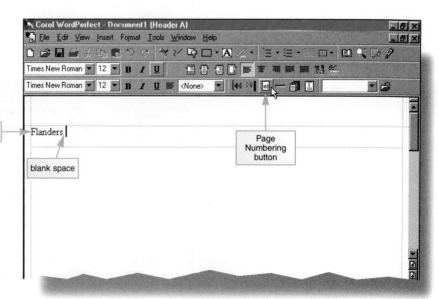

FIGURE 3-15

6 **Click the Page Numbering button. Point to Page Number.**

*WordPerfect displays the **Page Numbering drop-down menu** and recesses the **Page Number command** (Figure 3-16).*

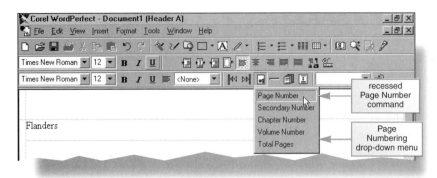

FIGURE 3-16

7 **Click Page Number. Point to the Justify Right button on the Format Toolbar.**

*WordPerfect displays the number 1 after the blank space following the name Flanders (Figure 3-17). Although not visible, a **Page Numbering Display code** is inserted in the document.*

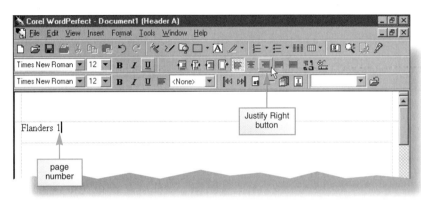

FIGURE 3-17

8 **Click the Justify Right button. Point to the Header/Footer Distance button on the Property Bar.**

*WordPerfect right-justifies the name and page number (Figure 3-18). The **Header/Footer Distance button** displays on the Property Bar.*

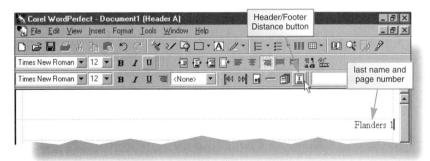

FIGURE 3-18

9 **Click the Header/Footer Distance button.**

WordPerfect opens the Distance dialog box (Figure 3-19). The default highlighted 0.167" setting displays in the Distance between text and header text box.

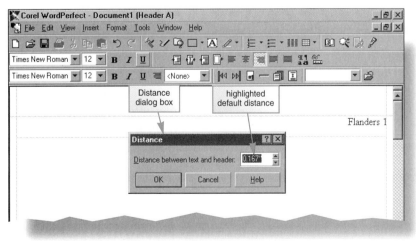

FIGURE 3-19

Type .303 **in the text box. Point to the OK button.**

WordPerfect displays the value .303 in the Distance between text and header text box (Figure 3-20). This value causes the first line of text to print one inch below the top of the page.

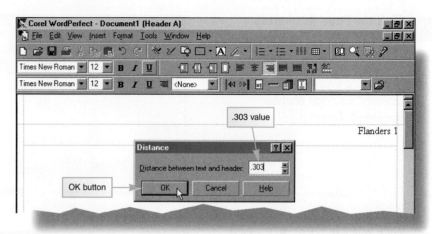

FIGURE 3-20

Click the OK button.

*WordPerfect closes the Distance dialog box (Figure 3-21). The insertion point displays to the right of the page number in the header and the Property Bar contains the buttons to work with the header. Although not visible, a **Header A code** and **Header Separator code** are inserted in the document.*

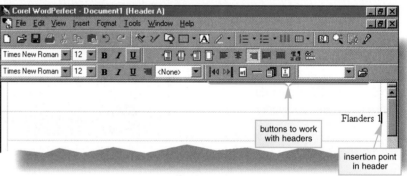

FIGURE 3-21

Click the blank line below the header area to move the insertion point.

WordPerfect removes the buttons designed to work with headers from the Property Bar, displays the original buttons, and moves the insertion point to the beginning of the first line in the document (Figure 3-22).

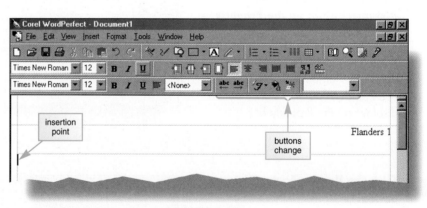

FIGURE 3-22

▶ *Other***Ways**

1. On Insert menu click Header/Footer, click Create, follow Steps 5 through 12

The header information will print .5 inch from the top the paper when you print the document. When text is typed on the blank line containing the insertion point and the document is printed, the line will print 1 inch from the top of the paper.

Changing the Line Spacing

The MLA style guidelines require all text in a term paper to be double-spaced. Thus, you should set the line spacing to double-space before entering text. Perform the following steps to set the line spacing to double-spacing.

Steps To Change the Line Spacing

1 **Click Format on the menu bar. Point to Line. Point to Spacing on the Line submenu.**

WordPerfect displays the Format menu and Line submenu and highlights the Spacing command on the Line submenu (Figure 3-23).

FIGURE 3-23

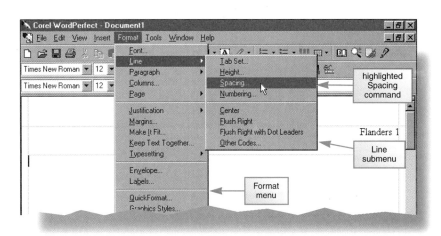

2 **Click Spacing. Type** 2 **in the Spacing text box. Point to the OK button.**

WordPerfect displays the Line Spacing dialog box (Figure 3-24). Before you typed a new value for the line spacing, the value 1.0 (indicating single-spacing) displayed in the Spacing text box and the sample document indicated the document was single-spaced. However, when the new line spacing value is typed, the value 2, indicating double-spacing, displays in the Spacing text box, and the mouse pointer points to the OK button.

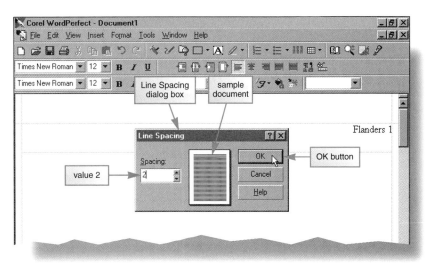

FIGURE 3-24

3 **Click the OK button.**

*The line spacing is set to double-space (Figure 3-25). Although not visible, WordPerfect inserts a **Line Spacing code** in the document.*

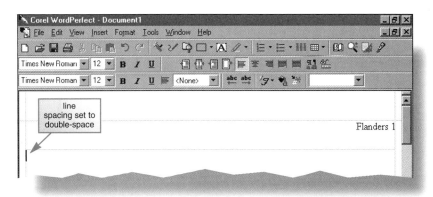

FIGURE 3-25

▶*Other***Ways**

1. Click Format on menu bar, point to Line, click Height, click Fixed, type height, click OK button

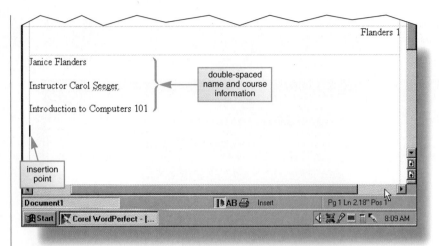

Flanders 1

Janice Flanders

Instructor Carol Seeger

Introduction to Computers 101

double-spaced name and course information

insertion point

Document1   AB   Insert   Pg 1 Ln 2.18" Pos 1

Start   Corel WordPerfect - [...   8:09 AM

FIGURE 3-26

Typing the Name and Course Information

According to the MLA style, you type the student's name on the first line of the term paper, instructor's name on the second line, course name and number on the third line, and current date on the fourth line (see Figure 3-2 on page WP 3.6). The steps to type the name and course information are summarized below.

TO TYPE NAME AND COURSE INFORMATION

1. Type Janice Flanders on the first line and then press the ENTER key.
2. Type Instructor Carol Seeger on the second line and then press the ENTER key.
3. Type Introduction to Computers 101 on the third line and then press the ENTER key.

The student name displays on the first line of the screen (Figure 3-26). The instructor name and course title are double-spaced below the student name. The insertion point is positioned at the left margin of the line following the course title.

More *About* the Date Format

A date format controls how the date looks when inserted in a document. Changing the date format allows you to display the date in other forms, such as 10/7/98, 7 October 1998, or Wednesday, October 7, 1998. Additional formats allow you to display the date and time, such as October 7, 1998 (1:15PM). To change the date format, click Insert on the menu bar, click Date/Time, click Date Format, select a format, and click the OK Insert button.

Inserting the Current Date

In Project 2, you inserted the date into the cover letter by entering the date from the keyboard. WordPerfect also allows you to insert the date using two other methods. The first method inserts the date using the Date code. The **Date code** causes the date in the document to change to the current date whenever you open or print the document even if it is at a later date. The second method inserts the date as text. As such, the date will remain the same and will change to the current date only if you select the **Automatic Update option** when you insert the date. Perform the following steps to insert the current date without automatically updating the date.

 Steps To Insert the Date

1. **Click Insert on the menu bar and point to Date/Time.**

    WordPerfect displays the Insert menu and highlights the Date/Time command (Figure 3-27).

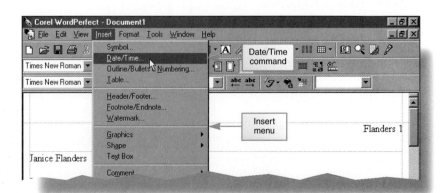

FIGURE 3-27

2 **Click Date/Time. Point to the Insert button in the Date/Time dialog box.**

WordPerfect displays the Date/Time dialog box (Figure 3-28). The dialog box contains the current date format (January 31, 1997) and a list box containing date and time formats. The first date format, January 31, 1997, is highlighted in the list box. The Automatic update check box should not be checked because the date and time is not to be updated when you open or print the document containing the date and time. The mouse pointer points to the Insert button.

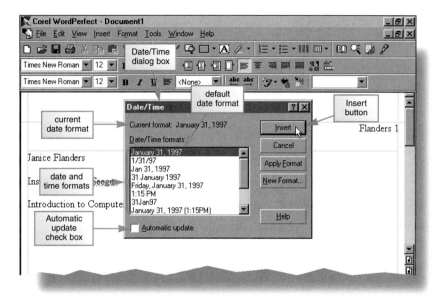

FIGURE 3-28

3 **Click the Insert button. Press the ENTER key.**

WordPerfect displays the current date (December 10, 1999) and a blank line (Figure 3-29).

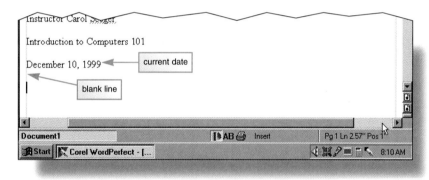

FIGURE 3-29

OtherWays

1. Press CTRL+D

Viewing Codes in the Term Paper

WordPerfect inserts codes in the document when you change the top margin, create a header, and change the line spacing. To view the codes, open the Reveal Codes window. The steps to view the codes in the document are summarized below.

TO VIEW THE CODES IN THE TERM PAPER

1 Right-click the first line (Janice Flanders) in the document.

2 Click Reveal Codes on the QuickMenu.

The Reveal Codes window displays (Figure 3-30 on the next page). The Top Margin code causes the top margin to be .5 inch. The Header A code causes the text in the header to be right justified and the last name and page number to display on each page of the term paper. The Header Separator code causes the first line of the text of the term paper to display .303 inch below the header. The Line Spacing code causes double-spacing.

After viewing the codes, close the Reveal Codes window by performing the following steps.

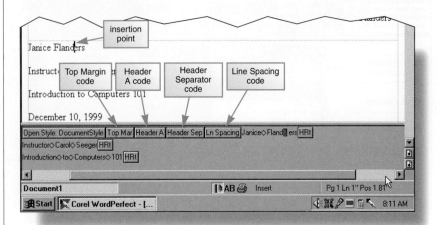

FIGURE 3-30

TO CLOSE THE REVEAL CODES WINDOW

① Right-click the text area.
② Click Reveal Codes on the QuickMenu.
③ Press the PAGE DOWN key to move the insertion point to the blank line following the date.

The Reveal Codes window closes and the insertion point is located in the text area.

Centering the Term Paper Title

After typing the identifying information, the next step is to type the title of the term paper centered on the line. The insertion point currently is positioned at the left margin of the blank line following the date. Perform the following steps to center and type the term paper title.

Steps **To Center a Line of Text Before Typing**

① Verify the insertion point is on the blank line following the date. Point to the Justify Center button on the Format Toolbar.

The Justify Center button displays on the Format Toolbar (Figure 3-31).

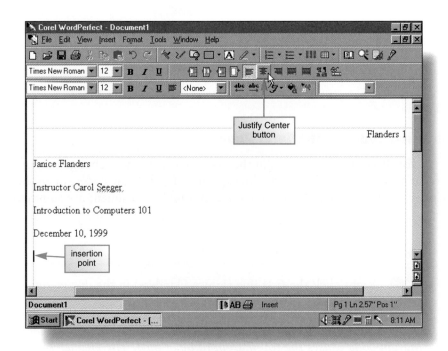

FIGURE 3-31

2 **Click the Justify Center button.**
Type Online Services and Internet Service Providers **and then press the ENTER key. Point to the Justify Left button on the Format Toolbar.**

WordPerfect recesses the Justify Center button, moves the insertion point to the center of the page, centers the term paper title as you type, and inserts a blank line following the title (Figure 3-32). The insertion point displays in the center, double-spaced below the title.

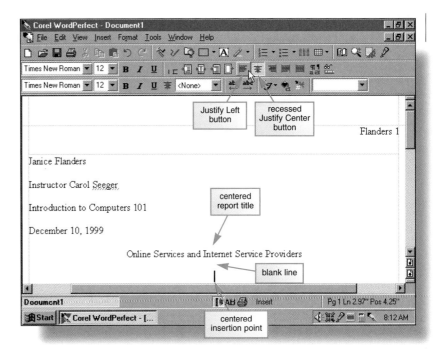

FIGURE 3-32

3 **Click the Justify Left button.**

WordPerfect recesses the Justify Left button and moves the insertion point to the left margin (Figure 3-33).

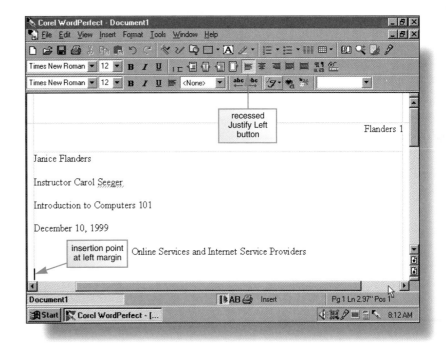

FIGURE 3-33

Indenting Paragraphs

According to the MLA style, the first line of each paragraph in the term paper is to be indented .5 inch. Indent the first line of a paragraph by pressing the TAB key. Because the **default tab setting** causes a tab stop to be set every .5 inch, pressing the TAB key moves the insertion point .5 inch to the right on the screen to the next tab stop on the line. After indenting, begin typing the first paragraph of the term paper. The step on the next page illustrates how to indent the paragraph and type the first three sentences of the first paragraph in the term paper.

> **Other Ways**
> 1. Right-click text area, click Center, type text
> 2. Click Justification button on Property Bar, click Center, type text
> 3. Click Format on menu bar, point to Line, click Center, type text
> 4. Press SHIFT+F7, type text

Steps To Indent the First Line of a Paragraph

1 **Press the TAB key. Then type the first three sentences of the first paragraph as shown in Figure 3-34.**

WordPerfect indents the first line of the paragraph .5 inch and the first three sentences of the paragraph are entered (Figure 3-34). The insertion point is located where the first footnote in the term paper should be entered.

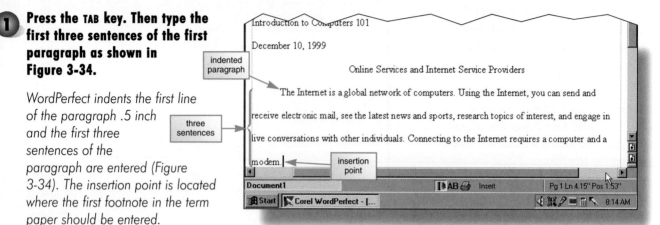

FIGURE 3-34

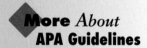

Formatting Standards for Explanatory Notes

Figure 3-35 contains the top portion of page one of the term paper and an explanatory note at the bottom of page one. The last sentence of the paragraph at the top of the page is followed by the smaller number 1 placed above the baseline, called a **superscript**. A superscript number 1 also precedes the explanatory note at the bottom of the page. The superscript number 1 associates the sentence in the term paper with the explanatory note.

According to the MLA style, explanatory notes are optional and may be placed in a report at the discretion of the author. Explanatory notes are called footnotes when they appear at the bottom of the page and **endnotes** when they appear at the end of the document. The superscript number associated with the footnote is called a **footnote number**. When placing an explanatory note at the bottom of a page, follow the MLA style guidelines described below.

1. Separate all footnotes at the bottom of a page from the text in the term paper with a two-inch horizontal line.
2. Indent the first line of the footnote .5 inch from the left margin.
3. Double-space the footnote.

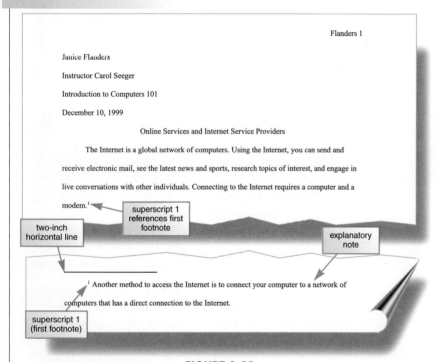

FIGURE 3-35

Creating a Footnote

When you create a footnote, WordPerfect assigns the appropriate number to the footnote, and then displays a two-inch **separator line** and the footnote number at the bottom of the page. You type the explanatory note following the footnote number. When you finish typing the explanatory note, WordPerfect places a footnote number in the text of the document where the insertion point was located before you created the footnote. The following steps illustrate how to create a footnote.

To Create the First Footnote

 Click Insert on the menu bar and point to Footnote/Endnote.

WordPerfect displays the Insert menu and highlights the Footnote/Endnote command (Figure 3-36).

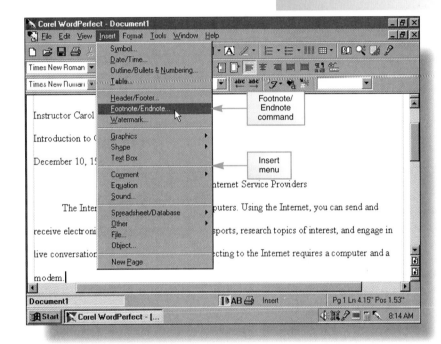

FIGURE 3-36

 Click Footnote/Endnote. Point to the Create button.

WordPerfect displays the Footnote/Endnote dialog box (Figure 3-37). The dialog box contains the selected Footnote Number option button and associated text box and the Endnote Number option button and associated text box. The highlighted value 1 displays in the Footnote Number text box.

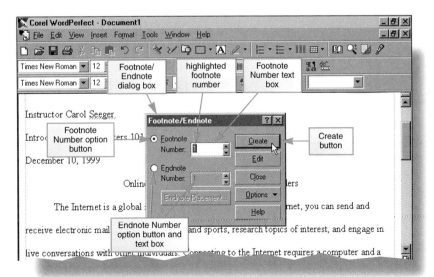

FIGURE 3-37

More *About* **Footnotes**

Several methods are available to delete a footnote. One method is to position the insertion point to the right of the footnote number in the text and press the BACKSPACE key. A second method is to position the insertion point to the left of the footnote number in the text and press the DELETE key. A third method is to open the Reveal Codes window and drag the Footnote code out of the Reveal Codes window.

3 **Click the Create button.**

WordPerfect changes the title in the document window to include the (Footnote) entry and displays a 2" horizontal line and the footnote number for the first footnote (1) at the bottom margin of the page (Figure 3-38). The footnote number 1 displays in superscript and is indented .5 inch from the left margin. Unless changed, the text of the footnote will be single-spaced.

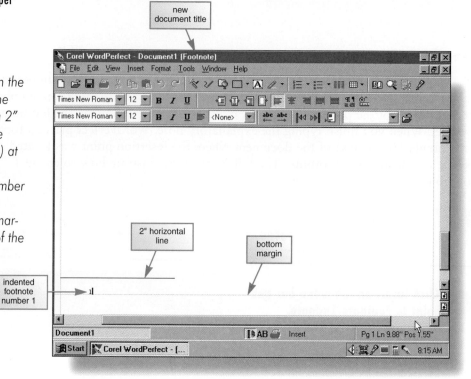

FIGURE 3-38

4 **Click Format on the menu bar. Point to Line. Click Spacing on the Line submenu. Type 2 in the Spacing text box. Click the OK button.**

The Format menu and Line submenu display, the Spacing command is clicked, the value 2 is entered, the OK button is clicked, and the line spacing of the footnote is changed to double-spacing (Figure 3-39).

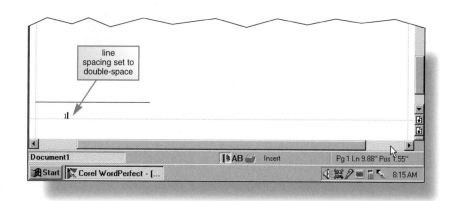

FIGURE 3-39

5 **Press the SPACEBAR. Type** Another method to access the Internet is to connect your computer to a network of computers that has a direct connection to the Internet. **as the footnote.**

The text of footnote number 1 begins one space to the right of the footnote number (Figure 3-40). Although not visible, WordPerfect inserts a Footnote code in the document.

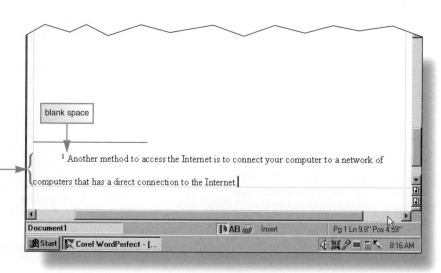

FIGURE 3-40

MLA Style Guidelines for Parenthetical Citations

Figure 3-41 illustrates the first two paragraphs on page one of the term paper and the top of the Works Cited page. The (Travis, 6 Nov. 1999) entry on page one is called a parenthetical citation. A **parenthetical citation** in a document indicates to the reader that a statement made in the term paper is related to information derived from a book, article, journal, or other reference material. The parenthetical citation contains the author's last name (Travis) and date (6 Nov. 1999).

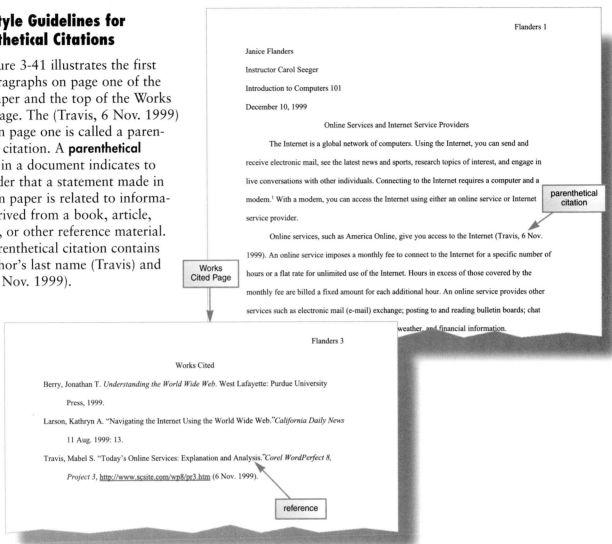

FIGURE 3-41

Each parenthetical citation in a term paper has a corresponding reference on the Works Cited page. Travis, Mabel S. "Today's Online Services: Explanation and Analysis.", the last reference on the Works Cited page, corresponds to the (Travis, 6 Nov. 1999) citation on the first page of the term paper.

When inserting a parenthetical citation in a term paper, follow the MLA style guidelines listed below.

1. Enclose each parenthetical citation within parentheses.
2. Include the last name of the author, a blank space, and a page or date reference.
3. When referencing multiple pages, list the beginning page number first, and then enter a hyphen (-) and the ending page number.

Typing the First Parenthetical Citation

Continue creating the term paper by typing the last sentence of the first paragraph and then typing the second paragraph. Perform the step on the next page to enter the text.

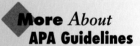

More *About* **APA Guidelines**

The APA style suggests the use of parenthetical citations instead of footnotes. An APA citation contains the author's last name, year of publication, and page number in a slightly different format from that of the MLA citation. An APA citation for a book written by Jonathan T. Berry in which information is taken from pages 12 through 14 would be (Berry, 1998, pp. 12-14). The equivalent MLA citation would be (Berry, 12-14).

Steps To Type a Parenthetical Citation

1 **Scroll the document window to make the superscript number 1 visible. Move the insertion point so that it follows the superscript number 1 in the first paragraph. Press the SPACE bar. Type the last sentence in the first paragraph. Press the ENTER key. Press the TAB key. Type the second paragraph and then press the ENTER key.**

WordPerfect moves the insertion point to the right of the superscript number 1 and a portion of the last sentence in the first paragraph and the second paragraph display in the document window (Figure 3-42). The first parenthetical citation displays at the end of the first sentence in the second paragraph.

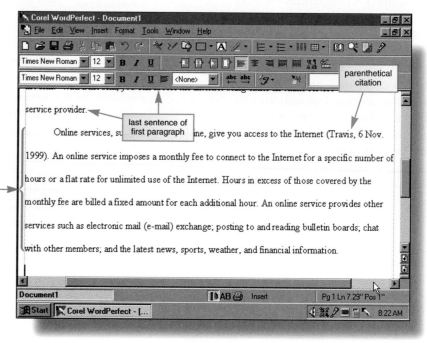

FIGURE 3-42

Saving the Term Paper

On a floppy disk or hard disk, you should periodically save the information you enter. Saving the document after you type several paragraphs will prevent the accidental loss of information if a power or computer failure should occur. To save the document, use the Save button on the WordPerfect 8 Toolbar and the filename, Internet Access. The steps to save the term paper are summarized below.

TO SAVE THE TERM PAPER

1 Insert the Corel WordPerfect 8 Files floppy disk into drive A.

2 Click the Save button on the WordPerfect 8 Toolbar.

3 When the Save File dialog box displays, type Internet Access in the File name box.

4 Click the Save in box arrow.

5 Scroll the Save in list until 3½ Floppy (A:) displays and then click 3½ Floppy (A:).

6 Click the Save button.

The partially complete term paper is saved on the Corel WordPerfect 8 Files floppy disk in drive A, and the Document1 entry in the Corel WordPerfect window title changes to include the A:\ Internet Access.wpd (unmodified) entry.

Soft Page Breaks

WordPerfect automatically creates a **soft page break** in a document if you type more information than can fit on one page of a printed document. In Page view, the soft page break displays as a thick gray horizontal line across the document window. The page break is described as "soft" because the position a soft page break occupies in a document may change when text is added or removed. Continue creating the term paper by typing the third paragraph.

More *About*
Soft Page Breaks

The soft page break displays as a thin black horizontal line in Draft view. The soft page break does not display in Two Pages and Web Page view.

Steps **To Create a Soft Page Break**

1 **Type the third paragraph as shown in Figure 3-42.**

As the third paragraph is typed, WordPerfect inserts a soft page break in the document, creates a second page and displays the header (Flanders 2) at the top of the second page. Although not visible in Figure 3-43, a Hard Return-Soft Page Break code is inserted in the document. The window title contains the Internet Access.wpd filename.

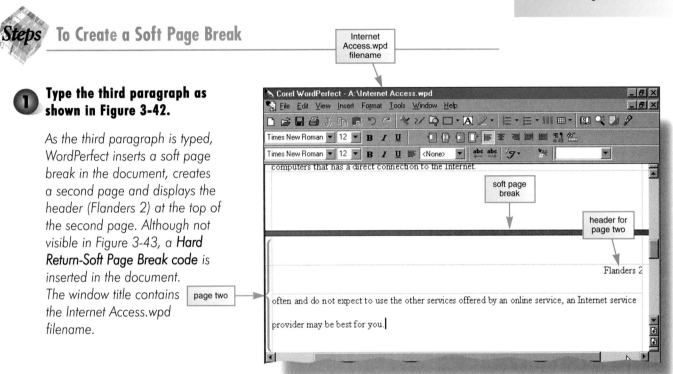

FIGURE 3-43

Completing the Entry of Text

The next task in the development of the term paper is to create the second footnote at the end of the third paragraph on page two. Then type the last two paragraphs. The steps to create the second footnote are summarized below.

TO CREATE A SECOND FOOTNOTE

1 Click Insert on the menu bar and click Footnote/Endnote.
2 Click the Create button.
3 Click Format on the menu bar. Point to Line. Click Spacing. Type 2 in the Spacing text box. Click the OK button.
4 Press the SPACEBAR. Type Before deciding on an online service or an Internet service provider, try several services and providers by calling and requesting a free introductory CD-ROM. as the footnote.

WordPerfect creates the second footnote (Figure 3-44 on the next page). Although not visible, WordPerfect displays footnote number 2 in the term paper.

More *About*
References

Common knowledge is commonly known or accessible to the reader. It does not have to be included as a parenthetical citation or listed in the bibliography. If you are unsure about information, include a parenthetical citation in the paper and a reference in the bibliography.

More *About*
Acknowledging Sources

Using someone else's ideas or words as your own is plagiarism and is a serious offense. Acknowledge all sources of information in a term paper. It is a matter of personal honesty and ethics.

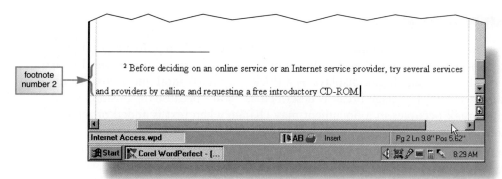

footnote
number 2

² Before deciding on an online service or an Internet service provider, try several services and providers by calling and requesting a free introductory CD-ROM.

Internet Access.wpd   AB   Insert   Pg 2 Ln 9.8" Pos 5.82"

Start   Corel WordPerfect - [...   8:29 AM

FIGURE 3-44

TO TYPE THE LAST TWO PARAGRAPHS

1 Position the insertion point following the superscript 2 in the document.
2 Press the ENTER key.

3 Type the fourth paragraph. Press the ENTER key.
4 Type the fifth paragraph. Press the ENTER key.

A portion of the fourth paragraph and the complete fifth paragraph display in the document window (Figure 3-45). Although the second parenthetical citation in the term paper (Larson 13) is not visible in the document window, the third parenthetical citation (Berry 12-14) displays in the fifth paragraph.

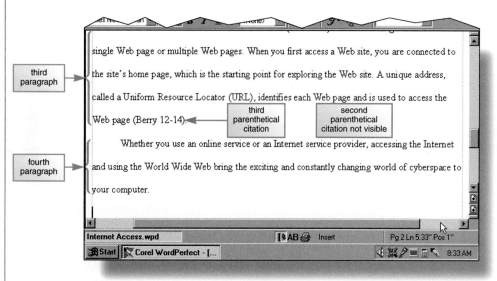

third paragraph

single Web page or multiple Web pages. When you first access a Web site, you are connected to the site's home page, which is the starting point for exploring the Web site. A unique address, called a Uniform Resource Locator (URL), identifies each Web page and is used to access the Web page (Berry 12-14).

third parenthetical citation

second parenthetical citation not visible

fourth paragraph

Whether you use an online service or an Internet service provider, accessing the Internet and using the World Wide Web bring the exciting and constantly changing world of cyberspace to your computer.

Internet Access.wpd   AB   Insert   Pg 2 Ln 5.33" Pos 1"

Start   Corel WordPerfect - [...   8:33 AM

FIGURE 3-45

Creating the Works Cited Page

Each parenthetical citation in a term paper has a corresponding reference on the Works Cited page. When creating the Works Cited page, follow the MLA style guidelines described below.

1. The list of works cited appears at the end of the term paper on a new page. The header with the last name and page number should appear in the upper right corner. The text on the page should be double-spaced.
2. The title, Works Cited, should be centered on the first line of the page.
3. Each reference should begin at the left margin. Subsequent lines should be indented .5 inch from the left margin.
4. The references should be in alphabetical order by the author's last name.

Figure 3-46 illustrates part of page two of the term paper and the top of the Works Cited page. Page two of the term paper contains a second footnote (footnote number 2) and the (Larson 13) and (Berry 12-14) parenthetical citations. The Works Cited page contains corresponding references for the parenthetical citations.

The Berry entry references a book. The MLA style indicates the reference for a book should contain the author's name (Berry, Jonathan T.), book title (Understanding the World Wide Web), city of publication (West Lafayette), name of the publisher (Purdue University Press), and year of publication (1999). A period should follow the author's name, book title, and year of publication. A colon should separate the city of publication and name of the publisher, and a comma should separate the name of the publisher from the year of publication.

The Larson entry references an article in a newspaper. The reference for a newspaper article should contain the author's name (Larson, Kathryn A.), article title (Navigating the Internet Using the World Wide Web), name of the newspaper (California Daily News), date of issue (11 Aug. 1999), and page number (13). A period should follow the author's name, article title, and page number. A colon should separate the year of publication from the page number.

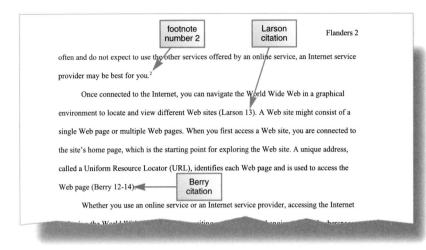

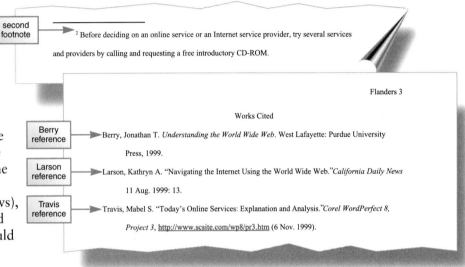

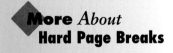

FIGURE 3-46

The Travis entry references an article on a Web page. The reference for an article on a Web page should contain the author's name (Travis, Mabel S.), article title (Today's Online Services: Explanation and Analysis), Web page title (Corel WordPerfect 8, Project 3), Web page address (http://scsite.com/wp8/pr3.htm), and date (6 Nov. 1999). A period should follow the author's name, article title, and date. A comma should separate the Web page title and Web page address.

Although not shown in this term paper, a reference for an article in a journal should contain the author's name, article title, journal title, volume number, year of publication, and page numbers. A period should follow the author's name, article title, and page numbers. A colon should separate the year of publication, which is enclosed in parentheses, from the page numbers.

Inserting a Hard Page Break

The list of works cited should be placed at the top of a new page in the term paper. To accomplish this, you must manually insert a hard page break in the document. A **hard page break** ends one page and begins another page. In Page view, the hard page break displays as a solid black and grey horizontal line. The page break is described as "hard" because the position of a hard page break in a document will not change regardless of any changes you make to the text in the document unless you delete it. Perform the steps on the next page to insert a hard page break in the term paper.

◆ **M**ore *About*
Hard Page Breaks

The hard page break displays as two thin horizontal lines in Draft view. The hard page break does not display in Two Pages or Web view. An alternative method to insert a hard page break is to hold down the CTRL key and press the ENTER key.

Steps To Insert a Hard Page Break

1 **If necessary, move the insertion point to the blank line following the last paragraph in the document. Click Insert on the menu bar and then point to New Page.**

WordPerfect opens the Insert menu and highlights the New Page command (Figure 3-47).

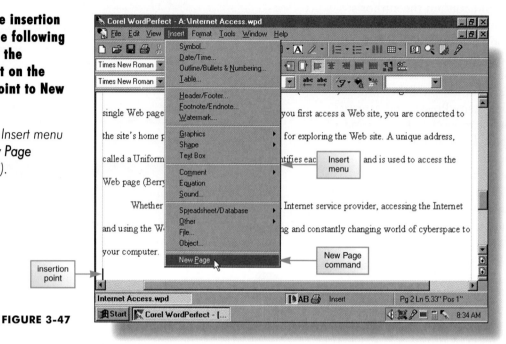

FIGURE 3-47

2 **Click New Page.**

WordPerfect displays a solid black and grey line across the document window, creates a third page, and displays the header (Flanders 3) at the top of the third page (Figure 3-48). The insertion point displays below the header at the beginning of the first line of the newly created page. Although not visible on the screen, a Hard Page Break code is added in the document when you insert a hard page break.

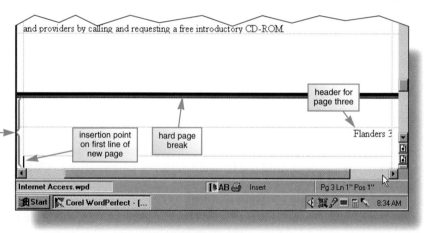

FIGURE 3-48

OtherWays

1. Press CTRL+ENTER

Centering the Works Cited Page Title

The title of the Works Cited page should be centered. One method of centering text before typing was shown earlier in this project. The steps to center the Works Cited title are summarized on the next page.

TO CENTER A LINE OF TEXT BEFORE TYPING

❶ Click the Justify Center button on the Format Toolbar.
❷ Type Works Cited and then press the ENTER key.
❸ Click the Justify Left button on the Format Toolbar.

WordPerfect centers the Works Cited title and displays the insertion point at the left margin of the line below the title (Figure 3-49).

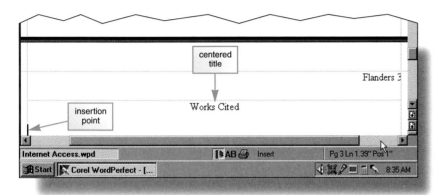

FIGURE 3-49

Creating a Hanging Indent

Each of the references on the Works Cited page should begin at the left margin, and subsequent lines of the reference should be indented .5-inch from the left margin. To accomplish this, you must create a **hanging indent** paragraph for each reference.

Although the parenthetical citations throughout the research paper are not in alphabetical order, the references on the Works Cited page must be in order by the author's last name. Before typing the references on the Works Cited page, you must establish the alphabetical order of the references. You should type the Berry reference first, Larson reference next, and Travis reference last. Perform the steps below and on the next page to type the references on the Works Cited page.

 Steps **To Create a Hanging Indent Paragraph**

❶ **Point to the Hanging Indent button on the Format Toolbar.**

*The Format Toolbar contains the **Hanging Indent button** (Figure 3-50).*

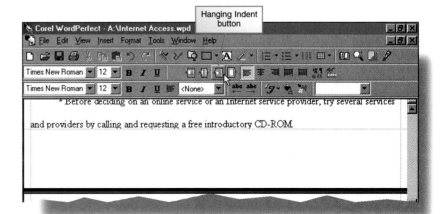

FIGURE 3-50

More *About*
**Deleting Hard
Page Breaks**

Several methods are available to delete a hard page break. One method is to position the insertion point at the beginning of the first line following the page break and press the BACKSPACE key. A second method is to position the insertion point at the end of the last line of text on the page preceding the page break and press the DELETE key. A third method is to open the Reveal Codes window and drag the Hard Page Break code out of the window.

More *About*
Indenting

Three types of indenting are available in WordPerfect: Indent, Double Indent, and Hanging Indent. Indent moves the left side of a paragraph one tab stop to the right. Double Indent moves the sides of a paragraph one tab stop in from both the left and right margins. A double indent is commonly used to format lengthy quotations. Hanging Indent moves all but the first line of a paragraph one tab stop to the right. A hanging indent is commonly used to format bibliography entries.

2 **Click the Hanging Indent button. Type** Berry, Jonathan T. Understanding the World Wide Web. West Lafayette: Purdue University Press, 1999. **and then press the ENTER key. Select the words, Understanding the World Wide Web, by dragging and then click the Italic button on the Format Toolbar. Click the blank line following the reference to remove the highlight.**

The first line of the Berry reference displays at the left margin (Figure 3-51). The second line of the reference is indented .5 inch from the left margin. Pressing the ENTER key terminates the hanging indent and moves the insertion point to the beginning of the next line.

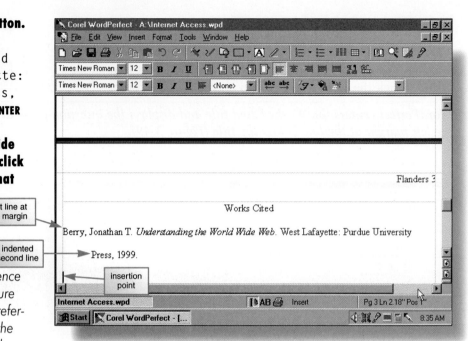

FIGURE 3-51

3 **Verify the insertion point displays at the beginning of the blank line following the first reference. Click the Hanging Indent button again. Type** Larson, Kathryn A. "Navigating the Internet Using the World Wide Web." California Daily News 11 Aug. 1999: 13. **and then press the ENTER key. Select the words, California Daily News, and then click the Italic button. Click the blank line following the reference to remove the highlight.**

The second reference displays on the screen (Figure 3-52).

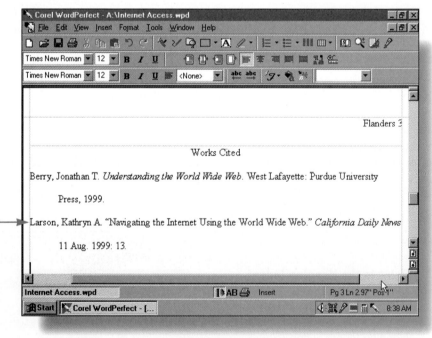

FIGURE 3-52

OtherWays

1. Click Format on menu bar, point to Paragraph, click Hanging Indent

2. Press CTRL+F7

Creating a Hyperlink

A **hyperlink** is a shortcut that allows you to jump quickly to another document on your computer, on your network, or on the World Wide Web. **Jumping** is the process of following a hyperlink to its destination. For example, clicking a hyperlink allows you to jump to another document on your computer, a network, or the World Wide Web. When you close the hyperlink destination page or document, you return to the original location in your WordPerfect document.

When you type the hyperlink text and press the spacebar to terminate its entry, WordPerfect formats the text as hyperlink text and an underline displays below the text. When you create a WordPerfect document and wish to create a hyperlink to a Web page, you do not have to be connected to the Internet.

In this project, one of the references is from a Web page on the Internet. When someone displays your research paper on the screen, you want him or her to be able to click the Web address in the term paper (hyperlink) and jump to the site for more information. Perform the steps to create a hyperlink as you type.

 Steps To Create a Hyperlink As You Type

1 **Verify the insertion point displays at the beginning of the blank line following the second reference. Click the Hanging Indent button again. Enter** Travis, Mabel S. "Today's Online Services: Explanation and Analysis." Corel WordPerfect 8, Project 3, http://www.scsite.com/wp8/pr3.htm **from the keyboard.**

The first part of the reference, including the hyperlink text, displays on the screen (Figure 3-53).

first part of Travis reference

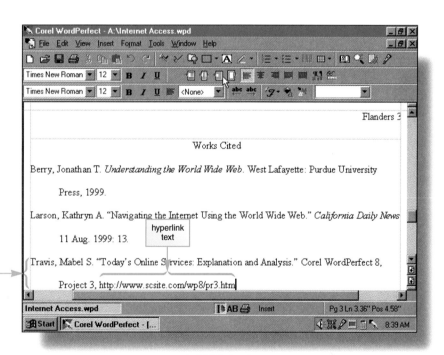

FIGURE 3-53

2 **Press the SPACEBAR and then type (6 Nov. 1999). to complete the entry of the reference. Press the ENTER key. Select the words, Corel WordPerfect 8, Project 3, and then click the Italic button. Click the blank line following the third reference to remove the highlight.**

When you press the SPACEBAR after typing the Web address, WordPerfect formats the address to indicate the address is a hyperlink (Figure 3-54). The third reference displays on the screen.

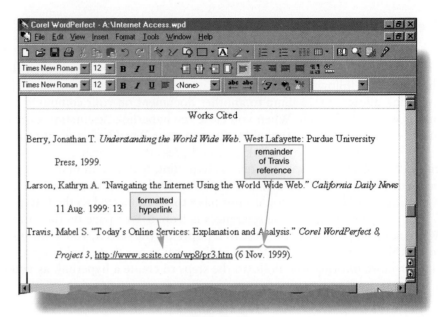

FIGURE 3-54

Using a Hyperlink to Jump to a Web Page

After creating a hyperlink in a WordPerfect document, you can easily jump to the Web site associated with the hyperlink by clicking the hyperlink in the document. If you are not connected to the World Wide Web, WordPerfect connects you using your default browser. After a few moments, the Web page with the URL, http://www.scsite.com/wp8/pr.htm, displays in your browser window. To return to the WordPerfect document, click the Close button in the browser window.

Saving the Term Paper Again

After completing the term paper, save the term paper again by using the Save button on the WordPerfect 8 Toolbar and the same filename (Internet Access.wpd). The step to save the term paper is summarized below.

TO SAVE THE TERM PAPER AGAIN

 Click the Save button on the WordPerfect 8 Toolbar.

WordPerfect saves the term paper on the floppy disk in drive A using the Internet Access.wpd filename. The document remains on the screen.

Hiding the Format Toolbar

Currently, the Format Toolbar displays in the document window. After creating the term paper, the Format Toolbar is no longer needed. The steps to hide the Toolbar are summarized on the next page.

TO HIDE A TOOLBAR

Format Toolbar removed

① Right-click any button on the Format Toolbar.
② Click Format on the QuickMenu.

WordPerfect hides, or removes, the Format Toolbar (Figure 3-55).

FIGURE 3-55

Editing the Term Paper

After completing and saving the term paper, you should **edit** the term paper; that is, review the term paper for any additions, deletions, or changes. You can edit while the term paper is on the screen, or you may find it easier to edit the paper if you print a copy and then edit the hard copy. When you have finished editing the hard copy, you can transfer the edits to the file on disk.

Moving Text

Upon reviewing a document, you may find that you wish to move text from one location to another location within the same document. The easiest method you can use to move text is **Drag and Drop Text**. The general steps for using Drag and Drop Text follow.

1. Select the text you wish to move.
2. Point to the highlighted text.
3. Hold down the left mouse button.
4. While holding down the left mouse button, position the insertion point at the location in the document where you wish to move the text.
5. Release the left mouse button.

To illustrate this process, assume you decide to move the words, research topics of interest, and the comma following them in the first paragraph on page one of the term paper so that they are placed before the words, see the latest news and sports, on the same line of the same paragraph (Figure 3-56). Before you can use Drag and Drop Text, you must locate the words you wish to move and display them on the screen.

More *About*
Moving Text

Drag and Drop allows you to move and copy text. If you want to copy text instead of move text, select the text, point to the text and hold down the left mouse button, position the shadow pointer in the new location, hold down the CTRL key and release the left mouse button. Then release the CTRL key. The text will display in both the original location and new location.

FIGURE 3-56

Moving the Insertion Point to Another Page

Assuming the insertion point is on page three (Works Cited page) and you know the sentence you wish to move is on page one, you can use the scroll bar to move through the document. A faster method to move the insertion point to another page in the same document is to use **Go To**. The following steps illustrate how to use Go To to move the insertion point to the top of page one in the term paper.

Steps To Move the Insertion Point to Another Page

1 Point to any area on either the vertical scroll bar or horizontal scroll bar.

The mouse pointer points to the area below the vertical scroll bar arrow (Figure 3-57).

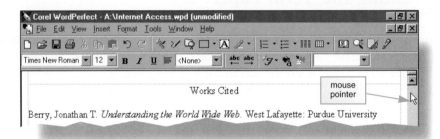

FIGURE 3-57

2 Right-click the vertical scroll bar. Point to Go To on the QuickMenu.

WordPerfect displays a QuickMenu and highlights the Go To command (Figure 3-58).

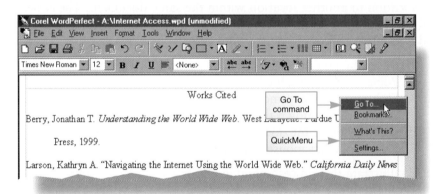

FIGURE 3-58

3 Click Go To.

WordPerfect displays the Go To dialog box (Figure 3-59) The Page number option button is selected and the page number of the page containing the insertion point (3) displays in the Page number text box.

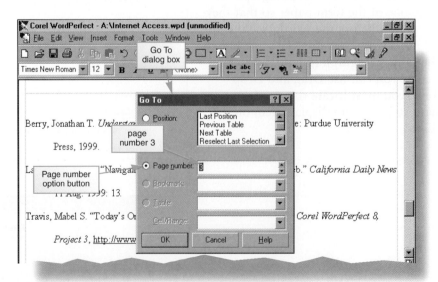

FIGURE 3-59

4 **Type** 1 **in the Page number text box. Point to the OK button.**

The number 1 displays in the Page number text box (Figure 3-60).

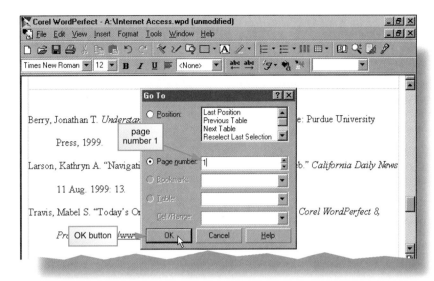

FIGURE 3-60

5 **Click the OK button.**

The top of the first page of the term paper displays (Figure 3-61). The insertion point is located at the beginning of the first line of the term paper on page one.

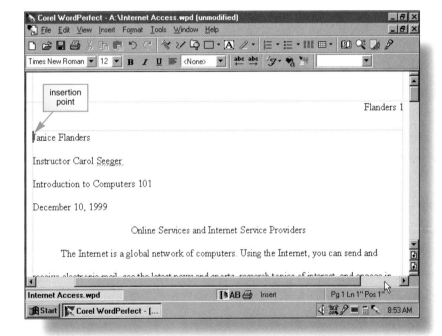

FIGURE 3-61

Other Ways

1. On Edit menu click Go To, type page number, click OK button
2. Scroll document
3. Press PAGE UP or PAGE DOWN keys repeatedly
4. Press CTRL+G

Finding a Word in a Document

Another method you can use to quickly move to a specific area in a document is Find and Replace. **Find and Replace** allows you specify one or more words you wish to locate in a document. In the following example, assume you are at the beginning of the document and you need to find the word, research, which is the first word in the text you wish to move to another location in the same document. Perform the steps on the next two pages to find the word, research.

Steps To Find a Word in a Document

1 **Click Edit on the menu bar and then point to Find and Replace.**

WordPerfect displays the Edit menu and highlights the Find and Replace command (Figure 3-62).

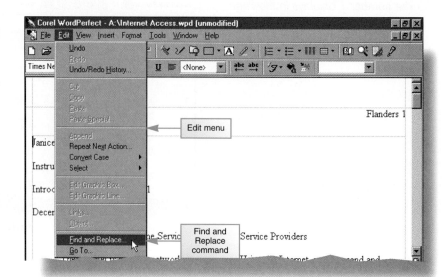

FIGURE 3-62

2 **Click Find and Replace. Type** research **in the Find box. Point to the Find Next button.**

*WordPerfect displays the **Find and Replace dialog box** (Figure 3-63). The word, research, displays in the Find box. Clicking the Find Next button will search from the insertion point toward the end of the document. Clicking the Find Prev button will search from the insertion point toward the beginning of the document. Both types of searches will search the main body of the document and all headers, footers, and footnotes.*

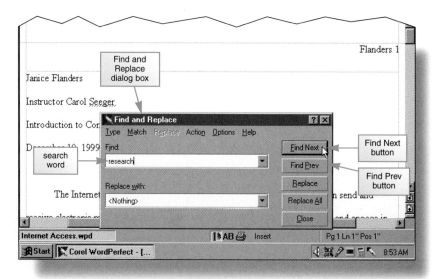

FIGURE 3-63

3 **Click the Find Next button. Point to the Close button.**

WordPerfect locates the first line where the word, research, occurs and highlights the word, research (Figure 3-64).

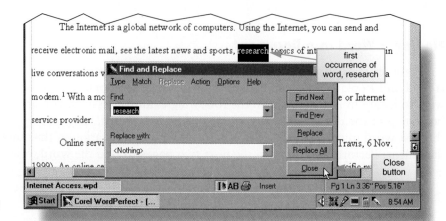

FIGURE 3-64

Click the Close button.

WordPerfect closes the Find and Replace dialog box (Figure 3-65). The word, research, remains highlighted.

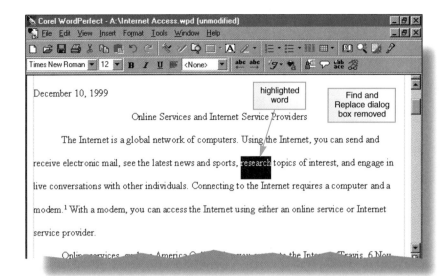

FIGURE 3-65

*Other***Ways**

1. Press F2 and make appropriate selection

2. Press CTRL+F or CTRL+F2 and make appropriate selections

Dragging and Dropping Text

After using Go To or Find and Replace to locate the words you wish to move in the document, use Drag and Drop Text to move the words to the new location. Perform the following steps to move the words, research topics of interest, and the comma following the words to a new location in the document.

 Steps To Move Text by Dragging and Dropping

Select the words, research topics of interest, and the comma following the words. Point to the highlighted text and then hold down the left mouse button.

The words are highlighted (Figure 3-66). When you point to the highlighted text and hold down the left mouse button, the mouse pointer changes to a **block arrow with an outlined rectangle.**

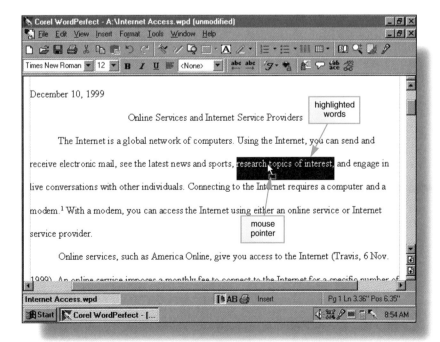

FIGURE 3-66

2 **Drag the mouse pointer to position the insertion point immediately to the left of the word, see, on the same line.**

The insertion point displays to the left of the word, see (Figure 3-67).

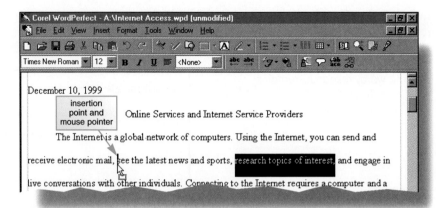

FIGURE 3-67

3 **Release the left mouse button. Click any area in the text to remove the highlight.**

WordPerfect moves the highlighted text to the new location and removes the highlight (Figure 3-68).

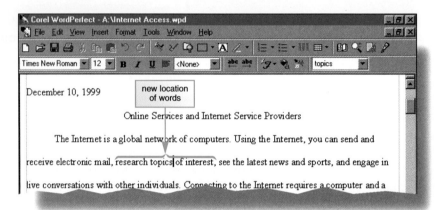

FIGURE 3-68

The Cut and Paste Buttons

Drag and Drop Text is more useful when the text you wish to move or copy and the location to which you wish to move or copy the text are in the same document and visible on the same screen. If you wish to move text from one page to another page or from one document window to another document window, you should use the **Cut button** and the **Paste button** on the Toolbar. The general steps to move text using the Cut button and Paste button are given below.

1. Select the text you wish to move.
2. Click the Cut button on the WordPerfect 8 Toolbar to cut the text out of the document and place it in a storage area of the computer called the **clipboard**.
3. Move the insertion point to the position where you wish the text to display after the move operation. If necessary, switch to another document window or scroll to another location in the same document to move the insertion point.
4. Click the Paste button on the WordPerfect 8 Toolbar to copy the text from the clipboard to the new location.

Finding and Replacing Text in a Document

Find and Replace was used earlier in this project to find a word in a document. This also can be used to find specific text in a document and replace it with new text. WordPerfect searches the text from the insertion point to the end of the document or if you select text, searches only the highlighted portion of the document.

In the term paper, you are to replace all occurrences of the word, see, with the word, view. In certain instances you will not want to replace the letters, see. Perform the following steps to accomplish this task.

More *About*
Finding and Replacing

You also can use Find and Replace to find and delete codes or find and replace codes with other codes. Instructions to find and replace a code and find and delete a code can be found using Help.

 Steps To Find and Replace Text in a Document

1 **Position the insertion point at the beginning of the document. Click Edit on the menu bar and then point to Find and Replace.**

WordPerfect displays the Edit menu and highlights the Find and Replace command (Figure 3-69).

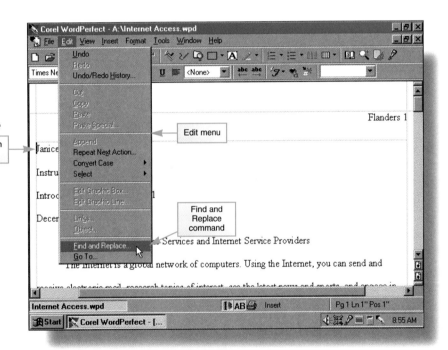

FIGURE 3-69

2 **Click Find and Replace.**

WordPerfect displays the Find and Replace dialog box (Figure 3-70). The word, research, displays in the Find text box because the find operation performed in Step 1 through Step 3 on pages WP 3.37 and WP 3.38 was to find the word, research. <Nothing> displays in the Replace with text box because no replacement word or words were typed.

FIGURE 3-70

③ Type see **in the Find box. Press the TAB key to move the insertion point to the Replace with box. Type** view **in the Replace with box. Point to the Find Next button.**

The word, see, and the word, view, display in the appropriate text boxes (Figure 3-71). Clicking the Find Next button searches from the insertion point toward the end of the document.

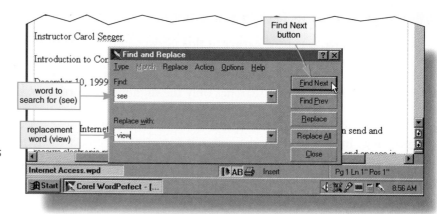

FIGURE 3-71

④ Click the Find Next button to find the first occurrence of the word, see.

WordPerfect locates and highlights the first three letters of the name, Seeger (Figure 3-72). Because the name, Seeger, contains the three characters, s-e-e, WordPerfect highlights those letters in the name, Seeger. The first three characters in the name, Seeger, should not be replaced with the word, view.

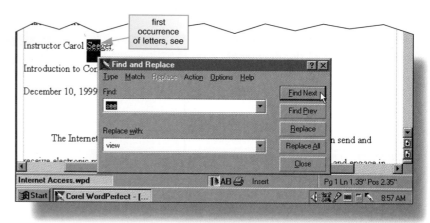

FIGURE 3-72

⑤ Click the Find Next button to leave the name, Seeger, unchanged and to find the next occurrence of the word, see. Point to the Replace button.

WordPerfect highlights the next occurrence of the word, see (Figure 3-73). This is an occurrence where you want to replace the word, see, with the word, view. For each occurrence where you want to substitute the word, view, for the word, see, click the Replace button. If you do not want to replace an occurrence of the word, see, click the Find Next button again. Continue this process until WordPerfect highlights each occurrence of the word, see, in the term paper.

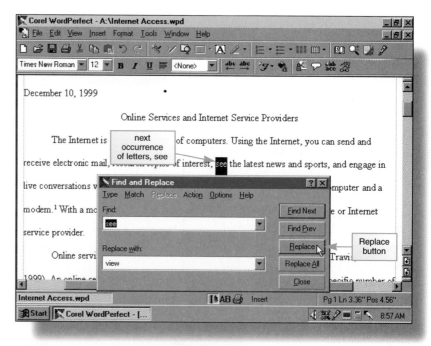

FIGURE 3-73

6 **Click the Replace button. Point to the No button.**

Although not visible in Figure 3-74, WordPerfect replaces the word, see, with the word, view. WordPerfect scans the term paper for additional occurrences of the word, see, until the entire document has been scanned. At that time, the Find and Replace dialog box displays on the screen (Figure 3-74). The Find and Replace dialog box contains the message, "see" Not Found, to indicate the entire document was searched and another occurrence of the word, see, was not found.

FIGURE 3-74

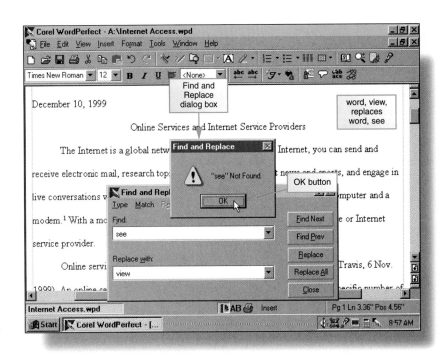

7 **Click the No button. Click the Close button to end the find and replace operation.**

The word, view, replaces the word, see, in the second sentence of the first paragraph (Figure 3-75).

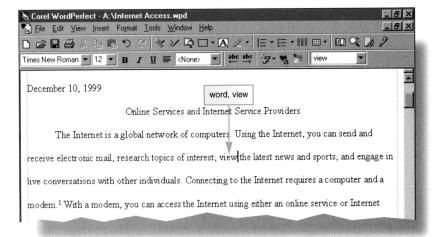

FIGURE 3-75

Find and Replace allows you to search for and replace a word or words, search for and replace a code, choose whether to search forward or backward through the document, and choose to search the entire document or search only the main body of text in the document.

WordPerfect Thesaurus

When writing a term paper, you may find instances where you want to replace certain words in the document with words of similar meaning, called **synonyms**, or with words of opposite meanings, called **antonyms**. To make these replacements, you can use the **WordPerfect Thesaurus**. A **thesaurus** is a dictionary of synonyms and antonyms. Perform the steps on the following pages to replace the word, imposes, with a synonym.

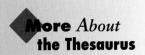

Other Ways

1. Press F2 and make appropriate entries

2. Press CTR+F, or CTRL+F2, and make appropriate entries

More About the Thesaurus

Double-clicking a word in the first list box in Figure 3-77 will display a list of synonyms and antonyms for the word in the second list box.

Steps To Use the Thesaurus to Replace a Word with a Synonym

1 **Scroll the document window to display the second paragraph. Position the insertion point in the word for which you want a synonym (the word, imposes, in the second paragraph). Click Tools on the menu bar and then point to Thesaurus.**

*The insertion point is located in the word, imposes. WordPerfect displays the **Tools** menu and highlights the **Thesaurus command** (Figure 3-76).*

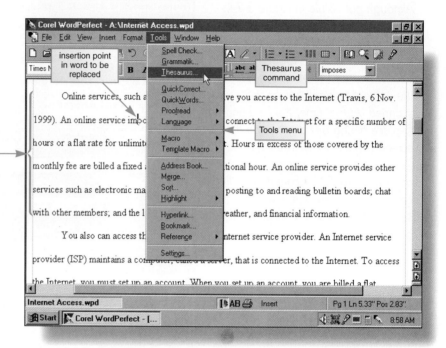

FIGURE 3-76

2 **Click Thesaurus.**

WordPerfect opens a window at the bottom of the document window (Figure 3-77). Three tabs display in the window (Spell Checker, Grammatik, and Thesaurus). The Thesaurus sheet contains the plural word, administers, in the Replace with box, singular word, impose, below the box, and three list boxes. The first list box contains the Synonym heading and a partial list of the synonyms for the singular word, impose. The first synonym in the list, administer, is highlighted. Unlike the plural word, imposes, each synonym is singular.

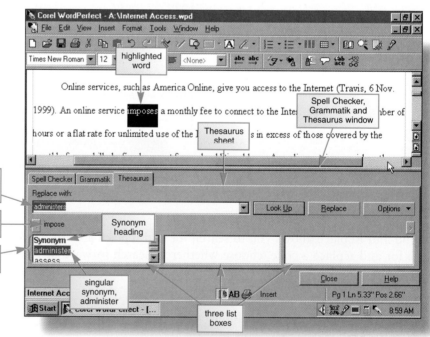

FIGURE 3-77

③ **Scroll the first list box to make the word, charge, visible. Click charge. Point to the Replace button.**

WordPerfect highlights the singular word, charge, in the first list box and displays the plural word, charges, in the Replace with box (Figure 3-78).

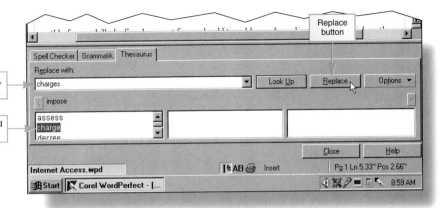

FIGURE 3-78

④ **Click the Replace button.**

The window closes and the plural word, charges, replaces the plural word, imposes, in the document (Figure 3-79).

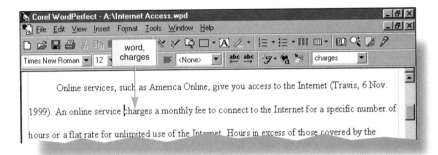

FIGURE 3-79

WordPerfect Spell Check

In Project 1, you corrected incorrectly spelled words that the Spell-As-You-Go and QuickCorrect features detected after you completed entering all the text. As mentioned in the same project, it is a matter of personal choice whether you correct misspelled words as you type or after you have finished typing.

If you prefer to wait until all the text is entered and you are working with a longer document, like the term paper, it may be easier to spell check the entire document using Spell Check. **Spell Check** allows you to check for misspelled words, duplicate words, and irregular capitalization in documents and parts of documents. Unless modified, Spell Check starts spell checking at the beginning of the document and continues until the end of the document is reached. The **Spell Check button** to spell check the spelling of an entire document displays on the WordPerfect 8 Toolbar.

Spell Checking the Term Paper

Assume that while entering the text of the term paper, you enter the incorrectly spelled word, moddem, instead of the correctly spelled word, modem, in the first paragraph of the term paper. The word, moddem, is incorrectly spelled and should be corrected. You should then perform the steps on the following pages to spell check the term paper.

OtherWays

1. Press ALT+F1, make appropriate choices

To Spell Check an Entire Document

1 Click the Spell Check button on the WordPerfect 8 Toolbar. Point to the Skip All button.

WordPerfect starts Spell Check, opens the Spell Checker, Grammatik, and Thesaurus window at the bottom of the document window and displays the Spell Checker sheet (Figure 3-80). Spell Check finds a word in the document (Seeger) that is not in the dictionary. The word, Seeger, is highlighted in the document and displays in the Not found text box in the window. A suggested replacement word (Seeder) displays in the Replace with text box and a list of other possible replacement words displays in the Replacements list box. The word, Seeger, is a proper name and is spelled correctly, so no replacement should be made.

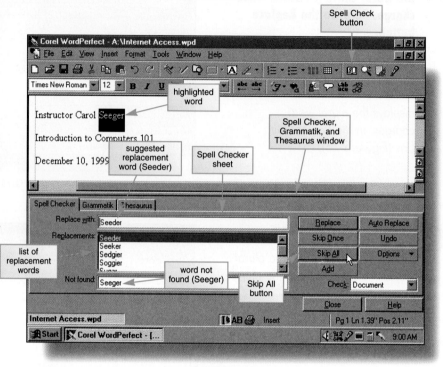

FIGURE 3-80

2 Click the Skip All button. Point to the Replace button.

Spell Check will ignore the word, Seeger, while spell checking the remainder of the document. Spell Check continues to check the spelling of the document until the misspelled word, moddem, is checked against the dictionary and no match is found. A suggested replacement word (modem) displays in the Replace with text box and a list of other possible replacement words displays in the Replacements list box. (Figure 3-81).

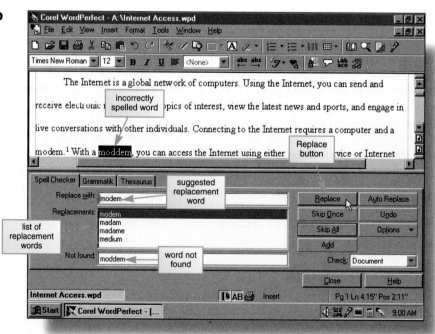

FIGURE 3-81

Click the Replace button. Replace any other words you may have misspelled. Point to the Yes button in the Spell Checker dialog box.

Spell Check replaces the misspelled word (moddem) with the suggested replacement word (modem) and continues to check the remainder of the document (Figure 3-82). WordPerfect opens the Spell Checker dialog box to indicate the remainder of the document has been checked.

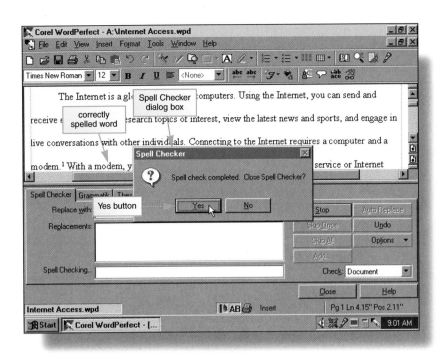

FIGURE 3-82

4 **Click the Yes button.**

WordPerfect closes the Spell Checker dialog box.

Spell Check also checks for duplicate words, irregular capitalization, and words containing numbers. If duplicate words are found in a document, you can delete the second occurrence of the word by clicking the Replace button. If an irregularly capitalized word, such as THinking, is found, you can replace the uppercase letter (H) with a lowercase letter (h) by clicking the Replace button. If a word containing a number, such as 2nd, is found, you can skip over any other occurrences by clicking the Skip All button.

OtherWays

1. Click Spell Check button on WordPerfect 7 Toolbar or WordPerfect 6.1 Toolbar and follow prompts
2. Right-click text area, click Spell Check and follow prompts
3. Press CTRL+F1 and follow prompts

Printing the Term Paper

After creating and editing the term paper, print the document on the printer. Perform the following steps to print the document.

TO PRINT THE TERM PAPER

1. Click the Print button on the WordPerfect 8 Toolbar.
2. If necessary, click the Print tab in the Print dialog box.
3. Click the Print button.
4. When printing is complete, retrieve the document.

WordPerfect prints the term paper on the printer. The printout is shown in Figure 3-1 on page WP 3.5.

Displaying Document Information

Document information includes a count of the number of characters, words, lines, sentences, paragraphs, and pages in a document and the average word length, average number of words per sentence, and maximum words per sentence. The document information includes the text in the headers, footers, and footnotes. Perform the steps on the next page to display this information about the term paper.

Steps: To Display Document Information

1 Right-click the text area. Point to Properties.

WordPerfect displays a QuickMenu and highlights the Properties command (Figure 3-83).

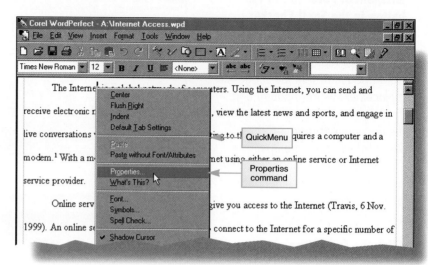

FIGURE 3-83

2 Click Properties. Click the Information tab.

WordPerfect displays the Properties dialog box, the Information sheet in the dialog box, and the document information on the Information sheet (Figure 3-84). The dialog box contains the character count (2561), word count (505), sentence count (36), line count (46), paragraph count (17), page count (3), average word length (5), average words per sentence (14), and maximum words per sentence (32).

3 Click the Close button.

WordPerfect closes the Properties dialog box.

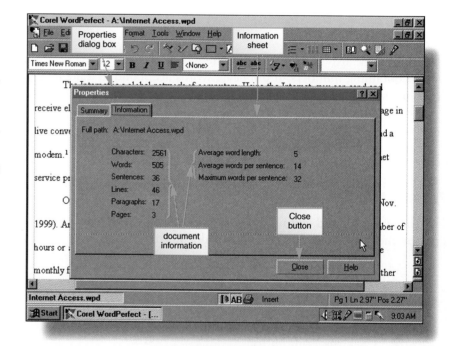

FIGURE 3-84

OtherWays

1. Click File on menu bar, point to Document, click Properties, click Information tab

Moving a Toolbar

The WordPerfect 8 Toolbar shown in Figure 3-85 displays below the menu bar of the Corel WordPerfect window. You can move a Toolbar so that it displays inside the Corel WordPerfect window or along the left, right, or bottom edge of the window. The following steps illustrate how to move the WordPerfect 8 Toolbar.

To Move the Toolbar

1 **Point to a blank area on the WordPerfect 8 Toolbar.**

When you point to a blank area on the Toolbar, the mouse pointer changes to a *four-directional pointer* (Figure 3-85).

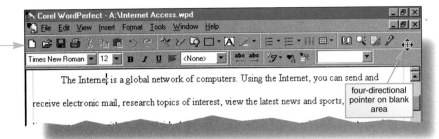

FIGURE 3-85

2 **Drag the Toolbar into the Corel WordPerfect window.**

As you drag the WordPerfect 8 Toolbar, an outline of the Toolbar displays in the window. After dragging, the WordPerfect 8 window containing a palette of buttons displays in the Corel WordPerfect window (Figure 3-86). The Toolbar name (WordPerfect 8) displays on the title bar.

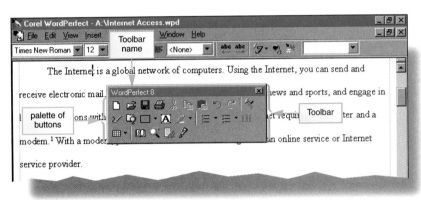

FIGURE 3-86

3 **Point to the title bar of the WordPerfect 8 window. Drag the WordPerfect 8 title bar to the left edge of the Corel WordPerfect window.**

As the Toolbar touches the left edge of the window, the buttons align vertically, and the WordPerfect 8 Toolbar displays along the left edge of the window (Figure 3-87).

4 **Experiment with the Toolbar by dragging it to the bottom edge of the Corel WordPerfect window. Then drag the Toolbar to the top edge of the window.**

The WordPerfect 8 Toolbar displays at the top of the Corel WordPerfect window.

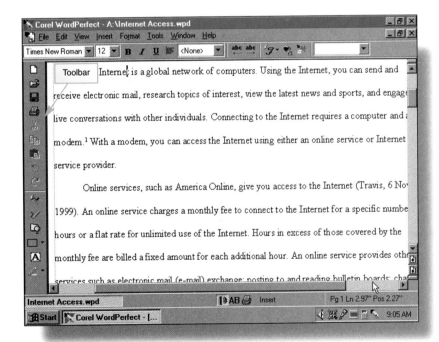

FIGURE 3-87

Quitting WordPerfect

After creating the term paper, save the file again, quit WordPerfect, and remove the Corel WordPerfect 8 Files floppy disk from drive A.

TO QUIT WORDPERFECT AND REMOVE THE FLOPPY DISK

1. Click the Close button in the Corel WordPerfect window.
2. Click the No button in the Corel WordPerfect dialog box.
3. Remove the Corel WordPerfect 8 Files floppy disk from drive A.

The Corel WordPerfect window is closed, changes to the term paper are not saved, WordPerfect is exited, and the Corel WordPerfect 8 Files floppy disk is removed from drive A.

Shortcut Keys and Insertion Point Movement

After you complete the term paper, you may wish to view the first page of the term paper again. In that event, open the file again. You can then display the first page of the term paper using Go To as explained earlier or you can use the CTRL+HOME shortcut key by holding down the CTRL key and pressing the HOME key. Table 3-1 summarizes the shortcut keys that are useful for moving the insertion point to various parts of a document.

You can also use the UP ARROW, DOWN ARROW, LEFT ARROW, and RIGHT ARROW keys to move the insertion point through a document.

Table 3-1

TASK	SHORTCUT KEYS
Move to the beginning of a document (before codes but after Open Style code)	CTRL+HOME, CTRL+HOME
Move to the beginning of a document (after most codes)	CTRL+HOME
Move to the end of a document (after codes)	CTRL+END
Move to the top of the screen (then up one screen at a time)	PAGE UP
Move to the bottom of the screen (then down one screen at a time)	PAGE DOWN
Move to the beginning of a line (after codes)	HOME
Move to the beginning of a line (before codes)	HOME, HOME
Move to the end of a line (after the codes, before the SRt or HRt code)	END
Move to the first line of the previous page	ALT+UP PAGE
Move to the first line of the next page	ALT+PAGE DOWN
Move one word to the left	CTRL+LEFT ARROW
Move one word to the right	CTRL+RIGHT ARROW
Move to the beginning of the next paragraph	CTRL+DOWN ARROW
Move to the beginning of the paragraph, or if you are at the beginning of a paragraph, move to the beginning of the previous paragraph	CTRL+UP ARROW

Project Summary

In Project 3, you created a term paper using the Modern Language Association (MLA) style. While typing the term paper, you created a header with page numbers, changed the line spacing to double-space, used footnotes to include explanatory notes in the term paper, typed parenthetical citations, and created a list of works cited at the end of the term paper.

While editing the term paper, you moved the insertion point to another location in the document, moved text using Drag and Drop Text, were instructed how to move and copy text using the Cut and Paste buttons, and searched for and replaced text using Find and Replace. In addition, you used Thesaurus to find a synonym for a word, used Spell Check to check for incorrectly spelled words, changed the position of a Toolbar, and displayed document information.

What You Should Know

Having completed this project, you now should be able to perform the following tasks:

▶ Center a line of text before typing *(WP 3.18), (WP 3.29)*

▶ Change the line spacing *(WP 3.15)*

▶ Change the top margin *(WP 3.9)*

▶ Close the Reveal Codes window *(WP 3.19)*

▶ Create a hanging indent paragraph *(WP 3.28)*

▶ Create a hyperlink as you type *(WP 3.31)*

▶ Create a second footnote *(WP 3.25)*

▶ Create a soft page break *(WP 3.25)*

▶ Create and format a header *(WP 3.11)*

▶ Create the first footnote *(WP 3.21)*

▶ Display a Toolbar *(WP 3.7)*

▶ Display document information *(WP 3.46)*

▶ Find a word in a document *(WP 3.36)*

▶ Find and replace text in a document *(WP 3.39)*

▶ Hide a Toolbar *(WP 3.33)*

▶ Indent the first line of a paragraph *(WP 3.20)*

▶ Insert a hard page break *(WP 3.28)*

▶ Insert the date *(WP 3.16)*

▶ Move text by dragging and dropping *(WP 3.37)*

▶ Move text using the Cut button and the Paste button *(WP 3.38)*

▶ Move the insertion point to another page *(WP 3.34)*

▶ Move the Toolbar *(WP 3.47)*

▶ Print the term paper *(WP 3.45)*

▶ Quit WordPerfect and remove the floppy disk *(WP 3.48)*

▶ Save the term paper *(WP 3.24)*

▶ Save the term paper again *(WP 3.32)*

▶ Spell check an entire document *(WP 3.44)*

▶ Start WordPerfect *(WP 3.7)*

▶ Type a parenthetical citation *(WP 3.24)*

▶ Type name and course information *(WP 3.16)*

▶ Type the last two paragraphs *(WP 3.26)*

▶ Use shortcut keys to move the insertion point *(WP 3.48)*

▶ Use the Thesaurus to replace a word with a synonym *(WP 3.42)*

▶ View the codes in the term paper *(WP 3.17)*

 Test Your Knowledge

1 True/False

Instructions: Circle T if the statement is true or F if the statement is false.

T F 1. The Modern Language Association of America (MLA) style is used to write the term paper in this project.

T F 2. The Format Toolbar contains a button to create a header.

T F 3 A header is special text that appears at the bottom of printed pages in a document.

T F 4. You can set line spacing using the Line Spacing button on the Property Bar.

T F 5. Explanatory notes are called endnotes when they appear at the bottom of the page in a term paper.

T F 6. You can use Go To to move the insertion point to another page in the same document.

T F 7. Drag and Drop Text allows you to move or copy text from one document to another document.

T F 8. A thesaurus is a dictionary of synonyms and antonyms.

T F 9. The synonym of a word has a similar meaning as the word.

T F 10. The only position the Toolbar can occupy is below the menu bar in the Corel WordPerfect window.

2 Multiple Choice

Instructions: Circle the correct response.

1. The _____ Toolbar contains the Hanging Indent, Page Margins, and Justify Center buttons.
   a. WordPerfect 8   b. Font
   c. Graphics   d. Format

2. A(n) _____ is special text that appears at the top of printed pages in a document.
   a. footer   b. header
   c. footnote   d. endnote

3. To indent the first line of a paragraph, _____
   a. drag the left margin marker 1/2 inch to the right on the Ruler
   b. click First Line Indent on the Insert menu
   c. press the TAB key
   d. press the ENTER key

4. A(n) _____ associates a sentence in the term paper with an explanatory note at the bottom of the page.
   a. superscript   b. subscript
   c. footnote   d. endnote

5. You insert a(n) _____ into a term paper to indicate a statement in the term paper has an associated reference on the Works Cited page.
   a. footnote   b. parenthetical citation
   c. explanatory note   d. endnote

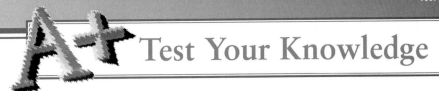

Test Your Knowledge

6. To insert a hard page break in a document, _____.
   a. click the Page Break button on the Format Toolbar
   b. hold down the ENTER key and then press the CTRL key
   c. press the ENTER key
   d. click New Page on the Insert menu

7. To center a line of text before typing, you click the _____ button, type the text, and click the _____ button.
   a. Justify Center, Justify Left
   b. Justify Center, Justify Full
   c. Justify Left, Justify Center
   d. Justify Center, Justify Center

8. When the text you wish to move and the location to which you to wish to move the text are visible on the screen, the easiest method to move the text is to use the _____.
   a. Drag and Drop Text feature
   b. Cut and Paste buttons
   c. Copy and Paste buttons
   d. Drag and Drop buttons

9. The words, charges and imposes, are _____.
   a. nouns
   b. synonyms
   c. antonyms
   d. adjectives

10. You change the position of a Toolbar by pointing to a blank area on the Toolbar and then _____ the Toolbar.
    a. right-dragging
    b. double-clicking
    c. dragging
    d. clicking

3 Knowing the Buttons on the Format Toolbar

Instructions: In Figure 3-88, arrows point to several buttons on the Format Toolbar. In the spaces provided, list the button name and button function of each one.

FIGURE 3-88

BUTTON NAME	BUTTON FUNCTION
1. _____	_____
2. _____	_____
3. _____	_____
4. _____	_____
5. _____	_____
6. _____	_____
7. _____	_____

 Test Your Knowledge

4 Creating a Footnote

Instructions: Given the partially entered term paper and the position of the insertion point in Figure 3-89, list the steps to create the first footnote in the term paper in the space provided.

Step 1: _____

_____

Step 2: _____

_____

Step 3: _____

_____

Step 4: _____

_____

Step 5: _____

_____

Step 6: _____

Step 7: _____

Step 8: _____

FIGURE 3-89

 Use Help

1 Reviewing Project Activities

Instructions: Perform the following tasks on a computer.

1. Start WordPerfect. Press the F1 key. Click the Contents tab. Double-click the How Do I...? book. Double-click the Repeat Text on Every Page book.
3. Click the first help topic (Learn About Headers/Footers) and then click the Display button to read about Headers and Footers. Click the Help Topics button when you have finished reading about the topic. Follow the same procedures for the next three Help topics. How do you replace a header or footer?
4. Click the Help Topics button to return to the Help Topics: WordPerfect Help window.
5. Double-click the Create and Edit Text book. Double-click the Search for Text book. Double-click the Find and Replace Text help topic. On which menu are the Case and Font options available?

Use Help

6. Click the Help Topics button. Double-click the Check for Mistakes book. Double-click the Check Spelling help topic. What is a user word list?

7. Click the Help Topics button to return to the Help Topics: WordPerfect Help window.

8. Click the Index tab. Type footnote and then double-click the edit topic. Read the information about editing footnotes. Click the Options button, click Print Topic, and click the OK button.

9. Click the Help Topics button. Type drag and drop and then double-click the drag and drop text topic. Double-click the To drag and drop text to another document help topic. What technique is used to make dragging and dropping text between documents easier?

10. Click the Help Topics button. Type thesaurus and then double-click the look up a word topic. How do you look up a word automatically?

11. Click the Help Topics button. Type hanging indent and then double-click the hanging indent topic. Double-click the About Indent topic. Click the To use QuickIndent button. Read the information about QuickIndent. Click the Options button, click Print Topic, and then click the OK button.

12. Close any open Help windows by clicking the Close button. Quit WordPerfect.

2 Expanding on the Basics

Instructions: Perform the following tasks using a computer, and then answer the questions.

Toolbars allow you to accomplish basic tasks, such as opening, saving, and printing a document without using a menu. Using Help, answer the following questions about Toolbars.

1. How can you add a button to a Toolbar?
2. How do you hide a Toolbar?
3. How do you create a Toolbar?

Headers are used to print information, such as a chapter heading, title, date, person's name, or company name at the top of a document. Using Help, answer the following questions about headers.

1. How do you edit a header?
2. How do you delete a header?
3. How do you stop a header from printing on subsequent pages?

A hanging indent was used during the creation of each entry on the Works Cited page. Using Help, answer the following questions about other forms of indentation.

1. What is the difference between an indent and a double indent? What is the difference between the previous two forms of indentation and a hanging indent?
2. Is there a difference between pressing the Tab key and clicking the Indent button? If your answer is yes, explain the difference?
3. How do you indent the first line of each paragraph automatically?

One proofreading tool provided by WordPerfect is Grammatik, a grammar checker. Use Ask the PerfectExpert to get detailed help about grammar checking. Answer the following questions about grammar checking.

1. How do you check the grammar of a document?
2. What is a rule?
3. What is a checking style?

Apply Your Knowledge

1 Editing a Word Processing Document

Instructions: The Computer_Systems.wpd file, located on the Corel WordPerfect 8 Web site, contains the text of a term paper. Perform the following steps to download the file and edit the document.

Part 1: Downloading and Opening the Computer Systems file

1. Start WordPerfect.
2. If you do not have access to the Internet, obtain a copy of the Computer_Systems.wpd file from your instructor, place the file on the Corel WordPerfect 8 Files floppy disk, and go to Step 5.
3. Click File on the menu bar. Click Internet Publisher. Click the Browse the Web button to start your browser. Type http://www.scsite.com/wp8 in the Location box. Press the ENTER key to display the home page of the Corel WordPerfect 8 Web site.
4. Click Project 5.
5. Click the Computer_Systems.wpd filename and follow the instructions to download the file to the Corel WordPerfect 8 Files floppy disk.
6. Close all Netscape windows.
7. Open the Computer_Systems.wpd document located on the Corel WordPerfect 8 Files floppy disk.

Part 2: Editing the Document

1. Find and replace the word, user, with the words, computer user. Change all occurrences of the word in the document.
2. Using Drag and Drop Text, switch the position of the words, system software, with the words, application software, in the fourth sentence in the first paragraph.
3. Using the Cut and Paste buttons, switch the position of the words, electronic spreadsheets, with the words, database management systems, in the last sentence of the first paragraph.

Part 3: Saving and Printing the Document

1. Save the document on the Corel WordPerfect 8 Files floppy disk using Edited Computer Systems.wpd as the filename.
2. Print the document.

1 **Preparing a Term Paper**

Problem: You are a college student enrolled in an introductory computer class. Your assignment is to prepare a short term paper about the history of graphical interfaces. The requirements are to prepare the term paper using the MLA style. Create the term paper shown in Figure 3-90 below and on the next page.

Part 1: Creating the Term Paper

1. Change the top margin to .5 inch. Change the line spacing to double spacing.
2. Create a header to number pages.
3. Type the name and course information at the left margin. Center and type the title.
4. Type the body of the paper as shown in Figure 3-90a and Figure 3-90b on the next page. Indent the first line all paragraphs. Insert footnotes and parenthetical citations as required.
5. Insert a hard page break following the body of the paper.
6. Create the Works Cited page as shown in Figure 3-90c on the next page.
7. Save the term paper on the Corel WordPerfect 8 Files floppy disk using Graphical Interface Revolution.wpd as the filename.
8. Print the term paper.

Part 2: Editing the Term Paper

Problem: After reading the term paper, you realize there are several changes you would like to make to the term paper. Follow the instructions on the next page to edit the term paper.

Farnsworth 1

Barbara Anne Farnsworth

Professor Carolyn Tagemann

Introduction to Computers 110

October 13, 1999

The Graphical User Interface Revolution

Bill Gates, founder of Microsoft, popularized the use of graphical user interfaces in the 1990s by introducing Microsoft Windows. Today, more than 90 million copies of Microsoft Windows are used in businesses worldwide.

As early as 1977, Gates realized the need for operating system changes. A key element missing in operating systems was the capability of application software to interface easily with a computer's input and output devices.[1] Although he recognized the need for change, it was several years before Bill Gates and Microsoft would take action.

At a 1982 computer convention, VisiCorp Corporation demonstrated a software interface called VisiOn. VisiOn contained many of the operating system changes Gates had imagined. In response to VisiOn, Microsoft began the development of what was called the Interface Manager (Cooper 56). A design team was formed and announcements were made that Microsoft was working on a product superior to VisiOn.

The graphical user interface concept used to develop the Interface Manager was a descendent of the experimental versions of the graphical user interface from Xerox's Palo Alto Research Center and the commercial version from Apple Computer's Macintosh.

Throughout 1983, Microsoft promoted the Interface Manager and the graphical user

---
[1] Bill Gates envisioned using software, called device drivers, to facilitate the communication between application software and the computer's input and output devices.

FIGURE 3-90a

(continued)

In the Lab

Preparing a Term Paper *(continued)*

1. Use Find and Replace to replace the word, Microsoft, with the words, Microsoft Corporation, where appropriate.
2. Use Drag and Drop Text to move the second sentence in the first paragraph to the beginning of the first paragraph.
3. Use the Thesaurus to replace the word, imagined, with a more appropriate word from the Thesaurus.
4. Check the spelling of the entire document.
5. Count the number of words, lines, and sentences in the term paper.
6. Save the modified term paper on the Corel WordPerfect 8 Files floppy disk using Edited Graphical Interface Revolution.wpd as the filename.
7. Print the term paper.
8. Write the total number of words, lines, and sentences in the term paper above your name on the term paper.

Farnsworth 2

interface revolution. The name Microsoft Windows was introduced when marketeer Rowland Hanson insisted on replacing the name Interface Manager with Microsoft Windows (Riley, 13 Jan. 1999). By late 1983, Windows was widely recognized even though the development of Windows would not be complete until 1985.

Microsoft released Microsoft Windows Version 1.0 in 1985. Version 2.0 followed in October 1987. When Microsoft released Version 3.0 in May 1990, Windows became a success (Caldwell 17-18).

In the year following the release of Microsoft Windows Version 3.0, more than three million copies were sold. In 1992, Microsoft released Version 3.1.[2] Microsoft Windows Version 3.0 and Version 3.1 marked the beginning of the widespread transformation to the graphical environment of Microsoft Windows.

Three years later, Microsoft released Microsoft Windows 95 and the migration to the graphical environment was completed. The acceptance of Windows 95 by business and personal users made Windows 95 the most popular and widely used operating system for personal computers.

[2] Computer magazine writers were quick to write about Windows Version 3.1. Articles in every computer magazine summarized new features and gave tips on how to use Windows.

FIGURE 3-90b

Farnsworth 3

Works Cited

Caldwell, Mark S. *The History of Microsoft Windows.* New York: Computer Publishing, 1999.

Cooper, Patricia L. "Reactions to the New VisiOn Software System." *Personal Computer Journal* 72 (1999: 56-59).

Riley, Christopher S. "Microsoft Windows Replaces Interface Manager." *Rochester Daily Gazette.* http://www.rochestergazette.com/pr1.htm (13 Jan. 1999).

FIGURE 3-90c

In the Lab

2 Preparing a Term Paper

Problem: You are a college student enrolled in an introductory Advertising and Marketing class. Your assignment is to prepare a short term paper about self-publishing using the MLA style. Create the term paper shown in Figure 3-91 below and on the next page.

Part 1: Creating the Term Paper

1. Change the top margin to .5 inch. Change the line spacing to double spacing. Create a header to number pages. Type the name and course information at the left margin. Center and type the title.

2. Enter the body of the paper as shown in Figure 3-91a and Figure 3-91b on the next page. Indent the first line of all paragraphs. Insert footnotes and parenthetical citations as required. Insert a hard page break following the body of the paper. Create the Works Cited page as shown in Figure 3-91c on the next page.

3. Save the term paper on the Corel WordPerfect 8 Files floppy disk using Self-Publishing.wpd as the filename. Print the term paper.

Perez 1

Alexander Perez

Professor Frank Wilson

Introduction to Advertising and Marketing 111

October 6, 1999

Self-Publishing

Self-publishing is the process of publishing a book you have written yourself. Self-publishing is not new. In 1884, Mark Twain wrote and published *Huckleberry Finn*. Today, consultants and experts regularly publish their own books as a way to establish their reputations. Professional authors often self-publish to maximize earnings from writing.

Self-publishing entails writing, producing, and selling a book (Peterson 34). A self-published book should be written clearly, well organized, and thorough. An editor with expertise in the subject matter should review the book and make suggestions on content, organization, and writing style. Next, a copyeditor with experience in proofreading should review the book for spelling and grammatical errors.

Production involves designing, laying out, and printing the book (Clancy, 10 Sept. 1998). A designer suggests page size, type of paper, text size and style, and may design artwork for the book. Next, an artist will lay out the book by placing the text and illustrations on each page. Typically, the artist uses desktop publishing software to lay out the pages of a book. Small print shops that specialize in printing 1,000 to 5,000 copies at a time are a good choice to print the book. Printing is the most expensive part of self-publishing.[1]

After producing a book, you must sell the book. Selling is a time-consuming project that

---

[1] Printing costs may vary from $1.49 per book to print 1,000 books to $1.29 per book to print 5,000 books. As the quantity printed increases, the price per book decreases.

FIGURE 3-91a

(continued)

In the Lab

Preparing a Term Paper *(continued)*

Part 2: Editing the Term Paper

Problem: After reading the term paper, you decide to make several changes to the paper. Follow the instructions below to edit the term paper.

1. Replace the word, authors, with the word, writers. In the second paragraph, move the words, well organized, in the second sentence to before the words, written clearly, in the same sentence. Replace the word, involves, in the third paragraph with a word recommended by the Thesaurus.
2. Check the spelling of the entire document. Save the modified term paper on the WordPerfect Document Files floppy disk using Edited Self-Publishing.wpd as the filename. Print the term paper.
3. Use Document Properties to calculate the average word length in the term paper. Write the average word length in the term paper above your name on paper.

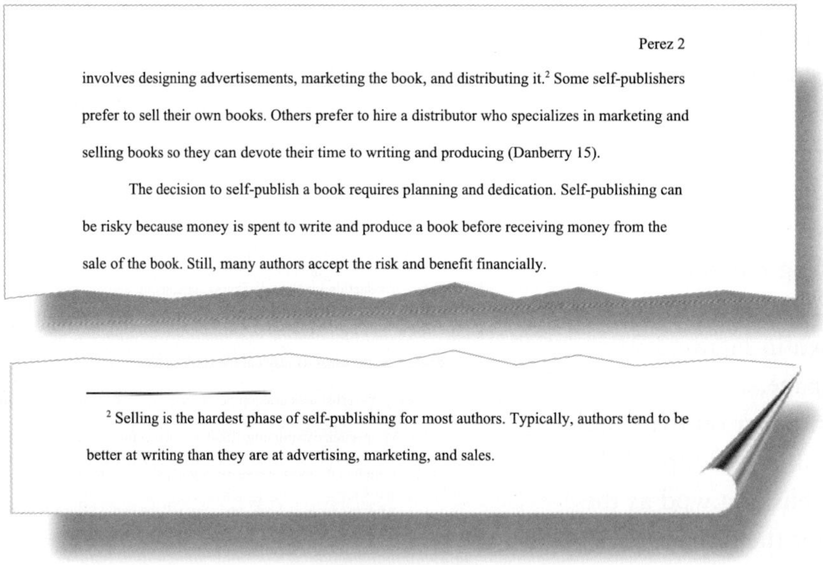

Perez 2

involves designing advertisements, marketing the book, and distributing it.[2] Some self-publishers

prefer to sell their own books. Others prefer to hire a distributor who specializes in marketing and

selling books so they can devote their time to writing and producing (Danberry 15).

    The decision to self-publish a book requires planning and dedication. Self-publishing can

be risky because money is spent to write and produce a book before receiving money from the

sale of the book. Still, many authors accept the risk and benefit financially.

---

[2] Selling is the hardest phase of self-publishing for most authors. Typically, authors tend to be

better at writing than they are at advertising, marketing, and sales.

FIGURE 3-91b

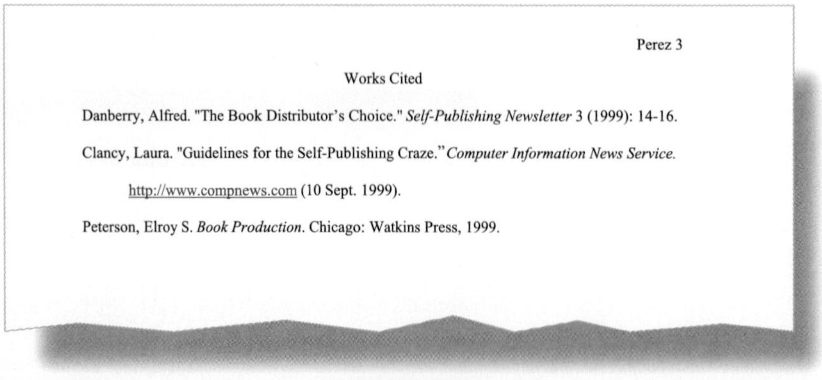

Perez 3

Works Cited

Danberry, Alfred. "The Book Distributor's Choice." *Self-Publishing Newsletter* 3 (1999): 14-16.

Clancy, Laura. "Guidelines for the Self-Publishing Craze." *Computer Information News Service.*

    http://www.compnews.com (10 Sept. 1999).

Peterson, Elroy S. *Book Production.* Chicago: Watkins Press, 1999.

FIGURE 3-91C

In the Lab

3 Preparing a Term Paper

Problem: You are a college student enrolled in a Software Applications class. Your assignment is to prepare a 450-500 word term paper about grammar checking software. Create the term paper shown in Figure 3-92 using the MLA style. Save the term paper using an appropriate name.

After reading the term paper, you decide to edit it by replacing the word, find, with the word, locate, where appropriate; moving the words, errors in grammar, in the first paragraph to before the words, weaknesses in writing style; and replacing the second occurrence of the word, archaic, with a word recommended by the Thesaurus.

Check the spelling of the entire document. Calculate the word count. If the length of the term paper is not within the 450-500 word requirement, edit the term paper to make the term paper longer or shorter. Save and print the modified term paper.

Rutkowski 1

Pam Rutkowski

Professor Andrew Findley

Software Applications 201

November 23, 1999

Grammar Checking Software

Grammar is the study of how words and their component parts and inflections combine to form sentences. Grammar checking software allows you to find and correct improper grammar in a written document.[1] Most grammar checking software packages detect three types of problems: weaknesses in writing style, errors in grammar, and mechanical mistakes.

Common grammatical errors include subject-verb disagreements, incomplete sentences, and double negatives (Sarandon 29). A grammar checker can recognize the missing subject and verb in the following incomplete sentence: For example, singing, dancing, and acting. A subject-verb disagreement causes a grammar checker to suggest substituting the word, were, for the word, was, in the following sentence: We was playing in the backyard. Also detectable by a grammar checker is a double negative such as the use of the words, not and no, in the following sentence: She does not have no money.

Grammar checkers also identify weaknesses in writing style that include using archaic words and the passive voice. Although common in the past, the word, Ofttimes, in the following sentence is archaic: Ofttimes, we go to the movies. Grammar software can detect the passive voice in the following sentence: The ball was thrown by Bob.

Grammar checkers can distinguish mechanical mistakes including double occurrences of a

[1] A wide variety of grammar checking software is available at a reasonable price at local software retail stores.

FIGURE 3-92A

(continued)

Preparing a Term Paper *(continued)*

Rutkowski 2

word, incorrect punctuation, and misuse of capitalization.[2] A double occurrence of the word, the,

occurs in the following sentence: I went to the the concert on Saturday. Incorrect punctuation

causes a grammar checker to find a missing apostrophe showing the possessive in the noun,

Freds, in the following sentence: It is Freds newspaper (Rochester, 20 Aug. 1999). A grammar

checker would detect the incorrect capitalization of the word, july, in this sentence: We go to the

beach in july.

      Grammar checking software allows a writer to check easily for common grammatical

errors (Beatrice 15-17). Regardless of your profession, grammar checking software provides help

for effective communication through well-written documents.

---

[2] In addition to grammar checking software, spell checking software packages also detect

double occurrences of a word and improper capitalization in a written document.

FIGURE 3-92b

Rutkowski 3

Works Cited

Beatrice, Candice D. *Easy-to-Use Grammar Checkers*. Saginaw: Saginaw Press, 1999.

Rochester, Daniel S. "Common Punctuation Errors." *Portland Daily News*.

    http://www.pdnews.com/page1.htm (20 Aug. 1999).

Sarandon, Patricia. "Grammar Checking for the Nineties." *Personal Computer Journal* 131

    (1999): 27-31.

FIGURE 3-92c

Cases and Places

The difficulty of these case studies varies: ❱ are the least difficult; ❱❱ are more difficult; and ❱❱❱ are the most difficult.

1 ❱ Designing Web pages for display on the Internet has become a popular and profitable business. Research the World Wide Web and determine the following: 1) what computer hardware and software is required to design a Web page; 2) how a Web page is designed and created; 3) how the Web page is connected to the Internet: and 4) who pays Web page designers to create Web pages. Write a term paper explaining the World Wide Web and Web page design. Prepare the term paper using the MLA style and the concepts and techniques presented in this project. Include at least two footnotes and three parenthetical citations in the term paper.

2 ❱ The three authorities recognized by WordPerfect for writing term papers are the Modern Language Association (MLA), Chicago Manual of Style (Tiburian), and American Psychological Association (APA). Research the Tiburian and APA styles. Write a term paper that summarizes the two styles. Prepare the paper using the MLA style and the concepts and techniques presented in this project. Include at least two footnotes and three parenthetical citations in the term paper.

3 ❱❱ Several companies advertise on the Internet that they sell term papers to high school and college students. Gather information about several of these companies using the Internet. Determine who writes the term papers, the price of the term papers, and the legality of using these term papers in school. Contact several teachers for their opinion of buying term papers. Write a brief report that summarizes your findings.

4 ❱❱ In WordPerfect, you can access the Spell Check, Grammatik, and Thesaurus proofreading tools when preparing documents. Using the Internet, a library, or any other resource, research the purpose of each proofreading tool. Write a brief report summarizing the three proofreading tools.

5 ❱❱❱ The MLA report Project (PerfectExpert) allows you to prepare a term paper using the MLA style. If possible, obtain a copy of the MLA Handbook for Writers of Research Papers (Fourth Edition 1995) from the library or a bookstore or download it from the MLA Web site. The URL is: http://155.43.225.30/mla.htm. Select one of the In the Lab assignments in this project that your instructor did not assign as homework. Use PerfectExpert (MLA Report project in the Education category) to prepare the term paper in that assignment.

Cases and Places

6 ▶▶ Microsoft Word 97, another word processor, also contains a spell checker, grammar checker, and Thesaurus. Choose one of these three proofreading tools and compare it to the same tool in Corel WordPerfect 8. Write a brief report summarizing the similarities and differences between the two tools.

7 ▶▶ For several years, mathematics teachers could not decide whether students should be allowed to use calculators in the classroom. Is the same thing happening to word processors and English teachers? Interview an English teacher at a junior high school, high school, and college to determine their policies on using word processors in the classroom and for homework assignments. Write a brief report explaining what a word processor is, how it can be used, and then summarize the policies and views of the teachers you interviewed.

Generating Form Letters, Mailing Labels, and Envelopes

Objectives:

You will have mastered the material in this project when you can:

▶ Understand the merge process
▶ Create and enter data into a data file
▶ Differentiate between fields and records
▶ Understand the function of markers in a data file
▶ Create the letter form file
▶ Insert merge codes into the letter form file
▶ Create and format a letterhead
▶ Add a horizontal graphics line to the letterhead
▶ Create a table
▶ Enter text and formulas into a table
▶ Apply a table style to a table
▶ Select and format a cell or group of cells in a table
▶ Insert or delete a row or column in a table
▶ Merge the data file and letter form file
▶ Print form letters
▶ Create the label form file
▶ Merge the data file and label form file
▶ Print mailing labels
▶ Create the envelope form file
▶ Merge the data file and envelope form file
▶ Print envelopes

FORM, FIT, *and* FUNCTION

Bathed in the golden glow of a full moon, a wizened old gypsy woman slowly stirs her bubbling cauldron. In time with her movements, she chants a chilling elegy:

*Many a man who is pure in heart
and says his prayers by night
May become a wolf when
wolfsbane blooms
Beneath the full moon's light.*

Suddenly, scudding clouds mask the moon, and from a distant forest comes a piercing howl. The scene cuts to a man writhing in the throes of transformation — changing from human form to that of a slavering werewolf, desiring human flesh.

This scene and many like it are the products of show business, catering to people's abiding fascination with things that change their form. Known as shapeshifters, these beings abound in literature, music, and films: Odo from the

database

merge

form letters

transform

television series *Deep Space Nine*; the *Flying Dutchman* of Wagnerian opera fame; Merlin, who often changed shapes to aid King Arthur; and even Bram Stoker's *Dracula*, who was transformed into a bat.

It is fun to be scared by fictitious monsters, but in Europe of the sixteenth century, people saw monsters around every corner. In France, 30,000 people were executed as werewolves in a single year!

Why is the shape of things so important? Psychologists say that because humans and animals depend on the form of a thing for recognition, they are puzzled and intrigued by those that seem to be what they are not. To classify an object, we identify it by its form. Going beyond physical appearance, we recognize intangibles such as the musical form in a sonata, the customs of etiquette, or the subtle characteristics of traditional values. Other identifiers include buying-habits of demographic groups, memberships in associations, or voter preferences.

In today's information age, PC software makes it possible to use this type of information to target specific groups of individuals. Organizations utilizing extensive databases can conduct mass mailings to promote products, offer services, and solicit data.

Corel WordPerfect provides a powerful mass mailing capability. You may need to mail a letter to a student club. Or when job-hunting after graduation, you might want to send a query letter to dozens of potential employers. After helping you create a database of names and addresses, WordPerfect provides a seamless merge process, generating personalized copies of your form letter and the associated labels or envelopes. All you need do is sign the letters. Then, watch as your correspondence shapes the decisions of those who you contact.

Devices that cause others to change are shapeshifters, too. Letters worded to influence are intended to change minds, which is a difficult task at best. In *Something Wicked This Way Comes*, Ray Bradbury gives us the ultimate shapeshifter, Mr. Dark, the man who is adept at changing people. Ray also teaches us to be careful of what we wish for, especially at carnival sideshows.

Corel
WordPerfect 8

Generating Form Letters, Mailing Labels, and Envelopes

Case Perspective

Harry McMurtrie is the customer representative for Anderson Autos. Every Monday morning, Harry reviews the list of new customers from the previous week and sends a letter to each new customer to thank them for buying a car and to inform them of their membership in the Anderson Customer Club. Harry creates a data file that contains the names, addresses, and new car purchases of each new customer. Realizing he can save time if he does not have to type a separate letter for each customer, Harry uses a form letter. The form letter, personalized with customer information from the data file, notifies the customer of their Customer Club membership and the discounts available for vehicle maintenance. Harry merges the data file with the form letter so that an individual letter prints for each new customer. Next, Harry generates mailing labels to use when he is preparing to mail the form letters.

Customer Club members receive a fifteen percent discount for all standard vehicle maintenance (3,000, 15,000, and 30,000 mile service). In addition, the 3,000 mile service is free if the customer brings the form letter when he or she delivers the vehicle for service. Harry includes his telephone number in the letter and makes the customer aware of the Anderson Autos Web site.

Introduction

Form letters are widely used by businesses and individuals who wish to send the same letter to a large group of people. Although the message being conveyed in a group of form letters is the same, form letters can be personalized with such information as the name, address, city, state, and zip code. A letter that is personalized is more likely to be opened and read than a letter addressed to Occupant or Resident. A business may generate form letters to announce a sale, address change, or sweepstakes. Individuals may generate form letters to apply for a new job, families can make relatives living out of town aware of recent family activities or send graduation announcements. After generating form letters, envelopes can be addressed or mailing labels generated for the envelopes.

Project Four—Form Letters, Mailing Labels, and Envelopes

Project 4 illustrates how to generate form letters. A form letter is sent to all new customers at Anderson Autos to inform them of their membership in the Customer Club and the associated discounts. Generating form letters involves creating a data file to contain new customer information, creating a letter form file to contain the form letter, and merging the contents of the two files to generate personalized form letters (Figure 4-1).

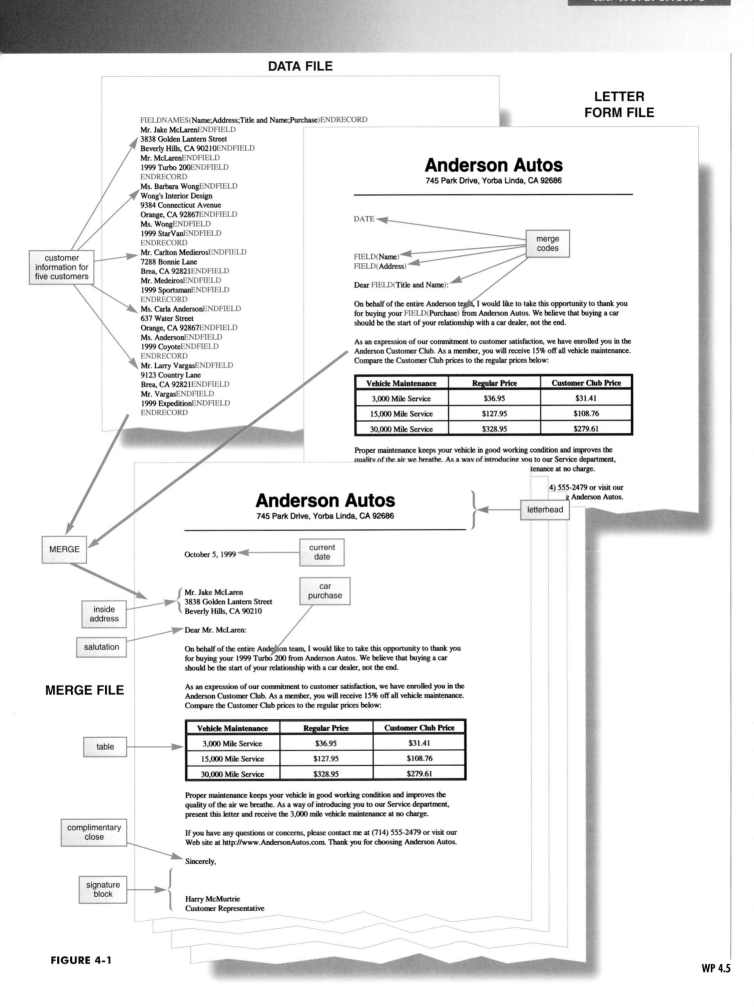

FIGURE 4-1

Document Preparation Steps

The following tasks will be completed in this project.

1. Start WordPerfect.
2. Create and save the data file.
3. Create and save the letter form file.
4. Associate the data file with the letter form file.
5. Merge the data file and letter form file to generate form letters.
6. Print the form letters.
7. Create the label form file.
8. Merge the data file and label form file to generate mailing labels.
9. Print the mailing labels.
10. Create the envelope form file.
11. Merge the data and envelope form files to generate envelopes.
12. Print the envelopes.

The following pages contain a detailed explanation of these tasks.

The Merge Process

You will use **Merge** to produce the form letters shown in Figure 4-1 on the previous page. Two sources are required to produce the form letters.

The first source of information (**letter form file**) controls the merge operation and is required in every merge operation. The letter form file illustrated in Figure 4-1 contains the text of the form letter and special **merge codes** required to perform the merge. The merge codes indicate the information that is missing from the form letter, where to obtain the missing information, and where to insert this information in the letter form file.

The second source of information, the **data source**, supplies information to the letter form file during the merge operation. The data source can be a data file or an Address Book. In this project, you will use a data file to generate the form letters. The **data file** contains information about each customer who will receive a form letter. In Figure 4-1, the data file contains the customer name, customer address, customer title and last name, and customer purchase for five customers.

After creating the data file and the letter form file, you will **merge** the customer information in the data file with the merge codes and text in the letter form file to produce a merge file. The **merge file** contains a personalized form letter for each customer in the data file.

At the top of each form letter is the Anderson Autos letterhead, containing the Anderson Autos name, address, and a horizontal line. Below the letterhead is the current date, inside address, and salutation. Each form letter is personalized with a customer name, address, and salutation. In addition, the first paragraph in the body of each form letter is personalized with a recent car purchase made by the customer.

In the middle of the form letter is a table. The table contains the Vehicle Maintenance, Regular Price, and Customer Club Price for the 3,000 mile service, 15,000 mile service, and 30,000 mile service.

At the bottom of the form letter is the complimentary close, consisting of the word, Sincerely, and a comma. The signature block below the complimentary close contains the signature, typed name of the customer representative (Harry McMurtrie), and his title (Customer Representative).

Starting WordPerfect

Before you can create the data file, you must start WordPerfect. The steps to start WordPerfect are summarized below.

TO START WORDPERFECT

① Click the Start button on the taskbar.

② Point to Corel WordPerfect Suite 8 on the Start menu.

③ Click Corel WordPerfect 8 on the Corel WordPerfect Suite 8 submenu.

④ If necessary, click the Maximize button in the Corel WordPerfect window.

⑤ If necessary, click the Maximize button in the Document1 window.

WordPerfect displays the maximized Corel WordPerfect application window and a blank document titled Document1 in a maximized document window.

The Data File

The first step in generating the form letters is to create the data source (data file). A portion of the data file is illustrated in Figure 4-2 as it appears in the document window. The data file contains the personalized information printed on each form letter (customer title and name, customer address, customer title and last name, and customer purchase).

The information about one customer is called a **record**. In the data file shown in Figure 4-2, there are five records. The first three records are visible, but the remaining two records are not visible. The **ENDRECORD marker** and the hard page break (double horizontal line) following the marker indicate the end of a record. The ENDRECORD marker displays in red text.

The information in each record is divided into fields. A field may contain one piece of information, such as customer name, or several pieces of information, such as the company name, street address, city, state, and zip. The **ENDFIELD marker** and a hard return indicate the end of a field. The ENDFIELD marker displays in red text. Figure 4-2 displays the fields in each record: (1) customer name; (2) customer address; (3) customer title and last name; and (4) customer purchase. The company name in the customer address field is optional and may not display in all records.

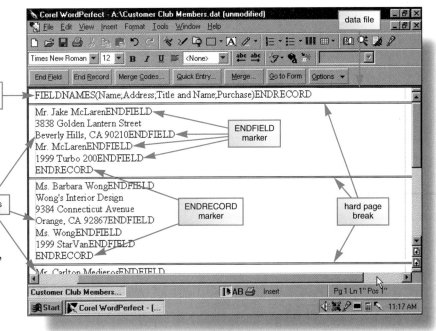

FIGURE 4-2

More *About*
Data Files

In this project, the data file you create is a data text file. A data text file organizes data into fields and records and marks the data with ENDFIELD and ENDRECORD codes. In addition, the data file you create can be a data table file. The data table file organizes the same fields and records into table columns and rows. In addition to using a WordPerfect document as the data file, you also can use other word processing files (Ami Pro or DisplayWrite), database files (dBASE or Paradox), or spreadsheet files (Quattro Pro).

The first line of the data file shown in Figure 4-2 contains the **FIELDNAMES marker**, which consists of the word, FIELDNAMES, followed by a list of the field names in each record of the data file separated by semicolons and enclosed in a set of parentheses. The list of field names is followed by an ENDRECORD marker. The word, FIELDNAMES, the parentheses, and the word, ENDRECORD, display in red text. A hard page break separates this line from the records in the file.

When you create a data file, WordPerfect inserts several codes in the document. WordPerfect inserts the MRG: ENDFIELD code for the ENDFIELD marker, MRG: ENDRECORD code for the ENDRECORD marker, and two revertible MRG:FIELDNAMES codes for the FIELDNAMES markers.

Creating the Data File

The first step in generating the form letters shown in Figure 4-1 on page WP 4.5 is to create the data file. Creating the data file involves designing and entering field names, typing a record for each customer, and saving the data file. Perform the following steps to create the data file.

Steps **To Create a Data File**

---

1 **Insert the Corel WordPerfect 8 Files floppy disk into drive A.**

2 **Click Tools on the menu bar and then point to Merge.**

*WordPerfect displays the Tools menu and highlights the **Merge** command (Figure 4-3).*

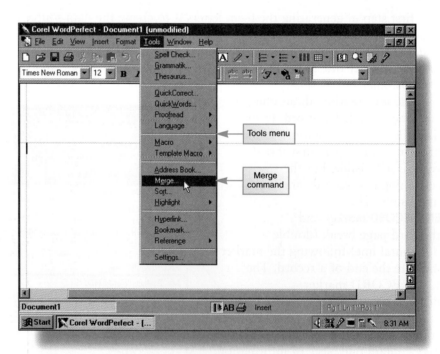

FIGURE 4-3

3 **Click Merge. Point to the Create Data button.**

WordPerfect displays the Merge dialog box containing three areas (Figure 4-4). Each area contains a button and a description of what occurs when you click the button. In addition, the Create Data area contains the Edit records in Corel Address Book for data source button. This button is not used to generate the data file in this project.

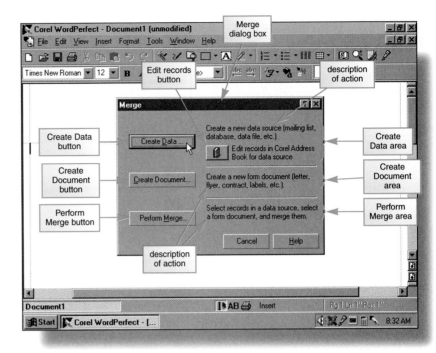

FIGURE 4-4

4 **Click the Create Data button.**

WordPerfect displays the Create Data File dialog box (Figure 4-5). The dialog box contains the Name a field text box containing the insertion point, Fields used in merge list box, Format records in a table check box, and several buttons. A message defining the type of name that should be used for a fieldname and the action the user should take displays at the bottom of the dialog box. The Format records in a table check box is not used to generate the data file in this project.

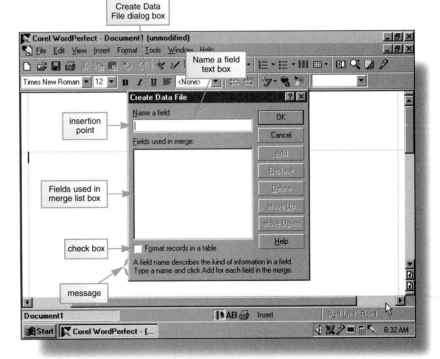

FIGURE 4-5

⑤ Type Name **in the Name a field text box. Point to the Add button.**

The field name, Name, displays in the Name a field text box (Figure 4-6).

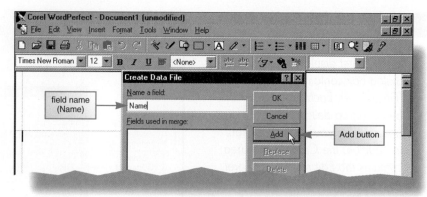

FIGURE 4-6

⑥ Click the Add button.

WordPerfect removes the field name, Name, from the Name a field text box and displays the field name in the Fields used in merge list box (Figure 4-7).

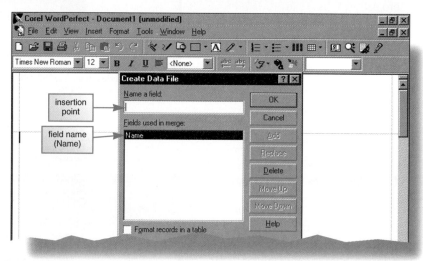

FIGURE 4-7

⑦ Type Address **in the Name a field text box and then click the Add button. Type** Title and Name **in the Name a field text box and then click the Add button. Type** Purchase **in the Name a field text box and then click the Add button. Point to the OK button.**

Four field names display in the Fields used in merge list box (Figure 4-8).

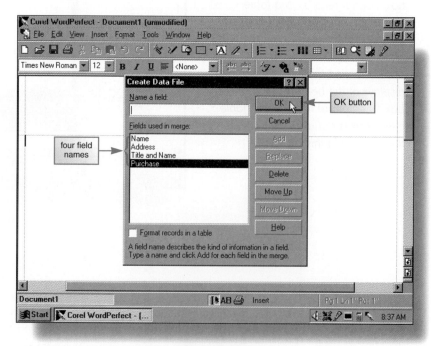

FIGURE 4-8

8 **Click the OK button.**

*WordPerfect removes the Create Data File dialog box, displays the Quick Data Entry dialog box, and displays the partially hidden **Merge Bar** (Figure 4-9). The dialog box contains a text box for each field name and scroll arrows display to the right of each text box. The dialog box displays on top of the first line of the data file that contains the FIELDNAMES marker and a hard page break. Although not visible, two **MRG: FIELDNAMES** codes, a **MRG: ENDRECORD** code, and a Hard Page Break code are inserted in the document.*

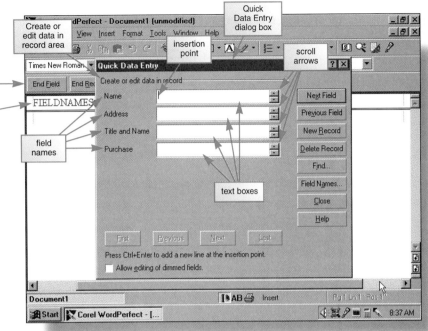

FIGURE 4-9

9 **Type** Mr. Jake McLaren **in the Name text box. Point to the Next Field button.**

The first customer name displays in the Name text box (Figure 4-10).

FIGURE 4-10

10 **Click the Next Field button. Type** 3838 Golden Lantern Street **in the Address text box.**

WordPerfect displays the first line of the address (street address) in the Address text box (Figure 4-11). As the message at the bottom of the Quick Data Entry dialog box indicates, holding down the CTRL key and pressing the ENTER key (CTRL+ENTER) allows you to enter an additional line in a text box.

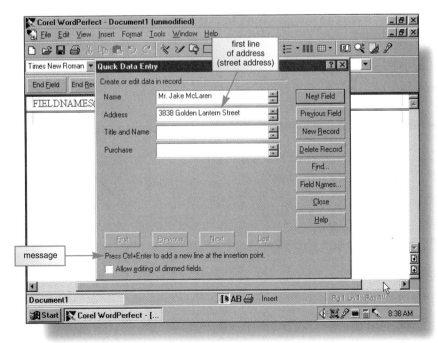

FIGURE 4-11

11 **Hold down the CTRL key and then press the ENTER key.**

WordPerfect scrolls the first line of the address in the Address text box up and displays the insertion point on a blank line (Figure 4-12).

FIGURE 4-12

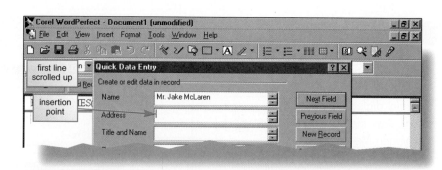

12 **Type** Beverly Hills, CA 90210 **in the Address text box and then click the Next Field button. Type** Mr. McLaren **in the Title and Name text box and then click the Next Field button. Type** 1999 Turbo 200 **in the Purchase text box. Point to the New Record button.**

The second line of the address (city, state, and zip code) displays in the Address text box, the title and last name display in the Title and Name text box, and the customer purchase displays in the Purchase text box (Figure 4-13).

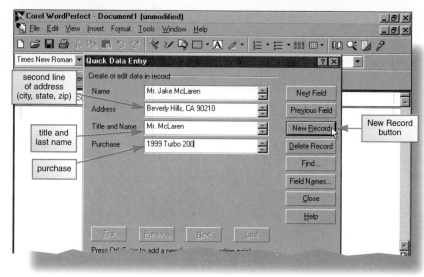

FIGURE 4-13

13 **Click the New Record button. Type** Ms. Barbara Wong **in the Name text box. Click the Next Field button and then type** Wong's Interior Designs **in the Address text box. Hold down the CTRL key, press the ENTER key, and type** 9384 Connecticut Avenue **in the Address text box. Hold down the CTRL key, press the ENTER key, and type** Orange, CA 92867 **in the Address text box. Click the Next Field button and then type** Ms. Wong **in the Title and Name text box. Click the Next Field button and then type** 1999 StarVan **in the Purchase text box. Point to the New Record button.**

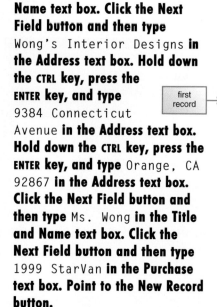

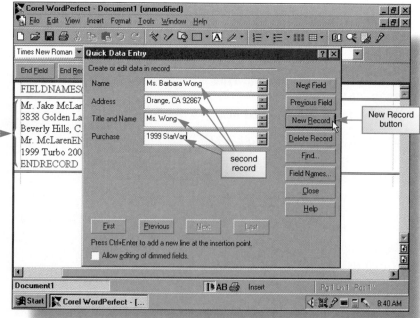

FIGURE 4-14

Although partially hidden, WordPerfect displays the first record in the document window (Figure 4-14). The fields in the second record display in the text boxes in the dialog box.

14 Click the New Record button. Type Mr. Carlton Medeiros in the Name text box. Click the Next Field button and then type 7288 Bonnie Lane in the Address text box. Hold down the CTRL key, press the ENTER key, and type Brea, CA 92821 in the Address text box. Click the Next Field button and then type Mr. Medeiros in the Title and Name text box. Click the Next Field button and then type 1999 Sportsman in the Purchase text box. Point to the New Record button.

Although partially hidden, WordPerfect displays the second record in the document window (Figure 4-15). The fields in the third record display in the text boxes in the dialog box.

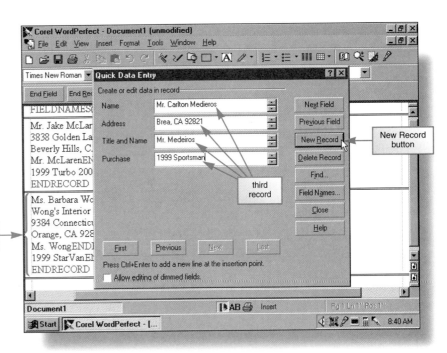

FIGURE 4-15

15 Click the New Record button. Type Ms. Carla Anderson in the Name text box. Click the Next Field button and then type 637 Water Street in the Address text box. Hold down the CTRL key, press the ENTER key, and type Orange, CA 92867 in the Address text box. Click the Next Field button and then type Ms. Anderson in the Title and Name text box. Click the Next Field button and then type 1999 Coyote in the Purchase text box. Point to the New Record button.

Although partially hidden, WordPerfect displays the third record in the document window (Figure 4-16). The fields in the fourth record display in the text boxes in the dialog box.

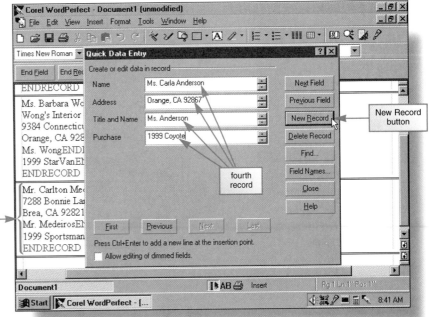

FIGURE 4-16

16 **Click the New Record button. Type** Mr. Larry Vargas **in the Name text box. Click the Next Field button and then type** 9123 Country Lane **in the Address text box. Hold down the CTRL key, press the ENTER key, and then type** Brea, CA 92821 **in the Address text box. Click the Next Field button and then type** Mr. Vargas **in the Title and Name text box. Click the Next Field button and then type** 1999 Expedition **in the Purchase text box. Point to the Close button in the dialog box.**

Although partially hidden, WordPerfect displays the fourth record in the document window (Figure 4-17). The fields in the fifth record display in the text boxes in the dialog box.

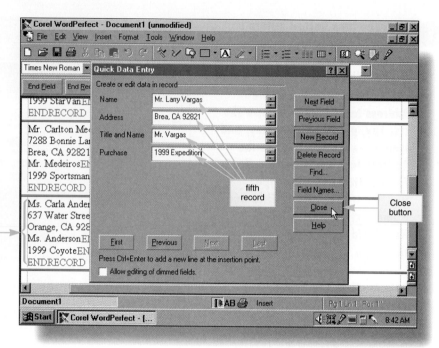

FIGURE 4-17

17 **Click the Close button. Point to the Yes button in the Corel WordPerfect dialog box.**

WordPerfect closes the Quick Data Entry dialog box, displays the Corel WordPerfect dialog box, makes the buttons on the Merge Bar visible, and displays the fifth record in the document window (Figure 4-18). The Corel WordPerfect dialog box contains a message and the Yes and No buttons. WordPerfect inserts the appropriate MRG: ENDFIELD, MRG: ENDRECORD, and Hard Page Break codes in the document.

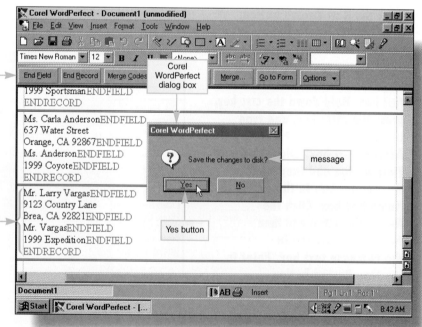

FIGURE 4-18

18 **Click the Yes button. When the Save File dialog box displays, type** Customer Club Members **in the File name box. Click the Save in box arrow. Scroll the Save in drop-down list until 3½ Floppy (A:) displays and then click 3½ Floppy (A:). Click the Save button.**

WordPerfect adds the .dat extension to the Customer Club Members filename, saves the Customer Club Members.dat file on the Corel WordPerfect 8 Files floppy disk, and changes the window title (Figure 4-19). The last two records and part of the third record display in the document window. The ENDRECORD marker displays on a line by itself at the end of each record and the ENDFIELD marker displays to the right of the last line of each field. The ENDRECORD and ENDFIELD markers display in red text.

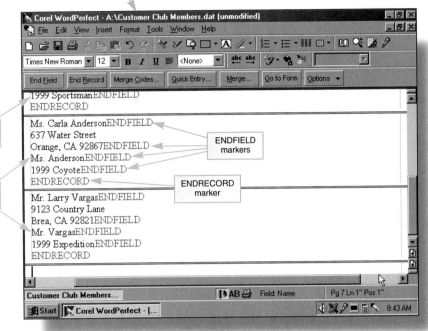

FIGURE 4-19

Editing the Field Names in the Data File

In the Create Data File dialog box (see Figure 4-5 on page WP 4.9), you can add, replace, delete, or reposition a field in a record. To add a field, type the field name in the Name a field text box and then click the Add button as shown in the steps on the previous pages. To change an existing field name, select the field name in the Fields used in merge list box, type the new field name in the Name a field text box, and click the Replace button. To delete a field, select the field name in the Fields used in merge list box and then click the Delete button. To reposition a field name within a record, select the field name in the Fields used in merge list box and then click the Move Up or Move Down button to move the field up one position or down one position in the list of field names.

Editing the Records in a Data File

To edit the data file, open the data file and then click the Quick Entry button on the Merge Bar to display the Quick Data Entry dialog box (see Figure 4-17). The dialog box allows you to view the records using the First button, Previous button, Next button, and Last button. In addition, you can add a record using the New Record button or delete a record using the Delete Record button. To change the text in a field, make the change in the appropriate text box.

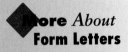

More About Form Letters

The cover letter you created in Project 2 for your resume may be created best as a form letter. Each cover letter will contain the same basic information about yourself, but it should be personalized for each potential employer. Thus, the cover letter will be the form file and the list of employers will be the data file.

More *About* Associating Data Files and Form Files

When you create an association, WordPerfect associates, or links, the data file name and the form file name. When you perform a merge operation using the form file, the associated source file is used. Although you usually associate a data file and form file as you create a form file, you also can create the association or change the association at a later time.

The Letter Form File

The next step in the generation of the form letters is to create the letter form file. The letter form file is created by associating the data file, Customer Club Members.dat, with the form letter and then creating the form letter. The association makes it possible for the letter form file to locate the customer information in the data file (Name, Address, Name and Title, and Purchase).

Associating the Data File with the Letter Form File

When an association is made between the data file and letter form file, WordPerfect gives you the option of creating the form letter in the current document window or opening a new document window. Perform the following steps to associate the data file with the letter form file in a new document window.

To Associate a Data File with a Letter Form File

1 **Click Tools on the menu bar and then point to Merge.**

WordPerfect displays the Tools menu and highlights the Merge command (Figure 4-20).

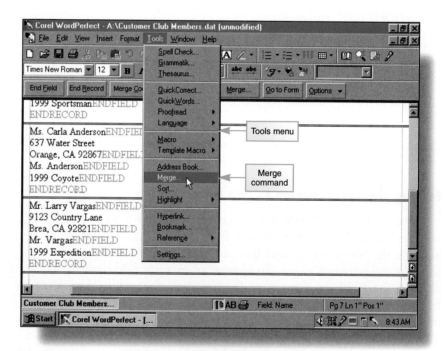

FIGURE 4-20

2 **Click Merge. Point to the Create Document button in the Merge dialog box.**

WordPerfect displays the Merge dialog box (Figure 4-21). The Create Document area contains the Create Document button.

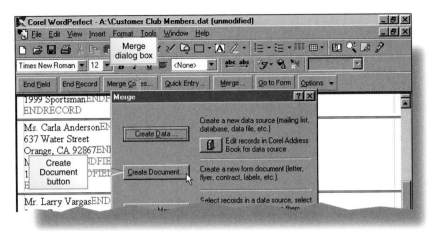

FIGURE 4-21

3 **Click the Create Document button. Point to the OK button in the Create Merge File dialog box.**

WordPerfect displays the Create Merge File dialog box (Figure 4-22). The selected New document window option button indicates a new document window will open to contain the letter form file.

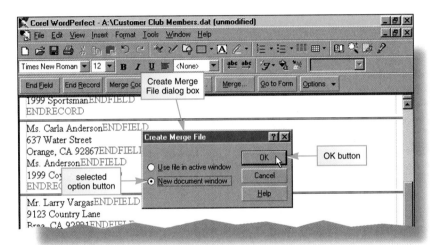

FIGURE 4-22

4 **Click the OK button. Point to the Select File button at the far right side of the Associate a data file text box.**

WordPerfect closes the Create Merge File dialog box, displays the Associate Form and Data dialog box, opens a second document window (Document2), and selects the Associate a data file option button (Figure 4-23). The insertion point is located in the Associate a data file text box. A message at the bottom of the dialog box reminds you to associate a data file, address book, or ODBC data source with the letter form file you are creating. The Merge Bar does not display in the new window.

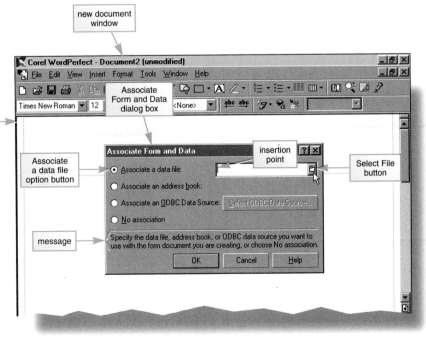

FIGURE 4-23

5 **Click the Select File button. Click Customer Club Members and then point to the Select button.**

WordPerfect displays the Select Data File dialog box (Figure 4-24). The Customer Club Members file-name is highlighted in the list box and displays in the File name box.

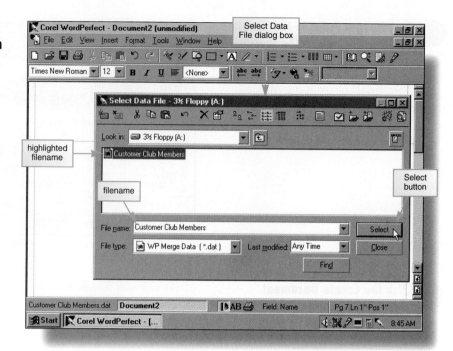

FIGURE 4-24

6 **Click the Select button. Point to the OK button.**

WordPerfect closes the Select Data File dialog box, opens the Associate Form and Data dialog box, and displays the location and part of the data file name (A:\Customer Club Members.da) in the Associate a data file text box (Figure 4-25).

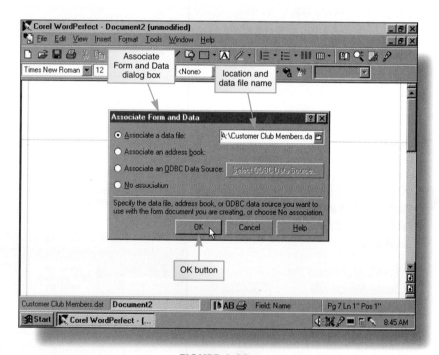

FIGURE 4-25

7 **Click the OK button.**

WordPerfect closes the Associate Form and Data dialog box and displays the Merge Bar in the Document2 window (Figure 4-26).

Merge Bar →

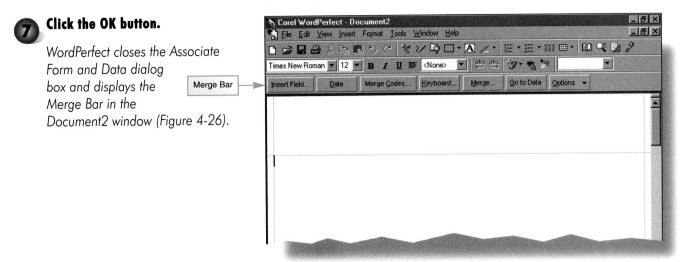

FIGURE 4-26

*Other***Ways**

1. Click Go to Form button on Merge Bar, click Create button

2. Press SHIFT+F9, click Create Document button

The Form Letter

Next, create the form letter by creating a letterhead, typing the text of the form letter, inserting the merge codes, and creating and formatting the table. The steps to create the form letter are given in the following sections.

Creating a Letterhead for the Form Letter

As explained in Project 2, a letterhead is the information at the top of the letter that usually contains a name, address, and phone number. You use graphics, such as horizontal lines, and different font faces, styles, and sizes to enhance the appearance of a letterhead. In Project 2, you created a letterhead when you selected a letterhead style while using PerfectExpert. In this project, you will create the letterhead illustrated in Figure 4-1 on page WP 4.5 without using PerfectExpert.

Displaying the Ruler and Setting the Margins

In the letterhead shown in Figure 4-1 on page WP 4.5, the Anderson Autos name should begin .75-inch down from the top of the page. The default setting for the top margin is 1 inch; therefore, you must change the top margin setting.

When creating a long letter (one full page or more) you should use a 6-inch wide line. A 6-inch line requires left and right margins of 1.25 inches on paper 8.5 inches wide. The default setting for the left and right margins is 1 inch; therefore, you must change the left and right margin settings.

Before you set the margins, you should display the Ruler. The Ruler makes it easy to see the new margin settings and is useful later in this project when you create the table in the letter form file. The steps to display the Ruler and set the margins were explained in previous projects and are summarized on the next page.

More *About* **Letterheads**

There are many designs used to create a letterhead. Some designs center the text and graphics in the letterhead at the top of the page, while others align text and graphics with the right or left margins. Other designs place the company name and logo at the top of the page and the address and other information at the bottom. One thing is certain, a well-designed letterhead adds professionalism and credibility to your business letters.

TO DISPLAY THE RULER AND SET THE MARGINS

① Click View on the menu bar and click Ruler on the View menu.

② Click Format on the menu bar and then click Margins.

③ Type 1.25 in the Left text box.

④ Type 1.25 in the Right text box.

⑤ Type .75 in the Top text box.

⑥ Click the OK button.

WordPerfect displays the Ruler above the Merge Bar, sets the margins, and displays new margin guidelines (Figure 4-27). As indicated by the position of the insertion point, Line entry (Ln 0.75") on the Application Bar, and top margin guideline, the top margin is .75 inch. As indicated by the left and right margin guidelines, Position entry (Pos 1.25"), and left and right margin markers (1.25-inch and 7.25-inch mark) on the Ruler, the left and right margins are 1.25 inch. Although not visible, three Margin codes are inserted in the document.

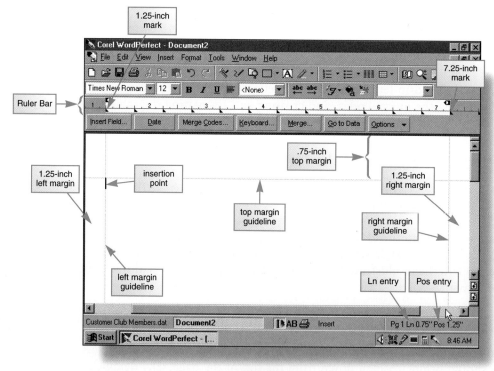

FIGURE 4-27

Typing the Text of the Letterhead

You are now ready to type the letterhead illustrated in Figure 4-1 on page WP 4.5. The agency name is centered and displays in Arial Bold 28-point font. The address is centered and displays in Arial 12-point font. A blank line follows the address. A single horizontal line displays below the blank line between the left and right margins. The steps to center the text of the letterhead as you type are summarized on the next page.

TO CENTER THE TEXT OF THE LETTERHEAD AS YOU TYPE

① Click the Justification button on the Property Bar and then click Center.

② Type `Anderson Autos` and then press the ENTER key.

③ Type `745 Park Drive, Yorba Linda, CA 92686` and then press the ENTER key.

④ Click the Justification button on the Property Bar and then click Left.

⑤ Press the ENTER key to insert a blank line.

WordPerfect centers the paragraphs containing the store name and address (Figure 4-28). The insertion point, positioned at the left margin on the line below the blank line, is located where the horizontal line is to be drawn.

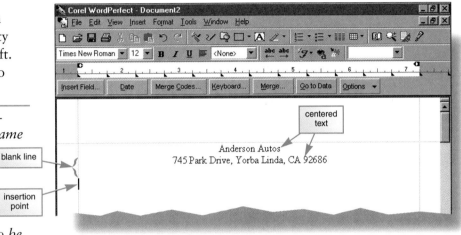

FIGURE 4-28

Adding a Horizontal Line

After typing the name and address, you should continue the creation of the letterhead by adding a **horizontal graphics line** at the position of the insertion point. The default horizontal line setting displays a .012-inch thick line between the left and right margins. Perform the following steps to add a horizontal graphics line to the letterhead.

 Steps **To Add a Horizontal Graphics Line to the Letterhead**

1 **Click Insert on the menu bar, point to Shape, and then point to Horizontal Line.**

*WordPerfect displays the Insert menu, highlights the Shape comand, displays the Shape submenu, and highlights the **Horizontal Line command** (Figure 4-29).*

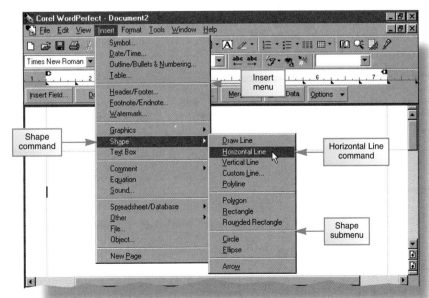

FIGURE 4-29

Click Horizontal Line. Press the ENTER key three times to end the graphics line and insert two blank lines.

WordPerfect draws a .012-inch thick, 6-inch long horizontal graphics line between the margins. Pressing the ENTER key three times ends the graphics line and inserts two blank lines below the line (Figure 4-30).

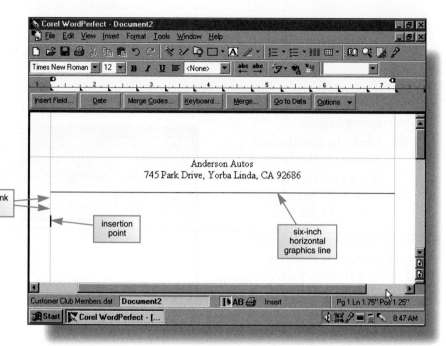

FIGURE 4-30

Formatting the Letterhead

After you have drawn the horizontal line, you should finish the letterhead by formatting the store name and address. In Project 1, you used the Font dialog box to format the paragraphs in an announcement. The following steps summarize how to format the two paragraphs containing the store name and address using the Font dialog box.

TO FORMAT THE STORE NAME IN THE LETTERHEAD

① Highlight the first paragraph (Anderson Autos).
② Right-click the first paragraph.
③ Click Font on the QuickMenu.
④ Scroll the Font face list box until Arial displays.
⑤ Click Arial.
⑥ Click Bold in the Font style list box.
⑦ Scroll the Font size list box until 28 displays.
⑧ Click 28.
⑨ Click the OK button.
⑩ Click anywhere off the highlighted text to remove the highlight.

WordPerfect formats the paragraph containing the store name using the Arial Bold 28-point font.

TO FORMAT THE ADDRESS IN THE LETTERHEAD

① Highlight the second paragraph (745 Park Drive, Yorba Linda, CA 92686).

② Right-click the second paragraph.

③ Click Font on the QuickMenu.

④ Scroll the Font face list box until Arial displays.

⑤ Click Arial.

⑥ Click the OK button.

⑦ Click anywhere off the highlighted text to remove the highlight.

The paragraph containing the agency name displays using the Arial 28-point font, and the paragraph containing the address displays using the Arial 12-point font (Figure 4-31).

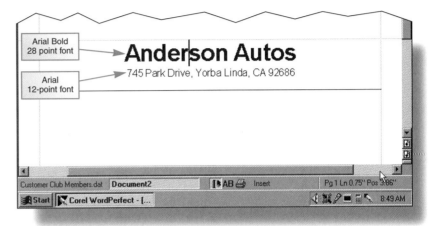

FIGURE 4-31

If there is a possibility the Anderson Autos letterhead will be useful at a later date to create additional business letters, you can save it in a file on disk. In the future, you can then open the letterhead document and use it to create a business letter. In this project, the letterhead will not be saved.

Inserting the Merge Codes

Earlier in this project you created the data file. In the process, you designed and entered four field names (Name, Address, Title and Name, and Purchase) in the data file. To link these field names to the letter form file, you must insert the corresponding merge codes in the form letter. The position a **merge code** occupies in the form letter determines where the customer information from the data file will display when the two files are merged.

The letter form file will contain five merge codes. The first merge code, the DATE code, indicates where the current date will display in each form letter after performing the merge operation. The FIELD(Name), FIELD(Address), FIELD(Title and Name), and FIELD(Purchase) merge codes indicate where the customer name, customer address, customer title and last name, and customer purchase from the data file will display in each form letter.

Inserting the DATE Code in the Letter Form File

First, insert the DATE code in the letter form file. The **DATE code** indicates where the current date will display in each form letter after performing the merge operation. Insert the DATE code into the letter form file by performing the steps on the next page.

Steps To Insert a Date Code in the Letter Form File

1 **Press the PAGE DOWN key to move the insertion point to the end of the document. Point to the Date button on the Merge Bar.**

WordPerfect moves the insertion point to the end of the document (Figure 4-32). The mouse pointer points to the Date button.

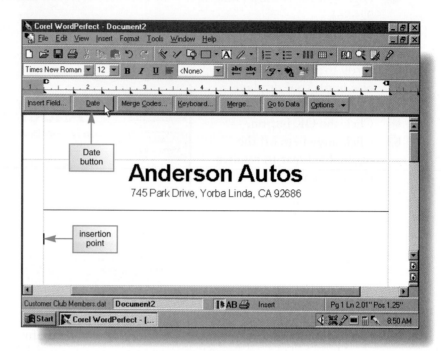

FIGURE 4-32

2 **Click the Date button. Press the ENTER key four times.**

*WordPerfect inserts the DATE code and three blank lines in the form letter (Figure 4-33). The DATE code displays in red text. Although not visible in the document window, the **MRG: DATE** code is inserted in the document.*

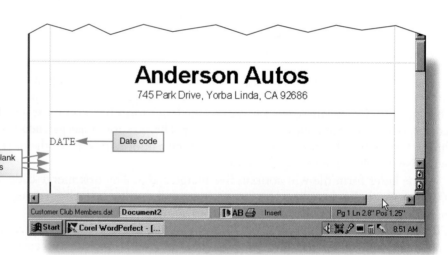

FIGURE 4-33

OtherWays

1. On Merge Bar click Merge Codes button, click DATE, click Insert button, click Close button

Inserting Field Merge Codes in the Letter Form File

Next, insert the FIELD(Name), FIELD(Address), FIELD(Title and Name), and FIELD(Purchase) merge codes in the letter form file. The FIELD merge codes indicate where in each form letter the customer information from the fields in the data file will display after performing the merge operation. Insert the five merge codes into the form letter by performing the following steps.

Steps To Insert Field Merge Codes in the Letter Form File

① Point to the Insert Field button on the Merge Bar (Figure 4-34).

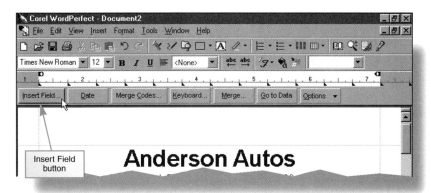

FIGURE 4-34

② Click the Insert Field button. Point to the Insert button in the Insert Field Name or Number dialog box.

WordPerfect displays the Insert Field Name or Number dialog box (Figure 4-35). The Customer Club Members.dat filename displays following the word, Filename, in the dialog box. Four field names display in the Field Names list box. The first field name, Name, is highlighted.

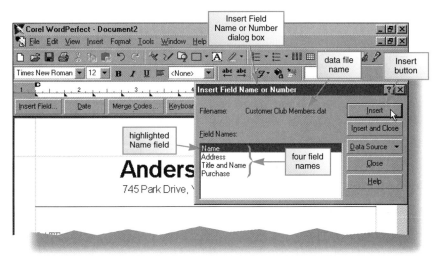

FIGURE 4-35

③ Click the Insert button. Press the ENTER key to move the insertion point to the next line in the document window.

WordPerfect inserts the FIELD(Name) code in the document and moves the insertion point to the next line (Figure 4-36). The word, FIELD, and the parentheses surrounding the field name display in red text. The dialog box remains on the screen. Although not visible, WordPerfect inserts two revertible MRG: FIELD codes in the document.

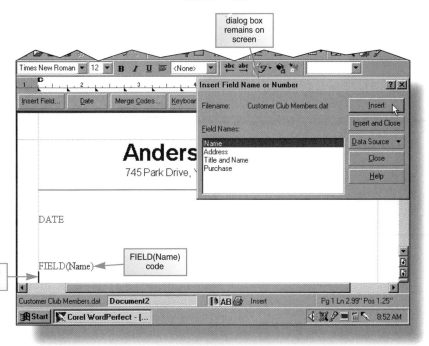

FIGURE 4-36

4 Click the Address field name in the Field Names list box and then click the Insert button. Press the ENTER key twice. Type Dear and then press the SPACEBAR. Click the Title and Name field name in the Field Names list box, click the Insert button, type : (colon) and press the ENTER key twice.

WordPerfect displays the FIELD(Address) code on one line, a blank line follows the code, and the word, Dear, a blank space, the FIELD(Title and Name) code, and a colon display on the next line (Figure 4-37). A blank line displays below the line containing the FIELD(Title and Name) code.

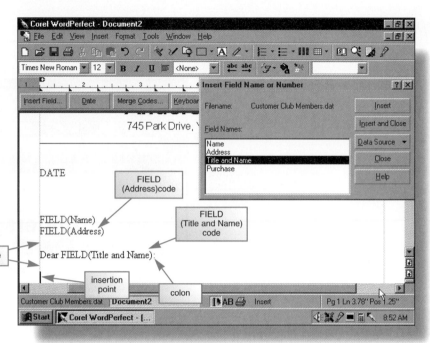

FIGURE 4-37

5 Type On behalf of the entire Anderson team, I would like to take this opportunity to thank you for buying your **and press the SPACEBAR. Click the Purchase field name in the Field Names list box, click the Insert button, and click the Close button. Type the remainder of the paragraph and the next paragraph as shown in Figure 4-38. Press the ENTER key two times.**

WordPerfect closes the Insert Field Name or Number dialog box, displays the two paragraphs, and inserts the FIELD(Purchase) code in the first paragraph (Figure 4-38).

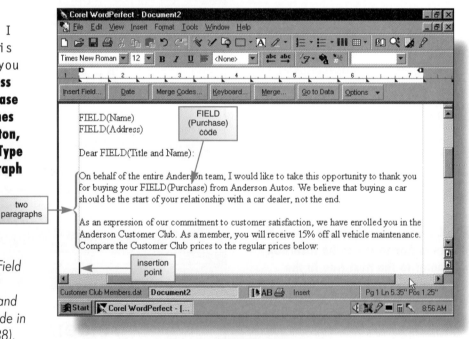

FIGURE 4-38

Tables

The table in the letter form file is illustrated in Figure 4-39. A **table** consists of **rows**, which run horizontally, and **columns**, which run vertically. Graphics lines divide the table into rectangular areas called **cells**. A cell can contain text, numbers, or graphics.

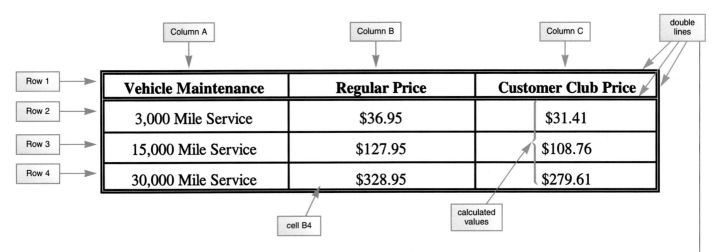

FIGURE 4-39

For the purpose of identification, rows are labeled numerically from top to bottom and columns are labeled alphabetically from left to right. The first column is column A, second column is column B, third column is column C, and so on. The first row is row 1, second row is row 2, third row is row 3, fourth row is row 4, and so on.

A **cell address**, consisting of a column letter and a row number, identifies each cell in a table. The cell that contains the entry, $328.95, which is located at the intersection of column B and row 4, has a cell address of B4.

The table contains three columns and four rows. The first row contains the headings (Vehicle Maintenance, Regular Price, and Customer Club Price). Rows 2, 3, and 4 contain the vehicle maintenance, regular price, and customer club price for the 3,000 mile service, 15,000 mile service, and 30,000 mile service, respectively.

The customer club prices in cells C2, C3, and C4 are calculated values. Each customer club price is fifteen percent off the regular price, or eighty-five percent of the regular price. The formula to calculate a customer club price is the regular price multiplied by .85 (85%). The customer club price in cell C2 ($31.41) is calculated by multiplying the regular price in cell B2 ($36.95) by .85 and rounding the answer to two decimal places. The customer club price in cell C3 ($108.76) is calculated by multiplying the regular price in cell B3 ($127.95) by .85 and rounding the answer. The customer club price in cell C4 ($279.61) is calculated by multiplying the regular price in cell B4 ($328.95) by .85 and rounding the answer.

The headings in row 1 display in bold text and the values in the table (Regular Price and Customer Club Price) are formatted using the currency format. **Currency format** causes a value to display with a dollar sign ($), a thousands separator (the comma separating the thousands value and hundreds value), a decimal point, and two positions to the right of the decimal point. All cells in the table are centered. The double line surrounding the table and below row 1 displays because the **Double Border Header table style** was applied to the table. All other lines in the table are single lines.

More *About* **Tables**

Older methods of organizing columns of data used the TAB key to organize the data into columns. Today, the WordPerfect Table feature is a preferred method of organizing data into columns. For emphasis, you can shade the cells in a table, add borders to a table, sort the contents of a table, or quickly add or delete an entire row or column.

Creating the Table

Next, create the 3-column, 4-row (3 x 4) table shown in Figure 4-39 on the previous page by performing the following steps.

Steps To Create a Table

1 Point to the Table QuickCreate button on the WordPerfect 8 Toolbar.

The WordPerfect 8 Toolbar contains the Table QuickCreate button (Figure 4-40).

FIGURE 4-40

2 Hold down the left mouse button.

WordPerfect displays a table sizing grid consisting of thirteen columns and ten rows (Figure 4-41). The message, No Table, displays above the table sizing grid.

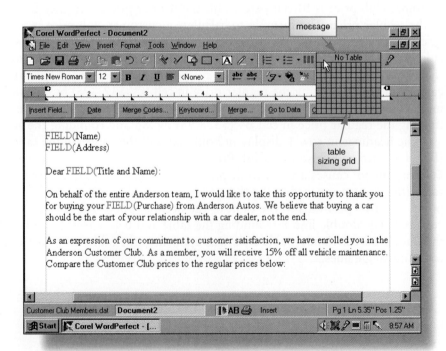

FIGURE 4-41

3 **Drag the mouse pointer onto the table sizing grid until three columns and four rows of the grid are highlighted and the entry, 3x4, displays above the grid.**

A three column by four row area of the table sizing grid is highlighted (Figure 4-42). The table size (3x4) displays above the grid.

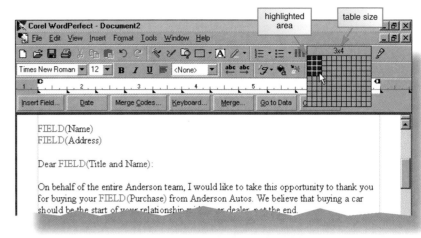

FIGURE 4-42

4 **Release the left mouse button. Scroll the document window to display the paragraph above the table and the table at the top of the document window.**

WordPerfect creates a 3x4 table (Figure 4-43). Because the insertion point is currently located in the table, the buttons on the Property Bar change to include buttons that make working with tables easier.

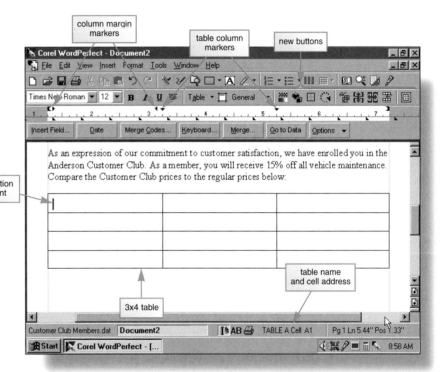

FIGURE 4-43

WordPerfect allows you to create multiple tables in a document. The first table you create is labeled Table A, the second table is labeled Table B, and so on. In Figure 4-43, the current table name and cell address of the insertion point (TABLE A Cell A1) display on the Application Bar.

Two **table column markers** on the Ruler define the width of each column as two inches wide. The two **column margin markers** on the Ruler above the first column indicate the first column contains the insertion point. Although not visible, WordPerfect inserts a **Table Definition code** when you create a table and a **Row code** and two Cell codes for each row in the table.

Other Ways

1. On Insert menu click Table, type number of columns, press TAB key, type number of rows, click Create button

2. Press F12, type number of columns, press TAB key, type number of rows, click Create button

Entering Text in a Table

After creating the table, enter the headings in cells A1, B1, and C1. To accomplish this, perform the following steps.

 Steps To Enter Text into a Table

1 **If necessary, click cell A1 to move the insertion point into cell A1. Type** Vehicle Maintenance **in cell A1 and then press the TAB key. Type** Regular Price **in cell B1 and then press the TAB key. Type** Customer Club Price **in cell C1 and then press the TAB key.**

The first heading (Vehicle Maintenance) displays in cell A1, the second heading (Regular Price) displays in cell B1, and the third heading (Customer Club Price) displays in cell C1 (Figure 4-44).The insertion point displays in cell A2.

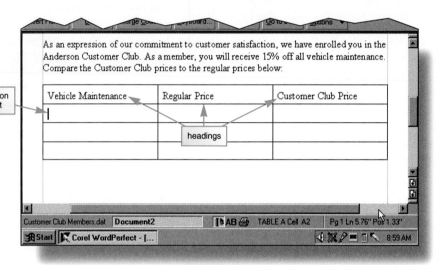

FIGURE 4-44

2 **Type** 3,000 Mile Service **and then press the TAB key. Type** 36.95 **and then press the TAB key.**

The vehicle maintenance (3,000 Mile Service) displays in cell A2 and the regular price (36.95) displays in cell B2 (Figure 4-45). The regular price, 36.95, will be formatted later in this project in the currency format.

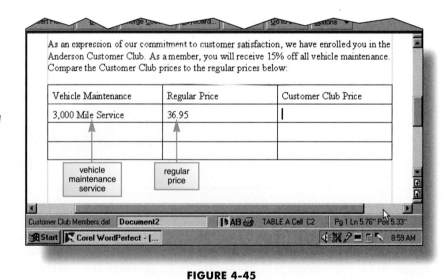

FIGURE 4-45

More *About*
**Entering Text
in a Table**

Within a table cell, text wraps within the margins of the cell just as text wraps within the margins of a document window. When text wraps within a table cell, the height of the row in which the cell occurs increases to accommodate the wrapped text.

Entering Formulas in a Table

The next step is to enter the formula for the customer club price in cell C2. The **Formula Bar** allows you to define a math formula, enter the formula into a cell, and then WordPerfect automatically calculates and displays the result of the calculation in the cell. A formula can include cell addresses, numbers, and the arithmetic operators.

The **arithmetic operators** are the plus sign (+) for addition, minus sign (–) for subtraction, asterisk (*) for multiplication, and slash (/) for division. The formula to calculate the customer club price in cell C2 is: B2*.85. The formula B2*.85 contains a cell address (B2), multiplication operator (*), and number (.85). When you insert the formula into cell C2, the value in cell B2 (36.95) is multiplied by the value .85 and the result (31.4075) displays in cell C2. The multiplication operator (*) causes multiplication to occur. Later in this project, you will format the customer club price (31.4075) with the currency format ($31.41).

Displaying the Formula Bar

Prior to entering the formula for the customer club price in cell C2, perform the following steps to display the Formula Bar.

 Steps To Display the Formula Bar

1 **Right-click the table and then point to Formula Toolbar on the QuickMenu.**

WordPerfect displays a QuickMenu and highlights the Formula Toolbar command (Figure 4-46).

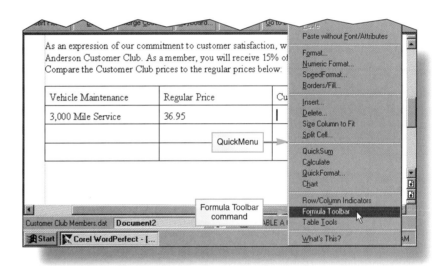

FIGURE 4-46

2 **Click Formula Toolbar.**

WordPerfect replaces the Merge Bar with the Formula Bar (Figure 4-47). The Toolbar contains the Address box containing the table name and cell address (TABLE A.C2), Cancel button, Insert button, Formula Edit text box, and several buttons.

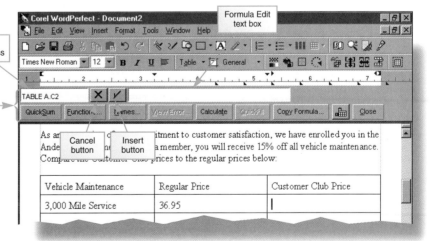

FIGURE 4-47

Entering a Formula into a Table Cell

After displaying the Formula Bar, enter the b2*.85 formula in cell C2 by performing the following steps.

Steps **To Enter a Formula into a Table Cell**

1 **Click cell C2 to move the insertion point into cell C2. Click the Formula Edit text box. Type** b2*.85 **in the Formula Edit text box. Point to the Insert button on the Formula Bar.**

The formula b2.85 displays in the Formula Edit text box and the message, Formula edit mode is on, displays to the right of the text box (Figure 4-48). The mouse pointer points to the **Insert button**. Clicking the Insert button accepts the formula, inserts the formula into cell C2, and displays the calculated value in cell C2.*

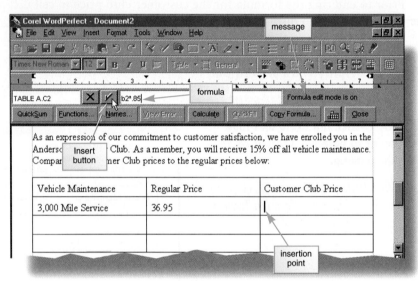

FIGURE 4-48

2 **Click the Insert button.**

The calculated customer club price (31.4075) displays in cell C2 and a plus sign is added to the formula in the Formula Edit text box (+B2*.85) (Figure 4-49). Although not completely visible, the message on the Application Bar changes to include the formula (TABLE A Cell C2 =+B2*.85). The value 31.4075 will be formatted later in this project in the currency format.

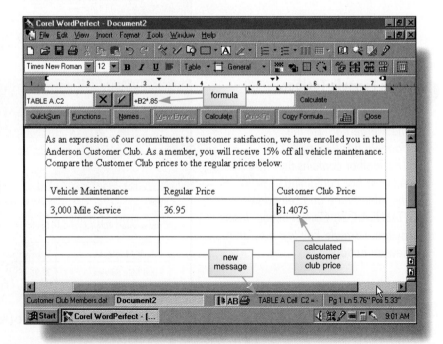

FIGURE 4-49

Completing the Entry of Text and Formulas

After entering the headings in row 1, entering text, a value, and a formula in row 2, complete the table by entering the text and formulas for rows 3 and 4 by performing the following steps.

 ### To Complete the Entry of Text and Formulas in the Table

1 **Press the TAB key. Type** 15,000 Mile Service **and then press the TAB key. Type** 127.95 **and then press the TAB key. Click the Formula Edit text box, type** b3*.85 **and click the Insert button.**

The vehicle maintenance service (15,000 Mile Service) displays in cell A3, the regular price (127.95) displays in cell B3, and the calculated customer club price (108.7575) displays in cell C3 (Figure 4-50).

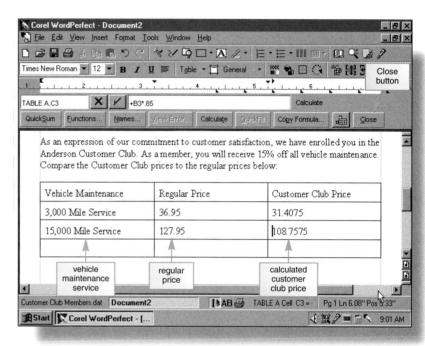

FIGURE 4-50

2 **Press the TAB key. Type** 30,000 Mile Service **and then press the TAB key. Type** 328.95 **and then press the TAB key. Click the Formula Edit text box, type** b4*.85 **and click the Insert button. Click the Close button on the Formula Bar.**

The vehicle maintenance (30,000 Mile Service) displays in cell A4, the regular price (328.95) displays in cell B4, the calculated customer club price (279.6075) displays in cell C4, and the Merge Bar replaces the Formula Bar (Figure 4-51).

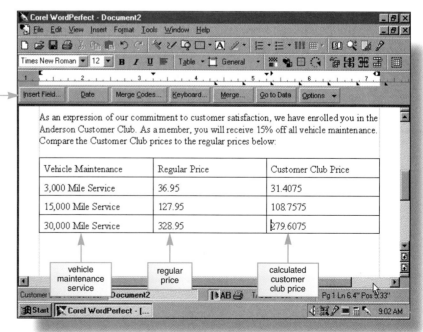

FIGURE 4-51

More *About* Table Styles

In addition to applying a table style to a table, you can create your own table style. To create a table style, create and format a table, right-click the table, click SpeedFormat, click the Create button, enter a name for the table style in the Name text box in the Create Table Style dialog box, and click the OK button. The table style name will display in the list of table styles in the TableSpeed dialog box.

Formatting the Table

After entering the text and formulas in the table, you should format the table. **Formatting** consists of applying the Double Border Header table style to the table, bolding the headings in row 1, formatting the cells containing the regular price and customer club price using the currency format, and centering the contents of the cells in rows 2, 3, and 4.

Displaying the Row and Column Indicators

Row and column indicators allow you to select a single row or column, multiple rows or columns, or the entire table easily. In preparation for formatting the table, perform the following steps to display the row and column indicators.

  To Display Row and Column Indicators

① **Right-click the table. Point to Row/Column Indicators on the QuickMenu.**

WordPerfect displays a QuickMenu and highlights the Row/Column Indicators command (Figure 4-52).

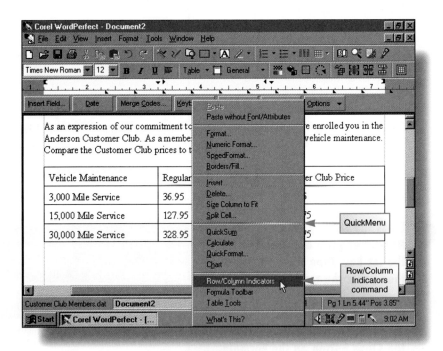

FIGURE 4-52

② **Click Row/Column Indicators.**

WordPerfect displays the row and column indicators for the table (Figure 4-53).

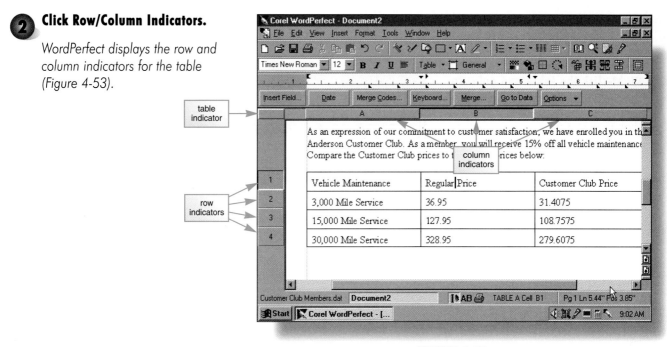

FIGURE 4-53

Clicking Row/Column Indicators on the QuickMenu displays the row, column, and table indicators (Figure 4-53). The **row indicators**, labeled 1 through 4, display to the left of each row in the table and the **column indicators**, labeled A through C, display above each column. Clicking a row or column indicator selects all the cells in the corresponding row or column. Clicking the **table indicator**, located to the left of the column indicators, selects all cells in the table.

Apply a Table Style Using Table SpeedFormat

The first step in formatting the table is to apply the Double Border Header table style to the table using Table SpeedFormat. The **Double Border Header table style** replaces the single line surrounding the table and the single line below row 1 with a double line, centers the headings in row 1, and makes a table header row consisting of the three headings in row 1. Although not used in this project, a **table header row** repeats itself at the top of each new page if the table displays on more than one page.

You select and apply a table style using Table SpeedFormat. **Table SpeedFormat** allows you to select and apply one of forty table styles designed to give the table a professional business or artistic appearance. Perform the steps on the next page to apply the Double Border Header table style.

Steps: To Apply a Table Style to a Table

1 Right-click the table and point to SpeedFormat on the QuickMenu.

WordPerfect displays a QuickMenu and highlights the SpeedFormat command (Figure 4-54).

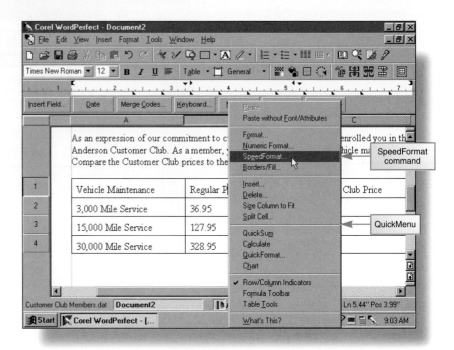

FIGURE 4-54

2 Click SpeedFormat. Scroll the Available styles list box until Double Border Header is visible. Point to Double Border Header.

WordPerfect displays the Table SpeedFormat dialog box (Figure 4-55). The dialog box contains the Available styles list box and a Preview box. The default table style (<None>) is applied to the table in the Preview window.

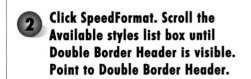

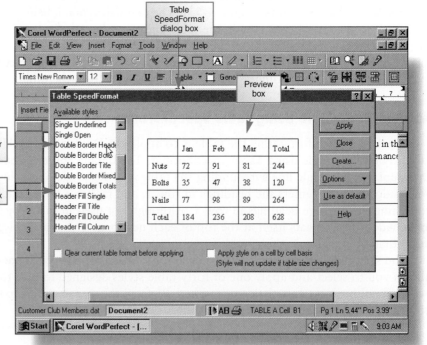

FIGURE 4-55

3 **Click Double Border Header and then point to the Apply button.**

WordPerfect highlights the Double Border Header table style and applies the Double Border Header table style to the table in the Preview window (Figure 4-56).

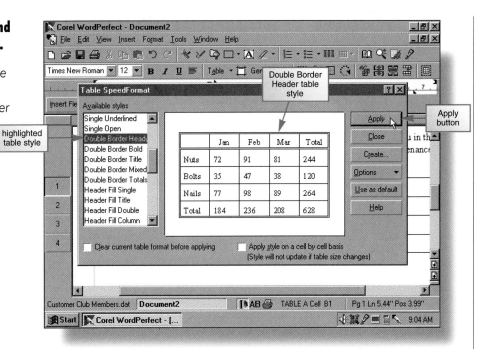

FIGURE 4-56

4 **Click the Apply button.**

WordPerfect closes the Table SpeedFormat dialog box and applies the Double Border Header table style to the table (Figure 4-57). The Double Border Header style centers the headings in row 1 and replaces the single line surrounding the table and the single line below row 1 with a double line.

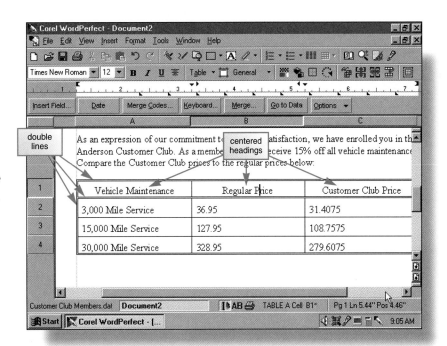

FIGURE 4-57

▶*Other*Ways

1. With insertion point in table, on Tables Toolbar click Table button, click SpeedFormat

Formatting the Cells in the Table

The remaining steps to format the table include bolding the headings in row 1, formatting the cells containing the regular price and customer club price using the currency format, and centering the contents of the cells in rows 2, 3, and 4. The first step, bolding the headings in row 1, is explained in the following two sections.

Selecting a Row of Cells

Before you can bold the headings in row 1, you must select the cells in row 1. One method of selecting a row is to click the row indicator to the left of the row. After selecting the row, you can bold the contents of the cells in the row using the Bold button on the Toolbar. Perform the following steps to select the cells in row 1.

 Steps To Select a Row of Cells

---

1 **Point to the row indicator to the left of row 1.**

*WordPerfect changes the mouse pointer to a **box with a horizontal arrow** (Figure 4-58).*

row indicator for row 1

box with a horizontal arrow

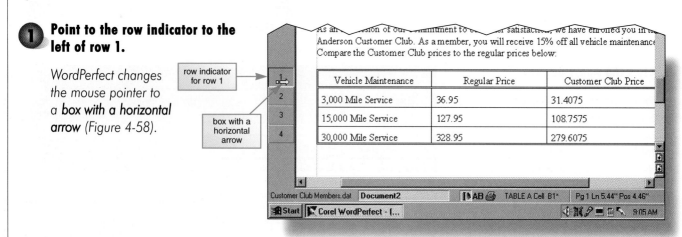

FIGURE 4-58

---

2 **Click the row indicator.**

WordPerfect highlights the cells in the first row and changes the color of the row indicator to gray (Figure 4-59).

highlighted row 1

gray row indicator

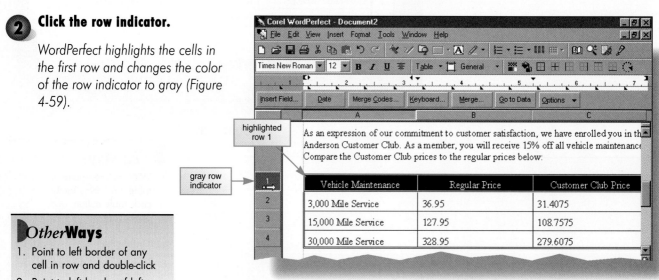

FIGURE 4-59

OtherWays
1. Point to left border of any cell in row and double-click
2. Point to left border of left-most cell in row, drag to right until all cells are highlighted

Bolding the Cells in a Row

After selecting the row, one method to bold the contents of the cells in the row is to click the Bold button on the WordPerfect 8 Toolbar. Perform the following step to bold the cells in row 1.

 Steps To Bold the Cells in a Row

1 **Click the Bold button on the WordPerfect 8 Toolbar. Click inside the highlighted text to remove the highlight.**

WordPerfect displays the headings in bold type (Figure 4-60).

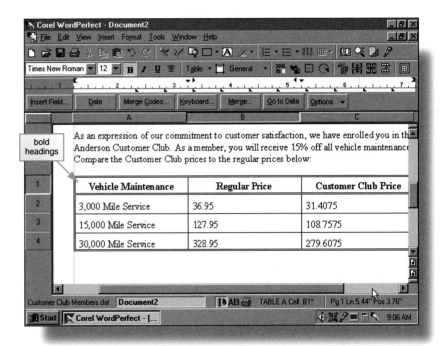

FIGURE 4-60

The next step in formatting the table is to format the regular prices and customer club prices in cells B2, B3, B4, C2, C3, and C4 using the currency format. Because the cells do not comprise a full row, full column, or entire table, you cannot use the row, column, or table indicators to select the cells. Instead, you must select the cells using other techniques. The following section explains other ways to select a cell or group of cells.

OtherWays

1. On Format menu click Font, click Bold, click OK button
2. Press CTRL+B

Selecting a Cell or Group of Cells

When you move the mouse pointer into a cell of a table, the mouse pointer changes to an I-beam. When you point to the left border of a cell, the I-beam pointer changes to a **horizontal selection arrow**. As it crosses the left border, it changes to a **vertical bar and double arrow** to indicate you can move the border by dragging. When you point to the top border of a cell, the I-beam changes to a **vertical selection arrow**. To select a cell or group of cells, point to the left or top border of a cell and click, double-click, or triple-click. Table 4-1 explains the techniques you can use to highlight a single cell; a row or column of cells; several cells, rows, or columns; or the entire table.

TABLE 4-1	
TO SELECT	*ACTION TO BE PERFORMED*
A cell	Point to the left or top border and click.
A row of cells	Point to the left border of any cell in the row and double-click.
A column of cells	Point to the top border of any cell in the column and double-click.
A group of cells, rows, or columns	Point to the left or top border of a cell in the table and drag until the desired cells, rows, or columns are highlighted.
All cells in the table	Point to the left or top border of any cell in the table and triple-click.

Selecting a Group of Cells in a Table

The next step in formatting the cells of the table is to format the regular prices and customer club prices in cells B2, B3, B4, C2, C3, and C4 using the currency format. The currency format causes values to display with a dollar sign ($), a thousands separator (the comma separating the thousands from the hundreds), a decimal point, and two positions to the right of the decimal point. Before you format the cells, you will need to select the cells using one of the techniques shown in Table 4-1. Perform the following steps to select and format the numeric values in cells B2, B3, B4, C2, C3, and C4.

 To Select and Format a Group of Cells

1 **Point to the left border of cell B2 and drag down and to the right until cells B2, B3, B4, C2, C3, and C4 are highlighted. Right-click the highlighted area of the table and then point to Numeric Format on the QuickMenu.**

WordPerfect highlights the group of cells (B2, B3, B4, C2, C3, and C4), displays a QuickMenu, and highlights the Numeric Format command on the QuickMenu (Figure 4-61).

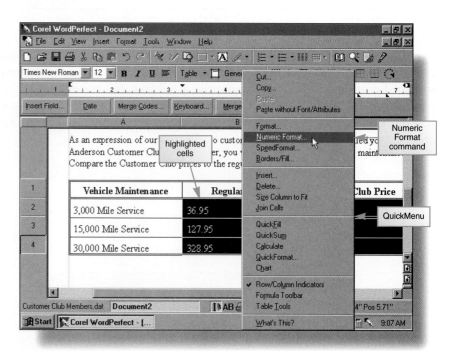

FIGURE 4-61

2 **Click Numeric Format. Point to the Currency option button.**

WordPerfect displays the Properties for Table Numeric Format dialog box (Figure 4-62). The Cell sheet displays in the dialog box to indicate you are formatting a cell or group of cells. The General option button is selected and the negative number -1234 displays in the Preview box to illustrate the general format. The dimmed value zero in the Number of decimal places text box indicates the general format displays numbers without decimal positions.

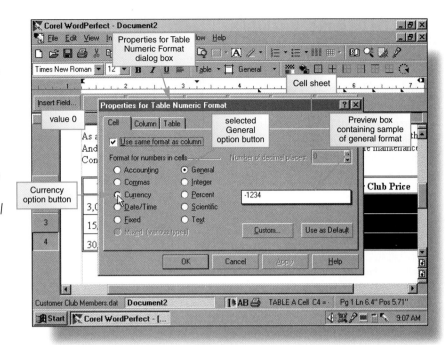

FIGURE 4-62

3 **Click the Currency option button. Point to the OK button.**

WordPerfect selects the Currency option button, displays the value 2 in the Number of decimal places text box, and displays the ($1,234.00) entry in the Preview box (Figure 4-63). The currency format causes the parentheses, dollar sign, thousands separator, decimal point, and two decimal places to display. The parentheses indicate the number is negative.

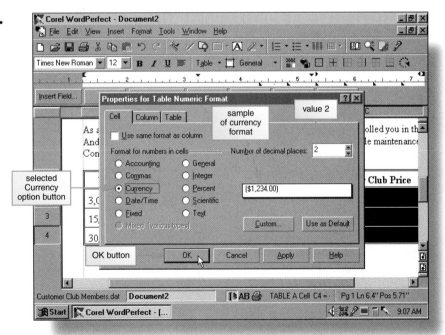

FIGURE 4-63

④ Click the OK button. Click outside the highlighted text to remove the highlight.

The regular prices and customer club prices display using the currency format (Figure 4-64). The values in the Customer Club Price column are rounded to two decimal places.

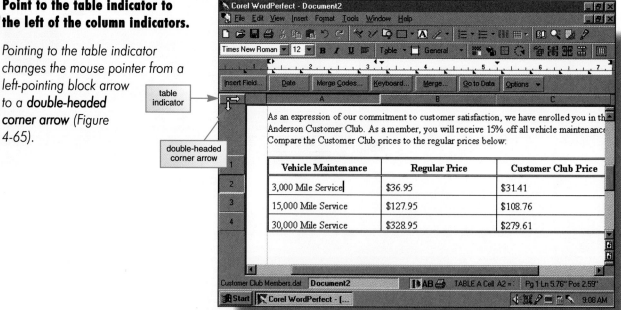

FIGURE 4-64

Selecting All Cells in a Table

Previously in this project, you applied the Double Border Header table style to the table. As a result, the headings in the first row are centered. The next step in the process of formatting the table is to center the remaining cells in the table. Before you can center the cells in the table, you must select the cells. Although several methods allow the cells to be centered, selecting and formatting the entire table instead of selecting individual rows may save time. Perform the following steps to select all the cells in the table.

Steps To Select All the Cells in a Table

① Point to the table indicator to the left of the column indicators.

*Pointing to the table indicator changes the mouse pointer from a left-pointing block arrow to a **double-headed corner arrow** (Figure 4-65).*

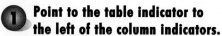

FIGURE 4-65

Click the table indicator.

WordPerfect highlights all cells in the table and changes the color of the row, column, and table indicators to gray (Figure 4-66).

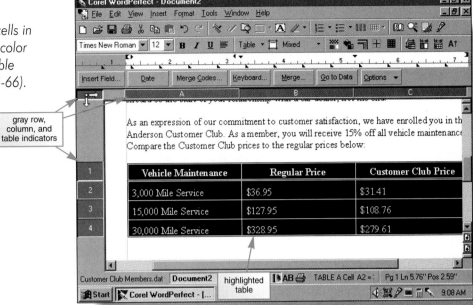

gray row, column, and table indicators

FIGURE 4-66

Centering All Cells in the Table

After selecting the cells in the table, you should center the contents of all the cells in the table. One method of centering text in a document was explained in a previous project and used the Justification button on the Property Bar. The steps to center a highlighted group of cells in a table are similar to the steps to center highlighted text in a document and are summarized below.

TO CENTER ALL CELLS IN A TABLE

① Click the Justification button on the Property Bar.

② Click Center.

③ Click anywhere inside the table to remove the highlight.

All the cells in the table are centered (Figure 4-67).

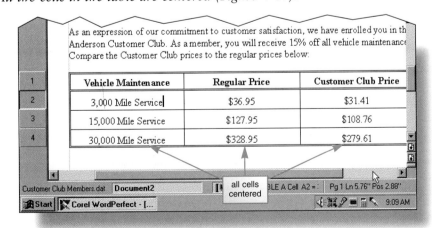

all cells centered

FIGURE 4-67

Other Ways

1. Click Select Table button on Tables Toolbar

2. Point to row 1 indicator and drag down to highlight all rows

3. Point to column 1 indicator and drag to right to highlight all columns

4. Point to left border or top border of any cell and triple-click

5. With insertion point in table, point to Select on Edit menu, click Table

Completing the Letter Form File

Next, complete the entry of the text of the form letter by typing the two paragraphs below the table, the complimentary close, and the signature block. The following steps summarize how to type the text.

TO TYPE THE REMAINING TEXT IN THE LETTER FORM FILE

1 Right-click the table and click Row/Column Indicators.

2 Click the blank line below the table and then press the ENTER key.

3 Type Proper maintenance keeps your vehicle in good working condition and improves the quality of the air we breathe. As a way of introducing you to our Service department, present this letter and receive the 3,000 mile vehicle maintenance at no charge. and then press the ENTER key twice.

4 Type If you have any questions or concerns, please contact me at (714) 555-2479 or visit our Web site at http://www.AndersonAutos.com. Thank you for choosing Anderson Autos. and then press the ENTER key twice.

5 Type Sincerely, and then press the ENTER key four times.

6 Type Harry McMurtrie and then press the ENTER key.

7 Type Customer Representative and then press the ENTER key.

The two paragraphs below the table, complimentary close, and signature block are shown in Figure 4-68.

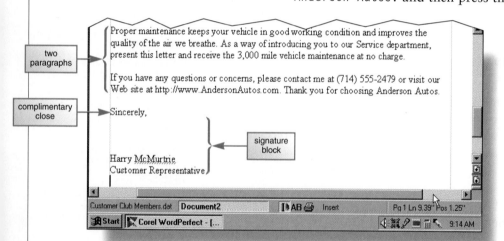

FIGURE 4-68

Spell Checking and Saving the Letter Form File

In previous projects, two methods were given to spell check a document. The first method was to review the document for words underlined with red diagonal lines and find the correct replacement word if the word was incorrectly spelled. The second method, used on longer documents, was to use Spell Check to find and replace the incorrectly spelled words. Spell check the form letter using either of these methods.

Before you perform the merge operation, you should save the letter form file on disk. Save the file using the Save button on the Toolbar and the Customer Club Letter filename. WordPerfect will automatically add the .frm extension to the filename and save the document using the Customer Club Letter.frm filename. The steps to save a file using the Save button were explained in Project 1 and are summarized on the next page.

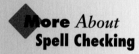

More *About*
Spell Checking

It is important for a form letter to be error free. Use Spell Checker to check for and correct misspelled words. Create and proofread the form letter for grammatical errors or poor wording, set the form letter aside for several days, and then proofread the form letter again.

TO SAVE THE LETTER FORM FILE

① Click the Save button on the Toolbar.
② When the Save File dialog box displays, type `Customer Club Letter` in the File name box.
③ Click the Save in box arrow.
④ Verify 3½ Floppy (A:) displays in the Save in box.
⑤ Click the Save button.

Windows 95 saves the form letter on the Corel WordPerfect 8 Files floppy disk in drive A and replaces the Document2 entry in the Corel WordPerfect window title with A:\Customer Club Letter.frm (unmodified).

Hiding the Ruler

After completing the letter form file, the Ruler is no longer needed and should be removed. The step to remove, or hide, the Ruler is summarized below.

TO HIDE THE RULER

① Click View on the menu bar and click Ruler on the View menu.

WordPerfect removes the Ruler.

Merging the Data File and Letter Form File

The data file and letter form file are complete. The next step is to merge the two files. **Merge** combines the customer information in the data file with the text and merge codes in the letter form file to produce the merge file. The **merge file**, or **merge document**, will contain a form letter for each customer in the data file. Perform the following steps to merge the form and data files to produce the merge document.

 To Merge a Data File and a Letter Form File

① **Click Tools on the menu bar and click Merge on the Tools menu. Point to the Perform Merge button in the Merge dialog box (Figure 4-69).**

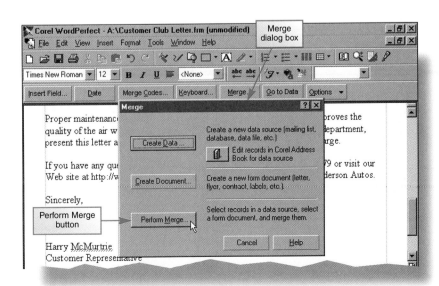

FIGURE 4-69

2 **Click the Perform Merge button. Point to the Merge button in the Perform Merge dialog box.**

WordPerfect removes the Merge dialog box and displays the Perform Merge dialog box (Figure 4-70). The message to the right of the Form document button, Current Document, indicates the letter form file is located in the current document window. The Data source text box to the right of the Data source button indicates the location (A:\) and filename (Customer Club Members.dat) of the data file. The message, New Document, to the right of the Output button indicates the merge document will display in a new document window. The message, All Records, indicates all records in the data file will be merged.

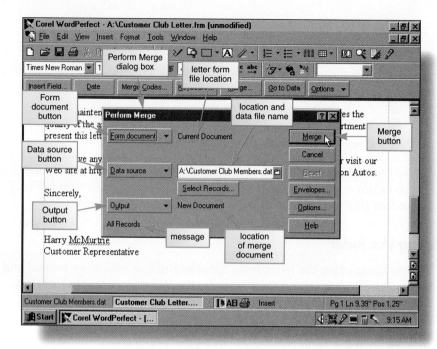

FIGURE 4-70

3 **Click the Merge button. Scroll the document window to make the letterhead of the first form letter visible.**

*While WordPerfect merges the form and data files, the Please Wait dialog box displays momentarily on the screen, and then a new window (Document3) containing the form letters opens (Figure 4-71). Currently, the date, customer name, customer address, salutation, and customer purchase for the first customer in the data file (Mr. Jake McLaren) display in the window. Although not visible, WordPerfect inserts a **Paper Size and Type code** in the document.*

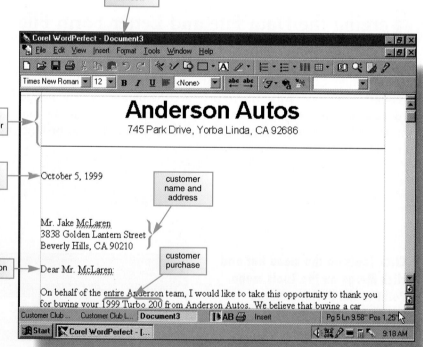

FIGURE 4-71

Other Ways

1. Click Merge button on Merge Bar, click Merge button

2. Press SHIFT+F9, click Perform Merge button, click Merge button

Printing the Form Letters

After generating the merge document, you can print the form letters or save the document on disk and print the form letters at a later time. The steps to print the form letters are summarized below.

TO PRINT THE FORM LETTERS

1. Click the Print button on the Toolbar.
2. Review the Print to dialog box to ensure the Full document option button is selected in the Print sheet and the value 1 displays in the Number of copies text box.
3. Click the Print button in the Print to dialog box.

WordPerfect displays the Corel WordPerfect dialog box momentarily and then prints the five form letters illustrated in Figure 4-1 on page WP 4.5.

Closing the Merge File and Letter Form File

After printing the form letters, close the document windows containing the merge document and letter form file. The steps to close the two windows are summarized below.

TO CLOSE MULTIPLE DOCUMENT WINDOWS

1. Click File on the menu bar.
2. Click Close on the File menu.
3. Click the No button in the Corel WordPerfect dialog box so the merge document will not be saved.
4. Click File on the menu bar.
5. Click Close on the File menu.

The two windows containing the merge document and letter form file close and the window containing the data file displays.

Addressing and Printing Mailing Labels

Next, create mailing labels for the form letters using the Customer Club Members data file. Each mailing label will contain the customer name on the first line of the label and the customer address on the remaining lines.

To create the mailing labels, an association must be made between the **label form file** containing the mailing labels and the data file, Customer Club Members. While making the association, WordPerfect offers the option of creating the mailing labels in the current document window or opening a new document window. The steps to associate a data file and letter form file were explained earlier in this project. The steps to associate the Customer Club Members data file and label form file are similar to those steps. The summarized steps are on the next page.

TO ASSOCIATE A DATA FILE WITH A LABEL FORM FILE

① Click Tools on the menu bar.

② Click Merge.

③ Click the Create Document button in the Merge dialog box.

④ Click the OK button in the Create Merge File dialog box.

⑤ Click the Select File button at the far right of the Associate a data file text box.

⑥ Click Customer Club Members.dat in the list box in the Select Data File dialog box.

⑦ Click the Select button.

⑧ Click the OK button in the Associate Form and Data dialog box.

WordPerfect opens a new document window (Document2) and displays the Merge Bar.

Creating the Label Form File

Next, create mailing labels by selecting a label definition and inserting the FIELD(Name) and FIELD(Address) merge codes into the newly created document window. The **label definition** determines the label sheet size, label size (width, height, and margins), number and position of labels on a sheet, and label type (laser printed or tractor-fed). Several predefined label definitions are available in WordPerfect. Perform the following steps to create the mailing labels using the Avery 5160 Address label definition.

Steps **To Create the Label Form File**

① **Click Format on the menu bar and then point to Labels.**

WordPerfect displays the Format menu and highlights the Labels command (Figure 4-72).

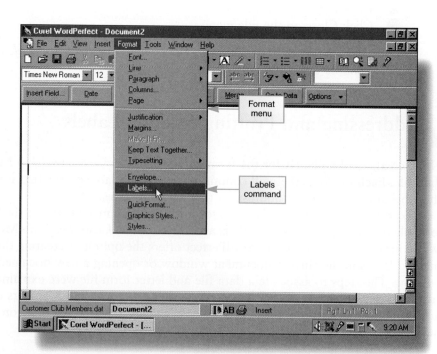

FIGURE 4-72

2 **Click Labels. Scroll the Labels list box in the Labels dialog box to display Avery 5160 Address and then click Avery 5160 Address. Point to the Select button.**

WordPerfect displays the Labels dialog box (Figure 4-73). The Labels list box contains a list of mailing label definitions that are compatible with your printer. The Avery 5160 Address label definition is high-lighted in the list box, the Label details area displays the details of the selected label definition, and a sample mailing label sheet displays in the List labels for area. Each printed sheet contains room for thirty labels: three labels across the page and ten rows down the page. If you have a dot matrix printer, the label definitions may be different.

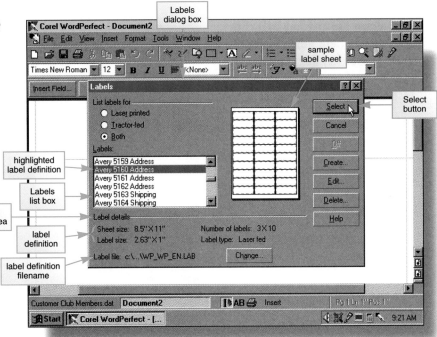

FIGURE 4-73

3 **Click the Select button. Click the Insert Field button on the Merge Bar.**

When you click the Select button, WordPerfect closes the Labels dialog box and displays a blank mailing label in the document window (Figure 4-74). When you click the Insert Field button, WordPerfect displays the Insert Field Name or Number dialog box. The Name field name is highlighted in the Field Names list box and the data filename (Customer Club Members.dat) displays above the list box.

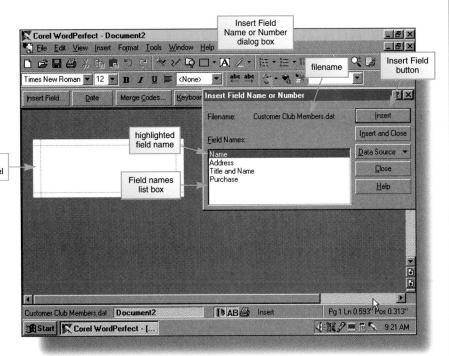

FIGURE 4-74

4 **Hold down the CTRL key and click the Address field name in the Field Names list box. Release the CTRL key and then point to the Insert and Close button.**

WordPerfect highlights the Address field name (Figure 4-75). Currently, the Name and Address field names are highlighted.

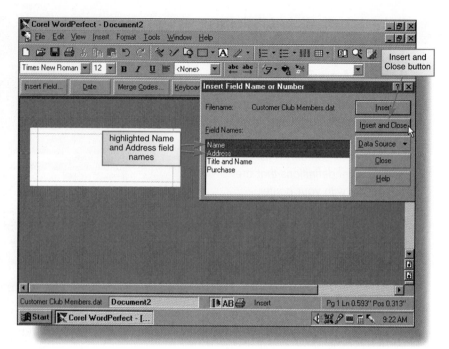

FIGURE 4-75

5 **Click the Insert and Close button.**

WordPerfect closes the Insert Field Name or Number dialog box and displays the FIELD(Name) and FIELD(Address) codes in the mailing label (Figure 4-76).

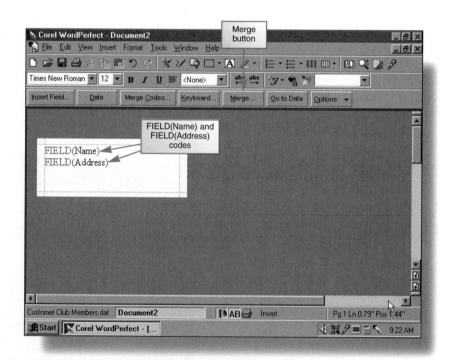

FIGURE 4-76

Merging the Data File and Label Form File

The next step in generating the mailing labels is to merge the data file and label form file to produce a merge document. The steps to merge a data file and form file were explained earlier and are summarized on the next page.

TO MERGE A DATA FILE AND A LABEL FORM FILE

1. Click the Merge button on the Merge Bar.
2. Click the Merge button in the Perform Merge dialog box.

WordPerfect merges the data file and label form file, opens a new document window (Document3), and displays the mailing labels in the window (Figure 4-77).

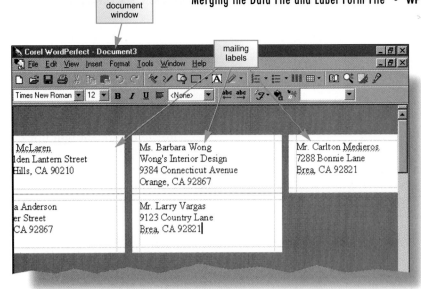

FIGURE 4-77

Printing the Mailing Labels

After merging the data and label form files, you can print the labels or save the document on disk and print the labels at a later time. The steps to print the labels are summarized below.

TO PRINT THE MAILING LABELS

1. Click the Print button on the Toolbar.
2. Review the Print to dialog box to ensure the Full document option button is selected in the Print sheet in the Print area and the value 1 displays in the Number of copies text box.
3. Click the Print button in the Print to dialog box.
4. When prompted by the printer, manually insert a mailing label sheet in the printer.

WordPerfect displays the Corel WordPerfect dialog box momentarily and then prints the mailing labels (Figure 4-78).

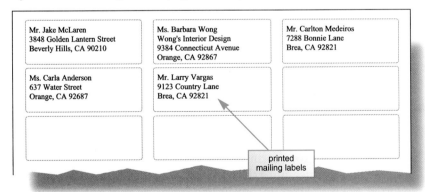

FIGURE 4-78

> ### ▶ More *About* Printing Labels
>
> To print individual labels or a range of labels, click File on the menu bar, click Print, click the Print drop-down list box arrow, click Advanced Multiple Pages, click the Edit button, type the number of each label or a range of labels in the Page(s)/Label(s) text box, click the OK button, and click the Print button. While entering the range of labels, you can type 3 to print the third label, type 3 8 to print the third and eighth label, or type 3- to print the third label and the remaining labels in the document.

Closing the Form Document and Merge Document

After you print the mailing labels, close the document windows containing the mailing label definition and mailing labels. The steps on the next page summarize closing the two document windows.

TO CLOSE MULTIPLE DOCUMENT WINDOWS

① Click File on the menu bar.

② Click Close.

③ Click the No button in the Corel WordPerfect dialog box so the merge document will not be saved.

④ Click File on the menu bar.

⑤ Click Close on the File menu.

⑥ Click the No button in the Corel WordPerfect dialog box so the mailing label definition will not be saved.

The windows containing the merge document and the mailing label definition close and the document window containing the data file displays.

Addressing and Printing Envelopes

If your printer has the capability of printing directly onto envelopes, you may wish to generate envelopes instead of mailing labels. To address and print envelopes, an association must be made between the data file and the **envelope form file**. While making the association, a new document window opens to create the envelopes. The following steps summarize how to associate the Customer Club Members data file and the envelope form file.

TO ASSOCIATE A DATA FILE WITH AN ENVELOPE FORM FILE

① Click Tools on the menu bar.

② Click Merge.

③ Click the Create Document button in the Merge dialog box.

④ Click the OK button in the Create Merge File dialog box.

⑤ Click the Select File button at the far right of the Associate a data file text box.

⑥ Click the Customer Club Members.dat filename in the list box in the Select Data File dialog box.

⑦ Click the Select button.

⑧ Click the OK button in the Associate Form and Data dialog box.

WordPerfect opens a new document window (Document2) and displays the Merge Bar in the new window.

Creating the Envelope Form File

Next, create the envelope form file by selecting an envelope definition and inserting the FIELD(Name) and FIELD(Address) merge codes into the envelope form file in the newly created document window. The **envelope definition** determines the envelope size (width and height), position of the name and address on the envelope, and the direction the envelope must be inserted into the printer. WordPerfect contains several predefined envelope definitions. Perform the following steps to create the envelope form file.

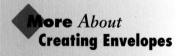

More *About*
Creating Envelopes

In addition to using the Envelope #10 Landscape envelope definition to create envelopes, other definitions include Envelope C5 Landscape, Envelope DL Landscape, and Envelope Monarch Landscape.

Steps To Create the Envelope Form File

1 **Click Format on the menu bar and then point to Envelope.**

*WordPerfect displays the Format menu and highlights the **Envelope command** (Figure 4-79).*

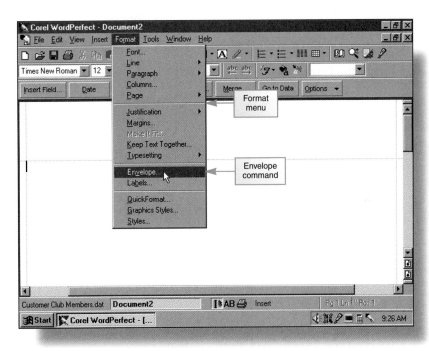

FIGURE 4-79

2 **Click Envelope. Point to the Print return address check box in the Return Addresses area of the Envelope dialog box.**

WordPerfect displays the Envelope dialog box (Figure 4-80). The Envelope dialog box contains areas to enter the return address and mailing address. A check mark displays in the recessed Print return address check box. The Envelope definitions area contains the Envelope #10 Land-scape envelope definition and the size of the envelope (4.13" X 9.5") below the box. A Preview box shows the blank envelope with a stamp.

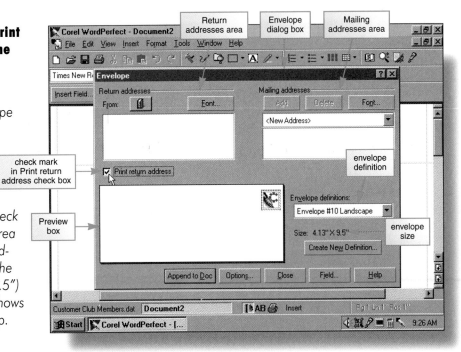

FIGURE 4-80

3 **Click the Print return address check box to remove the check mark in the check box. If necessary, click the Mailing addresses text box to move the insertion point to the text box. Point to the Field button.**

WordPerfect removes the check mark in the Print return address check box (Figure 4-81). The insertion point is located in the Mailing addresses text box.

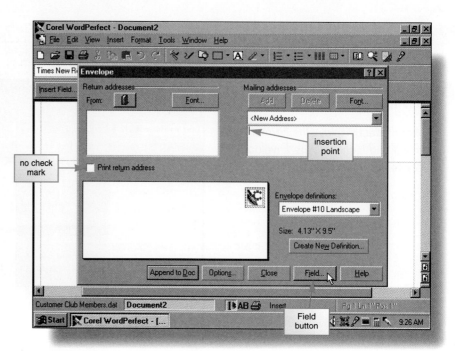

FIGURE 4-81

4 **Click the Field button. Hold down the CTRL key and click the Address field name in the Field Names list box to highlight the Address field name. Release the CTRL key. Click the Insert and Close button. Point to the Append to Doc button in the Envelope dialog box.**

WordPerfect displays the Insert Field Name or Number dialog box, highlights the Address field name in the Field Names list box, inserts the FIELD(Name) and FIELD(Address) codes in the Mailing addresses text box, and displays the Name and Address field names in the Preview box (Figure 4-82).

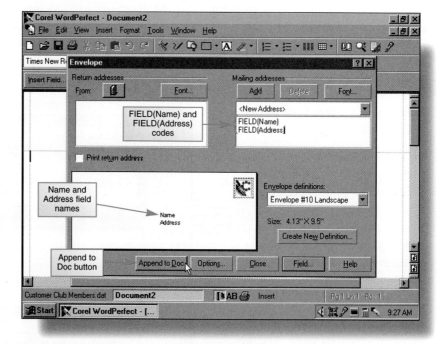

FIGURE 4-82

5 **Click the Append to Doc button.**

WordPerfect closes the Envelope dialog box and appends the envelope definition to the document in the window (Figure 4-83). The left margin changes to 4.5 inches and the left margin guideline changes position to display two Field codes 4.5 inches from the left edge of the envelope.

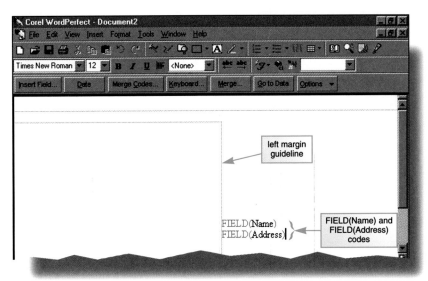

FIGURE 4-83

Merging the Data File and Envelope Form File

The next step in generating the envelopes is to merge the data file and envelope form file to produce a merge document. The steps to merge a data file and form file were explained earlier and are summarized below.

TO MERGE A DATA FILE AND AN ENVELOPE FORM FILE

1. Click the Merge button on the Merge Bar.
2. Click the Merge button in the Perform Merge dialog box.
3. Scroll the document window to display the first envelope.

WordPerfect merges the data file with the envelope form file (envelope definition), opens a new document window (Document3), and displays the envelope for the first customer in the data file in the window (Figure 4-84).

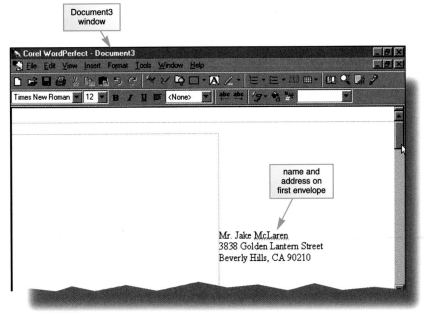

FIGURE 4-84

Printing the Envelopes

After merging the data file and envelope form file, you can print the envelopes or save the document on disk and print the envelopes at a later time. The steps to print the envelopes are summarized on the next page.

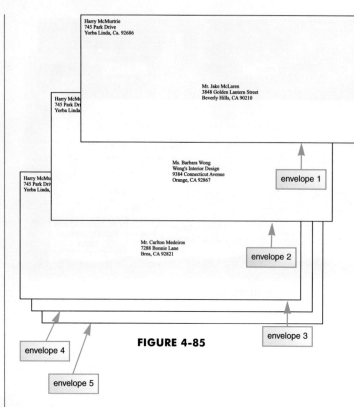

FIGURE 4-85

TO PRINT THE ENVELOPES

① Click the Print button on the Toolbar.

② Review the Print to dialog box to ensure the Full document option button is selected in the Print sheet in the Print area and the value 1 displays in the Number of copies text box.

③ Click the Print button in the Print to dialog box.

④ When prompted by the printer, manually insert each envelope.

WordPerfect displays the Corel WordPerfect dialog box momentarily and then allows you to print each envelope (Figure 4-85).

Closing the Merge Document and Envelope Form File

After printing the envelopes, close the document windows containing the envelopes, envelope definition, and data file. The following steps summarize closing the three document windows.

TO CLOSE MULTIPLE DOCUMENT WINDOWS

① Click File on the menu bar.

② Click Close.

③ Click the No button in the Corel WordPerfect dialog box so the merge document will not be saved.

④ Click File on the menu bar.

⑤ Click Close.

⑥ Click the No button in the Corel WordPerfect dialog box so the envelope definition will not be saved.

⑦ Click File on the menu bar.

⑧ Click Close.

WordPerfect closes the windows containing the envelopes, envelope definition, and data file.

TO QUIT WORDPERFECT AND REMOVE THE FLOPPY DISK FROM DRIVE A

① Click File on the menu bar.

② Click Exit on the File menu to exit WordPerfect.

③ Remove the Corel WordPerfect 8 Files floppy disk from drive A.

WordPerfect is exited and the Corel WordPerfect 8 Files floppy disk is removed from drive A.

More About Printing Envelopes

To print individual envelopes or a range of envelopes, click File on the menu bar, click Print, click the Print drop-down list box arrow, click Advanced Multiple Pages, click the Edit button, type the number of each envelope or a range of envelopes in the Page(s)/Label(s) text box, click the OK button, and click the Print button. While entering the range of envelopes, you can type 2 to print the second envelope, type 3 5 to print the third and fifth envelopes, or type 4 - to print the fourth envelope and all remaining envelopes in the document.

Project Summary

In Project 4, you generated form letters, mailing labels, and envelopes. You created a data file containing a record for each customer, a letter form file containing a business letter, and saved both files on disk. In the process of creating the letter form file, you created a letterhead with a horizontal graphics line, inserted merge codes in the form file, created a table, entered text and formulas into the table, applied a table style, and selected and formatted cells in the table. You used the Merge Bar to merge the data file and letter form file and produce the merge document containing the form letters. Then you printed the form letters on the printer.

You created the label form file, associated the data file and the label form file, merged the two files, and printed mailing labels. Then, you created the envelope form file, associated the data file and the envelope form file, merged the two files, and printed envelopes.

What You Should Know

Having completed this project, you now should be able to perform the following tasks:

- Add a horizontal graphics line to the letterhead *(WP 4.21)*
- Apply a table style to a table *(WP 4.36)*
- Associate a data file with an envelope form file *(WP 4.52)*
- Associate a data file with a label form file *(WP 4.48)*
- Associate a data file with a letter form file *(WP 4.16)*
- Bold the cells in a row *(WP 4.39)*
- Center all cells in a table *(WP 4.43)*
- Center the text of the letterhead as you type *(WP 4.21)*
- Close multiple document windows *(WP 4.47, WP 4.52, WP 4.56)*
- Complete the entry of text and formulas in the table *(WP 4.33)*
- Create a data file *(WP 4.8)*
- Create a table *(WP 4.28)*
- Create the envelope form file *(WP 4.53)*
- Create the label form file *(WP 4.48)*
- Display row and column indicators *(WP 4.34)*
- Display the Formula Bar *(WP 4.31)*
- Display the Ruler and set the margins *(WP 4.20)*
- Enter a formula into a table cell *(WP 4.32)*
- Enter text into a table *(WP 4.30)*
- Format the address in the letterhead *(WP 4.23)*
- Format the store name in the letterhead *(WP 4.22)*
- Hide the Ruler *(WP 4.45)*
- Insert a date code in the letter form file *(WP 4.24)*
- Insert field merge codes in the letter form file *(WP 4.25)*
- Merge a data file and an envelope form file *(WP 4.55)*
- Merge a data file and a label form file *(WP 4.51)*
- Merge a data file and a letter form file *(WP 4.45)*
- Print the envelopes *(WP 4.56)*
- Print the form letters *(WP 4.47)*
- Print the mailing labels *(WP 4.51)*
- Quit WordPerfect and remove the floppy disk from drive A *(WP 4.56)*
- Save the letter form file *(WP 4.45)*
- Select a row of cells *(WP 4.38)*
- Select all cells in a table *(WP 4.42)*
- Select and format a group of cells *(WP 4.40)*
- Start WordPerfect *(WP 4.7)*
- Type the remaining text in the letter form file *(WP 4.44)*

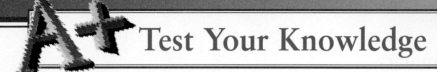 Test Your Knowledge

1 True/False

Instructions: Circle T if the statement is true or F if the statement is false.

T F   1. Merging is the process of combining information from two or more sources to produce an entirely new document.

T F   2. A field is divided into records.

T F   3. The ENDRECORD marker and hard page break indicate the end of a record in the data file.

T F   4. When you create a data file, holding down the CTRL key and pressing the ENTER key allows you to enter more than one line of text in a field.

T F   5. The DATE code in the form file indicates where the current date will display in each form letter after you perform the merge operation.

T F   6. You insert a Field merge code in a data file.

T F   7. A table consists of rows and columns.

T F   8. The address of the cell located at the intersection of the second row and third column is B3.

T F   9. The formula b2*.85 in cell C3 takes the value in cell C3, multiplies the value by .85, and places the result in cell B2.

T F   10. You select a row of cells by clicking the indicator to the left of the column indicators.

2 Multiple Choice

Instructions: Circle the correct response.

1. The process of combining information from two or more sources to produce an entirely new document is called _____.
   a. mass production
   b. sorting
   c. merging
   d. combining

2. The _____ file controls the merge operation.
   a. form
   b. data
   c. merge
   d. master

3. The _____ contains the Create Data, Create Document, and Perform Merge buttons.
   a. Merge Bar
   b. Merge dialog box
   c. Property Bar
   d. Tables Toolbar

4. The _____ command displays in the data file.
   a. FIELD(Name)
   b. DATE
   c. FIELD(Address)
   d. ENDFIELD

5. _____ does not display a horizontal graphics line.
   a. Pressing the HYPHEN (-) key four times and pressing the ENTER key
   b. Clicking Insert on the menu bar, pointing to Shape, and clicking Horizontal Line
   c. Pressing the EQUAL SIGN (=) key four times and pressing the ENTER key
   d. Pressing the F12 key

6. If cell B2 contains the value 36.95 and the formula b2*.85 is entered into cell C2, the value displayed in cell C2 is _____.
   a. 31.4075
   b. 31.40
   c. $31.40
   d. $31.4075

7. You apply a table style, such as the Double Border Header style, to a table using the _____.
   a. Table SpeedFormat
   b. Table Style Toolbar
   c. Tables menu
   d. DoubleBorder Header button

8. To select all the cells in a table, point to the top or left border of any cell in the table and _____.
   a. click
   b. double-click
   c. triple-click
   d. quadruple-click

9. After merging a data file with a letter form file, you print the form letters by printing the contents of the _____ file(s).
   a. form
   b. data
   c. merge
   d. form and data

10. Avery 5160 Address is a(n) _____.
   a. label definition
   b. envelope definition
   c. mailing label sheet
   d. type of envelope

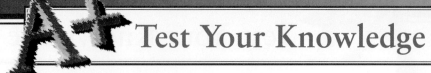

A+ Test Your Knowledge

3 Identifying the Objects that Display After Creating a Table

Instructions: In Figure 4-86, arrows point to objects that display in the document window when you create a table. Identify the various objects in the spaces provided.

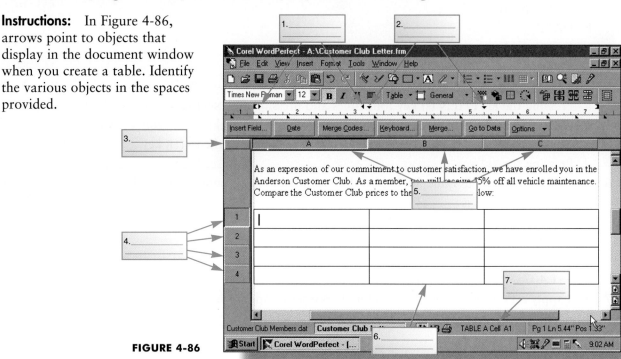

FIGURE 4-86

4 Formatting the Numeric Values in a Table

Instructions: Given the desktop shown in Figure 4-87, list the steps to select and format the numeric values in cells B2, B3, B4, C2, C3, and C4. Format the cells with the currency format.

As an ...sion of our ...mmitment to ...r satisfaction, we have enrolled you in t... Anderson Customer Club. As a member, you will receive 15% off all vehicle maintenance. Compare the Customer Club prices to the regular prices below:

Vehicle Maintenance	Regular Price	Customer Club Price
3,000 Mile Service	36.95	31.4075
15,000 Mile Service	127.95	108.7575
30,000 Mile Service	328.95	279.6075

Customer Club Members.dat   Document2   AB   TABLE A Cell B1"   Pg 1 Ln 5.44" Pos 3.76"

Start   Corel WordPerfect - [...   9:06 AM

FIGURE 4-87

Step 1: _____

Step 2: _____

Step 3: _____

Step 4: _____

Step 5: _____

Use Help

1 Reviewing Project Activities

Instructions: Perform the following tasks on a computer.

1. Start WordPerfect.
2. Create a 4x3 table by performing the following instructions: Point to the Table QuickCreate button on the WordPerfect 8 Toolbar, hold down the left mouse button, drag the mouse pointer onto the table sizing grid until four columns and three rows of the grid are highlighted and the 4x3 entry displays above the grid, and release the left mouse button.
3. Type the text and numbers shown in the following table into the table in your document window.

Table 4-2			
	1999	*2000*	*TOTAL*
Revenues (millions)	**13.7**	**14.5**	
Expenses (millions)	**8.6**	**7.9**	

4. Right-click the table and click Formula Toolbar on the QuickMenu to display the Formula Bar.
5. Position the insertion point in cell D2.
6. Click the Help button on the menu bar. Click Help Topics. Click Index. Type quicksum and click the Display button. Read about the QuickSum feature. Close the Corel WordPerfect Help window.
7. Click the QuickSum button on the Formula Bar. The +SUM(B2:C2) function and cell references display in the Formula Edit text box, the values in cells B2 and C2 are added together, and the sum of the values in cells B2 and C2 displays in cell D2.
8. Click the Help button on the menu bar. Click Help Topics. Click Index. Type copy and double-click the formula (in table) help topic. Read about copying formulas in a table. Close the Corel WordPerfect Help window.
9. Click the Copy Formula button on the Formula Bar, type D3 in the To Cell text box, and click the OK button. The formula in cell D2 is copied to cell D3 and the result of adding cells B3 and C3 displays in cell D3.
10. Click the Close button on the Formula Bar to remove the Formula Bar.
11. Print the document on the printer.
12. Click File on the menu bar, click Close on the File menu, and click the No button in the Corel WordPerfect dialog box so the document will not be saved.
13. Quit WordPerfect.

Use Help

2 Expanding on the Basics

Instructions: Perform the following tasks using a computer and answer the questions.

Two sources are required to generate form letters. The first source, called a data source, can be either a data file or the address book. Using Help, answer the following questions about using the Address Book as a data source:

1. When you use the Address Book as your data source, do you have to set up a data file?
2. What changes in the merge process when you use the Address Book instead of a data file?
3. What determines which records in the Address Book will be used during the merge process?

The second source to generate form letters is the letter form file. Using Help, answer the following questions about form files:

1. What name is linked to the form document when you make an association between a data file and a form file?
2. What merge code is used when performing a keyboard merge?
3. What happens when you perform a merge and WordPerfect finds the merge code mentioned in Step 2?

Tables allow you to organize and present text and numeric information in an easy-to-understand format. Using Help, answer the following questions about tables.

1. How do you convert a tabular column of text and numbers in a document into a table?
2. How do you join existing table cells into one cell?
3. How do you split an existing table cell into two cells?
4. How do you move a row to another location in the table?

Graphics lines allow you to separate text or graphics on a page and make documents easier to read and more visually appealing. Answer the following questions about graphics lines:

1. How do you insert a vertical graphics line in a document?
2. How do you create a .15-inch thick graphics line?
3. Can you move a graphics line within a document? If so, how?
4. What keyboard keys can you use to delete a graphics line?

Apply Your Knowledge

1 Editing a Table

Instructions: The Lane_Studios_Table.wpd file is located on the Corel WordPerfect 8 Web site. Perform the following steps to download and edit the file.

Part 1: Downloading a File

1. Start WordPerfect.
2. If you do not have access to the Internet, obtain a copy of the Lane_Studios_Table.wpd file from your instructor, place the file on the Corel WordPerfect 8 Files floppy disk, and go to Step 7.
3. Click File on the menu bar, click Internet Publisher, and click the Browse the Web button.
4. Type http://www.scsite.com/wp8 in the Location box.
5. Press the ENTER key to display the Corel WordPerfect 8 home page. Click Project 4.
6. Follow the instructions on the Web page to download the file to the Corel WordPerfect 8 Files floppy disk.
7. Click the Open button on the Toolbar and open the lane_studios_table.wpd document located on the Corel WordPerfect 8 Files disk.

Part 2: Entering Formulas Into the Table

1. Enter the formula for the total yearly revenues (B2+C2+D2+E2) in cell F2.
2. Enter the formula for the total yearly expenses (B3+C3+D3+E3) in cell F3.
3. Enter the formula for the first quarter profits (B2-B3) in cell B4.
4. Enter the formula for the second quarter profits (C2-C3) in cell C4.
5. Enter the formula for the third quarter profits (D2-D3) in cell D4.
6. Enter the formula for the fourth quarter profits (E2-E3) in cell E4.
7. Enter the formula for the total yearly profits (F2-F3) in cell F4.

Part 3: Formatting the Table

1. Apply the Header Fill Column table style to the table.
2. Format all numbers in the table using the currency format.
3. Save the file on the Corel WordPerfect 8 Files floppy disk.
4. Print the document on the printer.
5. Quit WordPerfect.

In the Lab

1 Generating Form Letters With a Table, Mailing Labels, and Envelopes

Problem: As the owner of California Tile Supply, you decide to send a letter to promote your tile business to each individual who has purchased a house from O'Connell Brothers builders in the past week. Then you decide to send it as a form letter to all these new home buyers.

Part 1: Create the Data File

1. Create a data file to contain the customer information shown in Table 4-3.

Table 4-3

	FIELD 1 (NAME)	FIELD 2 (ADDRESS)	FIELD 3 (CITY)	FIELD 4 (STATE)	FIELD 5 (ZIP CODE)	FIELD 6 (TITLE & NAME)	FIELD 7 (CREDIT)
Record 1	Mr. Arthur Morrow	834 Wandering Lane	Placentia	CA	92870	Mr. Morrow	$1700.00
Record 2	Ms. Susan Clarkston	793 Strawberry Lane	Brea	CA	92821	Ms. Clarkston	$2500.00
Record 3	Mr. & Ms. Vladdi Tsai	329 Oakwood Drive	Yorba Linda	CA	92887	Mr. & Ms. Tsai	$3400.00
Record 4	Mr. Taylor Norby	3875 Plank Road	Placentia	CA	92870	Mr. Norby	$1800.00
Record 5	Ms. Sandy Fleming	3563 Range Road	Yorba Linda	CA	92887	Ms. Fleming	$2300.00

2. Save the data file on the Corel WordPerfect 8 Files floppy disk using the Home Buyers filename.
3. Print the data file on the printer. The printed document will be six pages long.

Part 2: Create the Letter Form File

1. Create the letter form file illustrated in Figure 4-88 in a new document window.
2. Associate the Home Buyers data file with the letter form file.
3. Create the personalized letterhead shown in Figure 4-88. Use Arial Bold 24-point font for the name and Arial 10-point font for the address line. Add a blank line and a horizontal line below the address.
4. Insert the appropriate merge codes in the letter to display the current date, name, address, city, state, zip code, and design credit.
5. Create a 3x4 table in the form letter. Enter the text in the table. Enter the formula to calculate the values in column C (Our Price/Square Foot). The formula to calculate Our Price/Square Foot is: Retail Price/Square Foot *.83.
6. Apply the Header Fill Column table style to the table. Format all numbers using the currency format. Center all cells in the table.
7. Check the spelling of the form letter.
8. Save the letter form file on the Corel WordPerfect 8 Files floppy disk using Home Buyers Letter as the filename.
9. Print the form letter on the printer.
10. Merge the form and data files to create form letters.
11. Print the form letters on the printer.

In the Lab

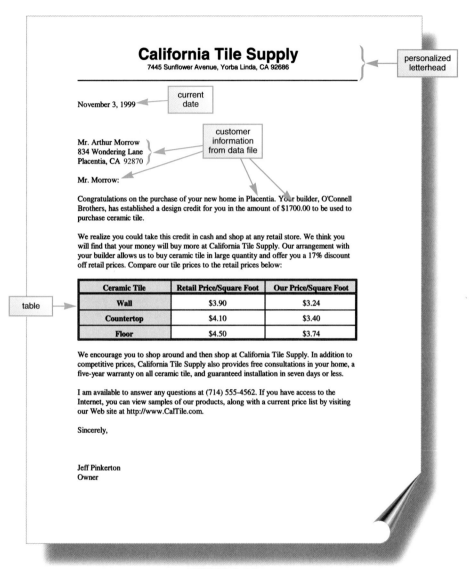

FIGURE 4-88

Part 3: Create the Label Form File and Envelope Form File

1. Create mailing labels using the same data file.
2. Save the mailing labels using Home Buyers Labels as the filename.
3. Print the labels.
4. If your printer allows, create envelopes using the same data file. Save the envelopes using the Home Buyers Envelopes filename. Print the envelopes.

In the Lab

2 Generating Form Letters With Tables, Mailing Labels, and Envelopes

Problem: As the president of the Jefferson High School Booster Club, you want to send a letter to each Booster Club member whose son or daughter is on a high school sports team and has asked to participate in the magazine sale. You decide to send a form letter to each member.

Part 1: Create the Data File

1. Create a data file to contain the member information shown in Table 4-4.

TABLE 4-4				
	FIELD 1 (NAME)	FIELD 2 (ADDRESS)	FIELD 3 (PLAYER MESSAGE)	FIELD 4 (SPORT)
Record 1	Mr. Collins	3674 Budding Blvd. Placentia, CA 92870	son, Brian,	basketball
Record 2	Mr. Kalcevich	738 Omega Dr. Placentia, CA 92870	daughter, Kim,	soccer
Record 3	Ms. Ford	9931 Fourth St. Placentia, CA 92870	daughter, Kristin,	football
Record 4	Ms. Dodge	5342 Park Rd. Placentia, CA 92870	son, Andrew,	water polo
Record 5	Mr. Begley	934 Circle Dr. Placentia, CA 92870	daughter, Jennefer,	tennis

2. Save the data file on the Corel WordPerfect 8 Files floppy disk using Booster Club Members as the filename.
3. Print the data file on the printer. The printed document will be six pages long.

Part 2: Create the Letter Form File

1. Create the letter form file illustrated in Figure 4-89 in a new document window.
2. Associate the Booster Club Members data file with the letter form file.
3. Create the personalized letterhead shown in Figure 4-89. Use Arial Bold 24-point font for the name and Arial 10-point font for the address. Add a blank line and a double horizontal line below the address line. (*Hint:* Click Insert on menu bar, point to Shape, click Custom Line, click Line style button, click Double in Styles list box, click OK button.)
4. Insert the appropriate merge codes in the letter to display the current date, name, address, player message, and sport.
5. Create a 4x4 table in the form letter. Enter the text in the table. Enter a formula to calculate the yearly savings in column D. The formula to calculate Yearly Savings is Newsstand Price – Booster Club Price.
6. Apply the No Lines Header table style to the table. Bold the table headings, center all cells in the table, and format all numbers using the currency format.
7. Create a 3x4 table in the form letter. Enter the text in the table. If necessary, apply the No Lines Header table style to the table. Bold the table headings and center all cells in the table. There are no formulas in the table.
8. Check the spelling of the form letter.

In the Lab

9. Save the letter form file on the WordPerfect Project Files floppy disk using Booster Club Sale Letter as the filename.
10. Print the form letter on the printer.
11. Merge the form and data files to create form letters.
12. Print the form letters on the printer.

Part 3: Create the Label Form File and Envelope Form File

1. Create mailing labels using the same data file.
2. Save the mailing labels using the Booster Club Labels filename.
3. Print the labels.
4. If your printer allows, create envelopes using the same data file. Save the envelopes using Booster Club Envelopes as the filename. Print the envelopes.

FIGURE 4-89

The figure shows a letter from Jefferson High School with the following annotations:

personalized letterhead

Jefferson High School
732 Central Avenue, Yorba Linda, CA 92887

August 31, 1999 — **current date**

Mr. Collins
3674 Budding Blvd.
Placentia, CA 92870 — **parent and student information from data file**

Dear Mr. Collins:

The Jefferson High School Booster Club is sponsoring a magazine sale to raise money to support the high school sports program. This year, your son, Brian, has chosen to compete on the basketball team and has asked to participate in this magazine sale. A sample of the magazines, newsstand prices, Booster Club prices, and yearly savings are illustrated below:

tables

Magazine	Newsstand Price	Booster Club Price	Yearly Savings
Cooking Monthly	$19.00	$11.75	$7.25
On the Internet	$25.00	$16.37	$8.63
Animal Kingdom	$19.00	$12.55	$6.45

As an incentive for students to sell magazines, the following awards will be given.

Subscriptions Sold	Sports Equipment	Booster Club Credit
1 - 10	Head or Wrist Bands	$10 Credit
11 - 20	Game Bag	$50 Credit
More 20	Athletic Shoes	$75 Credit

The Booster Club Credit can be used to pay sports or transportation fees. Thank you for your participation in the sale.

Sincerely,

Stella Henderson
Booster Club President

---

3 Generating Form Memos with a Table

Problem: You work at the corporate office of Brooks Department Store and want to send a memo to congratulate the department heads of the three departments that have increased their sales in each of the first three months of the year. You decide to send a personalized memo to each department head.

Part 1: Create the Data File

1. Create a data file to contain the sales information shown in Table 4-5.
2. Save the data file on the Corel WordPerfect 8 Files floppy disk using Department Managers as the filename.
3. Print the data file on the printer. The printed document will be four pages long.

TABLE 4-5

	FIELD 1 (MANAGER NAME)	FIELD 2 (DEPARTMENT)	FIELD 3 (MANAGER FIRST NAME)
Record 1	Alicia Brown	Television	Alicia
Record 2	Pete Blackburn	Household	Pete
Record 3	Marilyn Stoval	Lingerie	Marilyn

(continued)

In the Lab

Generating Form Memos with a Table *(continued)*

Part 2: Create the Memo Form File

1. Create the memo form file illustrated in Figure 4-90 in a new document window.
2. Associate the memo form file with the Department Managers data file.
3. Create the personalized letterhead shown in Figure 4-90. Use Arial Bold Italic 24-point font for the name and Arial 10-point font for the address line. Add a blank line and a horizontal line below the address.
4. Insert the appropriate merge codes in the letter to display the current date, manager name, department, and manager first name.
5. Create a 5x6 table in the memo.
   a. Enter the title, First Quarter Sales, in cell A1. Enter the remaining text and numbers in the table.
   b. Enter a formula to calculate the values in cells E3, E4, and E5 (Total Sales). The formula to calculate Total Sales is: Jan. Sales + Feb. Sales + Mar. Sales.
   c. Enter a formula to calculate the values in cells B6, C6, and D6 (Totals). The formula to calculate Totals is: Household Sales + Lingerie Sales + Television Sales.
   d. Enter a formula to calculate the value in cell E6 (Total Quarter Sales). The formula to calculate Total Quarter Sales is: Total January Sales + Total February Sales + Total March Sales.
   e. Apply the Fancy Fills table style to the table.
   f. Format all numbers in the table using the currency format.
6. Check the spelling of the letter.
7. Save the memo form file on the WordPerfect Document Files floppy disk using Department Managers Memo as the filename.
8. Print the form memo on the printer.
9. Merge the data file and memo form file to create the personalized memos.
10. Print the memos on the printer.

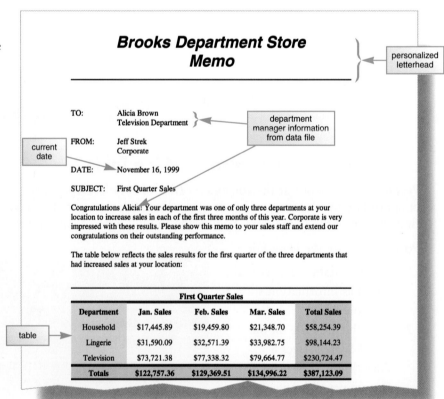

FIGURE 4-90

Cases and Places

The difficulty of these case studies varies: ❱ are the least difficult; ❱❱ are more difficult; and ❱❱❱ are the most difficult.

1 ❱ Every year, your city organizes a July 4th country fair on the Saturday before the holiday. The fair has booths that merchants, civic organizations, and youth sports groups may rent. As a city employee, it is your responsibility to rent the booths. The size of a small booth is 6 feet by 10 feet, and the size of a large booth is 10 feet by 20 feet. A small food booth rents for $400, a large food booth rents for $750, a small non-food booth rents for $250, and a large non-food booth rents for $500. Create a form letter to contact the organizations. The form letter should contain a letterhead and a table listing booth types, sizes, and prices. Create a data file that contains the names and addresses of five local organizations. Then, generate the form letters and accompanying mailing labels.

2 ❱ You are the owner of the Alligator Cafe, a very exclusive restaurant frequented by Hollywood actors, directors, and producers. You wish to advertise your weekday luncheon specials and offer a special twenty percent discount to groups of five or more. Create a form letter to send to the regulars that frequent your restaurant. The form letter should contain an appropriate letterhead and a table listing the weekday luncheon specials, regular prices, and discounted group prices. Create a data file containing the names and addresses of five regulars. Then, generate the form letters and accompanying mailing labels or envelopes.

3 ❱❱ Many businesses advertise their services and products by sending form letters or flyers to residences. Obtain three examples of advertisements that you or someone you know received in the mail. Write a brief report summarizing the advertisements. Include the good and bad features of each advertisement, ways to improve the advertisement, and what you believe makes a form letter effective.

4 ❱❱ Junk mail is on the increase! Have you ever wondered about the following questions? How companies obtain your name and address? How can you prevent junk mail? How can you eliminate your name and address from a database used to send junk mail? Are there companies that specialize in selling names and addresses? What do they charge? Who purchases these lists? What types of lists are available? Using the Internet, a library, or another resource, answer these questions and write a brief report summarizing your findings.

Cases and Places

5 ▶▶▶ Visit three businesses in your area that generate form letters to advertise their services or products. Talk to the individual who designs the letter form file, creates the data source, and generates the form letters. Write a brief report summarizing how each business generates form letters, where they get the data for the mailings, what software and hardware they use, what impact the mailings have on sales, and your suggestions to improve the process.

6 ▶▶▶ Use WordPerfect to create a survey to determine what people think about receiving personalized mail. Design the survey so it can be completed quickly by either limiting the number of questions or designing the survey using check boxes. Give the survey to five people in each of the following age categories: 20 to 29 years old; 30 to 49 years old; and 50 to 70 years old. Write a brief report summarizing the surveys in each age group, indicating how the responses in each age group are different or similar, and whether people like or dislike personalized mail.

7 ▶▶▶ Microsoft Office also has a mail merge feature to generate form letters. Visit a software store, friend's house, or local business to find a computer that has the Microsoft Office software. Use Mail Merge to create the data file and letter form file illustrated in Figure 4-1 in this project. Write a brief report comparing the two Mail Merge features.

Corel *WordPerfect 8*

Creating a Professional Newsletter

Objectives:

You will have mastered the material in this project when you can:

▶ Understand newsletter terminology
▶ Check a document for writing problems using Grammatik
▶ Create and format a newsletter title using TextArt
▶ Change the shape, font, and outline thickness of a TextArt image
▶ Change the text color and outline color of a TextArt image
▶ Remove a shadow from a TextArt image
▶ Create a newsletter subtitle, volume number, and date using a table
▶ Change the border style of a table
▶ Find and retrieve a file on disk using QuickFinder
▶ Define newspaper columns
▶ Format the subheads in a newsletter using QuickFormat
▶ Create a drop cap
▶ Insert a clipart image into a newsletter
▶ Wrap text around a clipart image
▶ Create a text box
▶ Create a pull-quote in a text box
▶ Change the border style and fill style of a text box
▶ Move text to the top of the next column

From Stones to E-mail

Express Messenger

In 1501, a Portuguese ship captain set sail for destinations unknown. Aware that he would be at sea for many years and wishing to send news of himself and his crew to those back home, he went ashore at the Cape of Good Hope on the southern tip of Africa and deposited a letter wrapped in pitch-covered canvas under a stone. On the stone, he inscribed a request to whoever found his message that they forward it to his homeland. This launched the tradition of the *post office stone*. Sea captains on their way to Europe — even bitter enemies of the writers — would pick up the letters and deliver them. This may have been the first example of global newsletter messenger service.

Humankind always has thirsted for information about news and events. Native Americans used smoke signals to convey news. Africans used drums. Some say Australian aborigines developed telepathic powers. The Spanish Conquistadores scratched their

PLEASE FORWARD

news onto Inscription Rock in New Mexico. Armies of old relied on mirrors and semaphores. Then, as technology progressed, the means of delivery grew more sophisticated, evolving from Pony Express and telegraph to modern fiber-optic cables, microwaves, and satellite relays.

Newsletters likewise have evolved into highly specialized vehicles that number in the thousands, addressing everything from astrology to investments to medicine to zoology. No matter what the association, cause, or subject, a newsletter for it is likely to exist. Besides the blizzard of hardcopy newsletters delivered by mail every day, e-mail and Web sites reach millions more.

A good reason for the explosive growth of newsletters is they get results. To unite people, organize an activity, persuade, or simply to pour out one's feelings, an attractive, well-written newsletter can boost sales, promote morale, raise money, or send your personal news to friends during the holiday season.

Snappy content, however, is not good enough. To reach out and seize someone's attention, newsletters must be more than merely attractive. Your newsletter must make a statement, provide appeal, and elicit interest.

In Corel WordPerfect, you have the ideal partner for creating dynamic newsletters. WordPerfect lets you produce crisp banner headlines, manipulate columns, fonts, and blocks of copy at will, then spice the whole thing with graphics. Once you have the newsletter just right, WordPerfect also provides the capability of merging names and addresses from a separate database, such as a student organization, your clients, or your family and friends.

Unlike that sixteenth century ship captain who had to rely on chance that someone would find the mail he deposited under the post office stone, once you finish that perfect (WordPerfect, that is) newsletter, you can whisk it on its way via the Internet or the corner mailbox — without getting pitch on your hands.

Project 5

Corel
WordPerfect 8

Creating a Professional Newsletter

Case Perspective

Sally McCormick is the newest member of the Board of Directors of the Michigan Historical Society. At the last board meeting, Sally suggested the society produce a monthly newsletter to send to all society members. She recommended that an interesting topic in Michigan history be presented each month, proposed several ideas for the first issue, and submitted *Michigan History* as the newsletter name. Paul Kowalski, society president, presented a motion that the society accept Sally's idea of producing a monthly newsletter and give her the total responsibility for writing, designing, and producing the newsletter. Selma Wigle, society treasurer, seconded the motion, and it passed.

Because Sally had just come back from a five-day lighthouse tour of the Lake Huron coastline, stopping at several lighthouses, visiting their towers and museums, and gathering historical information about each lighthouse, she decided the first issue would be about the Lake Huron lighthouses.

Introduction

Newsletters are an effective means of communication in today's world of information. Businesses use newsletters to advertise products and attract new customers. Schools use newsletters to communicate with parents, announce important dates, and highlight teacher and student performances. In the past, newsletters were produced using Ventura or PageMaker **desktop publishing software**. To create a newsletter, you opened an existing word processing document and formatted the document using the software's desktop publishing features. Today, Corel WordPerfect 8 contains many of these features and is the only software you will need to create professional newsletters.

Project Five—Producing a Newsletter

Project Five uses WordPerfect to produce the Michigan Historical Society's monthly newsletter illustrated in Figure 5-1. The newsletter includes a colorful title; horizontal lines to separate and highlight text; text displayed in two columns; a clipart image of a lighthouse; a pull-quote; and text formatted with different font faces, font styles, and font sizes. Grammatik, a grammar checking program, is used to check the text of the newsletter for writing problems. Techniques to search for and retrieve files for use in an existing document will be explained.

nameplate

MICHIGAN HISTORY

Michigan Historical Society   **Vol. I ● October 1999**

newsletter title

ruling lines, newsletter subtitle, volume number, and date

Historic Lighthouses

Michigan's 2,232 mile shoreline is the longest of any inland state in the United States and touches four of the five Great Lakes. Along those shores are the lighthouses on which lake navigators rely for safe passage through the Great Lakes. Among the lighthouses in Michigan, more than one hundred are located on the American side of Lake Huron. This issue of *Michigan History* spotlights ten of those historic Lake Huron lighthouses.

drop cap

Fort Gratiot Lighthouse

The Fort Gratiot Lighthouse, located on Coast Guard grounds in Port Huron, marks the point where Lake Huron empties into the St. Clair River. It was built in 1825, was the first lighthouse on Lake Huron, and is the oldest surviving lighthouse in Michigan. In 1828, during a violent storm, the lighthouse collapsed. It was rebuilt in 1829. The lighthouse was automated by the Lighthouse Service in 1933 and is active today.

subheads

Harbor Beach Lighthouse

The Harbor Beach Lighthouse, also known as the Sand Beach Lighthouse, was built in 1885 and marks the entrance to the artificial Sand Beach Harbor near Michigan's *thumb* region. The harbor was built by the U. S. Army Corps of Engineers as a refuge to ships traveling between Port Huron and Saginaw Bay.

Pointe Aux Barques Lighthouse

The Pointe Aux Barques Lighthouse was built in 1857 to mark the southern point where Lake Huron enters Saginaw Bay and to warn mariners of the shallow regions near the coast. It is located on the northeastern tip of the Michigan *thumb* in Huron City and is one of the tallest lighthouses on the Great Lakes. The lighthouse name, which translates to *point of the little boat*'s lighthouse, resulted from the many canoes used by the fur traders who frequented Saginaw Bay.

clip art image

Port Austin Reef Lighthouse

The Port Austin Reef Lighthouse was built in Port Austin in 1878. The lighthouse is located two and one-half miles from shore off the tip of the Michigan *thumb*. The lighthouse rests on the reef with the same name. The dangers of the waters surrounding the lighthouse are emphasized by the numerous shipwrecks that lay at the bottom of the lake near the lighthouse.

Tawas Point Lighthouse

The Tawas Point Lighthouse, built in 1853 in Tawas, marks the northern point where Lake Huron enters Saginaw Bay. Because the land on which the lighthouse was built had moved more than a mile due to shifting sands, the tower had to be moved in 1876. Currently, a cottage connected to the tower is the residence of the Coast Guard commander.

body copy

header

Page 2

Old Mackinac Point Lighthouse

...ouse was built in ...thouses built to...

Local folklore alleges that the lighthouse keeper drove his wife mad by locking her in the lighthouse. Today, you can hear her screams from inside the lighthouse on windy nights.

...ide the lighthouse ...New Presque Isle ...dred feet tall,

text box

...ghthouse

...Lighthouse, built with ...ed from Ohio, is located ...the Lake Huron shore and about 11 miles east of the Straits of Mackinac. Because of its remote location, it required four years to build and was the most expensive lighthouse built on the Great Lakes. This lighthouse was the featured Lake Huron lighthouse in the 1995 Great Lakes Lighthouse Series of United States postage stamps.

Cheboygan Crib Lighthouse

The Cheboygan Crib Lighthouse in Cheboygan was built in 1880 in Duncan Bay, marking the entrance to the Cheboygan River. Its foundation, or crib, settled over time and eventually, the tower and crib fell into the river. The citizens of Cheboygan recovered the light and placed it on the end of the pier on the western side of the Cheboygan River.

From 1892 to 1957, the Old Mackinac Point Lighthouse in Mackinaw City guided ships making the difficult passage through the Straits of Mackinac. The lighthouse also watched over a constant stream of car ferries shuttling to the upper peninsula and Mackinac Island. In 1957, the Mackinac Bridge was built to connect the lower and upper peninsulas of Michigan. As a result, ships began to set their courses by the lights of the Mackinaw bridge, and the lighthouse became unnecessary. With its unusual castle-like architecture and scenic location just east of the bridge, it remains an ideal spot for travelers to stop and watch the sunset.

pull-quote

Round Island Lighthouse

The Round Island Lighthouse on Mackinac Island, built in 1895, guards the shipping lanes near the Straits of Mackinac. The lighthouse served for 52 years and then was replaced by an automated beacon at the southern end of Mackinac Island.

Our Self-Paced Driving Tour

If you are interested in exploring these lighthouses, you can send for our free driving tour. This self-paced tour visits two dozen of the more popular lighthouses on Lake Huron. To receive information about the driving tour, contact the Michigan Historical Society at (810) 555-9283.

FIGURE 5-1

WordPerfect Newsletter Terminology

To produce a professional newsletter, it is important to be familiar with the newsletter terminology. In Figure 5-1, the **nameplate,** or **banner,** is the portion of the newsletter above the two columns. The first item in the nameplate is the **newsletter title** (Michigan History). Below the newsletter title is a horizontal line, the **newsletter subtitle** (Michigan Historical Society), the **newsletter volume number and date** (Vol. I ● October 1999), and second horizontal line. The two horizontal lines are called **ruling lines,** or **rules.**

The second page of the newsletter contains a **header** consisting of a horizontal line, the word, Page, and the page number. Below the nameplate on page one and continued below the header on page two is a single article about lighthouses. The text of the article, called the **body copy**, is subdivided into sections with each section identified by a **subhead**. The first letter of the paragraph below the first subhead is larger than the rest of the characters in the paragraph. The enlarged letter, called a **drop cap**, is used to draw attention to the beginning of the section.

The body copy is arranged in two columns. On the first page, a **graphics box** containing a **clipart image** of a lighthouse displays centered horizontally between the two columns. On the second page, a **text box** containing a quote displays centered horizontally between the two columns. The text inside the text box, called a **pull-quote**, is copied from the body copy to the text box and italicized. The text that wraps around the lighthouse image and text box is referred to as **wrap-around text** and the space surrounding the image and text box is called the **run-around**.

Document Preparation Steps

The following tasks will be completed in this project.

1. Start WordPerfect.
2. Download the Lake Huron Lighthouses article from the Internet.
3. Open the Lake Huron Lighthouses document.
4. Check the article for writing problems using Grammatik.
5. Create the nameplate.
6. Save the nameplate using Michigan History Nameplate.wpd as the filename.
7. Retrieve the Lake Huron Lighthouses article for use in the Michigan History Nameplate document.
8. Define a newspaper column as required for the two columns in the newsletter.
9. Format the newsletter.
10. Insert the clipart image and text box in the newsletter.
11. Save the newsletter using Michigan History - October 1999 as the filename.
12. Print the newsletter.

The following pages contain a detailed explanation of these tasks.

Starting WordPerfect

Before you can create the newsletter, you need to start WordPerfect. The steps to start WordPerfect are summarized below.

TO START WORDPERFECT

1. Click the Start button on the taskbar.
2. Point to Corel WordPerfect Suite 8 on the Start menu.
3. Click Corel WordPerfect 8 on the Corel WordPerfect Suite 8 submenu.
4. If necessary, click the Maximize button in the Corel WordPerfect window.
5. If necessary, click the Maximize button in the Document1 window.

WordPerfect displays the maximized Corel WordPerfect application window and a blank document titled Document1 in a maximized document window.

Checking the Lake Huron Lighthouses Article for Writing Problems

The Lake Huron Lighthouses article is illustrated in Figure 5-2. The article is typed using the default font (Times New Roman Regular 12 point). A blank line is inserted after each subhead and each paragraph. The article has been typed and stored on the Corel WordPerfect 8 Web site. Before you create the newsletter, you will download the Lake_Huron_Lighthouse.wpd file from the Web page, save it on the Corel WordPerfect 8 Files floppy disk, open it, and check it for writing problems.

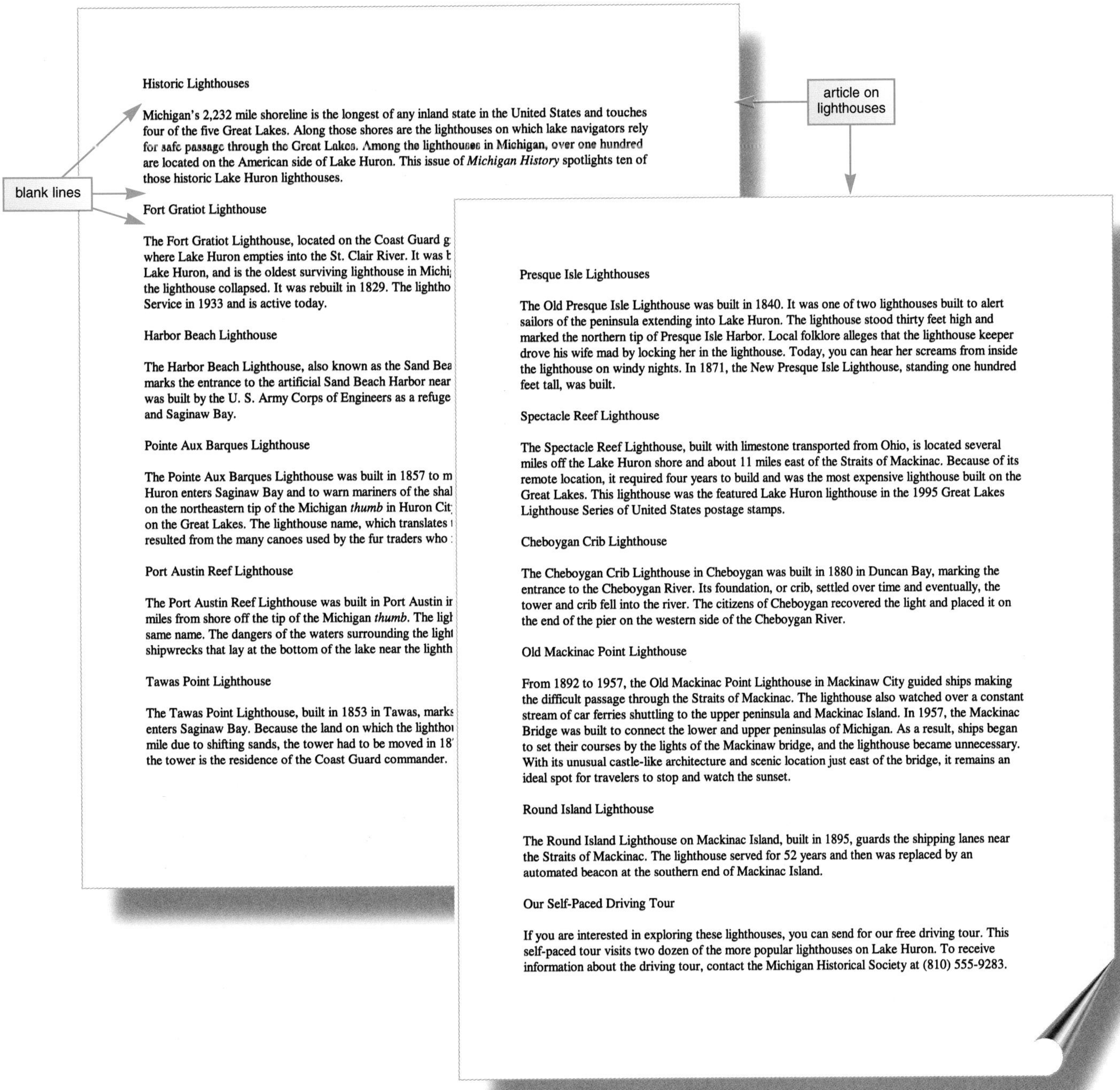

article on lighthouses

blank lines

Historic Lighthouses

Michigan's 2,232 mile shoreline is the longest of any inland state in the United States and touches four of the five Great Lakes. Along those shores are the lighthouses on which lake navigators rely for safe passage through the Great Lakes. Among the lighthouses in Michigan, over one hundred are located on the American side of Lake Huron. This issue of *Michigan History* spotlights ten of those historic Lake Huron lighthouses.

Fort Gratiot Lighthouse

The Fort Gratiot Lighthouse, located on the Coast Guard g where Lake Huron empties into the St. Clair River. It was b Lake Huron, and is the oldest surviving lighthouse in Michi; the lighthouse collapsed. It was rebuilt in 1829. The lightho Service in 1933 and is active today.

Harbor Beach Lighthouse

The Harbor Beach Lighthouse, also known as the Sand Bea marks the entrance to the artificial Sand Beach Harbor near was built by the U. S. Army Corps of Engineers as a refuge and Saginaw Bay.

Pointe Aux Barques Lighthouse

The Pointe Aux Barques Lighthouse was built in 1857 to m Huron enters Saginaw Bay and to warn mariners of the shal on the northeastern tip of the Michigan *thumb* in Huron Cit on the Great Lakes. The lighthouse name, which translates resulted from the many canoes used by the fur traders who

Port Austin Reef Lighthouse

The Port Austin Reef Lighthouse was built in Port Austin in miles from shore off the tip of the Michigan *thumb*. The ligh same name. The dangers of the waters surrounding the light shipwrecks that lay at the bottom of the lake near the lighth

Tawas Point Lighthouse

The Tawas Point Lighthouse, built in 1853 in Tawas, marks enters Saginaw Bay. Because the land on which the lightho mile due to shifting sands, the tower had to be moved in 18 the tower is the residence of the Coast Guard commander.

Presque Isle Lighthouses

The Old Presque Isle Lighthouse was built in 1840. It was one of two lighthouses built to alert sailors of the peninsula extending into Lake Huron. The lighthouse stood thirty feet high and marked the northern tip of Presque Isle Harbor. Local folklore alleges that the lighthouse keeper drove his wife mad by locking her in the lighthouse. Today, you can hear her screams from inside the lighthouse on windy nights. In 1871, the New Presque Isle Lighthouse, standing one hundred feet tall, was built.

Spectacle Reef Lighthouse

The Spectacle Reef Lighthouse, built with limestone transported from Ohio, is located several miles off the Lake Huron shore and about 11 miles east of the Straits of Mackinac. Because of its remote location, it required four years to build and was the most expensive lighthouse built on the Great Lakes. This lighthouse was the featured Lake Huron lighthouse in the 1995 Great Lakes Lighthouse Series of United States postage stamps.

Cheboygan Crib Lighthouse

The Cheboygan Crib Lighthouse in Cheboygan was built in 1880 in Duncan Bay, marking the entrance to the Cheboygan River. Its foundation, or crib, settled over time and eventually, the tower and crib fell into the river. The citizens of Cheboygan recovered the light and placed it on the end of the pier on the western side of the Cheboygan River.

Old Mackinac Point Lighthouse

From 1892 to 1957, the Old Mackinac Point Lighthouse in Mackinaw City guided ships making the difficult passage through the Straits of Mackinac. The lighthouse also watched over a constant stream of car ferries shuttling to the upper peninsula and Mackinac Island. In 1957, the Mackinac Bridge was built to connect the lower and upper peninsulas of Michigan. As a result, ships began to set their courses by the lights of the Mackinaw bridge, and the lighthouse became unnecessary. With its unusual castle-like architecture and scenic location just east of the bridge, it remains an ideal spot for travelers to stop and watch the sunset.

Round Island Lighthouse

The Round Island Lighthouse on Mackinac Island, built in 1895, guards the shipping lanes near the Straits of Mackinac. The lighthouse served for 52 years and then was replaced by an automated beacon at the southern end of Mackinac Island.

Our Self-Paced Driving Tour

If you are interested in exploring these lighthouses, you can send for our free driving tour. This self-paced tour visits two dozen of the more popular lighthouses on Lake Huron. To receive information about the driving tour, contact the Michigan Historical Society at (810) 555-9283.

FIGURE 5-2

Downloading and Opening the Lake Huron Lighthouses File

The steps to download a graphics file from the Internet were explained in Project 1. The steps to download a WordPerfect document file were explained in the Apply Your Knowledge assignment on page WP 1.74 at the end of Project 1 and are summarized in the steps that follow. If you do not have access to the Internet, obtain a copy of the Lake Huron Lighthouses.wpd file from your instructor, place it on the Corel WordPerfect 8 Files floppy disk, and skip the next steps.

TO DOWNLOAD A WORDPERFECT FILE FROM THE INTERNET

1. Insert the Corel WordPerfect 8 Files floppy disk into drive A.
2. Click File on the menu bar, click Internet Publisher, and click the Browse the Web button.
3. Click the Location box to highlight the URL.
4. Type http://www.scsite.com/wp8 in the box and press the ENTER key.
5. Click Project 5.
6. Click the Lake_Huron_Lighthouses.wpd filename.
7. Type Lake Huron Lighthouses in the File name box.
8. Click the Save in box arrow.
9. Scroll the Save in list box to display 3½ Floppy (A:) and then click 3½ Floppy (A:).
10. Click the Save button.
11. Click the Close button in the Netscape - [WordPerfect 8, Project 5] window.
12. Click the Close button in the Shelly Cashman WordPerfect 8 Netscape window.

WordPerfect saves the Lake Huron Lighthouses file on the Corel WordPerfect 8 Files floppy disk in drive A.

Next, open the Lake Huron Lighthouses document. The steps to open a document were explained in Project 1 and are summarized below.

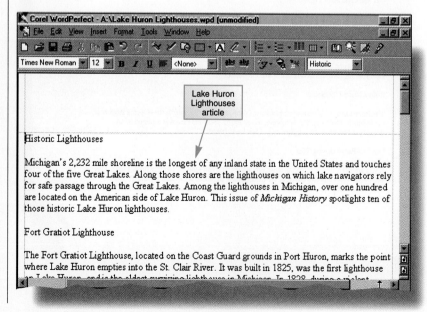

FIGURE 5-3

TO OPEN A DOCUMENT

1. Click the Open button on the Toolbar.
2. Click the Look in box arrow.
3. Scroll the Look in list box to display 3½ Floppy (A:) and then click 3½ Floppy (A:).
4. Click Lake Huron Lighthouses in the list box.
5. Click the Open button in the dialog box.

WordPerfect displays the first part of the Lake Huron Lighthouses article at the top of the document window (Figure 5-3).

Grammar Checking Using Grammatik

In previous projects, two proofreading tools, Spell Checker and Thesaurus, were used to check for possible misspelled words and to find a synonym for a word. A third proofreading tool, Grammatik, can be used to check for grammar mistakes.

Grammatik checks each sentence in a document for possible mistakes in grammar, style, usage, punctuation, and spelling. The rules that Grammatik uses to check for problems are organized into sixty-seven **rule classes**. Rule classes are further organized into three **rule class groups**: Style, Grammar, and Mechanical. The **Style rule class group** consists of rules relating to style and word choice such as passive voice, wordiness, and clichés. The **Grammar rule class group** consists of rules used to check for the correct use of parts of speech, such as subject/verb agreement, possessive form, and split infinitives. The **Mechanical rule class group** consists of rules used to check for errors in capitalization, spelling, double words, and punctuation.

Grammatik checks a document using one of ten predefined sets of rule classes, called **checking styles**. Each checking style has specific rule classes it uses to check a document. Checking styles include Spelling Plus, Quick Check, Very Strict, Formal Memo or Letter, Informal Memo or Letter, Technical or Scientific, Documentation or Speech, Student Composition, Advertising, Fiction, and Grammar-As-You-Go. The default checking style is the **Quick Check checking style**.

Each checking style has one of three **formality levels**: formal, informal, or standard. The **formal level** uses very strict rules of diction and usage and is often used with the Very Strict checking style. In contrast to the formal level, the **informal level** is very relaxed and is often used with the Advertising writing style. The **standard level** is appropriate for writing that contains everyday language and is targeted for a general audience. It is often used with the Student Composition writing style.

More About Grammar Checking

Grammatik also can analyze the grammatical structure of your writing and provide basic counts (syllables, words, sentences, and so on) and readability ratings (Flesch-Kinkaid grade level, percentage of passive/active voice, and degree of sentence and vocabulary complexity).

Checking a Document for Writing Problems

After opening the Lake Huron Lighthouses document, check the document for writing problems using the Quick Check checking style by performing the following steps.

 Steps To Check a Document for Writing Problems

1 **Click Tools on the menu bar and then point to Grammatik.**

WordPerfect displays the Tools menu and highlights the Grammatik command (Figure 5-4).

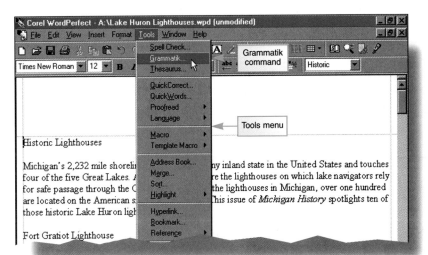

FIGURE 5-4

2 **Click Grammatik. Point to the Replace button in the Grammatik sheet.**

Grammatik starts checking the document. When the first problem is found, Grammatik highlights the word, over, in the problem sentence, opens the Spell Checker, Grammatik, and Thesaurus window, and displays the Grammatik sheet (Figure 5-5). The Replacements list box contains the suggested replacement words (more than) for the highlighted word (over). A replacement sentence displays in the New sentence list box with the words, more than, substituted for the word, over. The words, Questionable Usage, indicate the Questionable Usage rule class has been violated. A suggested change displays in the associated list box. You can remedy the problem by replacing the word, over, with the words, more than.

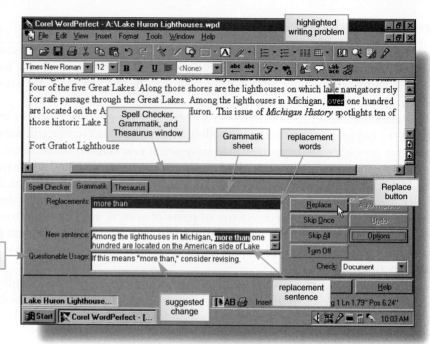

FIGURE 5-5

3 **Click the Replace button. Point to the Skip All button.**

Grammatik replaces the word, over, with the words, more than, in the document and then displays the next writing problem (Figure 5-6). Grammatik highlights the word, Gratiot, in the subhead, displays a list of replacement words and a suggested replacement sentence, and indicates the Spelling rule class has been violated. The word, Gratiot, is a proper name and is spelled correctly, so no replacement should be made, and other occurrences of the word should be skipped.

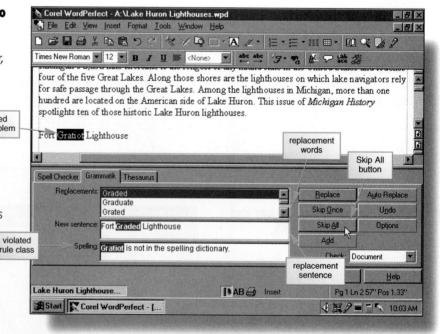

FIGURE 5-6

④ Click the Skip All button.

Grammatik displays the next writing problem (Figure 5-7). Grammatik highlights the number 2 in the 2½ entry, displays a replacement word (two), suggested replacement sentence, and indicates the Number Style rule class has been violated. To correct the problem, replace 2½ with the words, two and one-half.

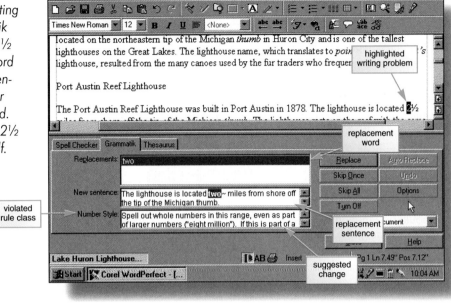

FIGURE 5-7

⑤ Move the insertion point to the left of the number 2 in the document window by clicking to the left of the number.

WordPerfect moves the insertion point to the left of the number 2 (Figure 5-8).

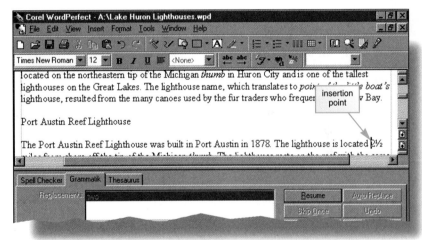

FIGURE 5-8

⑥ Press the DELETE key two times to delete the 2½ entry. Type two and one-half **and then point to the Resume button.**

The words, two and one-half, display on two lines in the document (Figure 5-9).

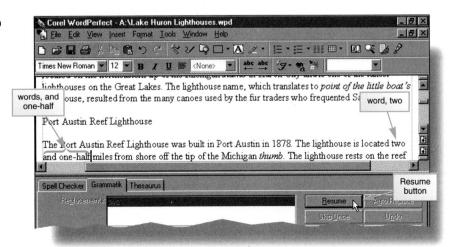

FIGURE 5-9

⑦ Click the Resume button. When the next problem is found, point to the Skip All button.

Grammatik highlights the word, Presque, in the document, displays <No Suggestions> in the Replacements list box and no replacement sentence in the New sentence list box, and indicates the Spelling rule class has been violated (Figure 5-10). The word, Presque, is a proper name and is spelled correctly, so no replacement should be made, and other occurrences of the word should be skipped.

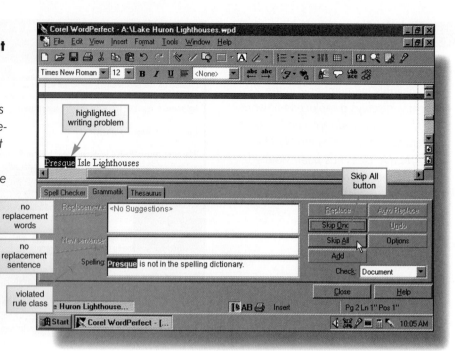

FIGURE 5-10

⑧ Click the Skip All button. When the next problem is found, point to the Skip All button.

Grammatik skips all occurrences of the word, Presque, and highlights the word, Cheboygan (Figure 5-11). The word, Cheboygan, is a proper name and is spelled correctly, so no replacement should be made, and other occurrences of the word should be skipped.

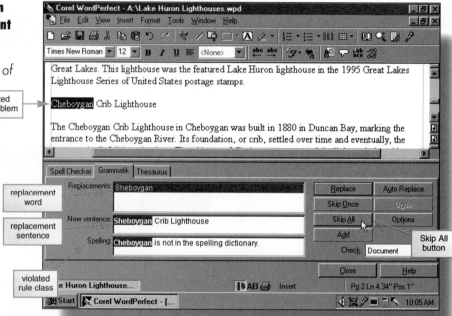

FIGURE 5-11

9 **Click the Skip All button. Point to the Yes button in the Grammatik dialog box.**

Grammatik skips all occurrences of the word, Cheboygan, and displays the Grammatik dialog box (Figure 5-12).

10 **Click the Yes button.**

WordPerfect closes the Grammatik dialog box and the Spell Checker, Grammatik, and Thesaurus window.

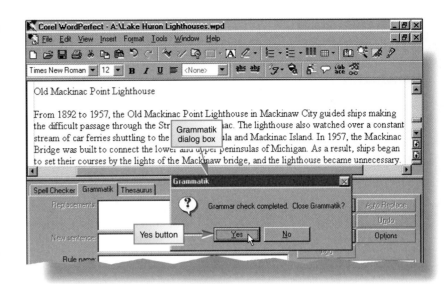

FIGURE 5-12

Saving the Modified Lake Huron Lighthouses Article

After correcting the problems in the Lake Huron Lighthouses article, save the modified document and close the document window. The procedures to save a modified document using the Save button on the WordPerfect 8 Toolbar and close a document using the Close button in the document window were explained in Project 1 and are summarized below.

TO SAVE A MODIFIED DOCUMENT AND CLOSE ITS WINDOW

1 Click the Save button on the Toolbar.
2 Click File on the menu bar and then click Close.

WordPerfect saves the modified Lake Huron Lighthouses.wpd file on the Corel WordPerfect 8 Files floppy disk in drive A, closes the document window, and displays the empty Document1 document window.

Creating the Michigan History Newsletter

After checking the article on lighthouses for problems and correcting them, the next step in the creation of the newsletter is to create the nameplate. The nameplate is again illustrated in Figure 5-13.

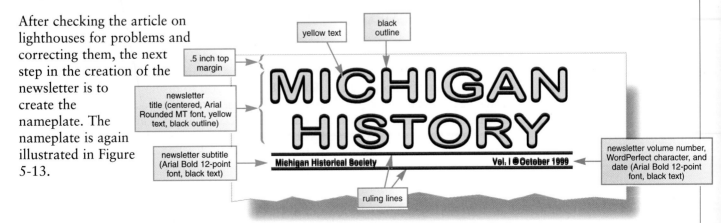

yellow text

black outline

.5 inch top margin

newsletter title (centered, Arial Rounded MT font, yellow text, black outline)

newsletter subtitle (Arial Bold 12-point font, black text)

newsletter volume number, WordPerfect character, and date (Arial Bold 12-point font, black text)

ruling lines

FIGURE 5-13

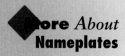

ore *About* Nameplates

A basic nameplate should contain at least the title and date of the newsletter. The newsletter title should display in as large a font size as possible and still be visually appealing. Nameplates also may contain a logo, a subtitle outlining the function of the newsletter, and a short table of contents.

The nameplate consists of the newsletter title (MICHIGAN HISTORY), ruling line, newsletter subtitle (Michigan Historical Society), newsletter volume number, WordPerfect character, and date (Vol. I ☻ October 1999), and a second ruling line. The newsletter title is created using TextArt. TextArt displays the centered newsletter title in the selected shape, Arial Rounded MT font, and yellow and black color. The newsletter subtitle, volume number, WordPerfect character, and date display in Arial Bold 12-point font in black.

The following general steps are used to create the nameplate. Read these steps without performing them.

1. Set the top and bottom margins to .5 inch.
2. Type and format the newsletter title using TextArt.
3. Type and format the newsletter subtitle, volume number, and date using a table.
4. Save the nameplate on the Corel WordPerfect 8 Files floppy disk using the filename, Michigan History Nameplate.

Changing the Margins

In Figure 5-13 on the previous page, the nameplate starts .5 inch down from the top of the page. Therefore, the top margin should be .5 inch. To maintain a balanced look in the newsletter, the bottom margin also should be .5 inch. The default setting for the top and bottom margins is 1 inch; therefore, you must change only the top and bottom margin settings. The procedure to change a margin using the margin guidelines was explained in Project 2 and is summarized in the following steps.

TO CHANGE THE TOP AND BOTTOM MARGINS

① Point to the top margin guideline.

② Hold down the left mouse button, drag the dotted top margin guideline up until the QuickTip indicates the margin is 0.5 inch, and then release the left mouse button.

③ Scroll the window to display the bottom margin guideline.

④ Hold down the left mouse button, drag the dotted bottom margin guideline down until the QuickTip indicates the margin is 0.5 inch, and release the left mouse button.

⑤ Scroll to display the top of the document in the document window.

WordPerfect repositions the top and bottom margin guidelines and changes the top and bottom margins to .5 inch. Although not visible, WordPerfect inserts two **Margin codes** *in the document.*

Using TextArt 8

When creating a newsletter or other color document, you may find instances where you wish to change the appearance of text dramatically to increase the visual impact of the document. **TextArt 8** allows you to display text in a document using special **text shapes**, such as waves, bow ties, crescents, circles, and pennants (Figure 5-14). TextArt 8 also allows you to specify the color and pattern of text, width and color of the outline (border surrounding the text), and color and direction of a shadow for the text. In addition, TextArt 8 allows you to rotate the text and create two-dimensional and three-dimensional images.

The nameplate you create in this project contains the newsletter title illustrated in Figure 5-13 on the previous page. You design the newsletter title using TextArt. The centered newsletter title displays in the selected text shape (square shape) and Arial Rounded MT font. The text color is yellow, the outline color is black, and the text is centered.

Object Linking and Embedding

TextArt 8 supports object linking and embedding (OLE). **Object linking and embedding** is the process of creating a document in one application, called the **client application**, that contains an object (text or graphics) created in another application, called the **server application**. When you make changes to the object in the server application, the object in the client application automatically changes.

TextArt designs, such as the newsletter title, are objects and can be created using TextArt (server application) without quitting WordPerfect (client application). To create a TextArt object in a WordPerfect document window, you start the TextArt application by clicking Insert on the menu bar, pointing to Graphics, and clicking TextArt.

When you start TextArt, the TextArt menu bar replaces the Corel WordPerfect menu bar, and an image box that will contain the object and the Corel TextArt 8.0 dialog box display. You create a TextArt object using the menus on the TextArt menu bar and the options in the Corel TextArt 8.0 dialog box. When you have finished, you click the Close button in the Corel TextArt 8.0 dialog box to quit TextArt. Quitting TextArt displays the WordPerfect menu bar and a graphics box containing the object, and links the TextArt object to the WordPerfect document. The following sections explain how to use TextArt to create the newsletter title.

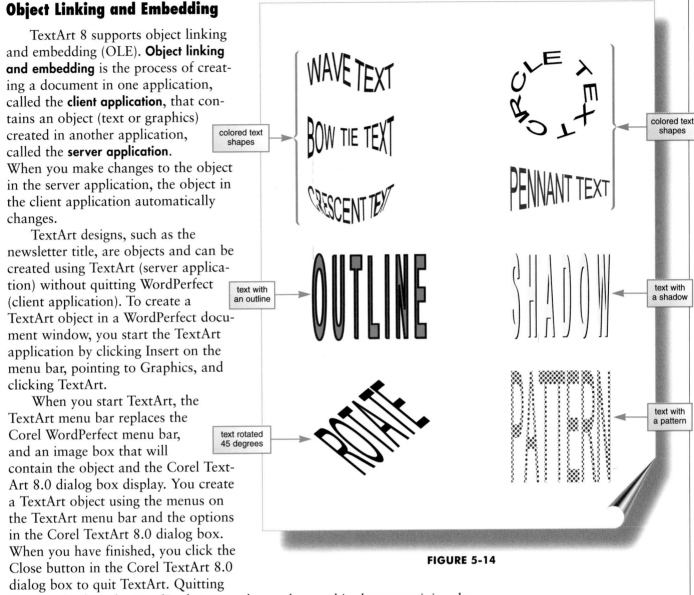

FIGURE 5-14

Creating the Newsletter Title Using TextArt

The next step in the creation of the newsletter is to create the nameplate by creating the newsletter title using TextArt and then creating the newsletter subtitle using a table. The steps to create the newsletter title are summarized below. Read these steps without performing them.

1. Start TextArt.
2. Enter the text of the newsletter title.
3. Change the shape of the text.
4. Change the font of the text.
5. Center the text.
6. Change the color of the text.
7. Remove the shadow from the text.
8. Add an outline to the text.
9. Quit TextArt.

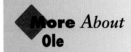

More *About* **Ole**

Because a TextArt image is an OLE object, you can copy or cut the object from one OLE application and paste it into another OLE application. Other OLE applications in the Corel WordPerfect Suite 8 include Corel Presentations 8 and Corel Quattro Pro 8.

Starting TextArt

The newsletter title will be created using TextArt. To start TextArt, perform the following steps.

Steps To Start TextArt

① Click Insert on the menu bar, point to Graphics, and then point to TextArt.

*WordPerfect displays the Insert menu, displays the Graphics sub-menu, and highlights the **TextArt command** on the Graphics submenu (Figure 5-15).*

FIGURE 5-15

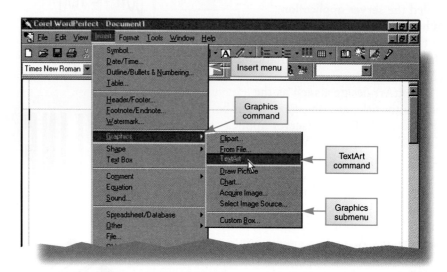

② Click TextArt.

*WordPerfect starts TextArt, removes the Toolbar and Property Bar, replaces the Corel WordPerfect menu bar with the **Corel TextArt menu bar**, displays an **image box** containing the word, Text, at the top of the document window, displays the Corel TextArt 8 dialog box below the image box, and changes the window title to Corel WordPerfect (TEXTART - Text Art 8 Document) - Document1 (Figure 5-16).*

③ Scroll the document window to display the right border of the image box. Drag the right border to the left to align with the right margin guideline.

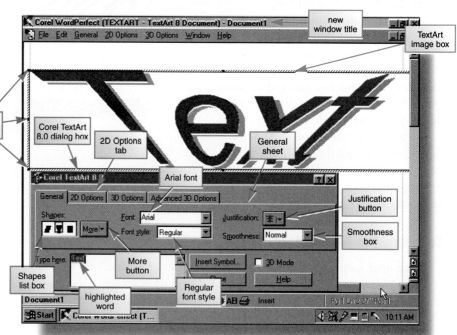

FIGURE 5-16

▷OtherWays

1. Click TextArt button on WordPerfect 6.1 or Graphics Toolbar

Sizing handles display at each corner and in the middle of each side of the image box. The word, Text, in the image box is formatted using the default TextArt settings. The **default TextArt settings** include the V-shaped text shape, Arial Regular font, center justification, royal blue text color, gray shadow, no text pattern, no text rotation, and normal smoothness.

In the **Corel TextArt 8 dialog box**, a red outline surrounds the second shape in the Shapes list box to indicate the current (default) text shape. The word, Arial, in the Font box and word, Regular, in the Font style box indicate the word, Text, displays using the Arial Regular font. The icon on the Justification button indicates the text is centered. Other settings in the 2D Options sheet indicate the text color is royal blue, and the text has a gray shadow with no text pattern, outline, or rotation.

Entering the Newsletter Title

Next, enter the words, MICHIGAN HISTORY, in the Type here text box by performing the following step.

 Steps To Enter the Newsletter Title

1 **If necessary, select the text in the Type here list box. Type** MICHIGAN **and then press the ENTER key. Type** HISTORY **to enter the remainder of the newsletter title.**

The newsletter title, MICHIGAN HISTORY, displays on two lines in the Type here text box and image box (Figure 5-17). The text in the image box is formatted using the default TextArt settings.

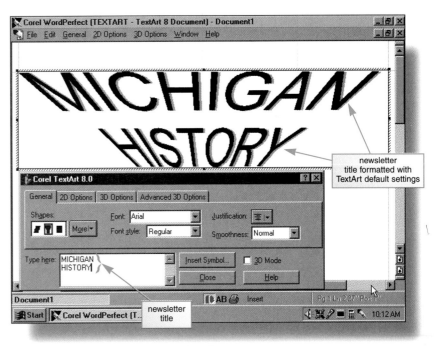

FIGURE 5-17

Changing the Shape of the Newsletter Title

There are fifty-seven different shapes you can use to design the newsletter title. Currently, the words (Michigan History) in the image box display in the default shape. The default shape arranges the words in a V shape. A square shape is used to design the newsletter title (see Figure 5-13 on page WP 5.13). Perform the steps on the next page to change the shape of the newsletter title.

To Change the Shape of the Newsletter Title

1 **Click the More button to the right of the Shapes list box. Point to the first shape in the first row of the Shapes palette.**

*WordPerfect opens the **Shapes palette,** which contains three rows and nineteen columns of shapes (Figure 5-18). A red square surrounds the current (default) shape box in the first row, and the first shape box in the first row is three-dimensional.*

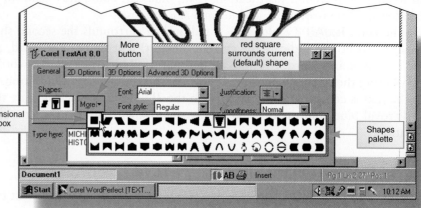

FIGURE 5-18

2 **Click the shape box.**

WordPerfect closes the Shapes palette, displays the new shape surrounded by a red square in the Shapes list box, displays the newsletter title in the image box using the new shape, and left-justifies the newsletter title in the image box (Figure 5-19). Because each shape has an associated justification, the icon on the Justification button changes to indicate the justification associated with the new shape is left-justification.

FIGURE 5-19

 OtherWays

1. Click a shape in the Shapes list box

Changing the Font of the Newsletter Title

TextArt allows you to display the text in the image box using one of almost two hundred display fonts. A **display font** is a decorative font face used primarily in headlines and advertisements. Unlike text fonts that are used primarily for body copy, only one font style is associated with each display font. Perform the following steps to change the font of the newsletter title from the default Arial Regular font to Arial Rounded MT font.

Steps **To Change the Font of the Newsletter Title**

① **Click the Font box arrow in the General tab. Point to Arial Rounded MT.**

WordPerfect displays the Font drop-down list and highlights the Arial Rounded MT font name in the Font box and Font drop-down list (Figure 5-20).

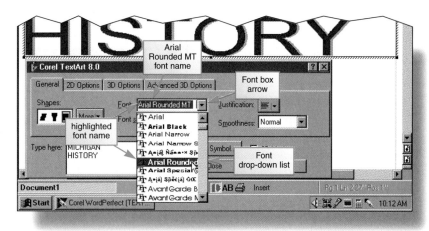

FIGURE 5-20

② **Click Arial Rounded MT.**

WordPerfect displays the newsletter title in Arial Rounded MT bold font (Figure 5-21).

FIGURE 5-21

Changing the Justification of the Newsletter Title

The next task in the process of creating the newsletter title is to center the title. TextArt allows you to left-, center-, and right-justify text in an image box. Full justification and all justification are not available. To center the newsletter title, change the justification from left justification to center justification by performing the steps on the next page.

More *About* **TextArt Justification**

When creating a TextArt image, justification is necessary only when there are two or more lines of text. A single line always expands to the full width of the image box.

Steps **To Change the Justification of the Newsletter Title**

1 **Click the Justification button in the General sheet. Point to the Center box on the Justification palette.**

*WordPerfect displays the **Justification palette** containing the left, center, and right boxes (Figure 5-22). An icon on each box identifies the justification associated with the box. A red square surrounds the first box and the icon on the Justification button indicates the text in the image box is left-justified. The Center box is three-dimensional.*

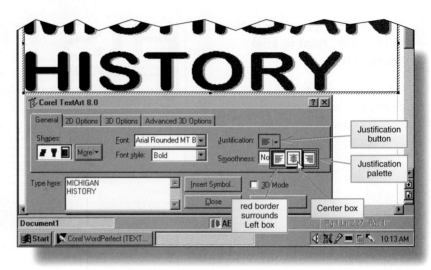

FIGURE 5-22

2 **Click the Center box.**

WordPerfect closes the Justification palette, centers the newsletter title in the image box, and changes the icon on the Justification button (Figure 5-23).

FIGURE 5-23

 ore *About* **Smoothness**

Using a very high smoothness setting greatly increases the size of the document.

The Smoothness box controls the smoothness of text curves. **Smoothness** refers to the number of segments used to shape a curved line. Smoothness settings include normal, high, and very high. A higher smoothness produces a more graceful line. The **default smoothness setting**, normal smoothness, is sufficient for the newsletter title. The default smoothness setting is not changed to create the letterhead.

Displaying the 2D Options Sheet

The 2D Options sheet in the Corel TextArt 8.0 dialog box contains the buttons to control the pattern, shadow, outline, text color, and rotation of the text in the image box. In preparation for changing the text color, removing the shadow and adding an outline to the newsletter title, display the 2D Options sheet in the Corel TextArt 8.0 dialog box by performing the following step.

Steps To Display the 2D Options Sheet

1 **Click the 2D Options tab in the Corel TextArt 8.0 dialog box.**

WordPerfect displays the 2D Options sheet in the Corel TextArt 8.0 dialog box (Figure 5-24).

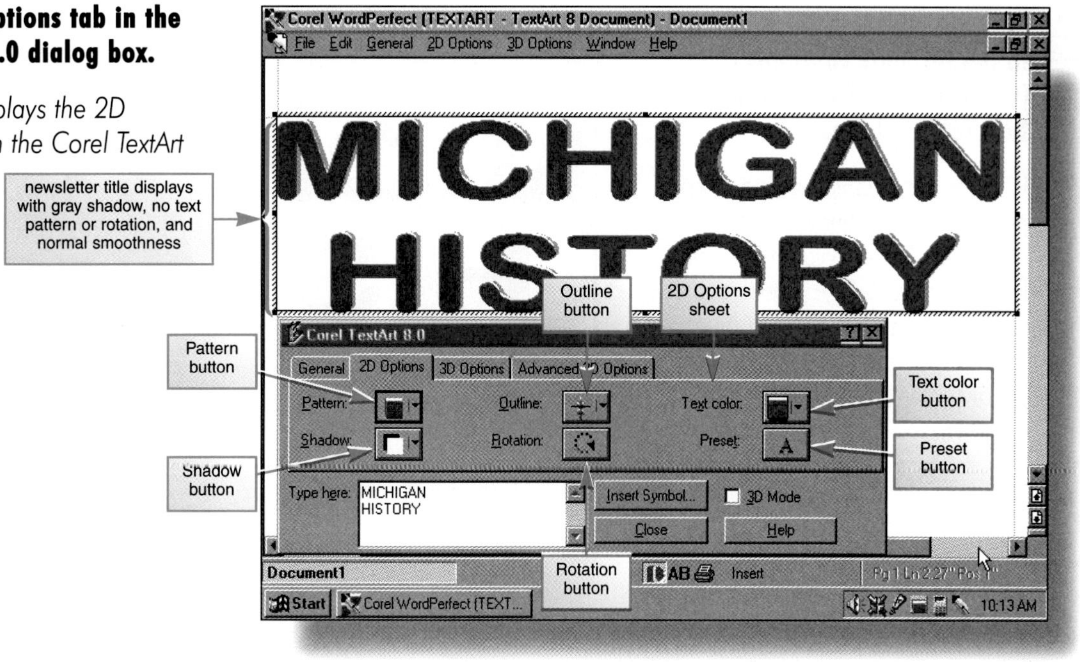

newsletter title displays with gray shadow, no text pattern or rotation, and normal smoothness

Pattern button

Shadow button

Outline button

2D Options sheet

Text color button

Preset button

Rotation button

FIGURE 5-24

The Pattern button, Shadow button, Outline button, and Rotation button control the pattern, shadow, outline, and rotation of the text in the image box. The Text color button indicates the text color is royal blue. The Preset button allows you to choose from five predefined 2D TextArt images and override the current TextArt image choices.

Currently, the newsletter title in the image box displays with a gray shadow and no outline, without a text pattern or text rotation, and with normal smoothness. To complete the newsletter title, you must change the text color to yellow, remove the gray shadow, and add a black outline. Although the newsletter title does not require a text pattern, the following section explains how to change the text pattern.

Text Patterns

TextArt allows you to display no pattern, display no fill, add one of thirty patterns, and change the background color of the pattern of the text in the image box. The **no fill pattern** makes the text invisible unless the text has an outline. The **default pattern setting** is to display no pattern. If a pattern is added, the default pattern setting displays a black pattern. The newsletter title does not require a pattern. If it did, you could add a pattern by clicking the Pattern button, clicking a pattern box in the Pattern palette, and clicking the OK button in the Pattern box.

Changing the Text Color of the Newsletter Title

TextArt allows you to display the text in the image box using one of the 256 predefined colors. The default text color is royal blue. Perform the steps on the next page to change the text color of the newsletter title to yellow.

Steps To Change the Text Color of the Newsletter Title

① **Click the Text color button. Point to the fifteenth color box (yellow) in the first row in the Text color palette.**

WordPerfect opens the Text color palette, which contains sixteen rows and sixteen columns of color boxes (Figure 5-25). A red square surrounds the default royal blue color box in the first row and the yellow color box is three-dimensional.

FIGURE 5-25

② **Click the yellow color box.**

The text color of the newsletter title changes to yellow (Figure 5-26). The gray shadow remains on the text, and the color box on the Text color button changes from royal blue to yellow.

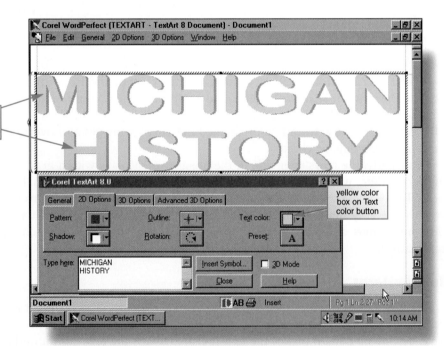

FIGURE 5-26

OtherWays

1. Click Pattern button, click Text color button, click color box, click OK button
2. Click Shadow button, click Text color button, click color box, click OK button
3. Click Outline button, click Text color button, click color box, click OK button

Removing the Shadow from the Newsletter Title

TextArt allows you to display no shadow, display one of twenty-four shadows, and change the color of the shadow. The **default shadow setting** displays a gray shadow on the right and bottom edges of the text. Because the newsletter title should not have a shadow (see Figure 5-13 on page WP 5.13), you must remove the shadow by performing the following steps.

Steps **To Remove the Shadow from the Newsletter Title**

① Click the Shadow button. Point to the shadow box in the center of the Shadow palette.

WordPerfect displays the Shadow box containing the Shadow palette with twenty-five shadow boxes, the Shadow color button, and the Text color button (Figure 5-27). The color boxes on the Shadow color button and Text color button indicate the default shadow color is light gray and text color is yellow. In the Shadow palette, a red outline surrounds the current shadow, and the center shadow box is three-dimensional. The center shadow box removes the shadow from the text in the image box.

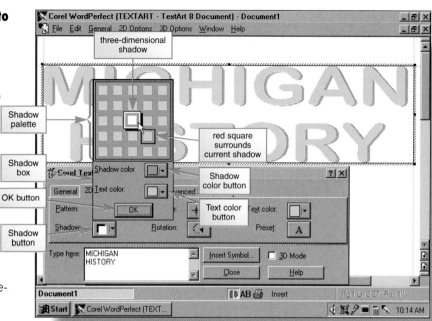

FIGURE 5-27

② Click the shadow box. Click the OK button in the Shadow box.

WordPerfect closes the Shadow box and removes the shadow from the newsletter title (Figure 5-28).

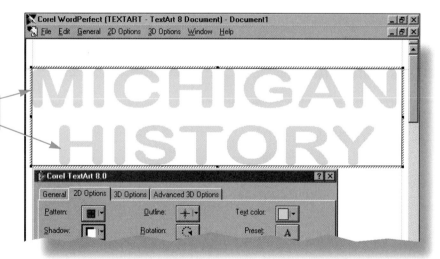

FIGURE 5-28

Adding an Outline to the Newsletter Title

TextArt allows you to display no outline or to select one of nine outline thicknesses and display the outline in one of 256 predefined colors. The **default outline thickness setting** is to display no outline. When you change the default setting and add an outline to the text in the image box, the **default outline color setting** is light gray. Because the newsletter title displays with a black outline (see Figure 5-13 on page WP 5.13), you must select an outline thickness and then select black as the outline color. Perform the steps on the next two pages to add a black outline to the newsletter title.

To Add an Outline to the Newsletter Title

1 **Click the Outline button. Point to the second thickness box in the third row in the Outline palette.**

WordPerfect displays the Outline box containing the Outline palette with its ten thickness boxes and the Outline color button and Text color button (Figure 5-29). The color box on the Outline color button indicates the current (default) outline color is light gray and the color box on the Text color button indicates the text color is yellow. In the Outline palette, the text color (yellow) displays in the background, the outline color (light gray) displays on each thickness, a red rectangle surrounds the first thickness box (None) in the first row to indicate no outline displays on the text in the image box, and the thickness box is three-dimensional.

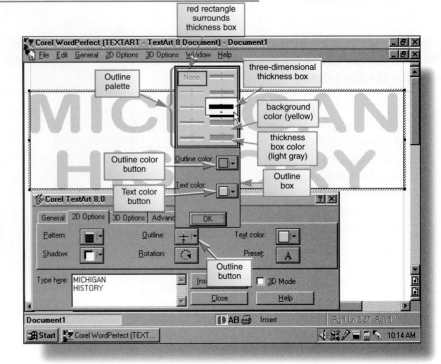

FIGURE 5-29

2 **Click the thickness box. Point to the Outline color button.**

Clicking the outline box moves the red rectangle to the second thickness box in the third row (Figure 5-30). The text in the image box changes when you click the OK button.

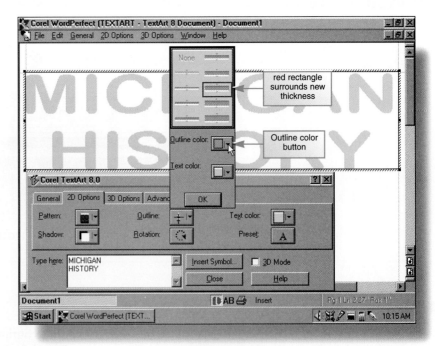

FIGURE 5-30

③ Click the Outline color button. Point to the first color box (black) in the first row of the Outline color palette.

*WordPerfect opens the **Outline color palette** containing 256 colors (Figure 5-31). A red square surrounds the current (default) outline color (light gray). The first color box (black) in the first row is three-dimensional.*

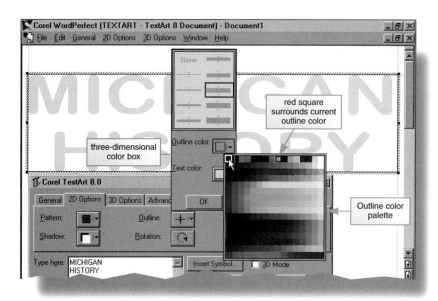

FIGURE 5-31

④ Click the color box. Point to the OK button in the Outline box.

WordPerfect changes the color of each thickness in the Outline palette and the color on the Outline color button to black (Figure 5-32). The text in the image box changes when you click the OK button.

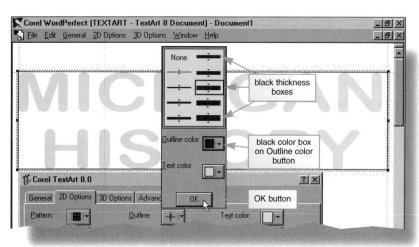

FIGURE 5-32

⑤ Click the OK button.

TextArt adds a black outline to the newsletter title (Figure 5-33).

FIGURE 5-33

Although the newsletter title does not require text rotation, the next section explains how to rotate a TextArt image.

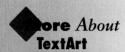

Text Rotation

TextArt allows you to rotate a TextArt image. The **default rotation setting** is no rotation of an image. If you want to rotate an image, either click the Rotation button and drag one of the rotation handles that display in the image box or double-click the Rotation button, click the degree of rotation, and click the Close button.

Quitting TextArt

After you change the shape and font of the newsletter title and text color, remove the shadow, and add an outline, the creation of the newsletter title is complete. When you quit TextArt, WordPerfect replaces the image box with a graphics box, displays the Toolbar and Property Bar, and replaces the Corel Text Art menu bar with the Corel WordPerfect menu bar. Perform the following step to quit TextArt.

 Steps To Quit TextArt

---

① **Click the Close button in the Corel TextArt 8.0 dialog box, and then click the blank line below the graphics box to deselect the box.**

WordPerfect closes the Corel TextArt 8.0 dialog box and deselects the graphics box containing the newsletter title (Figure 5-34). The insertion point is located where the newsletter subtitle, volume, and date should display. Although not visible, a Box code is inserted in the document.

FIGURE 5-34

Editing a TextArt Image

There are two methods to edit a TextArt image: 1) in-place editing; and 2) open editing. **In-place editing** allows you to edit the TextArt image in the document window containing the image without leaving WordPerfect. To in-place edit an image, double-click the image. When you have completed the editing, click the Close button in the Corel TextArt 8.0 dialog box.

Open editing lets you edit a TextArt image in a new document window. Open editing is useful when you wish to make editing a small image easier by making the image larger. To open edit an image, right-click the image, point to Corel Text-Art 8 Document Object, and click Open. WordPerfect displays the image in the TextArt 8 Document in Document1 - TextArt 8 window. When you have finished editing, click the Close button in the Corel TextArt 8 dialog box.

Creating the Newsletter Subtitle, Volume Number, WordPerfect Character, and Date

After creating the newsletter title, complete the nameplate by entering the newsletter subtitle, volume number, WordPerfect character, and date as illustrated again in Figure 5-35. The newsletter subtitle (Michigan Historical Society), newsletter volume number (Vol. I), and newsletter date (October 1999) display on the same line. The newsletter volume number and date are separated by a **WordPerfect character** (😊). A ruling line displays above and below the line. The newsletter subtitle, volume number, and date display in Arial Bold 12-point font. The newsletter subtitle is left-justified in the first cell of the table (cell A1), and the newsletter volume number, WordPerfect character, and date are right-justified in the second cell (cell B1).

You will create a two column, one row table to contain the newsletter subtitle, volume number, and date, and then change the borders of the table to create the ruling lines. To create the ruling lines, remove the outside border (left, right, top, and bottom) and the inside border (separates the cells) of the table. Then, increase the thickness of the top and bottom borders to display the two ruling lines.

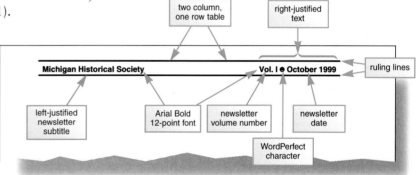

FIGURE 5-35

The WordPerfect character that separates the newsletter volume number and date is one of more than two thousand WordPerfect characters that are organized into fifteen character sets. Each **character set** is identified by a number from zero to fourteen. The **default character set**, the Iconic Symbols character set, is set number 5 and consists of 255 characters. Each WordPerfect character is identified by a character set number and a character number. The character numbers in each character set are numbered starting with the number zero.

The WordPerfect character separating the newsletter volume and date is identified by the entry, 5,8; the first number is the character set number and second number is the character number. Because character sets and characters are numbered starting with the number zero, the entry, 5,8, identifies the ninth character in the sixth character set.

Creating a Table

The first step in creating the newsletter subtitle is to create a table with two columns and one row. The steps to create a table were explained in Project 4 and are summarized on the next page.

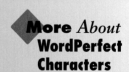

More *About*
WordPerfect
Characters

A WordPerfect character can be used as the bullet in a bulleted list. To find out how, search for the bulleted list topic and then click the change bullet character help topic.

insertion point

two cells in table

FIGURE 5-36

TO CREATE A TABLE

① Point to the Table QuickCreate button on the WordPerfect 8 Toolbar.

② Hold down the left mouse button and drag the mouse pointer onto the table sizing grid until two columns and one row of the grid are highlighted and 2x1 displays above the grid.

③ Release the left mouse button.

WordPerfect creates a 2x1 table (Figure 5-36). The insertion point is located in cell A1.

Entering the Newsletter Subtitle

After you create the table, enter the newsletter subtitle (Michigan Historical Society) in cell A1 of the table and then enter the volume number, WordPerfect character, and date in cell B1. Perform the following step to enter the newsletter subtitle in cell A1 and volume number in cell B1.

Steps **To Enter the Newsletter Subtitle and Volume**

① **Type** Michigan Historical Society **in cell A1. Press the Tab key, click the Justification button on the Property Bar, click Right, type** Vol. I **in cell B1, and press the** SPACEBAR.

WordPerfect displays the left-justified newsletter subtitle in cell A1 and right-justified volume number and blank space in cell B1 (Figure 5-37).

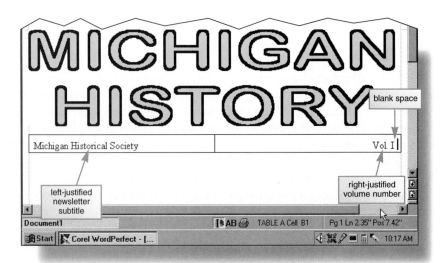

blank space

left-justified newsletter subtitle

right-justified volume number

FIGURE 5-37

Inserting a WordPerfect Character and Entering the Newsletter Date

Next, insert the WordPerfect character identified by the 5,8 entry following the newsletter volume, and then enter the newsletter date by performing the following steps.

Steps To Insert a WordPerfect Character

1 **Click Insert on the menu bar and point to Symbol.**

WordPerfect displays the Insert menu and highlights the Symbol command (Figure 5-38).

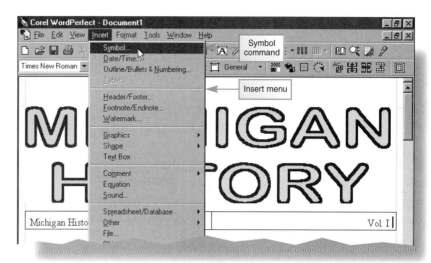

FIGURE 5-38

2 **Click Symbol. If the words, Iconic Symbols, do not display on the button in the Set area, click the button and then click Iconic Symbols. Click the second character in the second row in the Symbols list box. Point to the Insert and close button.**

WordPerfect displays the Symbols dialog box (Figure 5-39). The Set area contains the Iconic Symbols button, the Number area contains 5,8, and a blinking dotted square surrounds the selected character in the Symbols list box.

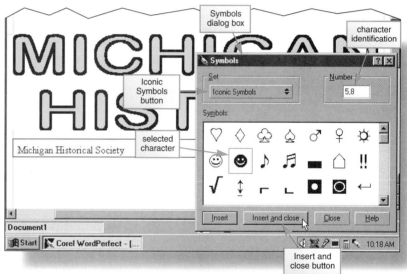

FIGURE 5-39

3 **Click the Insert and close button. Press the SPACEBAR and then type** October 1999 **as the date.**

WordPerfect displays the volume number, blank space, WordPerfect character, blank space, and newsletter date in cell B1 (Figure 5-40).

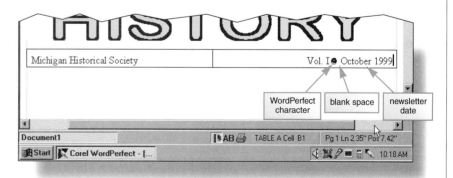

FIGURE 5-40

*Other***Ways**

1. Press CTRL+W

Formatting the Table

To complete the creation of the newsletter subtitle, volume number, WordPerfect character, and date, you must change the font of the text in the cells of the table to Arial Bold 12-point font and then change the border style of the table to display the two ruling lines. Perform the following step to change the font of the cells in the table.

Steps To Change the Font of the Table Cells

1 **Point to the left border of cell A1 and double-click to highlight cells A1 and B1. Click the Font Face button on the Property Bar. Click Arial on the Font Face drop-down list. Click the Bold button on the Property Bar.**

WordPerfect highlights the cells in the table and displays the text in the table cells in Arial Bold font (Figure 5-41).

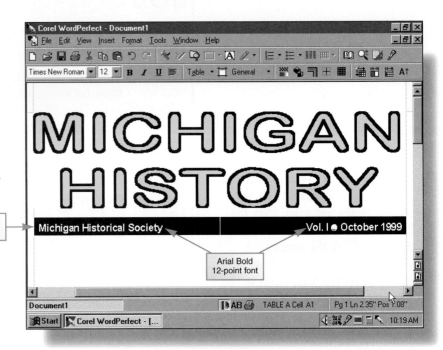

highlighted table cells

Arial Bold 12-point font

FIGURE 5-41

Changing the Border Style of a Table

The **default table border style** causes a single line to display as the outside border (left, right, top, and bottom) and inside border (separating two or more cells) of the table. To display the ruling lines above and below the newsletter subtitle, volume number, and date, you must change the border style of the inside and outside borders to display no lines and then select the border style of the top and bottom borders to display thick horizontal lines. Perform the following steps to change the border style of the table.

Steps To Change the Border Style of a Table

1 **Right-click the table and point to the Table Tools command on the QuickMenu.**

WordPerfect displays a QuickMenu and highlights the Table Tools command (Figure 5-42).

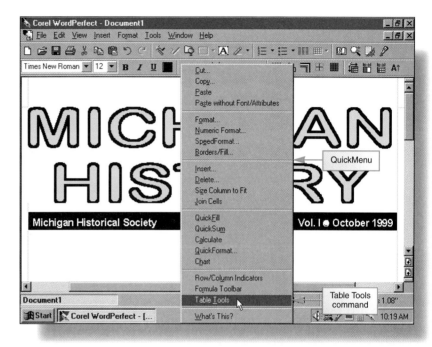

FIGURE 5-42

2 **Click Table Tools. Point to the Inside button on the Tools palette.**

*WordPerfect displays the **Tools palette** (Figure 5-43). The first six buttons control the border style of the left, right, top, bottom, inside, and outside borders of the highlighted cells. If no table cells are highlighted, the buttons control the border style of the **current cell**, which is the cell containing the insertion point. The icon on each button indicates the default border style for each border. The seventh button controls the fill style of the highlighted cells or current cell.*

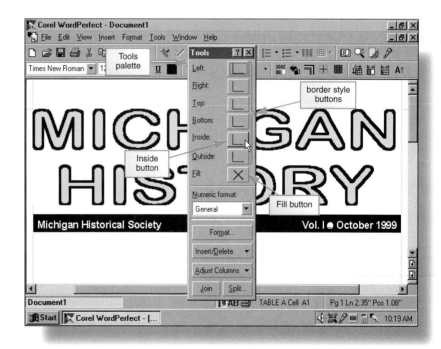

FIGURE 5-43

③ Click the Inside button. Point to the first border style box in the first row.

*WordPerfect displays the **Inside palette** containing thirty-two border style boxes (Figure 5-44). A red square surrounds the current inside border style. The first border style box (X) in the first row is three-dimensional, and the border style associated with the box (<None>) displays in the Border Style box.*

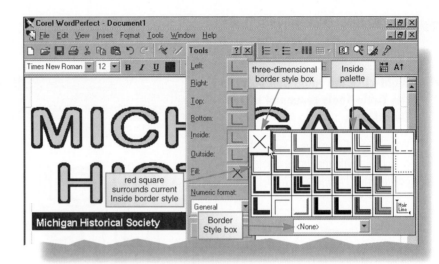

FIGURE 5-44

④ Click the border style box. Click the Outside button and then point to the first border style box in the first row.

*WordPerfect closes the Inside palette, removes the border between cells A1 and B1, displays an X on the Inside button, and opens the **Outside palette** (Figure 5-45). The inside border is not visible in the table. In the Outside palette, a red square surrounds the current border style, the first border style box (X) in the first row is three-dimensional, and the <None> border style displays in the Border Style box.*

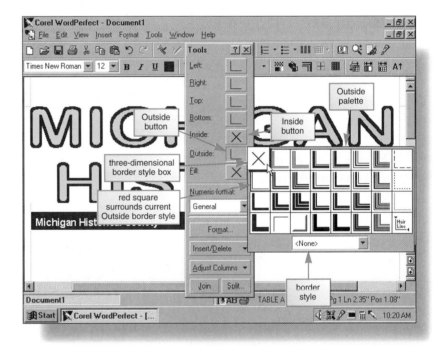

FIGURE 5-45

⑤ Click the border style box. Point to the Top button.

WordPerfect closes the Outside palette, removes the border surrounding the table, and displays an X on the Left, Right, Top, Bottom and Outside buttons (Figure 5-46). The outside border is not visible in the table because the cells are highlighted.

FIGURE 5-46

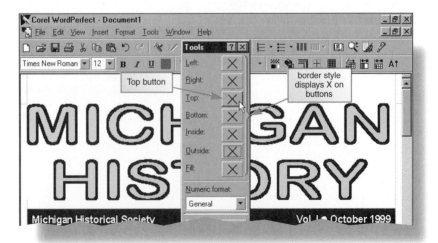

6 **Click the Top button. Point to the first border style box in the third row.**

WordPerfect opens the Top palette (Figure 5-47). A red square surrounds the current top border style, the third border style box in the first row is three-dimensional, and the Heavy border style displays in the Border Style box.

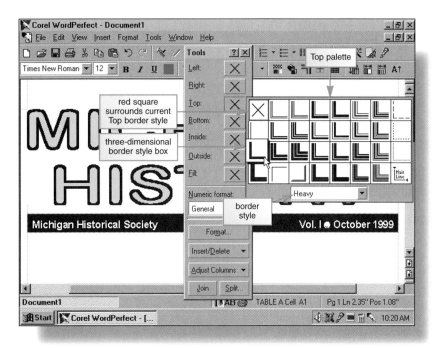

FIGURE 5-47

7 **Click the border style box. Click the Bottom button. Point to the first border style in the third row.**

*WordPerfect closes the Top palette, displays the top border using the heavy border style, displays the heavy border style icon on the Top button, and opens the **Bottom palette** (Figure 5-48). A red square surrounds the first border style in the first row, the first border style box in the third row is three-dimensional, and the Heavy border style displays in the Border Style box. The top border is not visible because the cells are highlighted.*

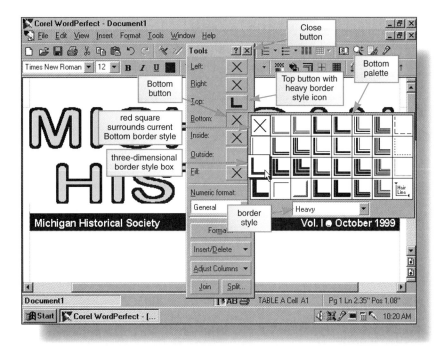

FIGURE 5-48

8 Click the border style box. Click the Close button in the Tools palette and then click the blank line below the table to move the insertion point below the table.

WordPerfect closes the Bottom palette, displays the bottom border using the heavy border style, displays the heavy border style icon on the Bottom button (not visible), closes the Tools palette, and removes the highlight from the table. The top and bottom borders display with the heavy border style and no other borders display (Figure 5-49).

FIGURE 5-49

*Other*Ways

1. Highlight table, click Table button on Property Bar or Tables Toolbar, click Borders/Fill, click border style button, select border style, click OK button

2. Highlight table, press SHIFT+F12

Saving the Nameplate

After you create the nameplate, save it on the Corel WordPerfect 8 Files floppy disk using the filename, Michigan History Nameplate. Once you save the nameplate, you can retrieve and reuse it when you produce next month's newsletter. Perform the following steps to save the nameplate.

TO SAVE THE NAMEPLATE

1 Verify the Corel WordPerfect 8 Files floppy disk is inserted into drive A.

2 Click the Save button on the Toolbar.

3 When the Save As dialog box displays, type `Michigan History Nameplate` in the File name box.

4 Verify 3½ Floppy (A:) displays in the Save in box.

5 Click the Save button.

WordPerfect saves the nameplate on the Corel WordPerfect 8 Files floppy disk in drive A and replaces Document1 in the Corel WordPerfect window title with A:\Michigan History Nameplate.wpd (unmodified).

Finding and Retrieving the Lake Huron Lighthouses Article

The next step in the preparation of the newsletter is to retrieve the article on Lake Huron lighthouses from the Corel WordPerfect 8 Files floppy disk and insert it into the Michigan History Nameplate document.

Sometimes after saving a document, you may forget the filename of the document. When this happens, you can use QuickFinder to search for a file on disk. **QuickFinder** can find a file knowing only a word or series of words in the file. For example, if you forget the filename of the file containing the article on Lake Huron lighthouses, you can use the word, lighthouse, to search through the files on disk. Perform the following steps to search for a file containing the word, lighthouse, and then insert the file into the Michigan History Nameplate document.

More *About*
Finding and Retrieving

In place of finding and retrieving a WordPerfect document, you also can find and retrieve other file types, such as a graphics file or Quattro Pro spreadsheet file.

Steps **To Find and Retrieve a File**

1 If necessary, position the insertion point on the line below the table and press the ENTER key to insert a blank line following the table. Click Insert on the menu bar and point to File.

*WordPerfect displays the Insert menu and highlights the **File command** (Figure 5-50). A blank line and the insertion point display below the table.*

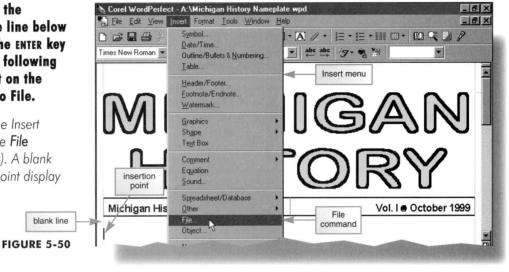

FIGURE 5-50

2 Click File. Type lighthouse in the File name box. Click the Look in box arrow. Scroll the Look in drop-down list box to display 3½ Floppy (A). Click 3½ Floppy (A). Point to the Find button.

*WordPerfect opens the **Insert File dialog box** (Figure 5-51). 3½ Floppy (A:) displays in the Look in box and the word, lighthouse, displays in the File name box and will be used in the search.*

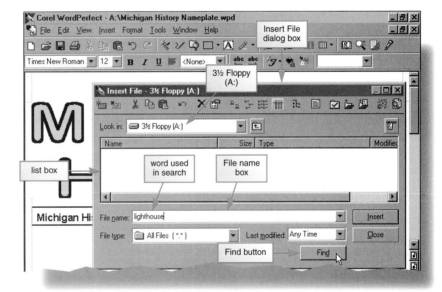

FIGURE 5-51

3 Click the Find button. Click the Lake Huron Lighthouses filename in the list box. Point to the Insert button.

QuickFinder searches the floppy disk in drive A for a file containing the word, lighthouse, and displays the highlighted Lake Huron Lighthouses filename in the list box and the filename in the File name box (Figure 5-52). The filename, file location, file size, file type, and date and time of the last modification display in the list box.

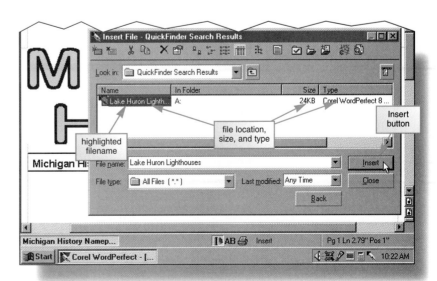

FIGURE 5-52

4 **Click the Insert button. Scroll the document window to display the Historic Lighthouses subhead at the top of the document window.**

WordPerfect retrieves the Lake Huron Lighthouses file from drive A and displays the article below the nameplate (Figure 5-53). The Historic Lighthouses subhead displays at the top of the document window, the insertion point is located to the left of the Historic Lighthouses subhead, and the article displays in Times New Roman 12-point font.

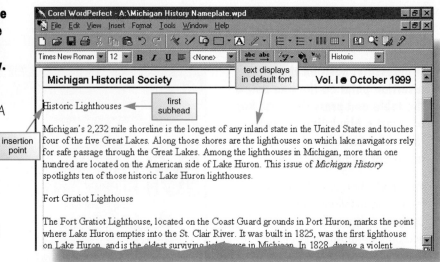

FIGURE 5-53

*Other*Ways

1. Click File on menu bar, click Open, type search word, selection location, click Find button

Newspaper Columns

As you can see in Figure 5-1 on page WP 5.5, the text in the newsletter displays in two columns. The text in the first column on page one flows from the bottom of the first column to the top of the second column. The text in the second column on page one flows to the top of the first column of page two. **Newspaper columns** allow text to flow from the bottom of one column to the top of another column and are frequently used for newsletters, newspapers, and brochures. The text in the newspaper columns is full-justified. **Full-justified** text is aligned between the left and right margins. WordPerfect adds space between the words on each line of text to fill the space between the left and right margins.

Two Pages View

Two Pages view allows you to display two consecutive pages side-by-side in the same document window. To change to Two Pages view, click View on the menu bar and then click Two Pages. Figure 5-54 illustrates the newsletter as it displays in Two Pages view. Although the choice of which view mode to use is purely a matter of personal preference, the remainder of the newsletter will be completed using Page view. Page view makes it easier to visualize the effects of defining newspaper columns, fully justifying the text in the columns, formatting the subheads, and inserting a clipart image and text box.

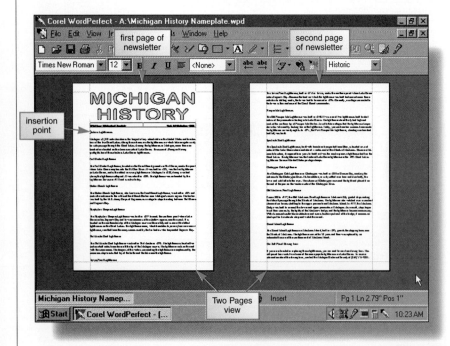

FIGURE 5-54

Defining Newspaper Columns

The next step in creating the newsletter is to define the newspaper columns. Perform the following steps to define the newspaper columns as two columns.

Steps To Define Newspaper Columns

1. **Verify the insertion point is located to the left of the Historic Lighthouses subhead. Click Format on the menu bar and point to Columns.**

   WordPerfect displays the Format menu and highlights the Columns command (Figure 5-55).

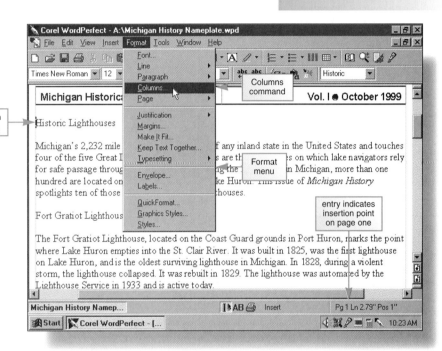

FIGURE 5-55

2. **Click Columns. Point to the OK button in the Columns dialog box.**

   *WordPerfect displays the Columns dialog box containing the **default column settings** (Figure 5-56). The number 2 in the Number of columns text box indicates two columns will be defined, and the selected Newspaper option button indicates the columns will be newspaper columns. The 0.500" entry in the Space between text box and Space text box indicate the space between the two columns will be one-half inch. The 3" entry in the Column 1 and Column 2 text boxes indicates the width of each column will be three inches. The preview box illustrates the newspaper columns.*

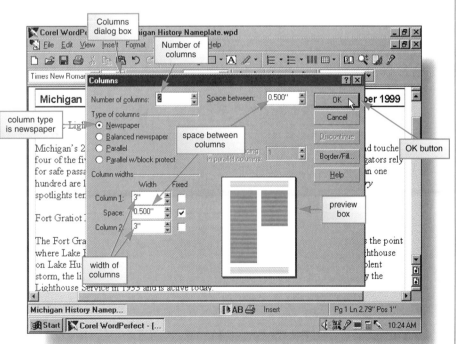

FIGURE 5-56

3 Click the OK button.

*WordPerfect arranges the body copy in two columns (Figure 5-57). The Col 1 and the Pg 1 entries on the Application bar indicate the insertion point is located in the first column on page one. Although not visible, a **Col Def** code is inserted in the document.*

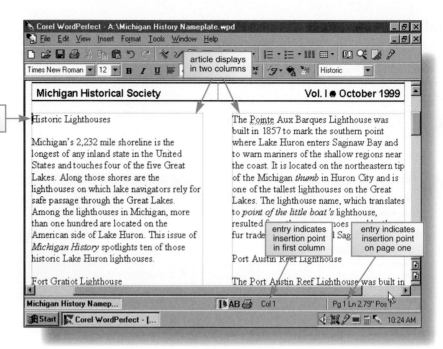

FIGURE 5-57

Formatting the Text in the Columns

The next step in creating the newsletter is to format the newsletter text. Formatting includes fully justifying the text, formatting the subheads, and creating a drop cap in the first paragraph. The procedures to accomplish these formatting tasks are explained in the following sections.

Full-Justifying the Text in Newspaper Columns

The text in the newspaper columns should be fully justified (see Figure 5-1 on page WP 5.5). The procedures to left-justify and right-justify text were explained in Project 1 and Project 2. The steps to full-justify text are similar to the steps to left-justify or right-justify text and are summarized below.

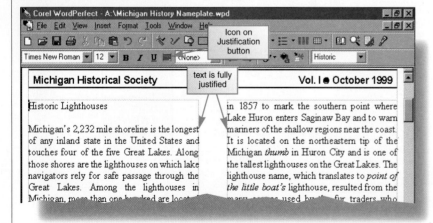

FIGURE 5-58

TO FULL-JUSTIFY THE NEWSPAPER COLUMNS

1. Verify the insertion point is located to the left of the Historic Lighthouses subhead.
2. Click the Justification button on the Property Bar.
3. Click Full.

The text in the newspaper columns is formatted in full justification (Figure 5-58). The icon on the Justification button indicates the text is fully justified.

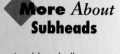

Formatting the Subheads Using QuickFormat

The next step in formatting the newsletter text is to format each subhead in the newsletter. One method of formatting the subheads is to format each subhead individually. A second and quicker method is to use QuickFormat. **QuickFormat** allows you to format one subhead in the document and then quickly copy the format of that subhead to the other subheads in the document.

To accomplish this, QuickFormat uses automatic paragraph styles. As explained in Project 1, a **style** provides an easy way to format similar types of text, such as headings or lists. One option of QuickFormat is to use a type of style, called the **automatic paragraph style**, to format and *link* the headings. **Linked headings** allow you to change the format of all headings automatically by changing the format of any one of the linked headings.

Each subhead in the newsletter should display in Arial Bold, Red, 14-point font. To quickly format the headings, highlight and format the first subhead in the first column (Historic Lighthouses), and then use QuickFormat to format the remaining subheadings in the newsletter.

Formatting the First Subhead

Methods to format text were shown in previous projects, and adding color to text was shown earlier in this project when you created the newsletter title. The steps to format the first subhead using Arial Bold, Red, 14-point font follow.

TO FORMAT A SUBHEAD

1. Select the Historic Lighthouses subhead.
2. Right-click the subhead.
3. Click Font on the QuickMenu.
4. Scroll the Font face list box to display Arial and then click Arial.
5. Click 14 in the Font size list box.
6. Click Bold in the Font style list box.
7. Click the Text color button.
8. Click the third color box (red) in the fifth row of the color palette.
9. Click the OK button in the Font dialog box.
10. Click anywhere in the document to remove the highlight from the subhead.

WordPerfect displays the Historic Lighthouses subhead in Arial Bold, Red, 14-point font (Figure 5-59).

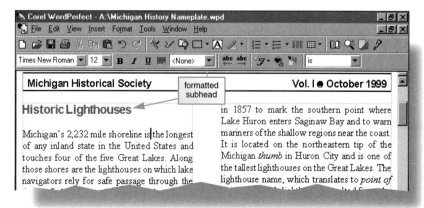

FIGURE 5-59

Formatting the Remaining Subheads

After formatting the first subhead, apply the format of the first subhead to the remaining subheads by performing the steps on the next two pages.

Steps To QuickFormat the Subheads

1 **Click the Historic Lighthouses subhead to position the insertion point in the subhead. Right-click the Historic Lighthouses subhead and then point to QuickFormat.**

WordPerfect displays a QuickMenu and highlights the QuickFormat command (Figure 5-60). The insertion point is located in the Historic Lighthouses subhead.

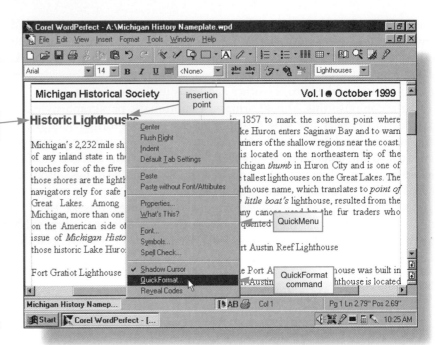

FIGURE 5-60

2 **Click QuickFormat. If necessary, click Headings in the QuickFormat dialog box. Point to the OK button.**

WordPerfect displays the Quick-Format dialog box and selects the Headings option button (Figure 5-61).

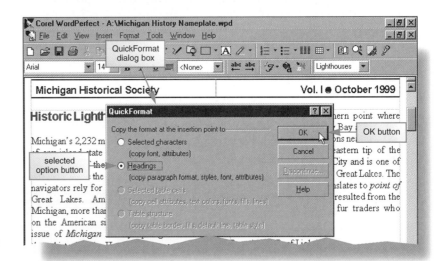

FIGURE 5-61

3 **Click the OK button.**

*WordPerfect closes the QuickFormat dialog box, changes the mouse pointer to an **I-beam with a paint roller,** and (QuickFormat1) displays in the Styles box on the Property Bar (Figure 5-62). Although not visible, two **Automatic Paragraph Style codes** and a **Style code** are inserted in the document.*

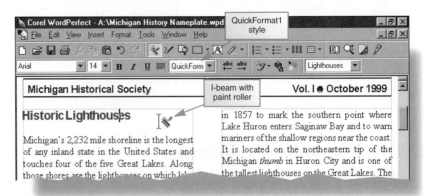

FIGURE 5-62

4 Scroll the window to display the Fort Gratiot Lighthouse, Port Austin Reef Lighthouse, Harbor Beach Lighthouse, and Tawas Point Lighthouse subheads. Position the tip of the roller over (point to) the Fort Gratiot Lighthouse subhead and click the subhead. Format the other three subheads in the document window by pointing to each subhead and clicking it.

QuickFormat formats the four sub-heads in Arial Bold, Red, 14-point and links the subheads (Figure 5-63). If, while formatting any of the later subheads, you format a subhead you do not want to format, click the Undo button on the WordPerfect 8 Toolbar to remove the formatting and start again.

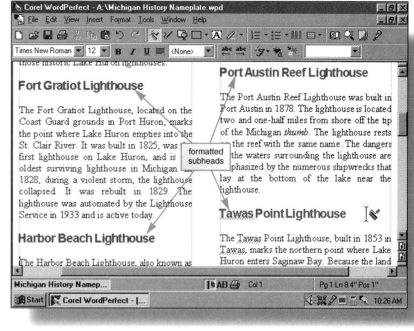

FIGURE 5-63

5 QuickFormat the remaining subheads in the newsletter by scrolling the document window, pointing to each subhead, and clicking the subhead.

All subheads in the newsletter are formatted and linked together (Figure 5-64). The I-beam with a paint roller icon continues to display. If you format text you do not want to format, follow the procedures listed in the step above.

6 Right-click anywhere in the body copy to display a QuickMenu and then click QuickFormat.

WordPerfect turns off QuickFormat and returns the mouse pointer to a left-pointing block arrow.

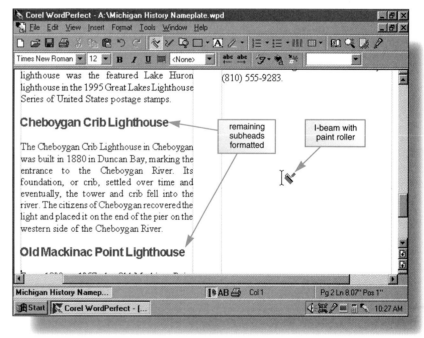

FIGURE 5-64

Changing the Format of Linked Subheads

Because of the ease with which you can format documents, it is not unusual to change the planned formatting as you create the document by trying different font faces, font styles, font sizes, and text colors to obtain the best design.

After formatting the subheads in the newsletter using QuickFormat, you can change the formatting of all subheads by changing the format of any single subhead. If, for example, you wished to change the font face from Arial to Courier New, you would select a subhead, right-click the subhead, click Font, change the font face to Courier New, and click the OK button in the Font dialog box. When you click the OK button in the Font dialog box, the font of all the subheads changes to Courier New.

Creating a Drop Cap

Next, continue to format the newsletter by creating a drop cap in the first paragraph. A **drop cap**, or **dropped capital letter**, displays larger than the rest of the characters in a paragraph and draws the attention of the reader to the beginning of the paragraph. The **Drop Cap** feature allows you to enlarge one or more of the first characters or words in a paragraph. In Figure 5-1 on page WP 5.5, the first paragraph of the newsletter contains a drop cap. Perform the following steps to create a drop cap for the first paragraph in the newsletter.

Steps   To Create a Drop Cap

1 **Scroll the document window to display the Historic Lighthouses subhead. Position the insertion point in the first paragraph of the newsletter. Click Format on the menu bar, point to Paragraph, and point to Drop Cap.**

The insertion point displays in the first paragraph and WordPerfect displays the Format menu, Paragraph submenu, and highlights the Drop Cap command on the Paragraph submenu (Figure 5-65).

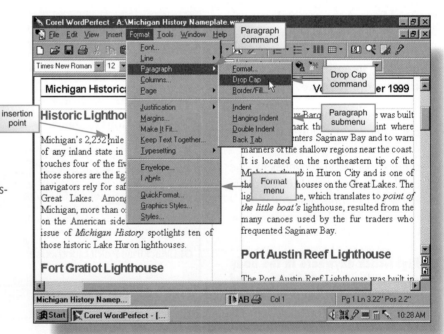

FIGURE 5-65

Click Drop Cap.

WordPerfect creates a drop cap in the first paragraph (Figure 5-66).

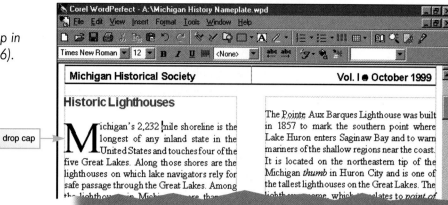

FIGURE 5-66

Clipart Images and WordPerfect Documents

In Project 1, you inserted a graphics image in an announcement. The file with the image (Huli_Tribesmen.jpg) contained a picture of two tribesmen you downloaded from the Internet. When you opened the file, WordPerfect displayed the Huli Tribesmen image in a graphics box. After inserting the box with the image, you moved the graphics box to the desired location in the document and sized it.

WordPerfect provides another type of graphics image, called **clipart**, for use in word processing documents. As a result of installing WordPerfect, thousands of clipart images are stored in the **scrapbook** on the Corel WordPerfect 8 CD-ROM disk. Other clipart images are stored on the Corel WordPerfect 8 Web site created by the publisher.

Downloading a Clipart Image

In this project, you will download the file with the clipart image (Shining_Lighthouse.gif) from the Corel WordPerfect 8 Web site established by the publisher of this book and store the graphics file on the Corel WordPerfect 8 Files floppy disk.

Another source for this file may be your network server. If your computer is connected to a network, ask your instructor if the file is available on the network server and how you can access the file. Your instructor can also obtain a CD-ROM with the file from the publishing company.

If you do not have access to the Internet or your computer network, ask your instructor how to obtain the file.

Perform the steps on the next page to download the Shining_Lighthouse.gif file to the Corel WordPerfect 8 Files floppy disk.

Other Ways

1. Position insertion point on a blank line, click Format on menu bar, point to Paragraph, click Drop Cap, type paragraph

2. Press CTRL+SHIFT+C

TO DOWNLOAD A GRAPHICS IMAGE FROM THE INTERNET

1. Verify the Corel WordPerfect 8 Files floppy disk is inserted in drive A.
2. Click File on the menu bar.
3. Click Internet Publisher.
4. Click the Browse the Web button. If the Netscape window is not maximized, maximize the window.
5. Click the Location box to highlight the URL.
6. Type http://www.scsite.com/wp8 in the Go to box.
7. Press the ENTER key.
8. Click Project 5.
9. Right-click the Shining_Lighthouse image.
10. Click Save Image As. Type Shining Lighthouse in the File name box. Verify 3½ Floppy (A:) displays in the Save in box. Click the Save button.
11. Click the Close button in each open Netscape window to close the windows.

WordPerfect saves the Shining Lighthouse file on the Corel WordPerfect 8 Files floppy disk in drive A.

Inserting the Light House Clipart Image

The next steps in preparing the newsletter are to insert the Shining Lighthouse clipart image between the two columns on the first page, wrap the text around the contour of the clipart image, and move and size the image. The text in the two columns should flow around the lighthouse image and be contoured to the shape of the image (see Figure 5-1 on page WP 5.5). Text that is wrapped around the contour of an image is called **contoured text flow**.

The size and position of the Shining Lighthouse image is shown in Figure 5-69 on page WP 5.46. The image is centered between the first and second columns and positioned in the paragraphs below the subheads at the top of the newsletter body. You insert a clipart image in a document by positioning the insertion point close to where the image should display, inserting the image in a graphics box, and moving the graphics box to its final position in the document and sizing it.

If you followed the steps to download the Shining_Lighthouse file, the file containing the lighthouse image is now located on the Corel WordPerfect 8 Files floppy disk in drive A.

Next, scroll the window to display the Historic Lighthouses subhead at the top of the document window, position the insertion point close to where the image should display, and insert the Shining Lighthouse clipart image in the newsletter. The procedures to scroll a document window, move the insertion point, and insert a graphics image were explained earlier and are summarized in the following steps to insert the clipart image in the document.

TO INSERT A CLIPART IMAGE

1. Scroll the document window to display the Historic Lighthouse subhead at the top of the window.
2. Move the insertion point to a place within the first line of the first paragraph of the newsletter.
3. Click Insert on the menu bar, point to Graphics, and click From File on the Graphics submenu.

④ Click the Look in box arrow in the Insert Image - ClipArt dialog box, scroll the Look in list box until 3½ Floppy (A:) displays, and click 3½ Floppy (A:).

⑤ Scroll the list box until the Shining Lighthouse filename displays, and then click Shining Lighthouse.

⑥ Click the Insert button.

WordPerfect inserts a graphics box containing the Shining Lighthouse image between the columns, wraps the text around the left and right sides of the graphics box, and changes the buttons on the Property Bar (Figure 5-67). The buttons on the Property Bar are designed to make working with graphics images easier.

FIGURE 5-67

The selected graphics box displays between the two columns, sizing handles display on the borders of the graphics box, and the text in both columns wraps around the two square sides of the box. Although not visible in the document window, a **Box code** is inserted in the document.

Contouring the Text Around a Graphics Box

The text in the two columns should flow around the lighthouse image and be contoured to the shape of the image. The **default text wrap setting** controls how the text in Figure 5-67 wraps around the graphics box. To contour the text around the graphics image, you must change the text wrap setting to Contour Both Sides. The steps to change the text wrap were explained in Project 1 and are summarized below.

TO CONTOUR THE TEXT AROUND A GRAPHICS BOX

① Scroll the document window to display the graphics box at the top of the window.

② Click the Wrap button on the Property Bar.

③ Click Contour Both Sides on the drop-down menu.

WordPerfect contours the text around the Shining Lighthouse image (Figure 5-68).

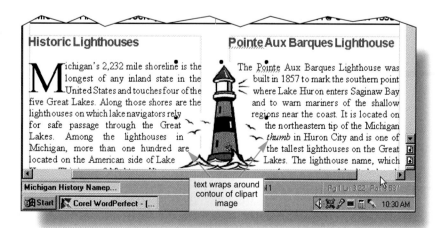

FIGURE 5-68

Moving and Sizing the Graphics Box

The Shining Lighthouse graphics image is close to the position it should occupy based upon the image in Figure 5-1 on page WP 5.5. Minor adjustments to the size and position of the image may be required. The procedure to move and size a graphics box were explained in Project 1 and are summarized below.

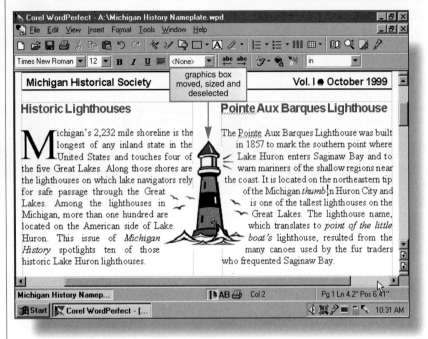

FIGURE 5-69

TO MOVE AND SIZE A GRAPHICS BOX

① To move the graphics box, point to the graphics box, hold down the left mouse button, drag the graphics box to its new position, and release the left mouse button.

② To size the graphics box, point to a sizing handle, and then drag it until the graphics box is sized correctly.

③ Repeat Step 1 and Step 2 until the clipart image looks like the one shown in Figure 5-69.

④ Click outside the graphics box to deselect it.

The Shining Lighthouse graphics box is moved, sized, and deselected (Figure 5-69).

Moving Text to the Top of the Next Column

After wrapping text and moving and sizing a graphics box, there is the possibility that a subhead, a subhead and a blank line, or a subhead and a single line of text will display at the bottom of a column. Because it would look better at the top of the next column, you can correct this situation by moving the subhead, or subhead and a blank line or line of text, to the top of the next column. To accomplish this relocation, move the insertion point to the end of the last line of text in the paragraph above the subhead, hold down the CTRL key, and press the ENTER key. Then remove the blank line that displays above the subhead at the top of the column by pressing the DELETE key. Holding down the CTRL key and pressing the ENTER key moves everything between the insertion point and the end of the column to the top of the next column.

Creating a Header

The second page of the newsletter contains a header (see Figure 5-1 on page WP 5.5). The header for the second page consists of the word, Page, and the right-justified page number followed by a horizontal line. The word, Page, and the page number display in the Arial 10-point font. Because the header should print only at the top of page two, the header must be created when the insertion point is positioned on page two. The procedure to create a header was explained in Project 3 and is summarized in the following steps.

TO CREATE A HEADER

① Scroll the document window to display page two at the top of the window.

② Click the paragraph below the Presque Isle Lighthouses subhead to move the insertion point into the paragraph.

③ Right-click the top margin and then click Header/Footer.

④ Click the Create button.

⑤ Type Page and then press the SPACEBAR.

⑥ Click the Page Numbering button on the Property Bar and then click Page Number.

⑦ Click the Justification button on the Property Bar and then click Right.

⑧ Select the header text, right-click the header text, click Font, scroll the Font face list box to display Arial, and click Arial. Click Bold in the Font style list box. Scroll the Font size list box to display 10 and then click 10. Click the OK button.

⑨ Move the insertion point to the end of the line containing the word, Page, and press the ENTER key.

⑩ Click Insert on the menu bar, point to Shape, and click Horizontal Line.

The header displays on the screen (Figure 5-70). The header will print .5-inch from the top edge of the paper on the second page of the newsletter when you print the document. Although not visible, a **Header A code** *is inserted in the document.*

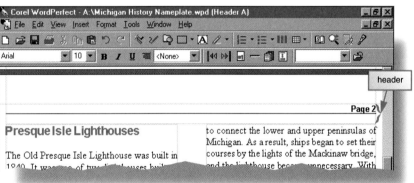

FIGURE 5-70

Text Boxes

The next task in preparing the newsletter is to create the text box shown in Figure 5-1 on page WP 5.5. The text box is centered between the two columns on page two and displays with a border, shadow, and 10% gray shading. **Gray shading** indicates how much black and white comprise the background color of a text box. Gray shading of 0% is an all-white background and gray shading of 100% is an all-black background. A shadow displays on the right side and bottom of the text box and gives the box a three-dimensional appearance. The text in the text box displays in Times New Roman Italic, Red, 12-point font.

Copying the Pull-Quote to the Clipboard

The **pull-quote** in the text box is copied from the paragraph below the Presque Isle Lighthouses subhead into the text box. To place the pull-quote in the text box, you select the text in the newsletter and then copy it to the clipboard using the **Copy button**. The **clipboard** is a temporary storage area used to hold text or graphics. Perform the steps on the next page to copy the text from the newsletter to the clipboard.

ore *About* **Text Boxes**

The Warning dialog box displays when the text you copy to a text box will not fit in the text box. A message in the dialog box indicates you should make the text box larger and clicking the Yes button enlarges the text box so that all the text displays in the text box.

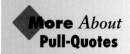

ore *About* **Pull-Quotes**

Use pull-quotes sparingly in a newsletter to jazz up otherwise boring columns of text.

Steps To Copy Text to the Clipboard

1 If necessary, scroll the document window to display the Presque Isle Lighthouses subhead at the top of the document window. Select the fourth and fifth sentences in the paragraph below the Presque Isle Lighthouses subhead. Point to the Copy button on the Toolbar.

The Presque Isle Lighthouses subhead displays at the top of the document window and the text to be copied to the text box is highlighted (Figure 5-71).

2 Click the Copy button. Click anywhere in the paragraph below the Presque Isle Lighthouses subhead to remove the highlight.

WordPerfect copies the text from the paragraph to the clipboard and deselects the highlighted text.

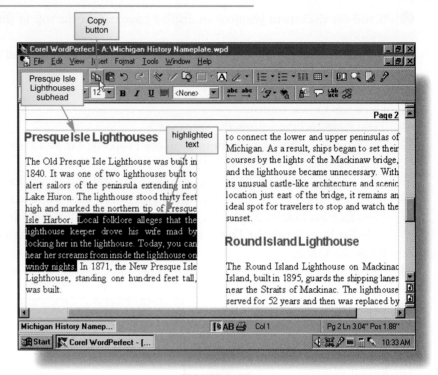

FIGURE 5-71

Creating a Text Box

Next, create the text box to contain the pull-quote by performing the following steps.

Steps To Create a Text Box

1 Verify the insertion point is located in the paragraph below the Presque Isle Lighthouses subhead. Point to the Text Box button on the WordPerfect 8 Toolbar.

The mouse pointer points to the Text Box button on the WordPerfect 8 Toolbar (Figure 5-72).

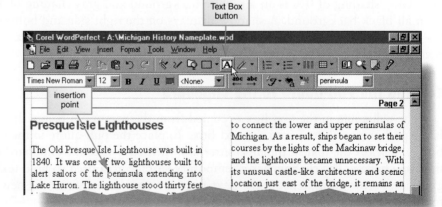

FIGURE 5-72

2 **Click the Text Box button.**

*WordPerfect creates a text box in the first column on page two (Figure 5-73). The **default border style** of the text box causes the top and bottom borders to display as thick horizontal lines. The insertion point is located at the left margin on the first blank line in the text box. Although not visible, WordPerfect inserts a Box code in the document.*

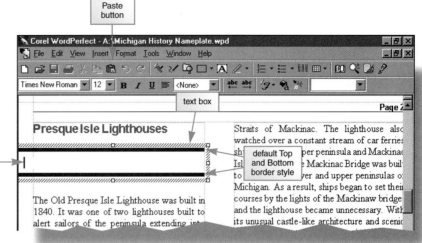

FIGURE 5-73

OtherWays

1. Click Insert on menu bar, click Text Box

2. Press ALT+F11

Copying Text from the Clipboard to the Text Box

After copying the text from the newsletter to the clipboard and then creating the text box, copy the text from the clipboard to the text box using the **Paste button**. Perform the following step to paste the text.

Steps **To Copy Text from the Clipboard to the Text Box**

1 **Click the Paste button on the Toolbar.**

WordPerfect copies the pull-quote to the text box (Figure 5-74).

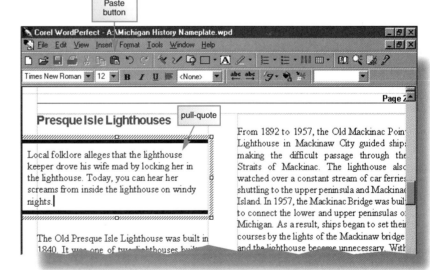

FIGURE 5-74

OtherWays

1. Position insertion point, click Edit on menu bar, click Paste

2. Press CTRL+V

Moving and Sizing the Text Box

The text box should display centered horizontally between both columns on page two (see Figure 5-1 on page WP5.5. To move a text box, point to any of the four borders that surround the text and drag the text box to its new location. To size a text box, point to any sizing handle and drag it to size the box. Perform the steps on the next page to move and size a text box.

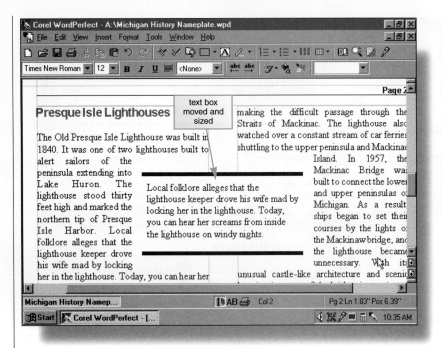

FIGURE 5-75

TO MOVE AND SIZE A TEXT BOX

① To move the text box, point to any border of the text box, and drag the text box to its new position.

② To size the text box, point to a sizing handle, and then drag it until the text box is sized correctly.

③ Repeat Step 1 and Step 2 until the text box looks like the text box in Figure 5-75.

④ Click outside the text box to deselect the text box.

The text box is moved, sized, and deselected (Figure 5-75).

Formatting the Text in the Text Box

After creating the text box, format the text in it by italicizing the text and changing the color from black to red. Perform the following steps to format the text.

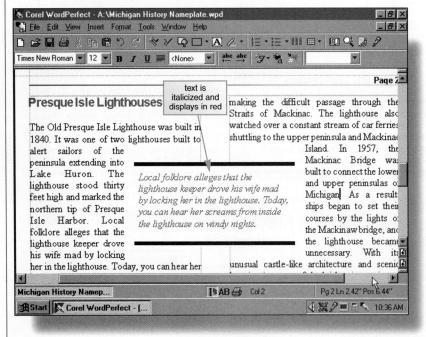

FIGURE 5-76

TO FORMAT THE TEXT IN A TEXT BOX

① Highlight the text in the text box.

② Right-click the highlighted text.

③ Click Font on the QuickMenu.

④ Click Italic in the Font style list box.

⑤ Click the Text color button.

⑥ Click the third color box in the fifth row (red color box).

⑦ Click the OK button.

⑧ Click anywhere outside the text box to remove the highlight.

The text displays in Times New Roman Italic, Red 12-point font (Figure 5-76).

Changing the Border Style and Fill Style of the Text Box

After creating the text box, change the border style and fill style by performing the following steps.

 Steps To Change the Border Style and Fill Style of a Text Box

1 **With the text box deselected, right-click the text box. Click Border/Fill on the QuickMenu. Point to the sixth border style in the first row.**

WordPerfect displays the Border sheet in the Box Border/Fill dialog box (Figure 5-77). The dialog box contains two additional tabs (Fill and Advanced), an Available border styles list box, a preview box, and several buttons. The current border style (default border style) displays in the preview box and the elements of the border style (color, line style, and drop shadow) display on the buttons to the left of the preview box. In the list box, a blue square identifies the current border style.

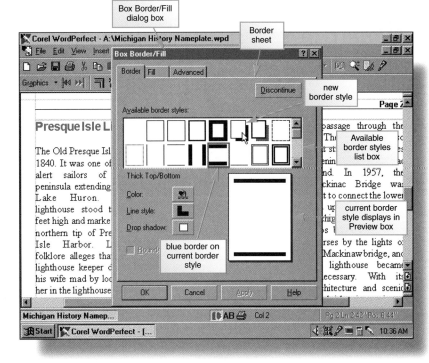

FIGURE 5-77

2 **Click the border style box and then click the Fill tab. Point to the third fill style box in the first row (10% fill style).**

WordPerfect moves the blue box to the new border style, changes the border style, displays the new border style in the preview box, and displays the Fill sheet (Figure 5-78). The Fill sheet contains an Available fill styles list box, a preview box, and several buttons. The current fill style (default fill style) displays in the preview box and the elements of the fill style (foreground, background, and pattern) display on the buttons to the left of the preview window. A blue square surrounds the current fill style (no fill style) in the list box.

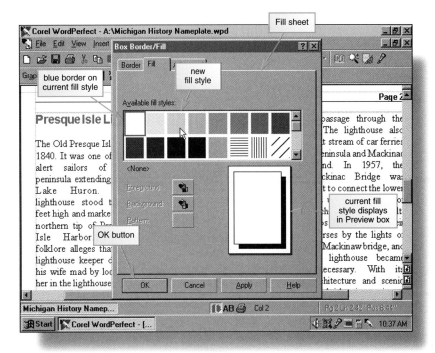

FIGURE 5-78

3 **Click the fill style box. Click the OK button in the Box Border/Fill dialog box.**

WordPerfect moves the blue box to the new fill style, changes the fill style, displays the new fill style in the preview box, closes the Box Border/Fill dialog box, and displays the text box with the new fill style (Figure 5-79).

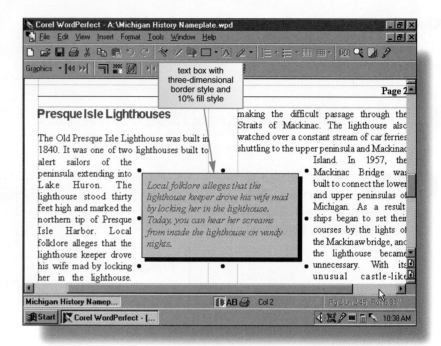

FIGURE 5-79

Editing a Text Box

After creating a text box, you can edit the text by clicking the text box. WordPerfect selects the text box and displays the insertion point in the text box. When you have finished editing the text, click anywhere outside the text box to deselect the text box.

Moving Text to the Top of the Next Column

Two conditions may exist so that you wish to move text to the top of the next column. First, there is the possibility that a subhead by itself, a subhead and a blank line, or a subhead and a single line of text display at the bottom of a column and will look better at the top of the next column. Second, there is more white space at the bottom of the second column than the first column and equalizing the text in the two columns would make the newsletter look more balanced.

You can correct either situation by moving the subhead and any lines below the subhead to the top of the next column. To accomplish this movement of text, position the insertion point on the blank line above the subhead, hold down the CTRL key, and press the ENTER key. Holding down the CTRL key and pressing the ENTER key moves the text between the insertion point and the end of the column to the top of the next column. In this case, a blank line will display above the subhead at the top of the second column. Remove the blank line above the subhead by pressing the DELETE key.

To balance the unbalanced columns on page two of the newsletter, move the Old Mackinac Point Lighthouse subhead and the text below the subhead at the bottom of the first column to the top of the second column on page two by positioning the insertion point, holding down the CTRL key, and pressing the ENTER key. Perform the following steps to move the text.

Steps To Move Text to the Top of the Next Column

1 **Scroll the document window to display the Old Mackinac Point Lighthouse subhead in the window. Position the insertion point on the blank line above the Old Mackinac Point Lighthouse subhead at the bottom of column one on page two.**

WordPerfect moves the insertion point to the blank line preceding the Old Mackinac Point Lighthouse subhead (Figure 5-80).

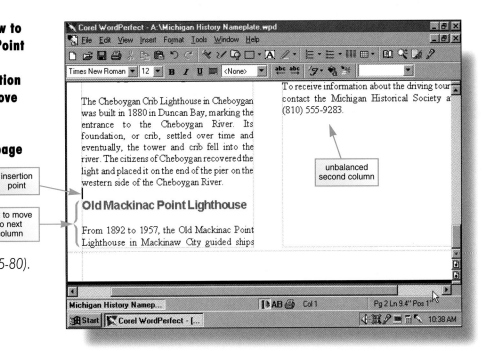

FIGURE 5-80

2 **Hold down the CTRL key and then press the ENTER key.**

WordPerfect moves the blank line, Old Mackinac Point Lighthouse subhead, and text below the subhead in the first column to the top of the second column (Figure 5-81). Although not visible, the bottom column guidelines adjust to the position of the new text. The insertion point is located on the blank line at the top of column two.

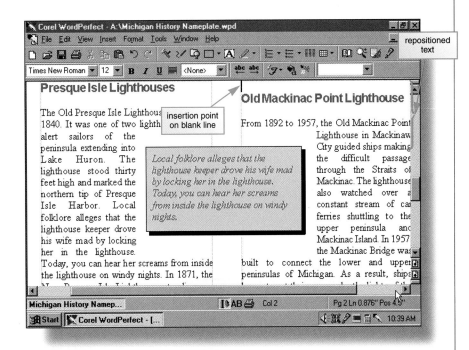

FIGURE 5-81

3 **Press the DELETE key to remove the blank line.**

The Old Mackinac Point Lighthouse subhead displays at the top of the second column on page two (Figure 5-82).

4 **Scroll the document window to verify the white space at the bottom of the two columns on page two appears more balanced.**

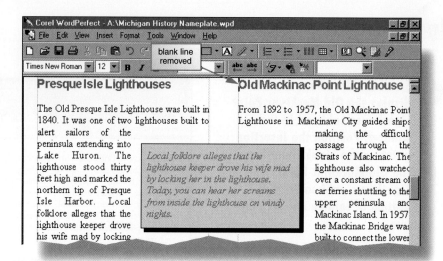

FIGURE 5-82

Saving and Printing the Newsletter

After you create the newsletter, you should save the newsletter on the Corel WordPerfect 8 Files floppy disk and print the document. Save the newsletter using the Save As command on the File menu and Michigan History - October 1999 as the filename. The procedure to save a document using a different filename was explained in Project 1. The procedure to save the newsletter using the Save As command is summarized below.

TO SAVE THE NEWSLETTER

1 Verify the Corel WordPerfect 8 Files floppy disk is inserted in drive A.
2 Click File on the menu bar.
3 Click Save As.
4 Type Michigan History - October 1999 in the File name box.
5 Click the Save button.

WordPerfect saves the newsletter on the Corel WordPerfect 8 Files floppy disk in drive A using the filename, Michigan History - October 1999.wpd. The newsletter displays on the screen with the new filename in the title bar.

Next, print the newsletter on the printer. To print the newsletter, perform the following steps.

TO PRINT THE NEWSLETTER

1 Click the Print button on the Toolbar.
2 Review the Print to dialog box to ensure the Full document option button is selected and the value 1 displays in the Number of copies text box.
3 Click the Print button in the Print to dialog box.

WordPerfect displays the Corel WordPerfect dialog box momentarily and then prints the two-page newsletter illustrated in Figure 5-1 on page WP 5.5.

Returning the Computer to Its Original State

In a school environment, you always want to return the computer to its original state before you quit your session with WordPerfect. Before quitting WordPerfect, close the document window, reset the TextArt settings you changed, and reset the Grammatik entries made while grammar checking the Lake Huron Lighthouses document. Perform the following step to close the document window.

TO CLOSE THE DOCUMENT WINDOW

1 Click File on the menu bar and then click Close to close the document window.

WordPerfect closes the document window containing the newsletter.

Next, start TextArt and reset the settings you changed. Perform the following steps to reset the text shape, font, text color, shadow, outline thickness, and outline color settings.

TO RESET THE TEXTART SETTINGS

1 Click Insert on the menu bar, point to Graphics and click TextArt.
2 Click the General tab. Click the More button to the right of the Shapes list box. Click the eleventh shape in the first row of the Shapes palette.
3 Click the Font box arrow. Scroll the Font drop-down list to display Arial and then click Arial.
4 Click the 2D Options tab. Click the Text color button and then click the tenth color box in the first row (royal blue).
5 Click the Shadow button, click the fourth shadow box in the fourth row, and click the OK button.
6 Click the Outline button and then click the first thickness box in the first row (None).
7 Click the Outline color button, click the ninth color in the first row (light gray), and click the OK button.
8 Click the Close button in the Corel TextArt 8.0 dialog box.
9 Click File on the menu bar and then click the Close button. Click the No button so that you do not save the changes to the document.

The TextArt settings are reset to the default settings.

While using Grammatik, the words Gratiot, Cheboygan, and Presque were highlighted, and you clicked the Skip All button to ignore these words in the remainder of the document. As a result, an entry was made in the user word list for each of these words. Perform the steps on the next page to remove these entries from the user word list.

TO REMOVE ENTRIES FROM THE GRAMMATIK USER WORD LIST

1. Click Tools on the menu bar and then click Grammatik.
2. Click the No button in the Grammatik dialog box.
3. Click the Options button in the Speller, Grammatik, and Thesaurus window.
4. Click User Word Lists on the QuickMenu.
5. Scroll the list box at the bottom of the User Word Lists dialog box to display the word, Cheboygan. Click Cheboygan. Click the Delete Entry button. Click Yes in the User Word List Editor dialog box.
6. Scroll the list box at the bottom of the User Word Lists dialog box to display the word, Gratiot. Click Gratiot. Click the Delete Entry button. Click Yes in the User Word List Editor dialog box.
7. Scroll the list box at the bottom of the User Word Lists dialog box to display the word, Presque. Click Presque. Click the Delete Entry button. Click Yes in the User Word List Editor dialog box.
8. Click the Close button in the User Word Lists dialog box.
9. Click the Close button in the Speller, Grammatik, and Thesaurus window.

The three entries for the words, Cheboygan, Gratiot, and Presque, are removed from the Grammatik user word list.

Quitting WordPerfect

Next, perform the steps below to quit WordPerfect and remove the Corel WordPerfect 8 Files floppy disk from drive A.

TO QUIT WORDPERFECT

1. Click File on the menu bar and then click Exit to quit WordPerfect.
2. Click the No button in the Corel WordPerfect dialog box.
3. Remove the Corel WordPerfect 8 Files floppy disk from drive A.

WordPerfect quits WordPerfect and the Corel WordPerfect 8 Files floppy disk is removed from drive A.

Project Summary

In Project 5, you learned newsletter terminology and how to create a newsletter. You used Grammatik to check a document for writing problems. In creating the newsletter, you performed a search to find a file on disk, inserted the text from a file into the document, defined newspaper columns, right-justified text in the columns, and moved text between columns. You created a drop cap and formatted the subheads using QuickFormat. You used TextArt to create and format the newsletter title and inserted a table to contain and format the newsletter subtitle, volume number, and date. This project illustrated the steps to insert a clipart image, create a text box, copy a quote to a text box, and format the text in a text box.

What You Should Know

Having completed this project, you now should be able to perform the following tasks.

▌ Add an outline to the newsletter title *(WP 5.24)*

▌ Change the border style and fill style of a text box *(WP 5.51)*

▌ Change the border style of a table *(WP 5.31)*

▌ Change the font of the newsletter title *(WP 5.19)*

▌ Change the font of the table cells *(WP 5.30)*

▌ Change the justification of the newsletter title *(WP 5.20)*

▌ Change the shape of the newsletter title *(WP 5.18)*

▌ Change the text color of the newsletter title *(WP 5.22)*

▌ Change the top and bottom margins *(WP 5.14)*

▌ Check a document for writing problems *(WP 5.9)*

▌ Close the document window *(WP 5.55)*

▌ Contour the text around a graphics box *(WP 5.45)*

▌ Copy text from the clipboard to the text box *(WP 5.49)*

▌ Copy text to the clipboard *(WP 5.48)*

▌ Create a drop cap *(WP 5.42)*

▌ Create a header *(WP 5.47)*

▌ Create a table *(WP 5.28)*

▌ Create a text box *(WP 5.48)*

▌ Define newspaper columns *(WP 5.37)*

▌ Display the 2D Options sheet *(WP 5.21)*

▌ Download a graphics image from the Internet *(WP 5.44)*

▌ Download a WordPerfect file from the Internet *(WP 5.8)*

▌ Enter the newsletter subtitle and volume *(WP 5.28)*

▌ Enter the newsletter title *(WP 5.17)*

▌ Find and retrieve a file *(WP 5.35)*

▌ Format a subhead *(WP 5.39)*

▌ Format the text in a text box *(WP 5.50)*

▌ Full-justify text in newspaper columns *(WP 5.38)*

▌ Insert a clipart image *(WP 5.44)*

▌ Insert a WordPerfect character *(WP 5.29)*

▌ Move and size a graphics box *(WP 5.46)*

▌ Move and size a text box *(WP 5.50)*

▌ Move text to the top of the next column *(WP 5.53)*

▌ Open a document *(WP 5.8)*

▌ Print the newsletter *(WP 5.54)*

▌ QuickFormat the subheads *(WP 5.40)*

▌ Quit TextArt *(WP 5.26)*

▌ Quit WordPerfect *(WP 5.56)*

▌ Remove entries from the Grammatik user word list *(WP 5.56)*

▌ Remove the shadow from the newsletter title *(WP 5.23)*

▌ Reset the TextArt settings *(WP 5.55)*

▌ Save a modified document and close its window *(WP 5.13)*

▌ Save the nameplate *(WP 5.34)*

▌ Save the newsletter *(WP 5.54)*

▌ Start TextArt *(WP 5.16)*

▌ Start WordPerfect *(WP 5.6)*

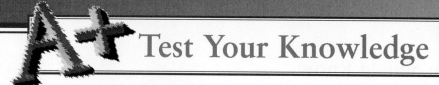

Test Your Knowledge

1 True/False

Instructions: Circle T if the statement is true or F if the statement is false.

T F 1. Newsletters are an effective means of communication in today's world of information.

T F 2. Grammatik checks a document for writing problems but does not check for misspelled words.

T F 3. Style, grammar, and mechanical are types of rule classes.

T F 4. Colored text should not be used when formatting a nameplate.

T F 5. QuickFinder allows you to search for a file using a word or series of words.

T F 6. You must know the name of the file you wish to retrieve and insert into a document.

T F 7. Two pages view allows you to display two consecutive pages side-by-side in the same document window.

T F 8. The easiest method to format the subheads in a newsletter is to format each one individually by selecting the subhead and then formatting it.

T F 9. When the insertion point is located in a newspaper column, holding down the CTRL key and pressing the ENTER key will delete the text between the insertion point and the end of the column.

T F 10. Clicking the Text Box button on the WordPerfect 8 Toolbar will create a text box.

2 Multiple Choice

Instructions: Circle the correct response.

1. The nameplate in this project contains a _____.
   a. newsletter title
   b. newsletter subtitle
   c. newsletter volume and date
   d. all of the above

2. Questionable Usage is an example of a _____.
   a. rule class
   b. checking style
   c. rule class group
   d. formality level

3. When Grammatik finds a writing problem, the _____.
   a. problem automatically is fixed by Grammatik
   b. Grammatik dialog box displays
   c. Error Detection window displays
   d. problem text is highlighted in the document

4. You format the newsletter title using _____.
   a. QuickFormat
   b. TextArt
   c. QuickFinder
   d. none of the above

5. The default table border style causes a _____ to display as the outside border and the inside border.
   a. double line
   b. single line
   c. pink dotted line
   d. none of the above

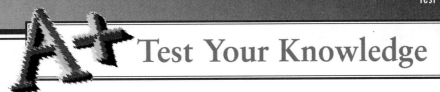

Test Your Knowledge

6. To search for a file and insert the file into another document, use the _____ command(s).
   a. QuickFinder   b. Retrieve   c. QuickFormat   d. Find and Retrieve

7. _____ columns allow text to flow from the bottom of one column to the top of another column.
   a. Parallel block protect   b. Newsletter   c. Table   d. Newspaper

8. A drop cap is a character that displays _____ the rest of the characters in a paragraph.
   a. larger than   b. smaller than   c. the same size as   d. none of the above

9. The _____ Toolbar contains both the button to insert a clipart image and the button to create a text box.
   a. Format   b. Table   c. Graphics   d. Features

10. Holding down the _____ key and pressing the _____ key causes the text from the insertion point to the end of the column to move to the top of the next column.
    a. CTRL, PAGE UP   b. CTRL, HOME   c. CTRL, ENTER   d. CTRL, END

3 Understanding the Grammatik Sheet

Instructions: In Figure 5-83, arrows point to objects on the Grammatik sheet in the Spell Checker, Grammatik, and Thesaurus window. Identify the objects in the spaces provided.

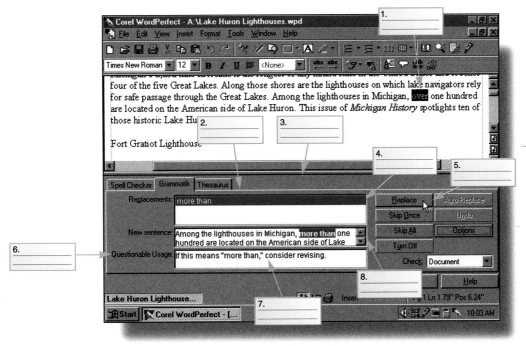

FIGURE 5-83

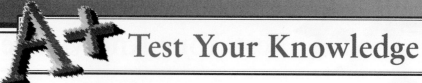

4 Understanding the Corel TextArt 8.0 Dialog Box and Image Box

Instructions: In Figure 5-84, arrows point to objects in the Corel TextArt 8.0 dialog box and image box. Identify the objects in the spaces provided.

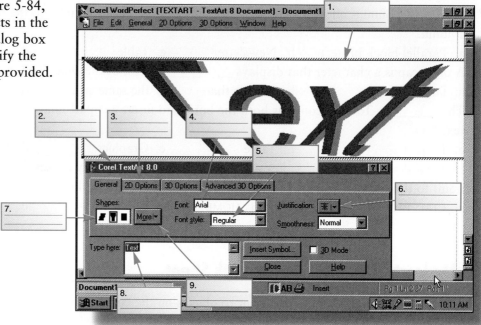

FIGURE 5-84

1 Reviewing Project Activities

Instructions: Perform the following tasks on a computer.

Part 1: Grammatik Help

1. Start WordPerfect.
2. Click Tools on the menu bar and then click Grammatik to start Grammatik. Click the No button in the Grammatik dialog box so you do not close Grammatik but leave the Spell Checker, Grammatik, and Thesaurus window on the screen.
3. Click the Help button in the Spell Checker, Grammatik, and Thesaurus window. Read the information about Grammatik in the About Grammatik screen.
4. Using Grammatik Help, record the definition of the term, user word list, in the space provided.

_____

_____

5. Using Grammatik Help, record the definition of the term, rule class, in the space provided.

_____

6. Using Grammatik Help, record the definition of the term, checking style, in the space provided.

_____

7. Click the Close button in the Grammatik Help window to quit Help.
8. Click the Close button in the Spell Checker, Grammatik, and Thesaurus window to close the window.

Part 2: Online Help

1. If you have access to the Internet, perform the following steps to obtain online help from the Corel Web site.
2. Click Help on the menu bar and click Corel Web Site.
3. Using information and hyperlinks on the Corel Web site, answer the following questions about Corel WordPerfect Suite 8.
4. What applications are included in Corel WordPerfect Suite 8? _____

_____

5. List five new features of Corel WordPerfect 8. _____

_____

6. What are the system requirements for using Corel WordPerfect Suite 8? _____

_____

7. What is the price of the full CD-ROM version of Corel WordPerfect Suite 8? _____

_____

8. What is the price of the competitive upgrade CD-ROM version of Corel WordPerfect Suite 8?

_____

9. What freebies and special offers are available for Corel WordPerfect Suite 8? _____

_____

10. Click the Close button in the Netscape window. _____
11. Quit WordPerfect by clicking File on the menu bar and then clicking Exit. Click the No button in the Corel WordPerfect dialog box so you do not save the changes.

2 Expanding on the Basics

Instructions: Perform the following tasks using a computer and then answer the questions on a separate piece of paper.

Grammatik allows you to check a document for writing problems. Using Grammatik Help, answer the following questions.

1. How do you turn off a rule while proofreading?
2. How do you skip a writing error once?
3. How do you automatically start Grammatik?
4. How do you add a rule class to a checking style?

(continued)

Use Help

Expanding on the Basics (*continued*)

TextArt allows you to create visually appealing images in a document. Use TextArt Help to answer these questions about TextArt.

1. How do you change text that has already been typed in a document into a TextArt image?
2. After creating a TextArt image in a document, how do you save the TextArt image in a separate file?
3. How do you rotate a 2D TextArt image?
4. Can you copy a TextArt image from one application to another application? If so, how?

WordPerfect allows you to create columns in a document to divide the text vertically on a page. Use Help to answer the following questions about columns.

1. What are the four types of columns?
2. What shortcut keys can you use to move the insertion point to the next column?
3. After creating newspaper columns, how do you delete the columns?
4. How do you insert a vertical line between newspaper columns?

Businesses, schools, and individuals use newsletters to communicate with groups of people. Use Help to answer the following questions about newsletters.

1. Can you create white text on black background? If so, how?
2. How do you import or link a spreadsheet to a newsletter?
3. How do you insert a chart in a newsletter?
4. What is meant by the phrase, *creating a published look?*

Apply Your Knowledge

1 Creating a Nameplate

Instructions: Create the Education Federation nameplate illustrated in Figure 5-85 by performing the following tasks.

1. Start WordPerfect.
2. Set the top and bottom margins to .5 inch.
3. Create the newsletter title (Education Federation) using TextArt. Use the Times New Roman Bold font. Use the thirteenth shape in the first row of the Shapes palette. Use the second color box in the first row of the Text color palette. Do not use a shadow, outline, or pattern.
4. Create a 2x1 table for the newsletter subtitle, volume, and date. In cell A1, type Newsletter of Concerned Educators (the newsletter subtitle). Left-justify the newsletter subtitle.

Apply Your Knowledge

5. Type Vol. III (the newsletter volume number), insert a WordPerfect character (5,48) from the Iconic Symbols character set, and type Fall 1999 (the date) in cell B1. Right-justify the newsletter volume number, WordPerfect character, and date.

6. Format the cells of the table using Arial Bold 12-point font and the color black.

FIGURE 5-85

7. Remove all borders from the table. Change the border style of the top and bottom borders to the Heavy Double border style (second border style in the second row).

8. Save the document on the Corel WordPerfect 8 Files floppy disk in drive A using the filename, Education Federation.wpd.

9. Print a copy of the nameplate on the printer.

10. Follow directions from your instructor for turning in the printed copy of the nameplate.

In the Lab

1 Checking for Writing Problems and Creating a Newsletter

Problem: As a computer graphics artist working at the Financial Investment Corporation, you are responsible for creating the first issue (Volume I, July 1999) of the *Successful Investor* newsletter. The article for the newsletter has been written and saved using the filename, Hard_Working_Money. The finished newsletter is shown in Figure 5-86a and Figure 5-86b on the next two pages.

Instructions: Check the Hard Working Money article for writing problems and then create the *Successful Investor* newsletter.

Part 1: Checking the Hard Working Money Article for Writing Problems

1. If you have access to the Internet, download the Hard Working Money.wpd file from the Corel WordPerfect 8 Web site to the Corel WordPerfect 8 Files floppy disk. Use the URL, http://www.scsite.com/wp8. Otherwise, obtain the file from your instructor.

2. Open the Hard_Working_Money.wpd file. Check the document for writing problems using the Quick Check checking style. The document displays in 14-point type.

3. Save the edited Hard_Working_Money file on the Corel WordPerfect 8 Files floppy disk using the same filename.

4. Close the document window containing the article.

(continued)

In the Lab

Checking for Writing Problems and Creating a Newsletter *(continued)*

Part 2: Creating the Nameplate

1. Set the top and bottom margins to .5 inch.
2. Create the nameplate title (Successful Investor) using TextArt. Use the Playbill Regular font, square shape (first shape in the first row of the Shapes palette), and red for the text color. The text should not have an outline, shadow, or pattern.
3. Create a 2x1 table. Type the newsletter subtitle (Your Guide to Successful Investing) in cell A1. Type the newsletter volume and number (Volume I), insert the WordPerfect character (5,37), and type the date (July 1999) in cell B1. Right-justify the text.
4. Format the cells of the table using Times New Roman Bold 12-point font.
5. Remove the inside and outside table borders. Change the border style of the top margin to the Thick border style.
6. Insert a blank line following the table.
7. Save the nameplate on the Corel WordPerfect 8 Files floppy disk using the filename, Successful Investor Nameplate.

Part 3: Creating the Newsletter

1. Insert the Hard_Working_Money file into the nameplate document.
2. Define the necessary newspaper columns.

Successful Investor

Your Guide to Successful Investing　　　　　　**Volume I ☎ July 1999**

This Month's Issue:

This month's issue of *Successful Investor* focuses on how to make money work harder. I want to show you four low-risk investments that increase your investment profits without increasing the risk associated with investing. All four investments make your money work harder by replacing low yield investments with high yield investments. By taking advantage of these investments, your yields will be as abundant as roses in the Rose Bowl Parade. Consider each one carefully.

Higher Yields

You don't have to accept low yields on bank CDs and T-bills. By moving your money into a higher yielding investment, you can improve your yield with little or no additional risk.

Money Market Accounts

Open a money market account with Wilmington Bank (P.O. 3748, Wilmington, DE 19885, (800) 555-3426). If you open an account before September 30, the bank guarantees a current rate that

is double what you will receive from most CDs and T-bills. The minimum initial deposit is $5,000. The bank insures each account up to $100,000.

Short Term Bond Funds

Transfer your money to my top choice short term bond fund, Western Federal Government Income Trust. Call (310) 555-0938 and ask for Frederick Rutherford. This is a no-load bond fund that invests in short-term paper issued by the governments of Mexico and Canada. The current yield is 150% higher than today's bank CDs.

Of course there will be fluctuations in the foreign currency rates of Mexico and Canada. Regardless, in the first eight months of this year, the fund's asset value per share increased from $10 per share to $10.23. I recommend buying the WFGIT fund at $10.18 or less.

Fixed Annuities

Open a fixed annuity with Federal Bank (P.O. Box 38478, Wilhelm, MI 48236),

FIGURE 5-86a

In the Lab

3. Full-justify the text in the news-paper columns.

4. Format the first subhead (Dear Subscriber:) using Times New Roman Bold, Italic 16-point font and the color red. Format the remaining subheads using QuickFormat.

5. If you have access to the Internet, download the Fist of Money file from the Corel WordPerfect 8 Web site to the Corel WordPerfect 8 Files floppy disk. Use the URL, http://www.scsite.com/wp8. Otherwise, obtain the file from your instructor.

6. Insert the Fist of Money clipart image between the two columns on page one.

7. Contour the text to wrap around the clipart image (contour both sides). Move and resize the clipart image to resemble the one illustrated in Figure 5-86a.

8. Create the header for page two. Type Page, press the SPACEBAR, and insert the page number. Format the text using Times New Roman Bold 12-point font and the color black. Right-justify the line containing the page number. Draw a black horizontal line.

Page 2

(616) 800-555-8394. Federal Bank offers a fixed annuity that pays a current yield that is 2.5% higher than the prime interest rate during the first year. The yield the second year jumps to 3% higher than the prime interest rate. Your tax-free earnings compound until you withdraw them. The Federal Bank is a strong financial institution with a long history of safe investment policies.

Minimum investment is $10,000.00. You can with draw up to 15% of your initial investment each year without a surrender charge. However, a federal penalty may apply if you withdraw money before the age of 59 1/2. Ask for an application from Nancy Stanford at the Federal Bank.

Utility Stocks

Many common stocks yield more than money market funds and bank CDs. The risk is much greater. Few common stocks can offer a safe yield with regular yearly increases like most electric company stocks.

Vancouver Power delivers 25% to 40% more income than American electric companies of similar quality. It's not a secret that Vancouver Power is my number one utility stock pick for 1998. Buy this utility now and lock up your savings for the years to come.

I do not suggest jumping into these investments all at once or immediately. Review your current investments, and decide which ones you can replace.

You can find the Vancouver Power stock on the Canadian exchange. Vancouver Power is my top pick for income-oriented investors. This stock should out perform easily its United States counterparts in the years to come.

Contact any investment broker who trades Canadian stocks to purchase Vancouver Power. If your broker doesn't trade them, contact Peter Reilly at Great Western Investments in Los Angeles at 1-714-555-9384. You should purchase Vancouver Power stock for $22 (Canadian) or less per share.

Your Success Depends on You

There you have it. Those are my four ways to make more money with your investments without increasing the risk. I do not suggest jumping into these investments all at once or immediately. Review your current investments, and decide which ones you can replace. Then resolve when you want to replace the investments.

Relax. These investments are solid investments. You have time to examine the options. I'll have more for you next time. The topic next month will be how to increase your investment returns by reducing the federal and state taxes you pay. Have a good day and a good return.

Kevin Stack

FIGURE 5-86b

---

9. Copy the third and fourth sentences in the paragraph below the Your Success Depends on You subhead to the clipboard. Create the text box at the bottom of page two. Paste the contents of the clipboard into the text box. Italicize the text in the text box. Change the border style of the text box to the Shadow Border style, and change the fill style to the 10% Fill style. Move and resize the text box to resemble the text box shown in Figure 5-86b.

10. Save the newsletter on the Corel WordPerfect 8 Files floppy disk using Successful Investor - July 1999 as the filename.

11. Return the computer to its original state before you quit your session with Windows by resetting the TextArt settings using the steps summarized on page WP 5.55.

12. Print a copy of the newsletter.

13. Follow directions from your instructor for turning in the assignment.

In the Lab

2 Checking for Writing Problems and Creating a Newsletter

Problem: You are Dr. Julian Whiting's business manager and responsible for creating the *Healthy Lifestyles* newsletter. The article for the newsletter has been written and saved using Basic_Nutrition.wpd as the filename. The complete newsletter is shown in Figure 5-87a and Figure 5-87b.

Instructions: Check the Basic_Nutrition article for writing problems and then create the Healthy Lifestyles newsletter.

Part 1: Checking the Basic_Nutrition Article for Writing Problems

1. If you have access to the Internet, download the Basic_Nutrition.wpd file from the Corel WordPerfect 8 Web site to the Corel WordPerfect 8 Files floppy disk. Use the URL, http://www.scsite.com/wp8. Otherwise, obtain the file from your instructor.

2. Open the Basic_Nutrition.wpd file. Check the document for writing problems using the Quick Check checking style.

3. Save the edited Basic_Nutrition article on the Corel WordPerfect 8 Files floppy disk using the same filename.

4. Close the document window containing the article.

Part 2: Creating the Nameplate

1. Set the top and bottom margins to .5 inch.

2. Create a 1x1 table. Type Dr. Julian Whiting's in cell A1. Format the words in the table using Times New Roman Bold, Italic 24-point font and the color black. Remove all borders from the table.

Dr. Julian Whiting's
Healthy Lifestyles

A Guide to Healthy Living   **Vol. 6, No. 7 ♥ September 1999**

DEAR READER:

Last month, we sent surveys to all our subscribers and announced a mountain bike contest. You were asked to pick four major health topics from a list of twenty health topics. Returning the survey entered you into our mountain bike contest. The most requested topic, Basic Nutrition, was chosen by 37 percent of the survey respondents. As a result, this month's issue of *Healthy Lifestyles* focuses on basic nutrition. Angie Chapman of Colorado is the winner of the Swartz mountain bike. Congratulations Angie!

BASIC NUTRITION

The *three major sources of calories* are carbohydrates, protein, and fat. Some foods, such as fruits and vegetables, easily fit into one category (carbohydrates). Other foods, such as meat, obtain their calories from more than one category (protein and fat). For simplicity, we place these foods into the category that supplies the most calories. For instance, meat is classified as a protein because the protein in meat accounts for the largest number of calories.

CARBOHYDRATES

The first major source of calories is carbohydrates. *Carbohydrates* are found in fruits, vegetables, and grains. Foods in this category contain about four calories per gram. For good nutrition, carbohydrates should account for approximately 50 to 60 percent of your daily caloric intake.

The two types of carbohydrates are simple carbohydrates and complex carbohydrates. *Simple carbohydrates* include refined products such as table sugar and candy. These carbohydrates do not offer the nutritional benefits of complex carbohydrates and should be limited in your diet. *Complex carbohydrates* offer many vitamins, minerals, and fiber and are found in unrefined grain products, vegetables, and fruits.

PROTEIN

The second major source of calories is protein. *Protein* is found in meat, fish, poultry, legumes, dairy products, and eggs. Protein is essential for the growth and maintenance of

Last month, we sent surveys to all our subscribers and announced a mountain bike contest. Angie Chapman of Colorado is the winner of the Swartz mountain bike. Congratulations Angie!

FIGURE 5-87a

3. Create the newsletter title (Healthy Lifestyles) using TextArt. Use Comic Sans MS font and the square shape (first text shape in the first row of Shapes palette). Use yellow (fifteenth color box in the first row) for the text color. Create an outline using the second outline thickness box in the second row. Use black (first color box in row one) for the outline color. The text should not have a shadow or pattern.

4. Create a 2x1 table. Type the newsletter subtitle (A Guide to Healthy Living) in cell A1. Type the newsletter volume (Vol. 6, No. 7), insert the WordPerfect character (5,170), and type the date (September 1999) in cell B1. Right-justify the text. Remove the inside and outside table borders. Change the border style of the top margin to the Thick border style by clicking the Top Margin button and clicking the first border style in the fourth row.

5. Format the cells of the table using Arial Bold 12-point font.

6. Save the nameplate on the Corel WordPerfect 8 Files floppy disk using the filename, Healthy Lifestyles Nameplate.

Part 3:   Creating the Newsletter

1. Insert the Basic_Nutrition.wpd file into the nameplate document.

2. Define the necessary newspaper columns.

3. Full-justify the text in the newspaper columns.

4. Format the first subhead (DEAR READER:) using Comic Sans MS Regular 14-point font and the color, royal blue. Format the remaining subheads using QuickFormat.

5. If you have access to the Internet, download the 10-Speed_Bicycle file from the Corel WordPerfect 8 Web site to the Corel WordPerfect 8 Files floppy disk. Use the URL, http://www.scsite.com/wp8. Otherwise, obtain the file from your instructor.

Page 2

human cells. Foods in the protein category contain four calories per gram. Studies show that protein should supply about 12 to 20 percent of your daily caloric intake.

Although protein is found in both animals and plants, only animal sources of protein contain *amino acids*, which the human body needs for good nutrition. Animal sources, however, also contain fat. Nutritionists warn that too much fat can be harmful and recommend limiting the consumption of animal protein. Besides providing protein, plant sources contain no cholesterol and are a good source of fiber.

FAT

The third major source of calories is fat. *Fat* is found in all animal food sources and contains nine calories per gram. Contrary to popular belief, fat is essential for good health. Because the calorie content of fat is more than twice that of carbohydrates and protein, the consumption of fat should be limited to no more than 30 percent of your daily calories.

WATER

Water is important for good nutrition. *Water* has zero calories, is inexpensive, and is necessary for the proper functioning of cells and organs in the human body. Nutritionists recommend that you consume eight 8-ounce glasses of water each day.

SODIUM

Sodium, a component of table salt, occurs naturally in many foods. Too much sodium can contribute to high blood pressure in certain individuals. Nutritionists advise against adding table salt to any food. Instead of using salt to enhance the flavor of food, season the food with natural herbs and spices.

ACTIVE LIFESTYLE

Advances in technology have replaced jobs requiring hard physical labor with jobs that require little or no physical effort. Although considered easier by many people, numerous jobs have eliminated, or greatly reduced, the amount of physical activity in the workplace. In the past, individuals moved about while performing their jobs. Today, the typical worker sits at a desk or in a meeting room.

We could learn a lesson from the animal kingdom when it comes to an *active lifestyle*. Consider the sleek cheetah. Known as the fastest land animal, the cheetah can achieve speeds up to seventy miles per hour for short periods of time. The survival of a cheetah depends on its speed and fitness.

In the not so distant past, housecleaning was hard, physical work. Today, vacuum cleaners and electric appliances have reduced greatly the need for physical activity while cleaning house. As helpful as technology is in today's world, technology also eliminates many opportunities to be physically active on a daily basis. Physical activity is essential to burn calories and keep the body's muscles in shape.

I hope you enjoyed this month's topic. Other highly rated topics from our survey will be covered in the months to come. Look for information about minerals and mineral supplements, vitamin therapy, heart attacks, and powerful antioxidants.

A naturally active lifestyle is a prerequisite for good health. An active lifestyle is the easiest way to improve your fitness and burn calories. Being naturally energetic involves making movement an integral part of your daily routine. When the amount of physical activity in a day increases, fitness increases.

FIGURE 5-87b   *(continued)*

In the Lab

Checking for Writing Problems and Creating a Newsletter *(continued)*

6. Insert the 10-Speed_Bicycle clipart image at the left margin of the paragraph following the Dear Reader: subhead. Contour the text to wrap around the right side of the clipart image (Contour/Right Side). Move and resize the clipart image to resemble the one illustrated in Figure 5-87a on page WP 5.66.

7. Create the text box at the bottom of column two on page one. Copy the first sentence in the first paragraph to the clipboard. Paste the text into the text box. Copy the last two sentences in the first paragraph to the clipboard. Paste the text into the text box. Italicize the text in the text box. Change the border style of the text box using the eighth border style in the second row of the Border palette and change the fill style to the 10% Fill style. Move and resize the text box to resemble the text box in Figure 5-87a.

8. Create the header for page two. Display the word, Page, and the page number. Format the text using the Arial Bold 12-point font and the color black. Right-justify the line containing the page number. Draw a black horizontal line.

9. If you have access to the Internet, download the Running_Cheetah file from the Corel WordPerfect 8 Web site to the Corel WordPerfect 8 Files floppy disk. Use the URL, http://www.scsite.com/wp8. Otherwise, obtain the file from your instructor.

10. Insert the Running_Cheetah clipart image between the two columns on page two. Contour the text to wrap around both sides of the clipart image (Contour/Both Sides). Move and resize the clipart image to resemble the one illustrated in Figure 5-87b on the previous page.

11. Use the Cut button on the Toolbar (not the Copy button) to cut the last paragraph in the newsletter to the clipboard. Create the text box at the bottom of column two on page two. Paste the text into the text box. Italicize the text in the text box. Change the border style of the text box using the fourth border style in the first row of the Border palette and change the fill style to the 10% Fill style. Move and resize the text box to resemble the text box in Figure 5-87b.

12. Save the newsletter on the Corel WordPerfect 8 Files floppy disk using Healthy Lifestyles - September 1999 as the filename.

13. Return the computer to its original state before you quit your session with Windows by resetting the TextArt settings using the steps summarized on page WP 5.55.

14. Print a copy of the newsletter.

15. Follow directions from your instructor for turning in the assignment.

Cases and Places

The difficulty of these case studies varies: ❱ are the least difficult; ❱❱ are more difficult; and ❱❱❱ are the most difficult.

1 ❱ The Student Government Organization at your school decided the school needs a monthly news-letter to convey information to the student body. You volunteer to design the newsletter and write the first issue. The newsletter should contain information of interest to the entire student body. Select a topic about your school, write an article for the newsletter, and then design and create the newsletter. Use an appropriate clipart image (or picture) and a pull-quote in the newsletter. Enhance the appearance of the newsletter using color.

2 ❱ Your high school Alumni club wishes to send a quarterly newsletter to its members to inform them of past and present happenings at the school. The president of the club calls to ask you to create the newsletter and write the first issue. The newsletter should contain current information about the high school and interesting news about former students. Write an article for the newsletter and then design and create the newsletter. Use an appropriate clipart image (or scanned photograph), create a pull-quote in the newsletter, and enhance the appearance of the newsletter using color.

3 ❱❱ Clipart images such as the Light House image used in the Michigan History newsletter in this proj-ect can be obtained from many different sources. Using the Internet, library, computer store, or another resource, develop a list of companies that sell clipart images. Your list should include the company name and address, type of storage media on which the images are stored, categories of the images, quantities and prices of images, and other relevant information. Write a brief report about how you compiled the list of sources and include the list in the report.

4 ❱❱ Newsletters are a common form of communication for many businesses and organizations. Local sources for newsletters include schools, government offices, hospitals, and financial institutions (banks, stock brokers, credit unions, and so on). Obtain three newsletters from various organizations in your area. Write a brief report summarizing the newsletters. Include the good and bad features of each newsletter, ways to improve the advertisement, and what you believe makes a newsletter effective.

Cases and Places

5 ▶▶▶ Obtain a copy of a newsletter distributed in your area. Using information found in the newsletter, obtain the name and telephone number of the individual or organization responsible for creating the newsletter. Contact the individual or organization to set up an appointment. Interview the person responsible for the newsletter to determine who writes and edits the articles, who designs and creates the newsletter, what software or hardware is used, who prints the newsletter, the cost of creating and mailing the newsletter, who receives it, and how many people get the newsletter. Write a brief report summarizing what you found.

6 ▶▶▶ A text box is one of eleven predefined graphics box styles available in WordPerfect. Using WordPerfect Help, obtain information about the other ten box styles. Write a brief report summarizing each graphics box style. Demonstrate your knowledge of each box style by creating each graphics box style in a WordPerfect document. Label each box style and include with your report.

7 ▶▶▶ Most software manufacturers, such as Corel WordPerfect, produce a newsletter for each software product they sell. The editors of *WordPerfect Magazine* in Orem, Utah produce a monthly newsletter for the Corel WordPerfect Suite 8 software. Your instructor may know of other newsletters about WordPerfect. Obtain a free copy of one of these newsletters by calling or writing the company that produces the newsletter. Write a brief report summarizing the contents of the newsletter, what features are discussed, and any other relevant information.

Index